21	Franz	Heuillard			Schiltach		21
2	Sch. Pr.	Hauptman				43	✝
3	Frz.	Delhonelle	Georg				✝
4	Sch. Fr.	Allemand				44	14
5	Frz.	Delfosse	André Josef				✝
6	Sch. Slo.	Potrebujes				8. 10. 43	3
7	Frz.	a la Rochefould		Mascara			4.
8	Franz	Ben-Haim	Leleven		22. 1. 21	23. 2. 44	Zurück
9	Franz	Ferrier	Marin	La Motte St. Mart.		23. 2. 44	Blank
30	Frz.	Wal	André François	Gray Rohr	12. 2. 05	23. 1. 44	✝
1	Franz	Dufour		Berge		11. 2. 44	Hellige
2	Slow.	Muhic	Johann		29. 12. 12	8. 10. 43	Luth
3	Franz	Oudin	Max	Leipholle	20. 6. 30	23. 2. 44	23. 3. 44
4	Rev.	Korolov	Kr.	Luciol	12. 1. 20	1. 10. 43	
5	Schreiz	Mortier		Tyro		23. 2. 44	
6	Sch. Fr.	Lefevre			98	23. 2. 44	
7	Franz	Anthom		Marney		2. 2. 44	
8	✗						
9	Jug.	Drasler	Valentin Peter	Laibach	4. 8. 22	8. 10. 43	8. 3. 44
40	Slov.	Jaksa		Solo	1. 11. 12	8. 10. 43	
1	Franz	Ben-Salem		Tunis		23. 2. 44	Bergen
2	Franz	Hugue	Alfred	St. Germain	2. 3. 94	23. 2. 44	✝ 19.
3	Frz.	Bach	Constant	St. Singolph	11. 11. 16	23. 2. 44	18.
4	Span.	Fernandez		Skain		1. 3. 44	
5	Franz	Benod				11. 1. 43	28. 2. 44
6	Sch. Fr.	Shadefaux	Marcel	Pontaillor	8. 1. 99	23. 2. 44	
7	Franz	Rohmer	Pierre Hans	Duisburg	3. 4. 03		10. 1. 44
8	Span.	Rone				11. 1. 44	3. 3. 44
		Kremzar		Laibach	4. 12. 13	8. 10. 43	4

The Impostor

THE IMPOSTOR

A True Story

Javier Cercas

TRANSLATED FROM THE SPANISH
BY FRANK WYNNE

Alfred A. Knopf

NEW YORK

2018

Grateful acknowledgment is made to Oxford University Press
for permission to reprint an excerpt of "Che Fece . . . II Gran Rifiuto"
from *C. P. Cavafy: Collected Poems*, new translation by Evangelos Sachperoglou,
edited by Anthony Hirst and Peter Mackridge (OWC, 2008).
Reprinted by permission of Oxford University Press.

Library of Congress Cataloging-in-Publication Data

Names: Cercas, Javier, [date] author. | Wynne, Frank, translator.
Title: The impostor : a true story / by Javier Cercas ; translated from the Spanish by
Frank Wynne.
Other titles: Impostor. English
Description: First edition. | New York : Alfred A. Knopf, 2018. |
"This is a Borzoi book" | Includes bibliographical references.
Identifiers: LCCN 2017044942 (print) | LCCN 2017045503 (ebook) |
ISBN 9781524732820 (ebook) | ISBN 9781524732813 (hardcover : alk. paper)
Subjects: LCSH: Marco, Enric, 1921—Fiction. | Impostors and
imposture—Spain—Fiction.
Classification: LCC PQ6653.E62 (ebook) | LCC PQ6653.E62
14713 2018 (print) | DDC 863/.64—dc23
LC record available at https://lccn.loc.gov/2017044942

For Raül Cercas and Mercè Mas

Si se non nouerit . . .

—*METAMORPHOSES*, OVID,
BOOK III, L. 348

Contents

PART I

The Onion Skin

I

I did not want to write this book. I didn't know exactly why I didn't want to write it, or rather I did, but didn't want to acknowledge it, or didn't dare acknowledge it; or not entirely. The fact is that for more than seven years I resisted writing this book. During that time, I wrote two others, but I never forgot this one; on the contrary: after my fashion, while I was writing those two books, I was also writing this one. Or perhaps, after its fashion, this book was writing me.

The first paragraphs of a book are always the last to be written. This book is finished. This paragraph is the last I am writing. And, since it is the last, I now know why I didn't want to write this book. I didn't want to write it because I was afraid. This is what I've known since the beginning but didn't want to acknowledge, or didn't dare acknowledge; or not entirely. What I didn't know until now is that my fear was completely warranted.

I met Enric Marco in June 2009, four years after he became the great impostor and the great pariah. Many people still remember his story. Marco was an octogenarian from Barcelona who, for almost three decades, had passed himself off as a *deportado*—a deportee—to Hitler's Germany and a survivor of the Nazi camps, for three years he had been president of the Amical de Mauthausen, the principal Spanish association for survivors of Mauthausen, he had given hundreds of lectures and dozens of interviews, he had received a number of significant official distinctions, and had addressed the Spanish parliament on behalf of his supposed companions in misfortune, until it was discovered in early May 2005 that he had not been deported and had never been a prisoner in a Nazi camp. The discovery was made by an obscure historian named Benito Bermejo, shortly before the commemoration ceremony at Mauthausen to mark the sixtieth anniversary of the liberation of the concentration camps, a ceremony at which, for the first time, a Spanish prime minister was to be in attendance and at which Marco was to play an important role, one he was forced to relinquish at the last minute after his imposture was exposed.

When I met Marco, I had just published my tenth book, *The Anatomy of a Moment*, but I was going through a difficult time. Even I didn't understand why. My family seemed happy, the book was a success; it's true that my father had died, but he had died almost a year earlier, more than enough time to have coped with his death. The fact is that, I don't know how, but I came to the conclusion that my recently published book was to blame for my depression: not (or not entirely) because it had left me physically and mentally exhausted; but also (or more importantly) because it was a curious book, a strange novel-without-fiction, a rigorously true story, devoid of the slightest trace of invention or imagination. I thought that this was what had killed me. Day and night I repeated a mantra to myself: "Reality kills, fiction saves." In the meantime I was struggling to deal with anxiety and panic attacks. I would go to sleep crying, wake up crying and spend the day hiding from people so that I could cry some more.

I decided that the solution was to write another book. Though I had no shortage of ideas, the problem was that most of them were for non-fiction narratives. But I also had ideas for fictions; three in particular: the first was a novel about a professor of metaphysics at the University of Pontificia de Comillas who, like a rutting boar, falls in love with a porn star and ends up travelling to Budapest to meet her personally, declare his love and ask her to marry him; the second was called *Tanga* and was the first of a series of crime novels featuring a detective called Juan Luis Manguerazo; the third dealt with my father and began with a scene in which I brought him back to life and we devoured fried eggs with chorizo and frogs' legs at El Figón, a restaurant in the Cáceres of his youth where we had often eaten together.

I attempted to write these three fictions; with all three I failed.

One day, my wife, Mercè, gave me an ultimatum: either make an appointment with a psychoanalyst, or she would make one with a divorce lawyer. I didn't have time to visit the psychoanalyst she recommended. He was a bald man, cold and twisted, with an unplaceable accent (sometimes he sounded Chilean or Mexican, sometimes Catalan, or maybe Russian), who, in our early sessions, constantly berated me for showing up at his surgery *in articulo mortis*. I have spent my life making fun of psychoanalysts and their pseudoscientific mumbo-jumbo, but I would be lying if I said that our sessions weren't useful: they at least gave me a place to sob uncontrollably; but I would also be lying if I didn't confess that, more than once, I felt like getting up from the couch and punching the psychoanalyst. He, for his part, attempted to guide me towards two conclusions. The first was that the blame for all my unhappiness was not my novel-without-fiction or true story, but my mother, which explained why I often left his consulting room with the urge to strangle her the next time I set eyes on her. The second conclusion was that my life was a charade and I was a charlatan, that I had chosen literature in order to have a free, happy and authentic life whereas actually my life was false, servile and unhappy, that I pretended to be a novelist, and succeeded by deceiving and cheating people; in reality I was nothing more than an impostor.

The latter conclusion eventually came to seem more plausible (and less hackneyed) than the former. And this prompted me to remember Marco, as well as a long-forgotten conversation about him in which I had been called an impostor.

Here I need to go back a few years, to the moment when the Marco scandal first broke. It triggered outrage that resonated around the world, but in Catalonia, where Marco had been born and had lived almost all of his life, and where he had been a very popular man, the revelation of his imposture made a greater impression than it did anywhere else. So it was logical that I, too, would be interested in his case. But there was another reason; furthermore, "interested" is an understatement: rather than simply being interested, I immediately wanted to write about him, as though I sensed in Marco some profound connection. This worried me; it produced a feeling of vertigo, an inchoate dread. Yet while the scandal played out in the media I devoured everything that was written about Marco and, when I discovered that a number of people close to me knew or had known Marco or had been aware of the man, I invited them to a dinner at my house to talk about him.

The dinner took place in mid-May 2005, shortly after the story broke. At the time, I was teaching at the University of Gerona and living in the suburbs in a little semi-detached house with a garden. To the best of my recollection, in addition to my son, my wife and my sister Blanca, those present that evening included two of my colleagues in the Faculty of Arts: Anna María García and Xavier Pla. My sister Blanca was the only one of us who knew Marco well. Years earlier she and he both had long served as vice-chair on the board of FaPaC—the Federation of Associations of Parents of Schoolchildren in Catalonia—she in the Gerona district, Marco in Barcelona. To everyone's surprise, over dinner, Blanca painted a picture of a charming, hyperactive, flirtatious and witty old man who was desperate to appear in photographs. Without bothering to hide the affection she had felt at the time for the great impostor and the great pariah, she recounted the projects, the meetings, the anecdotes and the trips she had shared with him. Anna María and Xavier did not know Marco personally (or knew him only superficially), but both had studied the Holocaust and the Deportation and seemed as fascinated by the case as I was. Xavier, a young professor of Catalan literature, loaned me various texts concerning Marco, including the two most comprehensive biographical accounts of his life. Anna María, a veteran historian who had never abandoned the noble concept of civic responsibility instilled in the intellectuals of her generation, had friends and acquaintances in the Amical de Mauthausen, the association for camp survivors of which Marco had been president, and had been in Mauthausen for the commemoration ceremonies a couple of days before the scandal exploded. She was among the first to hear of Marco's imposture; she had in fact had dinner with Benito Bermejo, the historian who had just unmasked him. As I remember it, when we talked about Marco in the garden of my house that afternoon, Xavier and I were more baffled than anything; Blanca somewhere between baffled and amused (though on the whole she tried to hide her amusement, perhaps for fear of shocking us); Anna María, simply outraged: over and over she said that Marco was a scoundrel, a compulsive, barefaced liar who had mocked the whole world, but in particular the victims of the most terrible crime in history. At some point, as though she had suddenly become aware of a blindingly obvious fact, Anna María said, her eyes boring into me:

"So, tell me, why did you organise this dinner? Why are you interested in Marco? You're not thinking of writing about him?"

The three point-blank questions caught me off-guard and I didn't know how to answer; it was Anna María herself who broke the silence.

"Listen, Javier," she said, very seriously, "the best thing to do about Marco is forget him. That would be the worst punishment for such a monstrous egotist." Then she smiled and added: "Let's stop talking about him."

I don't remember whether we changed the subject (I think so, though only briefly: later Marco made his presence felt again), but I remember that I didn't dare to publicly admit that Anna María's intuition was correct, that I was considering writing about Marco; I didn't even dare to tell the historian that, if I eventually were to write about Marco, it wouldn't be to talk about him but to try to understand him, to try to understand why he did what he did. A few days later (or perhaps it was the same day) I read something in *El País* that reminded me of the advice or warning Anna María had given me. It was a letter to the editor from a woman named Teresa Sala, the daughter of one of the Mauthausen deportados and herself a member of the Amical de Mauthausen. It was not the letter of an outraged woman, but rather one who felt devastated and humiliated; her letter said: "I do not think we need to understand the reasons for Señor Marco's deception . . . To spend time attempting to justify his behaviour is to disparage and to fail to understand the legacy of those who were deported . . . From now on, Señor Marco will have to live with his disgrace."

It was precisely the opposite of what I thought. I thought that our primary duty was to understand. Obviously, to understand does not mean to excuse or, as Teresa Sala said, to justify; to be more exact: it means the reverse. Thought and art, in my view, attempt to explore who we are, revealing our endless, ambiguous and contradictory variety, and in doing so, mapping out our nature: Shakespeare or Dostoyevsky illuminate every nook and cranny of the moral maze, demonstrate that love can lead to murder or suicide, and succeed in making us feel compassion for psychopaths and bastards. The duty of art (or of thought) consists in showing us the complexity of existence in order to make us more complex, in examining the mechanics of evil so that we may avoid it, and even the mechanics of good, perhaps so we may understand them both. I believed all these things, but Teresa Sala's letter betrayed a desolation that I found moving; I also remembered that, in *If This Is a Man*, Primo Levi had written with reference to Auschwitz, or to his experience of Auschwitz, "Perhaps one cannot, what is more one must not, understand what happened, because to understand is almost to justify." To understand is to justify? was the question I had asked myself years ago when I read this sentence by Levi, one I asked myself again when I read Teresa Sala's letter. On the contrary, is it not our duty? Is it not crucial to try to understand the bewildering diversity of the real, from the most noble to the most abject? Or does this universal imperative not apply to the Holocaust? Perhaps I was wrong and there is no need to try to understand terrible evil, still less someone who, like Marco, uses terrible evil to deceive.

These questions were still nagging at me a week later at another dinner with friends where, as I would remember years later when my psychoanalyst led me to the conclusion that I was an impostor, I was called an impostor. The dinner took place at Mario Vargas Llosa's house in Madrid. Unlike the dinner at my house, this gathering had not been arranged in order to talk about Marco, but inevitably we did end up talking about him. I say "inevitably" not simply because all those present—there were only four of us, in addition to Vargas Llosa and his wife, Patricia—had been following the case more or less attentively, but also because our host had just published an article in which he ironically paid tribute to Marco's masterful talents as an impostor and welcomed him to the guild of story-tellers. Since irony is not a strong suit of the holier-than-thou (or since the holier-than-thou jump at any opportunity to be shocked, flaunting their ersatz virtue and attributing ersatz sins to others), various hypocrites had testily responded to Vargas Llosa's piece, as though he were celebrating the lies of the great impostor in his article, and it is likely that our conversation about Marco over dessert came about because of this pseudo polemic. Whatever the case, we spent some considerable time talking about Marco, about Marco's lies, about his remarkable talents for fabrication and performance, about Benito Bermejo and the Amical de Mauthausen; I also remember we talked about an article by Claudio Magris, published in the *Corriere della Sera*, entitled "The Liar Who Tells the Truth" in which he quoted and discussed a number of Vargas Llosa's observations about Marco. Naturally, I took the opportunity to recount what I had found out about the case thanks to Xavier, Anna María and my sister Blanca, and at some point Vargas Llosa interrupted me.

"But Javier!" he roared, suddenly excited, his hair tousled, jabbing two peremptory arms towards me. "Don't you get it? Marco is one of your characters! You have to write about him!"

I was flattered by Vargas Llosa's spirited comment, but for some reason I didn't understand it then. I also felt uncomfortable; to hide my self-conscious satisfaction, I carried on talking, suggesting that Marco was not only fascinating in himself, but for what he revealed about others.

"It's as though we all have something of Marco in us," I heard myself say, caught up in the moment. "As though to some extent we are all impostors."

I trailed off and, perhaps because no-one knew what to make of this statement, there was a long, awkward silence. It was then that it happened. Among the guests at this dinner was Ignacio Martínez de Pisón, a friend of mine and a writer known among his acquaintances for his fearsome Aragonese bluntness, and he broke the spell with the devastating quip:

"Yes: especially you."

Everyone laughed. I laughed too, though less heartily: it was the first time in my life I had been called an impostor; though not the first time I had been linked to Marco. A few days after the story broke, I read an article online in the newspaper *El Punt* which did precisely that. It bore the headline "Lies," and the writer, Sílvia Barroso, said that Marco's case had caught her unawares while reading the last pages of one of my novels in which the narrator announces his decision to "lie about everything, but only to better tell the truth." She added that I often explored the boundaries between truth and lies in my novels and that on one occasion she had heard me say that, sometimes, "to get to the truth, it is necessary to lie." Was Barroso bracketing me with Marco? Was she insinuating that I too was a fraud, an impostor? No, thankfully, because she went on to say, "The difference between Cercas and Marco is that the novelist has a licence to lie." But that night at Vargas Llosa's house, I silently wondered, What about Pisón? Was his comment tongue-in-cheek, intending only to make us laugh and defuse the awkward silence, or did his quip betray an inability to hide his true feelings behind the screen we call politeness? And Vargas Llosa? What had he meant when he said Marco was one of my characters? Did Vargas Llosa think I was an impostor too? Why had he suggested that I write about Marco? Because he thought there is no-one better than an impostor to write about another impostor?

After the dinner was over, I spent hours tossing and turning in bed in my hotel room in Madrid. I was thinking about Pisón and about Sílvia Barroso. I was thinking about Anna María García, Teresa Sala, Primo Levi and I was wondering whether, if to understand is almost to justify, anyone had the right to attempt to understand Enric Marco and thereby justify his lies and feed his vanity. I thought to myself that Marco had already told enough lies and therefore it would be impossible to reach the truth about him through fiction but only through truth, through a novel without fiction, a rigorously true story without the slightest trace of invention or imagination, and that any attempt to fashion a story from Marco's history was doomed to failure: firstly because I remembered Vargas Llosa had written, "the true story of Marco will probably never be known" (Claudio Magris had likewise written "we shall never know the private truth about Enric Marco, his need to invent a life for himself"); and secondly because of something Fernando Arrabal said, a paradox I also remembered: "The liar has no history. No-one would dare tell the history of a lie or present it as a true story. How could one tell the story without lying?" So it was impossible to tell Marco's story; or at least impossible to tell it without lying. In which case, why tell it? Why try to write a book that could not be written? Why set oneself an impossible task?

That night, I decided not to write this book. And in making the decision, I felt a great weight lift from my shoulders.

2

His mother was insane. Her name was Enriqueta Batlle Molins and, although Marco always believed that she had been born in Breda, a quiet little village in the Montseny massif, in fact she was from Sabadell, an industrial city near Barcelona. On January 29, 1921, she was admitted to the Sant Boi de Llobregat insane asylum for women. According to the asylum records, this was three months after she had separated from her husband, who had abused her; during this period, according to the records, she earned her living going from house to house doing domestic work.

She was thirty-two years old and six months pregnant. When the doctors examined her, she seemed confused, she contradicted herself, and she was plagued by paranoid thoughts; her initial diagnosis read: "Persecution mania with degenerative symptoms"; in 1930 this was changed to "dementia praecox": what nowadays we know as schizophrenia. On the first page of the dossier there is a photograph of her, possibly taken on the day she was admitted. It shows a woman with long, straight hair and strongly marked features, a generous mouth and pronounced cheekbones; her dark eyes are not looking at the camera, but everything about her radiates the dark, melancholy beauty of a tragic heroine; she is wearing a knitted black cardigan, and her back, her shoulders and her lap are covered with a shawl that she gathers into her hands over her belly, as though she were trying to conceal her inconcealable pregnancy, or trying to protect her unborn child. This woman does not know that she will never again see the outside world that has abandoned her to her fate, locking her away and leaving her to become utterly engulfed by her madness.

There is no less dramatic way to say it. In the thirty-five years that
Marco's mother spent in the asylum, the doctors examined her only
twenty-five times (typically once a year, but after her initial admission,
eight years went by without her being examined), and the only treat-
ment they prescribed consisted of forcing her to work in the laundry,
"with excellent results," according to a note from one of the doctors
treating her. There are many such notes; though not all are as cynical,
all are curt, vague and heartbreaking. In the beginning they record
that the patient is in good physical condition, but they also record her
self-centredness, her hallucinations (particularly auditory hallucinations), her sporadic violent outbursts; later, her deterioration gradually affects her physically, and by the late 1940s the notes describe a
woman who is bedridden and has completely lost all sense of direction, her memory and any sign of her own identity; she is reduced to
a catatonic state. She died on February 23, 1956, as a result of "angor
pectoris," according to her file. Even this diagnosis was inaccurate:
no-one dies of chest pain; it is likely that she died of a heart attack.

Marco's mother gave birth to him in the asylum, on April 14,
according to him; this is the date that appears on his identity card and

his passport. But it is false: Marco's fiction begins here, on the very day he came into the world. In fact, according to his mother's case file and his own birth certificate, Marco was born on April 12, two days earlier than the date he would claim. Why lie then, why change the date? The answer is simple: because, after a certain point in his life, this allowed him to begin his talks, his speeches and his living history classes with the words "My name is Enric Marco, and I was born on April 14, 1921, exactly ten years before the declaration of the Second Spanish Republic," which in turn made it possible for him to present himself, implicitly or explicitly, as a man of destiny who has witnessed first hand the major historical events of the century and encountered its principal protagonists, as an emblem, a symbol or the very personification of his country; after all, his personal biography was a mirror image of the collective biography of Spain. Marco claims that the purpose of his lie was merely didactic; it is difficult, however, not to see it as an ironic wink at the world, as a blatant way of implying that, since his date of birth coincided with a momentous day in the history of his country, the heavens or the fates were signalling that this man was destined to play a decisive role in that history.

From the dossier in Sant Boi asylum, we know one more thing: on the day after he was born, Marco's mother watched as her son was forcefully taken from her and given to her husband, the man she had fled from because he abused her, or because she said that he abused her. Did Marco ever see his mother again? He claims he did. He says one of his father's sisters, his aunt Catherine—who breastfed him, since she had lost a child a few short weeks before he was born—took him to see his mother once or twice a year when he was a boy. He says that he clearly remembers these visits. He says that he and Aunt Catherine would wait in a huge bare white-walled room with the families of other patients for his mother to appear. He says that after a while his mother would emerge from the laundry rooms wearing a blue-and-white-striped apron, her eyes staring vacantly. He says that he would give her a kiss, but that she never kissed him back, and that in general she did not address a word to him, to his aunt Catherine, to anyone. He says that she often talked to herself, and that she almost always talked about him as though he were not there in front of her, as though she had lost him. He says that he remembers at the age of about ten or eleven, his aunt Catherine pointing to him and saying to his mother: "See what a handsome lad you have, Enriqueta: he's named Enrique, after you." And he says he remembers his mother fiercely wringing her hands and saying: "Yes, yes, he is a handsome lad, but he is not my son"; and, pointing to a two-year-old boy scampering around the room, he says she added: "my son looks like him." He also says that at the time he didn't understand, but that in time he realized his mother said this because her only memory of him was when he was no more than two or three years old, when she still had a vestige of lucidity. He says that he would sometimes bring her food in a lunch box and that sometimes he managed to exchange a word or two with her. He says that one day, after eating what he had brought in the lunch box, his mother told him that she worked hard in the laundry, that it was gruelling work but she didn't care, because they had told her if she worked hard, they would give her back her son. He says he doesn't remember when he stopped going to visit his mother. He says it was probably when his aunt and uncle stopped bringing him, perhaps when he reached adolescence, by which time the Civil War had already begun, perhaps earlier. In any event, he says, after that, he never again visited her, never again felt the slightest desire to see her, never worried about her—he forgot her completely. (This is not entirely true: many years later, Marco's first wife told her daughter Anna María that she persuaded Marco to go and see his mother at the asylum after they were married; she also told her that they visited once or twice, and that all she remembered of these visits was the woman smelled strongly of bleach and did not recognise her son.) He tells me that he knows his mother died in the mid-1950s, but cannot even remember attending her funeral. He tells me that he cannot understand how he could have left her in an asylum for more than thirty years, how he could have left her to die alone, although he adds that there are many things from that period he doesn't understand. He says he thinks about his mother often now, that he dreams of her sometimes.

3

I did not reconsider writing about Enric Marco until four years after the scandal broke. I had just finished writing *The Anatomy of a Moment*, a true story or a novel without fiction that had nothing to do with Marco, and, with the help of my psychoanalyst, I had reached the conclusion that I was an impostor, remembering my friend Pisón calling me an impostor in Vargas Llosa's house in Madrid. At the time, I was in a terrible state and I felt that what I needed to get through it was a fictitious rather than a true story—fiction saves, reality kills, I told myself over and over—and that my account of Marco could only be a true story, because Marco had already told enough lies about his life and to add fiction to these fictions would be redundant, irrelevant in literary terms; I also remembered the reasons with which, four years earlier, during a sleepless night in a hotel in Madrid, I had convinced myself to abandon my book about Marco before I had even begun. But I also remembered Vargas Llosa's flattering enthusiasm at his house in Madrid, and it occurred to me that perhaps he was right, perhaps Marco was one of my characters, perhaps only an impostor could tell the story of an impostor and that, if I truly were an impostor, perhaps no-one was better placed than I to write Marco's story. Besides, in the four years I had spent writing the book that had just been published, I had never completely forgotten Marco, never forgotten he was there, in the background, disturbing, mesmerising and dangerous, like a grenade that, sooner or later, I would have to throw so it would not blow up in my hands, like a story that, sooner or later, I would have to tell in order to be free of it. I resolved that now was the moment to make the attempt; or at least that it was better to try than to carry on trudging through the slough of despond.

My resolve barely lasted a week, the time it took once again to become engrossed in the story and—thanks to the internet—to discover, to my surprise, that no-one had written a book about Marco, but also, to my disappointment (and my private relief), that a film about him had just been released. *Ich bin Enric Marco* was the work of two young Argentinean directors, Santiago Fillol and Lucas Vermal, and had been premiered at a film festival. My disappointment was the result of a sudden certainty: if someone had recounted Marco's stories in images, it made no sense for me to do so in words (hence my relief). In any case, I was interested to see the film, and I realised that one of the directors, Santiago Fillol, lived, like me, in Barcelona. I managed to get his mobile number, I called him, we met.

The meeting took place in a restaurant on the plaza de la Virreina in the Gràcia district. Fillol turned out to be a short, swarthy, unkempt man in his thirties sporting a sparse moustache and intellectual glasses; he was also one of those Argentineans who seem to have read every book, seen every film and who would rather have his hand cut off than use a cliché. He brought me a copy of his film on DVD While we ate, we talked about the film, about the mechanics behind it, of living cheek by jowl with Marco for several weeks. Mostly we talked about Marco. It was not until we came to dessert that Santi asked if I was thinking of writing about him. I told him I wasn't.

"You guys have already told the story," I argued, savouring my *flan* and nodding towards his film. "Why would I tell it again?"

"No, no," said Santi, hurriedly contradicting me. He had passed on dessert and ordered coffee. "We just shot a documentary, we didn't tell the whole story of Enric. That still remains to be done."

I was about to say that perhaps it was impossible to tell the whole story of Enric and to quote Vargas Llosa, Magris and Arrabal. I said:

"Yes, by this stage I thought at least a dozen Spanish writers would have written about Marco. Yet from what I can see, no-one has."

"Not that I know of," Santi confirmed. "Well, I think one of them made an attempt, but got scared. Are you surprised? I'm not. Everyone in Enric's story comes off badly, first and foremost Enric, followed by the journalists and the historians and lastly the politicians: basically, the whole country. To write Enric's story would mean poking people in the eye, and no-one wants that. No-one wants to be a wet blanket, am I right? Least of all Spanish writers."

Santi must have been worried that my reaction would be patriotic or show solidarity with my compatriots because he immediately offered a vague apology. I told him he had nothing to apologise for.

"No, I know that, it's just . . . Well"—a mischievous smile played on his lips beneath the thin moustache that was stained with coffee—"you know what? I love literature, I read a lot, but to be perfectly honest with you, Spanish writers these days seem a bit insubstantial, not to say chicken: they don't write from their gut, they write what they think they should write, what they think will please the critics, and the result is that they never get past style and snobbery."

I didn't tell him that I was no better than my colleagues, realising just in time that if I did so, he might feel obliged to lie, to tell me I was different. Santi encouraged me to watch his film so I would see that my book was not incompatible with it, and offered to give me the documentation he had amassed during the shoot, and any help I needed.

"I don't know," I said, having thanked him for his generosity. Then I talked to him about the book I had just published, about my true story, and I apologised: "To be frank, I'm tired of reality. I've come to the conclusion that reality kills and fiction saves. So right now I need a little fiction."

Santi gave a loud laugh.

"Well, with Enric you'll tire of it soon enough!" he explained. "Enric is pure fiction. Don't you realise? Everything about him is a fiction, worse still, a fiction embedded in reality, he is fiction incarnate. Enric is like Quixote: he couldn't resign himself to a mediocre existence, he wanted to live life on a grand scale; and since he didn't have the wherewithal, he invented it."

"You talk about Marco as though he were a hero," I pointed out.

"Because he is: he is both hero and villain; or hero and villain and picaresque character. That's how complicated the story is, and how fascinating. I don't know if your other fictions can wait, but this one can't: Enric is eighty-eight. He might die any day, and his story would go untold. Anyway," he concluded, "do what you want. I hope you like the film."

I didn't just like the film, I liked it a *lot*. And I realised that Santi was right, that he and Lucas Vermal had decided not to tell the whole story of Marco; in fact this may have been the major asset of the film. It simply contrasted the story fabricated by Marco—according to which he had surreptitiously escaped to France at the end of the Civil War, had been imprisoned by Pétain's forces in Marseille before being delivered up to the Gestapo, deported to Germany and interned in the Flossenbürg camp near Munich—with the true story—according to which he had indeed gone to Germany, but as a volunteer under a scheme agreed between Hitler and Franco, and he had indeed spent several months in gaol, though in the ordinary prison in Kiel, in northern Germany. But there were countless stories yet to tell and countless questions in the air: Where had Enric Marco come from? What had his life been like before and after the scandal triggered by the discovery of his deception? Why had he done what he had done? Had he lied only once, about his time in Flossenbürg concentration camp, or had he spent his whole life lying? In a nutshell: who was Enric Marco really? In spite of its brilliance, or because of it, the film by Santi and Lucas Vermal did not offer answers to these questions, it did not exhaust nor did it claim to exhaust the subject of Marco's character, so much so that, after I had watched it, I called Santi, congratulated him on his work and asked him to mediate with Marco to grant me an interview.

"So, you're going to write the book?" asked Santi.

"Maybe," I said. "At least I'm going to try."

"The Spaniard's got balls, man!" I heard him say, as though talking to someone else, then he went on, "Don't sweat it. I'll get in touch with Enric today. I'll go with you to meet him."

The interview took place some days later in Sant Cugat, a little town near Barcelona. Santi and I took the train and, from the station, we walked to Marco's house, a top-floor apartment on the rambla del Celler in the new part of town where, from what Santi told me, our man had lived until some years ago with his wife and two daughters, and where he now lived alone with his wife. I don't know whether it was she or Marco who opened the door to us, but I do remember that my first impression of Marco was unpleasant, a little monstrous: he looked to me like a gnome. A swarthy, balding, thickset, burly, moustachioed gnome who was constantly sitting down only to get up again to fetch papers and books and documents and, as he bustled between the dining room and a veranda whose picture windows gave onto a terrace open to the sunny skies of the summer afternoon, he never for a moment stopped talking about himself, about my sister Blanca, about the documentary he had made with Santi and about my books and my journalism, in an attempt to flatter me or to ingratiate himself.

It seemed incredible to me that this walking whirlwind could be eighty-eight years old. Despite his diminutive size and the liver spots that mottled his skin, what was most striking was his ferocious energy and the youthful vitality radiated by his eyes, by his every gesture; he might not have had much hair left on his head, but he sported a thick moustache without a single grey hair; pinned to the chest of his sweater, he wore a little flag of the Second Republic. His wife, whose name was Dani, shook hands with Santi and with me and chatted to us for a moment, though I don't remember what she talked about because, listening to her and looking at her, I could not help but wonder what she must have felt, this tiny, gentle, smiling woman much younger than Marco, when the scandal erupted and her husband became the great impostor and the great pariah, what she must have thought when she realised that for decades he had deceived her just as he had deceived everyone. Then Marco's wife left us. By this time, Santi had been pacing up and down behind Marco, attempting to stanch his unrelenting torrent of words in order to explain the reason for our visit. As I watched Santi, I felt a mixture of gratitude, admiration and pity: gratitude for his efforts to help me; admiration, because he looked like a lion tamer vainly trying to break a wild beast; pity, because, in order to make his documentary, he had had to put up with Marco day and night during weeks of shooting. As for me, the powerful physical revulsion I had initially experienced on meeting Marco became a powerful sense of moral disgust: standing in the dining room of his home, watching him come and go, with Santi chasing after him, I wondered what the hell I was doing here, and with all my soul I despised myself for having come to meet this shameless con artist, this out-and-out liar, this utter scoundrel, and for being prepared to spend weeks listening to his story in order to write my wretched book, rather than spending the time with my mother, a woman who, whatever my psychoanalyst said, had never hurt a fly in her life and, despite that, still went to confession and took communion every week, and if there was anything she needed now that she was a widow, it was for her son to listen to her. I thought that Santi and Lucas Vermal were not simply brave, they were heroes. I thought that I was in no position to match their feat. I thought that, truth be told, I was as shameless as Marco, and in that moment, with a renewed sense of relief, I decided that I would not write a book about him for love or money.

Of the remainder of that meeting in Sant Cugat I remember only two things, but I remember them very clearly. The first is that, to justify the trip, Santi, Marco and I ate at La Tagliatella, an Italian restaurant just opposite Marco's house, and that, to make up for having wasted their time, I paid the bill. The second is that, during the meal, while I wolfed down pasta arrabiata and drained large glasses of red wine, Marco unleashed on Santi and on me a torrent of shameless self-aggrandisement and absurd justifications (in which, I noted with some astonishment, Marco would sometimes shift from first person to third person, as though he were not talking about himself): he was a great man, generous, loyal and profoundly humane, a tireless fighter for good causes, and this was why so many people said wonderful things about him. "Be careful," he warned me from the outset. "If you speak ill of Enric Marco, you are going to come across a lot of people who will tell you: 'You don't know Enric Marco: he is a truly extraordinary, amazing person with many great qualities.'" He warned me later, "Honestly, the day they broadcast the news that Enric Marco is dead, the plaza de Catalunya won't be big enough to hold the crowds that will gather to mourn him." This was how it was: everyone loved and admired him, his family worshipped him, he had dozens, hundreds of friends who, in spite of everything, had not turned their backs on him, people who were prepared to do anything for him. He had given countless demonstrations of courage and dignity, he had been a leader everywhere he went, in the *barrio* where he lived as a child, in the army as a young man and in his years in Germany; and later as a grown man: in the years of secret struggle against the Franco regime, in the university, in the C.N.T.—the anarcho-syndicalist union of which he had been secretary general during the 1970s—in FaPaC—the confederation of school parents' associations of which he had been vice-president during the '80s and '90s—and also in the Amical de Mauthausen. Not that he had sought to be a leader, quite the contrary: he felt no need to be a leader, he was not an egotistical or conceited person, this was something he needed to make clear from the outset. It was others who had pushed him to accept leadership positions, others who had constantly pleaded with him: "You do it, we wouldn't dare"; "You give the speech, you've got a way with words, you've got so much energy, and you're so intelligent and you know how to charm and move and persuade people." And he sacrificed himself and did as they asked. All his life he had been pursued by fame, by recognition, by the admiration of others, though he had always shunned them, admittedly with scant success. In such circumstances, it was not easy to be humble, yet somehow he had managed. For example, people seemed determined to see him as a hero, it had always been the case, it was a veritable mania; he, on the other hand, had always hated the idea, and had done everything in his power to avoid it, he did not like the idea of being put on a pedestal, being elevated, he had always been a modest, unassuming man. But the pupils and the teachers in schools where he gave talks when he was president of the Amical de Mauthausen would always insist he was, and sometimes would say, "Although you claim you're not a hero, you are a hero; you are a hero precisely because you say you are not a hero." And he would get angry and say, "Enric Marco is not a hero in any sense. He is an unusual person, I agree, that much I will agree, but not exceptional. Honestly, the only thing that he has done throughout his life is struggle tirelessly, with all his might, oblivious to danger and to his own self-interest, for peace, for solidarity, for freedom, for social justice, for human rights, for the dissemination of culture and of memory. That is all." This is what he would say to them. And it was true. He had always been where the need was greatest, had never failed to help anyone, nor to do and to promote what was good, he had always been an exemplary fighter, a model worker, friend, husband and father, and a man who had given his all for others. And how had he been repaid? With contempt, with silence, with the ignominious banishment that had been his lot since the scandal broke. Had he made mistakes? Had he said he had been imprisoned in a Nazi concentration camp when in fact he had not been? Who has not made mistakes? Who had the right to cast the first stone? A lot of people, it seemed, because in his case it was not simply a single stone, but thousands, he had been stoned, he had been pitilessly annihilated and humiliated, he had been the victim of an unspeakable lynching. And it was true, he acknowledged, that he had made a mistake, but he had done so for a good cause. He had not lied, he was not a fraud or an impostor as people said; he had simply altered the facts slightly: everything he had said about the horrors of the Nazi regime was true and well documented, even if he had lied; everything he had said about himself was true, even if he had altered the setting. He had made a stupid mistake, because he had no need to fabricate a past as a resistance fighter and a victim of the Nazis, he really had been arrested by the Gestapo, he really had been a prisoner in Nazi Germany, in a prison rather than a concentration camp, but what was the difference between them? All this was also well documented, perhaps I had not watched Santi's film? And then: how could the victims dare to say that he was not one of them simply because he had not been in a Nazi camp but in a Nazi gaol? He had said things that were not true, granted, he had embroidered or embellished or altered the truth a little, granted, but he had done it not out of egotism, but generosity, not out of vanity, but altruism, to educate younger generations about the horrors, to unearth the historical memory of this amnesiac country; he had been one of, if not *the* greatest advocate for the recovery of historical memory in Spain, the memory of the victims of the war and the post-war period, the victims of Franco, of fascism, of the Nazis, and when he joined the Amical de Mauthausen those who had survived the Nazi death camps were dead, or they were old and washed up, how was their message to be passed on? And who better than he to do so, since he was still young, he still had energy, and besides he was a historian? Did I know that he had studied history at university? Who better than he to give a voice to those who had none? Should he have allowed the last Spanish witnesses to the Nazi barbarism to remain silent, and everything that they had suffered be consigned to oblivion and the lessons of it be lost for ever? It was true that he, too, might have been a great historian, his professors at university had often told him so, but he had not wanted to be a historian. And did I know why? Because history is a cold, arid, lifeless subject, an abstraction devoid of any interest to young people; he kindled in them a love of history, he brought it to life: in the countless talks he gave, he presented history to schoolchildren in the flesh, living, breathing, never sparing them the blood, the sweat, the guts, he offered them history in all its colour, its emotion, its adventure and its heroism, he was history incarnate and he relived it for them, and thanks to his strategy, schoolchildren had acquired a knowledge and an understanding of the past. Was that wrong? Had he done something wrong? Why was he being condemned with no trial, no appeal? He had played a decisive role in the Amical de Mauthausen, he had advocated for the recovery of historical memory, he had taught a sense of history to teenagers, had fought for the rights of workers, for improvements to public education, for the freedom of his country, risking his life and suffering torture during the terrible years of the Franco regime, he had fought first for the triumph of the Second Republic and, during the war and the post-war period, against Franco, and this was why they were punishing him? Had he done no good in his life? Did he deserve such a punishment? Was it fair that he had been turned into a criminal? Surely there were genuine criminals for people to condemn? What about Kissinger? And Bush? And Blair? And Aznar? Anyhow, he had no intention of asking for forgiveness, he had done nothing wrong, he had committed no crime, he was not looking to be rehabilitated. This was something else he needed to make clear. He would have no truck with public redemption, he had no need of such a thing, the love of his wife, the love of his daughters and his friends were enough for him. He was not claiming that he would regain hard-won public recognition that had been stolen from him, the respect, the affection and the admiration of all, his reputation as an exceptional man who had made an exceptional contribution to understanding the past and to bettering humanity. No. He knew only too well that the world was indebted to him, but he had no intention of calling in that debt. All he wanted was to regain his voice, to take off the muzzle, to be allowed to defend himself, to tell the truth, or at least his version of the truth, to be able to tell it to the young and the not so young, to all those who had trusted him, acclaimed him, loved him. To leave his name unsullied for his family and be allowed to die in peace. This was all he wanted. And in this, I, who was a great writer, who wrote such wonderful books and articles, whom he knew and loved before he had even met me, because he knew and loved my sister Blanca, could be of great help. Careful: not only could I be of great help to him, that was the least of it; I could be of great help to everyone, by writing a book that recounted his true story.

"So . . ." Santi said as soon as we left Marco at the door of La Tagliatella and were walking back towards the train station, "what did you think of the old guy?"

I waited until we were far enough away from Marco before I said, before I almost screamed:

"A monster. A complete monster!"

On the return journey to Barcelona I vented: I told Santi exactly what I thought of Marco. I told him that not only was he a consummate liar; he was a manipulative, obsequious, utterly unscrupulous parasite who wanted to use me to whitewash his lies and his misdeeds. I told him I had absolutely no intention of writing Marco's story, because I thought he was a horrible person and because Marco was not a fiction, he was a terrifying reality, and what I needed was a fiction. I told him that, besides, it would be impossible to tell Marco's story, and now I did quote Vargas Llosa and Magris and even Arrabal and his theory that a liar has no story, or that it's impossible to tell it without lying. I told him that, even if it were possible to tell Marco's story, it did not have to be told, it was an immoral act, because to tell it—and here I quoted Primo Levi and Teresa Sala—would mean trying to understand Marco, and to try to understand Marco was almost to justify him, and lastly I said—possibly quoting Anna María García—that the best thing anyone could do with this monstrous egotist was not to write a book about him, but leave him to rot in his ignoble isolation. Santi listened patiently, laughing now and then, making no attempt to dispute my arguments, vainly attempting to calm my rage with steady doses of Argentinean irony and, when we got off the train in Barcelona, he suggested we get a coffee.

"Out of the question!" I said, almost shouting again. "Right now I am going to see my mother!"

At the end of that same year, *Ich bin Enric Marco*, the film by Santi Fillol and Lucas Vermal, was released in cinemas, and on December 27, I wrote an article about it in *El País*. It was headlined "I am Enric Marco," and it read:

"On May 11, 2005, the truth was discovered: Enric Marco was an impostor. For the previous twenty-seven years Marco had claimed to be prisoner No. 6448 from the German concentration camp of Flossenbürg; he had lived this lie and had made it live: for almost three decades, Marco gave hundreds of talks about his experiences of the Nazi regime, he was president of the Amical de Mauthausen, the association of Spanish survivors of the Nazi camps, he was awarded notable honours and medals and on January 27, 2005, he moved many of the members of both houses of the Spanish parliament to tears as they gathered in the Congreso de los Diputados to pay tribute for the first time to the almost nine thousand Spanish Republicans deported to the Third Reich. Only the last-minute discovery of his deception prevented Marco, three and a half months after this spectacular performance, from outdoing himself by giving a speech at Mauthausen concentration camp in the presence of the prime minister, José Luis Rodríguez Zapatero, and other important dignitaries at a memorial for the sixtieth anniversary of the end of the Nazi horrors. Many of you will remember the story, which was reported all over the world and filled newspapers with articles teeming with insults about Marco; one exception was the article by Mario Vargas Llosa entitled 'Monster and Genius.' The first word is obviously accurate; so too is the second: it takes a genius to manage to fool everyone for almost thirty years, everyone including family, friends, members of the Amical de Mauthausen and even a former internee of Flossenbürg, who came to recognise him as a companion in suffering.

"Genius, or something akin to genius. Because the truth is that it is difficult not to believe that a collective weakness facilitated the success of Marco's deception. This, from the outset, was the result of two parallel and unassailable forms of prestige: the prestige of the victim and that of the witness; no-one dares question the authority of the victim, no-one dares question the authority of the witness: the craven capitulation to this double blackmail—the first, moral, the second intellectual—oiled the wheels of Marco's deception. It was further helped by at least two other things. The first is our relative ignorance of the recent past generally and of Nazism in particular: although Marco promoted himself as a remedy for this national failing, in fact he was the finest proof of its existence. The second is perhaps less obvious. There can be little doubt that, at the moment, the greatest enemy of the left is the left itself; meaning: left-wing kitsch; meaning the transformation of left-wing discourse into a hollow shell, into the hypocritical, meaningless sentimentalism that the right call do-goodism. Moreover, in his public speeches, Marco succeeded in brilliantly embodying this prostitution, or this failure of the left; in other words: Marco's lies satisfied a massive vacuous leftist demand for toxic sentimental fodder seasoned with historical good conscience. The implications of Marco's case, however, are not simply political or historical, they are also moral. For some time now, psychology has maintained that we can barely live without lying, that man is an animal that lies: life in society demands a measure of falsehood that we call politeness (and which only hypocrites mistake for hypocrisy); Marco horribly exaggerated and distorted this basic human need. In this sense, he is like Don Quixote, or like Emma Bovary, two other great liars who, like Marco, cannot reconcile themselves to the greyness of their real lives and so invent and live out fictitious, heroic lives; in this sense there is something in Marco's fate that profoundly touches us all, as there is in those of Quixote and Bovary: all of us play a role; all of us are other than we are; in some way, we are Enric Marco.

"Perhaps this explains why Santiago Fillol and Lucas Vermal have given more or less this title to a documentary about Marco released this week: *Ich bin Enric Marco*. The film has many virtues, but I have space only to highlight two of them. The first is its humility: Fillol and Vermal make no attempt to exhaust all the complexities of the character; it is this restraint that gives the film its power. The second virtue is no less essential. As any good liar knows, a lie will prevail only if it is buttressed by truth; Marco's lie was no exception: it was true that he had been in Nazi Germany during the war, but it was not true that he was there as a Republican prisoner, rather he was one of Franco's volunteers; it was true that the Nazis imprisoned him, but it was not true that they imprisoned him in Flossenbürg concentration camp, but rather in the city of Kiel, nor was he imprisoned for anti-fascist resistance but probably for simple defeatism. Fillol and Vermal have the good sense to lead Marco to lies via the truth, rather than the reverse, and in doing so, they show him not only struggling fiercely with his lies, but struggling to justify the truth of his lies, struggling to vindicate himself as a victim, struggling for himself. Struggling. He is a fascinating character. It is a fascinating film. Go and see it."

4

Since his mother was committed to an asylum, Marco's childhood involved constantly moving from one family to another, from one home to another, which meant that he had neither family nor home. His father, Tomás Marco, had moved to Barcelona from Alfaro in the province of La Rioja, "city of storks and freethinkers," Marco would invariably add whenever it was mentioned. He was a libertarian, a mason and a printer, and although he consequently belonged to the cultural elite of the working class (or perhaps precisely because of it), he was a member of the union of graphic arts, a part of the C.N.T., the anarchist organisation. He was not a demonstrative man, or at least Marco doesn't remember him as such: he doesn't remember his father ever taking his hand, ever showing a sign of affection, ever buying him a toy (in fact, he remembers having only one toy: a cardboard horse which was later given to a female cousin). The only things his father had in the house were books and magazines, and this explains how Marco became such a precocious and omnivorous reader.

But it only partly explains it. Marco's father lived with a woman whose name was Teodosia, though she obviously did not like the name and had people call her Felisa. Marco remembers her as a coarse, violent woman who did not think twice about hitting him, fighting with his father, or whipping out a pair of scissors in an argument with the neighbours; he also remembers her as an alcoholic. Marco loathed her with every fibre of his being because, he says, she made his childhood a nightmare. He says that she would spend whole days lying in bed, ordering him to run down to the *taberna* on the corner to fetch the wine or the *aguardiente* she drank in outrageous quantities. He says she was illiterate and that, having no other form of entertainment, she would ask him to read to her from the books in the house, and so at an early age he was reading books by Cervantes, Rojas, Vargas Vila, Hugo, Balzac, Sue, books that often he did not fully understand, or did not understand at all. Sometimes he would read to his stepmother in the bedroom she shared with his father while, from the bed, she would listen, or laugh, or comment on his reading; at other times he would read to her in the dining room, a small, dark room lit only by a Petromax, wreathed by the smell of burning paraffin. But he says she was always drunk, and he was afraid of her. She would frequently beat him, humiliate him, insult him, and more than once, tired of being mistreated, he left the house, slamming the door behind him, and went to the offices of Editorial Sopena, where his father worked, sat outside the door and waited for him. When his father finally emerged, minutes or hours later, Marco would tell him what had happened, and from that point, the same sequence would invariably be played out: the two would go home and he would stand in the doorway, waiting, as he listened to his father and his stepmother screaming, in the hope that this argument would end in a happy separation.

The break-up never came, or at least he never witnessed it. His father and stepmother remained together for many years. In their own way, perhaps they loved each other: at least he remembers hearing them at night, laughing and screwing; or perhaps, as he tends to think now, so many years later, this horrible woman suited his father: she cooked his food, washed and darned his clothes, managed the house. Despite all this, the house was always terribly untidy, and on one occasion the neighbours reported his stepmother's beatings and a magistrate was obliged to intervene. This marked the beginning of his wanderings as a Dickensian orphan, from one family to another, from one home to another. The families were those of his aunts, for the most part his father's sisters. He insists that they all treated him much better than his stepmother, but adds that for most of his childhood he couldn't shrug off the mortifying sense that he was not wanted anywhere, that everyone wanted to be rid of him. He lived in various neighbourhoods in Barcelona: in Los Corts, with his father and his stepmother; with his uncle Francesc and his aunt Caterina in La Trinidad, where they had a grocer's shop, and where he felt more at home than he did anywhere else. It was here that he also spent his summers with his uncle Ricardo, his father's brother, who was a militant member of the socialist U.G.T. union, in the historic district of the city (on the calle del Tigre and the calle de la Luna) and also in Ensanche (on the calle Diputación, between Aribau and Muntaner). It was here that he was caught up in the so-called "unrest" of October 1934,[*] when, in the midst of a nationwide uprising by the Spanish left against the right-wing government of the Second Republic, the autonomous Parliament of Catalonia, the *Generalitat*, declared a Catalan State within the Spanish Federal Republic. The uprising, quickly quelled by the army, failed almost immediately, but not before causing forty-six fatalities, an unknown number of casualties and the imprisonment and subsequent prosecution of more than three thousand people, among them the President of the Generalitat and his entire cabinet.

Of these days, Marco retained two vivid memories. The first is rather confused. The Catalan uprising occurred while he was staying with his uncle Ricardo, who at the time worked for *La Humanitat*, a publication based on the calle Tallers near the Rambla; *La Humanitat* was the newspaper of the Republican Left of Catalonia, the party of the rebel government, and so the offices were shut down and the staff interned on the prison ship *Uruguay*. Marco didn't live far from the newspaper offices and, hearing rumours of what was happening there, and spurred on by his innate anxiety and the audacity of his thirteen years, he rushed out into the street to look for his uncle. From this point, Marco's memories, in addition to being confused, are fragmented: he says that on some of the streets he saw barricades, or the remnants of barricades; he says that he managed to make it as far as plaza Universidad and there stumbled on several machine-gun emplacements manned by soldiers who refused to let him pass; he says that he retraced his steps and attempted to take a roundabout route, taking the Rambla de Catalunya as far as the plaza de Catalunya and the Rambla, and that he saw people from Estat Català, the pro-independence party, being arrested outside a café called Oro del Rhin on the corner of the Gran Vía and the Rambla de Catalunya;

---

[*] On October 6, 1934, Lluís Companys, President of the Generalitat of Catalonia, proclaimed the Catalan State of the Spanish Federal Republic.

he says that he doesn't remember how long he spent wandering the streets but that, try as he might, he could not reach the calle Tallers and was eventually forced to go home without news of his uncle.

The second memory is more brutal and less vague. It related to an incident that must have occurred days or hours later, still in the midst of the warzone that gripped the city during those bloody days. With his uncle Ricardo incarcerated aboard the prison ship *Uruguay*, his relatives sent the boy to the house of his uncle Francesc in La Trinidad, perhaps hoping that the violence would not reach the suburbs; the evidence shows that it was a vain hope. Early one morning, the family were woken by the noise of screams and gunfire. The noise was coming from the house next door, inhabited by a father and his daughter, a young woman who tutored Marco every evening since he could not go to school while in La Trinidad; he had to help his uncle in the grocer's shop. Marco leapt out of bed and raced to his teacher's house and found her in the yard, in the darkness, sobbing bitterly as she cradled her dead father in her arms. Marco maintains that the teacher's father was shot by officers of the Guardia Civil, he assumes because the man was a militant Catalanista; he also says that he loved his teacher and that he remembers standing there, devastated and motionless in the yard, oblivious to the crowds of people milling around them, spellbound by the tears, the inconsolable grief of this goodhearted woman. And he says that it was incidents such as this that kindled his militant anarcho-syndicalism at an early age.

It's impossible to determine whether the dramatic memories of Marco I have just recounted are true or a product of his imagination—there are no surviving witnesses to attest to these events, I haven't managed to locate a single corroborating document, and very much doubt that they exist; all I can say for certain is that, although Marco's imagination tends towards the dramatic, these particular events fit with the general history of the period. For the rest, it is unnecessary to bring up such brutal events as the death of his teacher's father to understand Marco's political affiliations. He was from a working-class family, grew up in working-class neighbourhoods, was put to work early—firstly, as I have mentioned, in his uncle Francesc's shop, later at the workshop of a tailor he remembers as red-haired and forbidding, and later still at a laundry, the Tintorería Guasch, where he was a delivery boy. His father and various other members of his family were militant C.N.T. members, and he received a sporadic but dutiful liberal education at various schools, cultural associations and anarchist cooperatives; furthermore Barcelona had more C.N.T. members than any other Spanish city—the union was an overwhelming presence in the areas where he grew up. But, according to Marco, what definitively converted him to the cause of anarchism was none of these things, but rather the influence of one of his hated stepmother's brothers.

His name was Anastasio García, and he was the closest thing to a father Marco had in his life, and perhaps an idol or a role model. Again, according to Marco's version of events, in the 1920s, Uncle Anastasio had been a man of action, he had been a member of—or had links with—Los Solidarios, the legendary anarchist group run by Buenaventura Durruti, Francisco Ascaso and Juan García Oliver—"the finest terrorists of the working class," as García Oliver himself once called them—and had worked with them in Spain, in France and in South America. So Uncle Anastasio was clearly a tough guy, although by the time Marco had any dealings with him he had become domesticated, not to say diminished and possibly alcoholic: he was living with a woman, Aunt Ramona, was working as a painter for Transmediterránea, a Barcelona-based shipping company dedicated to transporting cargo and passengers, and had become a member of the shipping branch of the C.N.T. He had no children and, when he met Marco, not only did he become fond of the boy, he also gave him a home for long periods, perhaps to protect him from the abuses of his sister.

Uncle Anastasio and Aunt Ramona lived on calle Conde del Asalto, next to the Palacio Güell and almost opposite Edén Concert, a music hall that hosted the most glittering stars in the artistic firmament at the time, and where Marco sometimes says he managed to see Josephine Baker and Maurice Chevalier, though at other times he says he did not see them in the fabled dance hall where he may never even have set foot (after all, shortly after the war it was converted into a cinema), but coming and going from the nearby Eden Hotel, where his aunt Ramona worked and where he spent his days lazing about, lured by the scent of opulence and the shimmer of celebrity.

The fact remains that Uncle Anastasio adopted Marco; he also taught him: at this point Marco had completed his autodidactic education as an indiscriminate reader and took classes in French, music, theatre and Esperanto in school, cultural associations and libertarian cooperatives, and in the home of the unfortunate teacher in La Trinidad; now his uncle Anastasio forced him to learn penmanship, typing and shorthand. He wanted to turn him into a useful citizen, but mostly he wanted to turn him into a good libertarian: and so began instilling in him a rationalist, anti-political, violent, self-righteous, egalitarian, redemptive, anachronistic, puritanical, public-spirited and sentimental idealism of a particular variety of Spanish anarchism; and this is why he took him everywhere with him. And this is also why when, on July 18, 1936, as he had been expecting for months, a group of military units staged a coup against the government of the Second Republic and the following day a libertarian uprising erupted in Barcelona to face them down, Uncle Anastasio and Marco joined the fight; and, a few short weeks later, joined the war that was to devastate the country for the next three years.

5

By early 2013, four years after I met Marco and having abandoned, for the second time, the idea of writing a book about him, everything had changed for me. The previous autumn, I had published a novel with fiction entitled *Outlaws*, and since that time I had done little other than travel in Spain and the United States. I felt reasonably happy in my own skin. A few months earlier I had told my psychoanalyst to go to hell and I felt as though fiction had healed me; or perhaps it was simply that I had become accustomed to life without a father. For her part, my mother had resigned herself to life without a husband. My wife and my son, finally, seemed happy, particularly my son.

Raül had been ten years old when the Marco scandal first broke; he was now about to turn eighteen and thought himself a bit of a tough guy. In the past fourteen months he had lost twenty kilos. He was strong and healthy and constantly playing sports. Next year, he would go to university, though he was still not sure whether he would take a degree in film studies or in something else. But his greatest love was cars, and what the two of us enjoyed more than anything was to climb into a car—our own or rented—and drive for miles, listening to music, and talking about everything under the sun, but especially about our ultimate idols: Bruce Willis and Rafa Nadal.

One day in early January, while Raül and I were aimlessly zigzagging along the winding roads of Ampurdán, he asked me whether I had started writing my next book. This was an unusual question, since Raül did not read my books, nor did we generally talk about them, and in that moment I suddenly realised that I had spent almost six months not writing and that, against all logic, I was not remotely worried. I told him the truth.

"You've been a bit lazy lately, haven't you?" Raül said.

I looked at him for a moment: he was staring out the windscreen, his lips curled into a sardonic smile.

"You take care of your own affairs," I advised, turning back to the road, "and I'll take care of mine."

"OK, man, don't get mad at me," he said, satisfied that he had managed to put me on the defensive, "I was only asking out of curiosity, OK?"

As I've said, my son was a little full of himself, to use a polite expression. But, perhaps because there was a jokey competitiveness to our relationship and I wanted to prove to him that, if I had not started writing again, it was not for want of inspiration but because I did not want to write or had not found the right moment, I began to reel off possible subjects for my next book, and when I mentioned Marco's case, summoning it from the limbo of my abortive projects, Raül interrupted me.

"That's a good subject," he said.

"You remember Marco?" I asked, surprised.

"Of course," he said. "The old guy who said he'd been in a concentration camp but it turned out he was a liar, yeah?"

"Exactly."

"Interesting guy," he mused. "You can't be that much of a liar and not be interesting."

Although I realised he was playing the tough guy again, he was right. Marco was extraordinary, I thought. Suddenly I felt that, though I had twice given up on the story, it had been through a lack of courage, because I sensed something hiding in the old man that interested me, or that profoundly concerned me and I was afraid to discover what it was. Raül said something I didn't hear; I asked him to say it again.

"I said I could help you."

"To write a book about Marco?"

"Sure. You'll have to talk to Marco, won't you? I mean, so he can tell you his life story. Well, I can film you guys while you're talking.

That way you only have to worry about what he's saying, and you'll have the whole thing on tape and you can watch it whenever you like. And this way, I can see whether the whole cinema thing is cool or not."

I pretended that I appreciated his offer, though in fact I was thinking that not only had I twice given up on Marco's story because I sensed it involved deeply personal issues that I was afraid to investigate, but worse, I had given up because of a fear I could barely admit: the fear that I would be accused of playing into Marco's hands, of trying to understand him and in doing so, to forgive him, of being complicit with this man who had mocked the victims of the worst crime in human history. I remembered Teresa Sala's cautionary words: "I do not think we need to understand the reasons for Señor Marco's deception"; I also remembered Primo Levi's words: "Perhaps one cannot, what is more one must not, understand what happened, because to understand is almost to justify." More than once in the previous four years, while I was writing my novel with fiction, I had thought about both quotes, particularly what Primo Levi had written and the manifest incoherence that he should have written this while at the same time he had spent his whole life attempting to understand the Holocaust through his books (to say nothing of the fact that he had also written things like the following: "For a secular man like me, the essential is to understand and to make others understand"). To understand is to justify, I thought every time I remembered this phrase. Should we forbid ourselves from understanding, or did we rather have a duty to understand? Until one day, a few days or weeks before my conversation with Raül, I accidentally came across Levi's phrase again and found the solution.

I came across it in a book by Tzvetan Todorov. In it, Todorov argued that what Levi meant (and, I extrapolated, what Teresa Sala meant) was valid only for Levi himself and the other survivors of the camps (including, presumably, Teresa Sala who, though not a survivor, was the daughter of a survivor, and therefore a victim of the camps): they did not have to try to understand their executioners, Todorov said, because understanding relies on some degree of identification, be it partial or temporary, with the perpetrator and that could be highly damaging. The rest of us cannot spare ourselves the effort of understanding evil, particularly extreme evil, because, as Todorov concludes, "Understanding evil is not to justify it, but the means of preventing it from occurring again." And so, I thought as I drove through Ampurdán with Raül, pretending to think about his offer, to understand Marco was not to justify him, but, at most, to acquire the means to prevent the emergence of another Marco. Besides, I was now intrigued to discover what it was in Marco that so affected me it frightened me, and in that instant I knew that I felt strong enough and brave enough to try to find out. Was it possible to find out? Was it possible to tell Marco's story? And was it possible to tell it without lying? Was it possible to present an account of Marco's lie as a true story? Or was it impossible, as Arrabal probably thought? Vargas Llosa and Magris had supposed that we could never know the profound truth about Marco, but surely this was the best reason for writing about him. Was this not knowing, or this difficulty of knowing, not the best possible reason for attempting to know? And, even if a book about Marco was an impossible book, as Arrabal—and perhaps Vargas Llosa and Magris—thought, surely that was the perfect reason to write it? Surely it is the impossible books that are most necessary, perhaps the only ones truly worth trying to write? Was this not what Vargas Llosa had really meant when he said I had to write about Marco, that night at his house in Madrid? Is noble failure the best a writer can aspire to?

"He might be dead," I said to Raül.

"What?"

"Marco might be dead," I said. "When I met him he was nearly ninety, and that was four years ago."

"And we didn't hear that he died? After everything he did? Not very likely."

That very afternoon, I telephoned Marco from my mother's house in Gerona, where we spent most weekends. He was alive. Not only was he alive; he still seemed possessed by the same agitation, the same feverish logorrhoea he had four years earlier. He talked about our only meeting, about Santi and about my sister Blanca, but mostly he talked about himself, about the injustice he had suffered, about his tireless solidarity, about everything he had given to so many people only to get nothing in return. As I listened, I was reminded of the talent of Santi and Lucas Vermal and I wondered whether, like them, I would be able to put up with this never-ending self-justifying torrent, but I told myself I could not give up at the first hurdle and, plucking up my courage, I managed to interrupt him: I told him that I had decided to resume the idea of writing a book about him.

"Oh, really?" he asked, as though there might be some other reason I was calling him. "I suppose we did leave things up in the air, didn't we?"

Before he had time to go on the attack again, I asked whether we could meet to talk about the idea. Without a flicker of hesitation, Marco agreed. It was Friday. We agreed to meet on Monday.

Convinced that Marco would agree to my writing a book about him—because his vanity would trump all possible reservations about the project—that night, I printed out Vargas Llosa's article, my own, and an article published in *El País* by José Luis Barbería, and gave them to my son.

"I'm seeing Marco on Monday," I said. "It's just an initial meeting, to get back in touch and explain what I want to do. Next week, we start recording, assuming that he accepts. If you're going to do it, you'd better read up on him."

Raül took the pages and, after dinner, lay on the sofa in the dining room and started reading them. I sat in an armchair, with him on one side and my mother on the other; I was vaguely listening to my mother, who was holding my hand, and watched the news on television while glancing at my son out of the corner of my eye. When he had finished reading, he smiled.

"The guy's insane," he said, letting the pages fall onto the rug.

I did not ask who he was referring to; I asked:

"You think so?"

"Who are you talking about?" my mother interrupted.

"Just some guy." Raül raised his voice to compensate for his grandmother's deafness. "He claimed he was in a concentration camp, but it was a lie."

My mother stared at him blankly, then she looked at me. I summed up Marco's story, though I had not even finished when she asked:

"And you think all that lying could be true?"

Raül laughed. I told my mother that this was precisely what I planned to try and find out. My mother squeezed my hand, as though she approved of what I had said, and Raül went on.

"Marco lives in a fantasy world, one that's more interesting and more fun than reality. That's the definition of being insane, surely?"

"I suppose so," I said. "It's like Don Quixote. Although Don Quixote is also sane. What I mean is, he's mad as a box of frogs, but he's also the most sensible man in the world. Except on the subject of books about chivalry."

"And Marco is like him?"

"I don't know. I don't even know if he has books about chivalry. That's something else I have to find out. Or rather that we have to find out. If all goes well, we'll start next week. Pay attention while you're filming, and afterwards you can tell me what you think of him. Alright?"

Raül shifted on the sofa, put a cushion under his head and pulled a face that to me seemed sceptical, though perhaps not.

"OK," he said.

On Monday, at the appointed hour, I showed up at Marco's house in Sant Cugat. I was on my own; Marco and his wife greeted me. At first glance, I could see no difference between the Marco I had met four years ago and this man; perhaps he was a little shorter, a little more wrinkled, but he still looked like a man of sixty, not one who was over ninety. As though he could read my thoughts, one of the first things he said was that his health had deteriorated, that he had heart trouble. "I thought I'd make it to a hundred," he said, his voice hoarse and anguished, "but I know now I won't get there." Then he launched into a torrent of self-glorification, showering me with the usual mixture of vindication and victimisation: he had had an amazing life, had been everywhere, met everyone, he had been a defender of the republic, a fervent anti-fascist during the war, a clandestine resistance fighter during the Franco regime, a regular victim of the prisons of dictatorship, a union leader, a civic leader, a campaigner for justice, liberty and historic memory; it was true that at the end of his life he had made the mistake of passing himself off as a survivor of the Nazi camps, though deep down it had not been a mistake, he had not lied but merely distorted the truth, and moreover he had distorted it for a good cause, to expose the horrors of the century; what had happened to him when the scandal blew up was unforgive- able, he had been insulted, slighted, trampled, lynched, as though he were vermin rather than a great yet humble man who had given his life for others, as though it were he who was indebted to the world when in fact the world owed him a debt . . . I let him ramble on while his wife bustled about the house and though she wasn't interested in what Marco was saying, or had heard it many times, meanwhile I was wondering what she thought about my idea of writing a book about her husband. When I realised that Marco was not going to stop talk- ing unless I interrupted him, I tried to do so. I almost had to shout to interrupt his peroration to say that I had come to see him because I wanted him to tell his whole story, but all in due time.

"If you tell me everything now, there will be nothing left to tell!" I all but shouted. Marco fell silent; it was like a miracle. We were sitting on the veranda, facing each other, separated by a large, rectangular wooden table; behind the table were shelves filled with books, maga- zines and box files. His wife had just appeared by his side, silent as a cat. Returning to my usual tone of voice, I asked: "Would you like me to tell you about my project?"

I told him. I said again that my idea was to write a book about him. I assured him that, in order to write it, I would need his help. I repeated that, in the first instance, I would need him to recount his life in detail from beginning to end. I told him that, if he did not object, my son would film our sessions and that, if he preferred, we could film them right here, in his house.

"No, not here," he said peremptorily, "I am me and my family is my family."

"In that case, we can film in my office," I said. "We won't be dis- turbed there."

I told him that, although I was a writer of fictions, I was propos- ing to write an absolutely accurate account, a novel without fiction. I added that, aside from what I had just said, I could not give him any advance idea of how the book would turn out once it was written.

"All the same," I warned him, "you shouldn't expect it to be a defence. I'm not going to pull the wool over your eyes: you shouldn't expect either rehabilitation or exoneration from me; but nor should you expect a condemnation. What I want is to know who you are and why you did what you did. That's what I want: not to rehabilitate you, but to understand you."

Marco looked at me with his dark, sunken, inquisitive eyes; I held his gaze. I repeated that I had no doubt that he could help me with my project: it was enough to know what he had done and to spend five minutes in his presence to be certain that he was a man who would prefer people to speak ill of him than not to speak of him at all. And I was about to go on to say, with hypocritical magnanimity, that if he did not wish to accept the arrangement, I would completely understand, when he spoke up.

"Truthfully, I do not need anyone to rehabilitate me," he said, although I was convinced that there was nothing he longed for more than rehabilitation. "All I need is for someone to listen to me. To make me understood."

"I will listen to you," I assured him.

Marco continued to stare at me; his wife stared too.

"I read an article about myself in *El País*," said Marco, and in that moment I regretted having written the article. "It was not well-informed."

I looked at his wife, then back at him and once again resorted to hypocrisy (or sarcasm).

"Were there errors in it?" I asked.

"No," Marco said. "But it wasn't me. Honestly, I am much more complex."

"I'm sure you're right," I said, this time sincerely, taking the way out he offered. "That is precisely why I want to write the book: to give a portrait of you as you are in all your complexity. And for that, we need to talk, you need to tell me your life story. Later, you'll be able to help me in other ways: you could provide me with documents, accompany me to places where you lived, give me phone numbers and addresses of people you knew . . ." I turned back to his wife and said, "One day, I would also like to talk to you, if you don't mind."

"I don't mind," his wife said. She smiled and got to her feet as though she had heard all she needed to hear. "But on condition that you don't film me. I am only Enric's wife, and you heard what my husband said: he is himself, and his family is his family."

For a moment, Marco gazed, entranced, as his wife left the veranda. I took advantage of his silence to ask:

"What do you say we start tomorrow?"

We started three days later. During the intervening period I again immersed myself in Marco's case, I re-read everything I had read about him and searched the internet for new information, where I discovered countless articles, recordings, interviews and comments. On the eve of our first session, I almost suffered a panic attack.

"Shit," I said to Raül, "we can't film in my office."

"Why not?" he asked.

"Because there's no lift. How do you expect a ninety-two-year-old man to climb the stairs to the third floor?"

I immediately telephoned Marco, thinking that, if we couldn't film in my office or in his house, we would have to postpone our first day's work, which seemed to me a bad omen. Marco was irritated by my call.

"You take care of your side of things, Javier," he said. "The stairs are my concern."

I think this was the first time he called me by my given name, and for a very uncomfortable second I felt as though Marco were talking to me the way I talked to my son.

The following day, before 4:00 p.m., Raül and I were in my office in the Gracia district waiting for Marco. The previous evening, my son had shown me how the camera worked—he had to leave late in the afternoon and we needed to be sure I knew how to operate it after he left—and now he set it on a tripod and set the tripod next to me, facing the armchair where Marco was to sit. At about four thirty, the doorbell rang. It was Marco; he had come with his wife. Although she was almost thirty years his junior, Marco was first to reach the top of the stairs, determined and panting for breath. I don't remember what his wife was wearing; as for Marco, the footage we shot that day shows him wearing a dark flat cap, a striped shirt and a polka-dot sweater with the sempiternal Republican flag pinned to it. Marco greeted me and began talking to Raül; I chatted with Dani. Once the preamble was over, I had Marco sit in the armchair facing the camera, Dani sat on a chair, Raül perched on a seat behind the camera and I sat in my office chair facing Marco. Next to me on the desk I had a notepad filled with questions for him, but in the first half-hour I was barely able to formulate a single one since Marco filled the time with a classic vindictive harangue full of self-congratulation and complaints. We listened patiently until, thanks in part to the intervention of his wife, I managed to get him to start recounting his life from the beginning.

It was at this point that the first interview really began. It ended some three and a half hours later, shortly before eight o'clock. By this time, Marco and I had been alone in the office for some time; Raül and Dani had left, first Dani, then Raül. That night, over dinner, my wife, my son and I talked about Marco. I asked Raül what he thought of him, what impressions he had gathered, whether he still thought the man was crazy.

"He's crazy and he's not crazy," he said without stopping to think, without looking up from his plate, and I guessed that this wasn't a spontaneous response. "He's like Don Quixote, he plays the fool, but he's no fool. And he's not like Don Quixote. He's much better."

I waited for him to explain, but he was chewing a piece of food, or perhaps mulling over his idea; it was my wife, unable to contain her impatience, who asked for an explanation.

"It's obvious," said Raül, as he finished swallowing or finished thinking or both. "Nobody takes Don Quixote seriously, he doesn't manage to fool anyone; but Marco, he fooled everyone." He finally looked up from his plate and looked at his mother. "Don't you get it? Everyone!" Then he turned to me with an excited gleam in his eyes, pointed the fork at me and said, "He's the fucking master!"

6

The bloodiest battle fought during the first days of the Civil War took place in Barcelona, on Sunday July 19, 1936. On Saturday, news had reached the city of a military uprising in Morocco and all day the streets and the cafés were filled with rumours. The air was thick with eve-of-war tensions. In the afternoon, Lluís Companys, the President of the autonomous Generalitat de Catalunya, refused to give weapons to the workers, who wanted to defend the current left-wing Popular Front government, but the C.N.T., the anarchist union that represented the majority of workers in the city, refusing to accept this refusal, looted the army depots, armed its members and prepared to fight.

At dawn the following day, the war broke out. In accordance with the strategy devised by those planning the coup d'état—a group of military officers, including Frances—a number of rebel columns armed to the teeth began to stream from the major barracks in the city—from Pedralbes, from calle Tarragona, from Travessera de Gracia and Sant Andreu—converging on the city centre, on the Plaza de Catalunya and the Rambla. But the operation was so poorly organised and met with such fierce resistance from the C.N.T., and detachments of the Guardia de Asalto, that the rebels never reached their target, or reached it only to be forced to surrender: they were hampered by barricades of paving slabs, by sniper fire, by home-made grenades launched from rooftops, by suicide trucks crashing straight into them. By midday, the whole city had become a battlefield, there were people fighting on every corner, there were corpses everywhere, and most of the churches and the convents were ablaze. In the afternoon, the tide of the battle shifted towards the anti-fascist forces: the local leader of the rebels, General Goded—who had arrived by hydroplane from Majorca at noon—surrendered unconditionally and was forced to put out a call to his men to lay down their weapons; at about 2:00 p.m., after some hesitation, the guardia civil pledged their loyalty to the legitimate government; at more or less the same time (perhaps a little earlier or a little later), on Avenida Icaria, a group of workers managed to convince rebel soldiers from the Regimiento de Artillería de Montaña No. 1, armed with a battery comprising two 75mm cannons, that their leaders had lied to them, and persuaded them to turn their guns on their own men, and from this point, the rebel forces, which had seen occasional defections to the enemy since morning, began to desert en masse. By nightfall, the rebels held only the Atarazanas barracks near the port and the barracks at Sant Andreu some kilometres from the centre, in which the largest cache of weapons in Barcelona was stored.

Marco had been at the Sant Andreu barracks for some hours, or he says he was there. At the time, he had just turned fifteen, he had spent a few days in La Trinidad, helping his uncle Francesc and his aunt Caterina in the shop and, like everyone else, he knew that something was brewing, perhaps the outbreak of the revolution, perhaps a military coup, perhaps both at once. On Sunday morning, as the sirens in every factory in the city wailed, he heard about the military uprising and the pitched battles being fought since dawn, and he received instructions, or he says he received instructions, from the workers' parties and the unions (not just the C.N.T., to which he claims he belonged), instructions telling all those with guns to proceed to the city centre with the aim of stopping the uprising; those without weapons were to go to the nearest barracks to get them, or at least to show the military that the people were opposed to the coup.

The barracks closest to La Trinidad was the Maestranza barracks in Sant Andreu, and so this is where Marco went. He doesn't remember what time he arrived, but he remembers that when he did, there were already people at the gates prepared to confront the rebels, people not only from Sant Andreu and La Trinidad, but also from Santa Coloma, from La Prosperidad and other suburban districts of Barcelona. He says that among this diverse, angry crowd, he met someone who, over the years, would become one of his closest friends: a militant anarchist named Enric Casañas. He says he doesn't remember how long he was there, waiting for who knew what, but that at some point a Republican plane appeared in the skies and dropped a rain of pamphlets over La Maestranza while several soldiers fired at it. He says that the plane immediately disappeared, only to reappear over the barracks a little later, this time browbeating those inside to surrender and dropping a few bombs that, he says, produced more dust and noise than anything. But, he says, it was at this point that the barrack gates opened and, as one man, the crowd launched an attack, although what the attackers found inside was not what they had expected: there was only a bunch of drunken, frightened soldiers wandering like idiots through courtyards and through mess halls full of half-finished food and drink, who gave up without a fight. Among other weapons stored in the Sant Andreu barracks that day were 30,000 rifles, and Marco says that people helped themselves to whatever they wanted, and that he ended up with a musket. And this is all that Marco remembers of that day, or all that he says he remembers.

Of the days that followed, he remembers almost nothing other than the jubilation of the triumph of the workers in Barcelona, but what he does remember or says he remembers is that three weeks later, in the midst of the exceptional euphoria of that tumultuous summer, his uncle Anastasio took part in the Conquest of Majorca.

It was one of the most senseless operations in this senseless war. The British historian, Antony Beevor, manages to sum it up succinctly in a single paragraph: "The largest operation in the east at this time was the invasion by Catalonian militia of the Balearic Islands. Ibiza and Formentera were taken easily and on 16 August 8,000 men with the support of the battleship *Jaime I* and two destroyers invaded Majorca under the command of an air force officer, Alberto Bayo, later to be Fidel Castro's guerrilla trainer. The invaders established a bridgehead unopposed, then paused as if in surprise. For once the militia had artillery, air and even naval support, yet they gave the Nationalists[*] time to organise a counter-attack. Modern Italian aircraft arrived and strafed and bombed the invading force virtually unopposed. The withdrawal and re-embarkation, ordered by the new minister of marine, Indalecio Prieto, turned into a rout. The island then became an important naval and air base for the Nationalists for the rest of the war."

What more is there to be said? That the operation was utter chaos. That the operation included not only armed militiamen, but also women, old men and children. That although the secretary of the navy gave the order to retreat, no-one had informed him of the operation, just as no-one had informed the minister of war, nor even the president of the Republic. That the expeditionary force lacked medical services, field hospitals and adequate supplies, and that, when they retreated, they left the beaches strewn with corpses and the island in the hands of an Italian fanatic with a thick red beard named Arconovaldo Bonaccorsi, nicknamed "Count Rossi," who, in his black fascist uniform with a white cross on the collar, spent several months crisscrossing the island in a crimson racing car accompanied by a chaplain of the Falange,[†] ordering the summary execution of workers. And that, in spite of what Beevor calls the "crushing defeat" of the Catalonian militiamen, when they returned home, Radio Barcelona announced: "The heroic Catalan columns have returned from Majorca after a glorious campaign. Not a single man suffered during a campaign that Capitan Bayo, with incomparable tactical skill, managed to accomplish magnificently, thanks to the morale and the discipline of our invincible militiamen."

Marco was one of them; by which I mean, one of the invincible militiamen who suffered a crushing defeat. Or so he insists. His memories of this farce, however, are scant and unclear. He claims that he eagerly joined the fight because, despite being barely fifteen years old, he was an impetuous and idealistic youth, very different from boys nowadays, he contends, but just like most boys of the time,

* The Nationalist forces, or fascists, had supported the failed military coup.

† Among the Nationalists was the party Falange Española Tradicionalista y de las JONS, which later became, under Franco, the only legal political party in Spain.

caught up in the dream of building a happy and just world, or at least a better world; but he admits that his main reason for joining was following in the footsteps of his uncle Anastasio, who, as an employee of Transmediterránea, sailed every week to the Balearic Islands, where he had friends and acquaintances and who, on discovering that the archipelago had fallen into the hands of the fascists, felt it was his duty to help. Marco says he shipped out on the *Mar Negro*, which may have belonged to Transmediterránea, and came home on the *Jaime I*. He says that his principal memory is one of utter confusion and constant improvisation, with everyone giving orders that no-one obeyed. He says that he shipped out clinging to the real protection of his uncle Anastasio and the illusory protection of the musket that he had taken from Sant Andreu barracks and barely knew how to use. He says that, during the crossing, he joined a group of young boys like him who were called the Musketeers, because they wore tricorn hats. He says that he thinks he remembers them, protected by the warship and the destroyers, landing at Son Cervera, but he also says that he barely set foot on land because his uncle forbade him and he spent hours playing war games with the rest of the Musketeers on the deck of the ship. He says that when they arrived they realised they were not the only ones who had come to liberate the islands, and that a similar expedition had set out from Valencia (or had already arrived from there), under the command of an officer from the Guardia Civil named Uribarri. He says that the exhilaration of the first days quickly turned to unease when they began to receive news that the militiamen who had gone ashore had been met, not by people elated at the prospect of being liberated, but by deserted towns and villages whose inhabitants had fled, and that unease turned to disappointment (though not to panic or to a sense of defeat) when the retreat began, a retreat that, to him, seemed no more disorganised than the shipping out and which left the beaches strewn, not with corpses, as I have written in accordance with the accounts of witnesses and historians, but with military equipment. He says he remembers nothing of the voyage home except that everyone aboard blamed the failure of the operation on disagreements between Bayo and Uribarri.

Back on the mainland, he says, they disembarked not in Barcelona but in Valencia, and he also says that they had to make their way back to

Barcelona by train. He says that he doesn't remember how much time he spent in Barcelona, but that days or weeks later, he and his uncle re-enlisted as volunteers, this time in the Columna Roja y Negra, a column (Marco does not say this; I am saying it) comprising anarchist militiamen who had taken part in the Majorca expedition that, under the command of the union leader, García Pradas, and Capitán Jimé-nez Pajarero, joined the Huesca front* in mid-September. He says that it was here he discovered what war really was. He says that it was here he first saw a man die, and here, in the midst of a gun battle or an aerial bombardment, while he was lying under a truck attempting to protect himself, he saw another man running across the road carrying his intestines in his hands and screaming for someone to help him put them back in his belly. He says that later the same day he discovered the man had died, and that the scene left him transfixed with horror, but that he quickly grew accustomed to the horror as, he says, hap-pens to everyone during a war. He says that at some point, he doesn't remember when, his uncle Anastasio was wounded, a minor injury that nonetheless left him with a noticeable limp; and he says that this unforeseen incident triggered the end of his uncle's war. But it wasn't the only cause, he says: his uncle was old, he was tired; besides, like so many anarchists, he scorned the government's disbandment of the militias which resulted in the Columna Roja y Negra being integrated with the 28th Division of the People's Republican Army. As a result, having voluntarily enlisted in the militias, Uncle Anastasio voluntarily resigned. His nephew did likewise, he said.

Back in Barcelona, Marco says that he started working as a mechanic in the Ford factory. Since the factory had been collectivised, Marco can justly claim that he contributed to the war effort, mend-ing cars, trucks and vans. He says that he was still a member of the C.N.T. and that he held a position in the union; he also says that he remembers little of his war years in the Republican rearguard, except that he was involved in civil defence and that, one day in the spring of 1938, when an Italian bomb was dropped on Gran Vía, opposite the Coliseum cinema, on a truck carrying four tons of TNT, he helped to dig out of the ruins of the bombed-out buildings the bodies of

* A Republican offensive against the Nationalist-held city of Huesca.

almost a thousand victims killed in the blast, including 118 children. As for his uncle Anastasio, when he came back injured from Huesca, he managed to get a job as caretaker of a building on the corner of Lepanto and Travessera de Gracia, in the district of El Guinardó. There, with Aunt Ramona, the elderly anarchist lived for almost two years; he still limped, he was worn out and he drank heavily. He died in autumn 1938. Marco didn't attend the funeral, because by then he was once more fighting at the front. Or so he says.

7

Is it possible to catch out a liar? The liar is sooner caught than the cripple, so runs the old Spanish proverb, but like so many proverbs—Spanish or otherwise—this is false: especially with a liar as expert as Enric Marco. When the Marco scandal broke, many people assumed that, because Marco had lied about being interned in Flossenbürg, he had lied about everything else. This is a fallacious assumption and one that betrays a spectacular ignorance about the nature of great lies and great liars: great liars do not traffic only in lies, but in the truth, and big lies are composed of little truths; to quote *Ich bin Enric Marco*, "As every great liar knows, a lie can triumph only if it is shored up by truths." Was the lie about his time in Flossenbürg the only one that Marco told? What were the truths that shored up Marco's lie or lies, whether triumphant or not?

For almost a year and a half, I worked full-time attempting to identify them; by which I mean: I attempted to reconstruct the real life of Enric Marco. The first thing I did was listen to Marco, giving him my undivided attention, in long filmed sessions which I tried to steer towards my ends, sessions that initially took place in my office in Gracia but were later continued in his house, in conversations in bars and restaurants and on walks through the places of his childhood, his youth and his maturity. Santi Fillol and Lucas Vermal loaned me the recordings of the dozens of hours they had spent talking to Marco in order to make their documentary. I engaged two assistants, one in Barcelona—Xavier González Torán—and another in Berlin—Carlos Pérez Ricart—thanks to whom I was able to read countless articles, interviews and news reports published about Marco, together with the documents detailing his life in Spain and in Germany. I watched and listened to innumerable radio and television interviews Marco had given and, after a certain point, I was allowed to consult his personal archive, which contained all manner of things, from articles and documents about him, to letters and autobiographical or pseudo-autobiographical writings. I read books about psychology, about philosophy, about sociology, about history—especially about history. I talked with historians specialising in the Civil War, the anarchist movement, Nazi Germany, with former and current members of the C.N.T., of FaPaC, of the Amical de Mauthausen, with former and current neighbours and relatives of Marco, with bar owners, friends and pupils who had known him fifty years earlier, with lifelong friends and mortal enemies, with workers, doctors, lawyers, neurologists, with journalists and police officers. In general, I conducted these investigations alone, but sometimes I was accompanied by my son and also, now and then, by my wife. This was weird: like Marco, as a rule, I kept my family and my work separate; but in this case, the three of us frequently discussed Marco, we argued about him, joked about him. I am incapable of writing a book without it becoming an obsession, sometimes an unhealthy obsession (which is cured only when the book is completed), but I think I had never before been as obsessed with a character as I was with Marco. There came a moment when everything happening to me had something to do with Marco, or referred me back to him, or contrasted with him. During this period, I regularly dreamed about Marco, and in those dreams, or rather those nightmares, I was arguing with this man, who, to defend himself, constantly accused me of being a liar and a charlatan, of being like him, of being much worse than him, sometimes even of being him.

Naturally, one of the first people I talked to when I began investigating the life of Enric Marco was Benito Bermejo, the historian who had exposed his deception. The majority of our conversations took place on the telephone, and these calls rarely lasted less than an hour. On one occasion I travelled to Madrid especially to see him. That day, Bermejo told me many things, including that he had not given up on writing a book about Marco but that, for the moment, he had shelved the idea, perhaps mostly because he had moral qualms: he was tired of being a wet blanket, denouncing a liar was a thankless task, he had already done his work, to continue investigating Marco's life might do damage to Marco and his family. Bermejo also relayed two important pieces of information, or rather one fact and one suspicion. The fact was that, contrary to what everyone, including Marco's family, believed, he had not had two wives—Danielle Olivera, his current wife, and María Belver, his previous wife, with whom he had lived for twenty years, from the mid-Fifties to the mid-Seventies—but three. He told me that, some time after the story blew up (or he caused it to blow up), he had been nosing around in the archive in Alcalá de Henares and there, in the documentation of the Spanish volunteer workers sent by Franco to help Hitler in the 1940s, he had found a file on Marco recording his marriage to a woman named Ana Beltrán Ribes. Intrigued, he looked up the name in the Barcelona telephone directory, but he did not find her; he did, however, find a woman named Ana María Marco Beltrán and, thinking that she might be Marco's daughter, he called her. The woman said that it was true, she was Marco's daughter; she also told him that her mother and Marco had been married in the Forties, but she said that it was a subject she didn't wish to discuss, that for her the matter was closed and no good could come of reopening it; in the end, she asked Bermejo to leave her in peace. He left her in peace. However, the following day, he received a call from a man who said he was the son of this woman, the grandson of Marco, and, although this man insisted that he *did* want to discuss the subject, because he didn't understand why his grandfather had hushed up his first family, the historian had decided to let it lie.

This was Bermejo's fact. As to his suspicion, it had to do with Marco's role in the C.N.T., the anarchist union of which he became secretary general in the mid-seventies, during the shift from dictatorship to democracy. That day, in Madrid, Bermejo mentioned—initially in his house, and later in a bar in the Chamberí area where he took me for lunch—the testimony of numerous anarchists who, long before Marco was unmasked, had publicly and privately, verbally and in writing, cast doubt, not only on his clandestine resistance during Franco's dictatorship, but also on his conduct after the arrival of democracy while he was secretary general of the union. As Bermejo explained:

"From a completely reliable source, I discovered that Marco

was drawing a type of pension—known as *Pensiones de Clases Pasivas*—generally drawn only by civil servants or by those who had fought in the war (though it is also paid to victims of terrorist attacks and similar incidents). Marco says that he fought in the war, though I doubt it, for various reasons, including the fact that he was born in 1921 and those drafted in the last conscription by the Second Republic, the Quinta del Biberón—the Baby's Bottle Call-Up—were born in 1920."

This was in mid-February 2013, I had spent barely a month and a half immersing myself in Marco's life, so I said:

"Was Marco a civil servant?"

"Not as far as I know," said Bermejo, "unless . . ."

Bermejo trailed off, and I stared at him, unable to work out what he was getting at. Eventually, he finished the sentence:

"Unless he is drawing the pension as a former police officer."

"You're saying Marco was a snitch?"

"I'm not saying that," Bermejo corrected me. "A lot of other people have said as much, including some of his old comrades; or at least they have insinuated it. And I'm not saying it's true: I'm simply raising the possibility. A possibility that, incidentally, would help to explain some of the disasters that befell the C.N.T. in the 1970s, and almost destroyed what had been the most powerful union in the country during the Second Republic and became an inconvenient factor in the transition from dictatorship to democracy. Just imagine the damage a police informant within the union could have done to the anarchists back then. But, all in all, this is simply conjecture; maybe you can confirm it."

That evening, I left Madrid in a state of anguish, and in the following weeks I was plagued by a doubt I had managed to keep at bay from the moment I decided to begin a serious investigation of Marco's life. The anguish and doubt didn't relate to the possibility that Marco might have been a police informant, something I thought astonishing but not implausible, but the very act of writing a book about him. Was I entitled to write such a book? Bermejo was right, just as Santi Fillol had been three years earlier: I already knew enough about Marco's story to know that everyone comes off badly, that telling it would mean being a wet blanket, it would mean poking in the eye not just Marco and his family, but the entire country. Did I want to do that? Was I prepared to do that? Was it right to do it? Was it enough that Marco had given me his permission and was collaborating with me? Did I have the gall to write a book in which Marco's wife and children would find out that he had had another wife, other children, or that he had been a police informant? What else would they find out, what else would I end up recounting in this book, what else might I discover if I carried on with my investigation? Was I not doggedly trying to write a book that was not simply impossible, but reckless? Was my idea not immoral, not because it would mean playing into Marco's hands, sanctioning or suppressing his lies (or attempting to absolve him of them), but precisely the opposite, because it would mean putting an end to his lies, telling the truth? Was it not better to give up, to abandon the book, to leave Marco to the fiction that, over the years, had saved him, without bringing to light the truth that could kill him?

8

Marco claims he re-enlisted in the Republican army in the spring of 1938, in response to an appeal by the Autonomous Catalan Government for young men to join the ranks. The Civil War was in its penultimate year, and the Francoists had just broken through the Aragon front and were threatening Catalonia, so Marco was sent to the front at Segre, a river almost three hundred kilometres in length that formed the longest line of defence for Catalonian Republicans, and had been the scene of heavy fighting from early April.

Marco's memories of this particular phase of the war are more detailed and more abundant than those of earlier periods. He says that he travelled to the front in a truck with boys just like himself, volunteers just as he was, including his childhood friend Antonio Fernández Vallet, the son of a barber from La Trinidad. He says that, when they arrived at the front, they were divided into various units and, unfortunately, he and Fernández Vallet were not assigned to the same unit. He says that he clearly remembers his unit: third Company of the third Battalion of the 121st Brigade of the 26th Division—formerly the Durruti Column. He says that the unit held positions in the hills of Montsec, the villages Sant Corneli and La Campaneta. He says that he was the youngest soldier in his unit. He says he remembers some of the other soldiers: Francesc Armenguer, from Les Franqueses; Jordi Jardí, from Anglès; a lad named Jorge Veí or Vehi or Pei; a boy named Thomas or Tomás. He also says that he remembers the *comisario* of his unit, Joan Sants, and obviously Ricardo Sanz, the head of his division and a friend of Buenaventura Durruti. He says that most of his comrades had not been to school and couldn't read or write and that he wrote the letters that they sent to families, girlfriends and friends, just as he often wrote on the so-called *diario moral*, a board that offered news of interest to members of the unit. He says that sometimes he dared to do things few soldiers dared to do: sometimes, he said, he wandered deep into no-man's-land and shouted questions to the fascists, questions that his comrades had suggested he ask, what town or village they were from, whether they knew some friend or relative. He says that through such favours he became popular and admired by his comrades in arms. For years, he told another story (though one he didn't tell me). He said that on the frontlines in Segre he met "Quico" Sabaté, the legendary anarchist guerrilla who fought with the Republican Army for three years and who, after the defeat, continued to wage war against the Franco regime until 1960, when, after twenty-one years spent fighting a personal war against the dictatorship, he was gunned down near the French border. Marco wrote more than once about his relationship with Sabaté. For example, in a letter to the editor of *El País* in the early 2000s, he wrote: "I met 'Quico' personally. It was in the summer of 1938, one day when he visited the trenches held by the 26th Division, the Durruti Column, high up in the sierra de Montsec, and he proposed that a group of boys coordinate guerrilla actions in the fascist rearguard. At the time 'Quico' was setting up a guerrilla unit with the 11th Army Corps. We settled on a few boys: Pei, from Poble Sec; Jardí from Anglès; a short, scrawny Salamancan we called Gandhi; Francesc Armenguer, an intelligent, dependable lad from Les Franqueses who was killed some months later while crossing the río Segre between Soses and Torres de Segre, just after being appointed comisario of the unit; and myself. It was exciting to find yourself on 'the other side' wearing an enemy uniform, gathering information, cutting communications, helping in the escape of a number of Asturian prisoners forced to build defensive works."

Marco also remembers (or says he remembers) that during his time at the Segre front, he attended the Escuela de Guerra (the army's war school). He says that attendance meant climbing down from the summit of Sant Corneli and La Campaneta two days a week to the village where the classes were held, Vilanova de Meià, or Santa María de Meià, he doesn't remember exactly, or he says he doesn't remember. He says that here he was taught things such as Morse code, and that he remembers a number of his teachers, among them a Capitán Martín. He says he doesn't remember precisely when his time at the school ended, but he does remember that he graduated with the rank of corporal. He says the atmosphere in the trenches was poisoned by the civil war within the civil war in which communists and anarchists were embroiled, especially since they had clashed on the streets of Barcelona in May of the previous year, and that those like him who were militant in the anarchist union, the C.N.T., felt constantly under scrutiny by the S.I.M., the intelligence service, which was dominated by communists, who used the organisation as a political police force. He says that, one day, a leaflet arrived from the C.N.T. informing them that, following the signing of a pact three days earlier in Munich by the Western democracies with Nazi Germany and fascist Italy, victory was assured for Francoism in the Spanish Civil War, and the same leaflet recommended that, when the war was over, militant union members should organise a resistance underground, and offered instructions as to how to go about this. He says that, from that day on, he and his comrades remained in the trenches more out of a sense of camaraderie and duty than out of conviction. He says that, with or without conviction, at some point during that autumn, he and his unit crossed the río Segre and that this offensive—probably the same one that held Seròs, Aitona and Soses on the left bank of the river for several days in November—was intended to alleviate pressure on the Ebro front, where one of the largest, bloodiest and most decisive battles of the war was being fought. He says that he has some memories of the days he spent on the far bank of the río Segre, including Francesc Armenguer dying as he crossed the river, and Jordi Jardí being shot in the arse; he also remembers (or says he remembers) a homosexual adjutant named Antonio who was scared to death and who, in the course of a night march, was lost in the darkness and never seen again. He says he also remembers being promoted to sergeant during this fleeting Republican advance and, in one of the numerous autobiographical (or supposedly autobiographical) writings in his personal archive—Marco is not only a compulsive talker, but an obsessive writer—he wrote that the commander of his unit promoted him to officer on the battlefield "for repeated displays of valour in the performance of his duties." But what he most remembers, or says he remembers, is that one afternoon, during heavy shelling by the enemy artillery, an explosion lifted him into the air and he lost consciousness.

From this point, Marco's memories of the war become confused. He is unable to give the precise nature of his injury, which, moreover, left no scar on his body; he says only that, from what he knows, it caused internal damage, that it affected his bronchia and his lungs and forced him to take a long convalescence during which he was constantly spitting blood. He says that, afterwards, he was sent back from the front and that one rainy evening he crossed the river, carried on a stretcher over a pontoon bridge, close to a first-aid post where he spent the night. He says that he later spent time in various field hospitals behind the lines, in Manresa, possibly in Agramunt, definitely in the convent at Monserrat where he spent a month, a month and a half, perhaps longer. He says he barely remembers anything of his peregrinations as a convalescent soldier, except the spitting blood, the constant fever, the whispering voices of the nurses, and the shame of being naked in front of these women. He says that he arrived back in Barcelona in a truck packed with soldiers, shortly before the city was captured by Franco's troops on January 26, and that he remained there rather than taking the route towards exile as many of his comrades did. He says that, in his case too, the logical thing would have been to go into exile, given that he had been a warrant officer in the Republican army and a militant member of the C.N.T. and as a result would have been exposed to all manner of reprisals from the *franquistas*, but that he didn't leave because he had still not fully recovered, and also so that he could follow the instructions of the union, which recommended remaining in the country and organising a resistance. He says that his comrades dropped him off in the centre of the city, on la Diagonal, that he made his own way to El Guinardó and that, when he reached the corner of Lepanto and Travessera de Gracia, he rang the bell of the building where his uncle Anastasio and aunt Ramona lived when he had last been in Barcelona on leave only a few months earlier, just before he received his corporal's stripes. He says that it was his aunt Ramona who opened the door and who, after her initial surprise, hugged him, smothered him in kisses and ushered him inside. And he says that from that day, he spent a long time holed up in his aunt Ramona's place, not simply holed up but in hiding, not setting foot outside, to rest and allow Aunt Ramona's attentions to heal his invisible wounds before plunging into the clandestine armed struggle against the triumphant fascists with the same self-sacrifice and the same courage with which he had fought throughout the war.

9

This, in summary, is the story of Marco's exploits during the war as Marco has always related them, or at least as he has related them since, after decades of silence, he once again began to talk about the war towards the end of the 1960s, when Francoism was crumbling, and Franco's advancing years made it possible to envisage, or to imagine, an end to the dictatorship. The story, in broad outline, is plausible. Is it also truthful? Or is it merely the fruit of Marco's self-serving imagination, incited by the death rattle of the Franco regime and the first glimpses of freedom, which were gradually turning the dim and distant fact of having fought alongside the vanquished into a virtue?

It is very probable that, when I began researching Marco's life, most people believed—as Benito Bermejo believed—that it was not true that Marco fought in the war; in any event, nobody had located a single document proving that he had. Not even Marco himself, who, as both he and his wife insisted, had searched in vain for his military record in the late 1970s. I now searched for it, but I found no mention of his name in any of the Civil War archives: neither in Salamanca, nor in Ávila, Segovia or Guadalajara. This absence proves nothing, of course, such archives are incomplete and there are people who fought in the war who do not appear in any of them. Marco knew this. What he did not know, or pretended not to know, was the fact that he was drawing a military pension as a former warrant officer in the Republican army also did nothing to corroborate the account he was so eager to propose to demonstrate that he had not invented the story of his war years as he had his time in Flossenbürg concentration camp. Because in the Seventies and Eighties, after the dictatorship,

the new democratic authorities awarded such financial benefits without asking too many questions, and indeed without requiring claim-
ants to provide supporting documentation; all that was required to
claim such pensions was the testimony of former comrades in arms,
or former officers from the routed army, and these were sometimes
falsified. And so, Bermejo was correct: Marco was indeed drawing a
Pensión de Clases Pasivas; but he was not entirely correct, or at least his
inference appeared to be mistaken: Marco was not drawing a pension
as a former police officer—that is to say a police informant—but as
a warrant officer of the Second Republic. Or was he doing so both
as a warrant officer and as an informant, I wondered. Had Marco
genuinely been a warrant officer of the Second Republic? Or had he
hoodwinked the authorities in order to receive the pension? Could
Marco have invented his entire war record for the same reason he had
invented his stint in Flossenbürg, to gild his biography with an epic
lustre?

This is what most people believed ever since Bermejo had
unmasked Marco; but there were people who had been thinking this
for quite some time. In 1984, twenty-one years before the scandal
erupted, when the reputation of the great impostor and the great
pariah was still intact, or almost intact, his predecessor as secretary
general of the C.N.T., Juan Gómez Casas, published a book about the
union in which he cast doubt on Marco's record as a militant anarchist
during the dictatorship, and in which he revealed that, although our
man insisted he had fought during the war, "given his age" he could
not have done so. This was also Bermejo's argument; an argument that
nonetheless has a flaw: it is true that the last mobilisation announced
in 1938 by the Second Republic was the 1941 call-up of those born in
1920, the so-called Quinta del Biberón ("The Baby's Bottle Call-Up"),
and that Marco was born in 1921 and therefore belonged not to this
mobilisation but to the next (the Quinta del Biberón was the penultimate rather than the last mobilisation by the Second Republic: the
last was the 1942 call-up, the so-called Quinta del Chupete—"The
Baby's Pacifier Call-Up"—but this was not relayed to C.N.T. members until January 1939, by which time the war had already been lost,
and few obeyed the order to mobilise); nevertheless, the possibility
remains that, as he claims, Marco voluntarily enlisted and lied about

his age since, technically, all volunteers had to be over eighteen years old and he was only seventeen. Is this what happened? Did Marco fight as a volunteer? Or was all this a fabrication?

I quickly realised that this would be very difficult to prove either way, because there were no documents and very few witnesses (at least I couldn't find them); this meant everything, or almost everything, depended on Marco's testimony, and on the inconclusive, not to say problematic investigations that I could make, such that I resigned myself to remaining in the territory of hypothesis in this part of his biography. I did, however, succeed in finding some witnesses. Enric Casañas, for example. Casañas was the young militant anarchist Marco claims to have met on July 19, 1936, during the siege of the Sant Andreu barracks, and who he says immediately became his life-long friend. Casañas was still alive, and Marco gave me his telephone number, though not before sending him a letter informing him of my impending visit, and reminding him of their friendship and of the explosive events of the memorable day on which they had apparently met. As soon as I had Casañas' telephone number, I called him. His wife answered, her name was María Teresa. I told her I wished to speak to her husband, and I explained why. His wife told me there was nothing to be gained by talking to Casañas, because he had lost his memory; nonetheless, she did not object to my visiting.

And so, one afternoon in late September 2013, I visited him in his apartment on the calle Francolí in Barcelona. At the time, Casañas was ninety-four, two years older than Marco, a tall, wiry man with thinning, snow-white hair, physically well preserved. He had fought for three years, spent decades in exile in Brazil, and returned to Spain after the death of Franco; he, too, had been a member of both the C.N.T. and the Amical de Mauthausen, where, with his conciliatory disposition and his spotless reputation as a clandestine resistance fighter, an eternal exile, and a libertarian, he had defended Marco when his charade was discovered, something that won him Marco's enduring gratitude. When I stepped into Casañas' apartment that afternoon, I discovered that his wife had told me the truth. The elderly anarchist spent most of the two hours I was there poring over a photograph of Marco, a photo from an identity card I had given him in the hope of jogging his ruined memory; it was all in vain: he did not recognise

Marco, and though he still had wisps of memory of July 19, 1936, none of these included our man. While Casañas tried to remember, with help from me and from his wife, from time to time I chatted with her. She knew Marco, of course, but she believed that their friendship had been formed during their time in the Amical de Mauthausen, or perhaps in the C.N.T. in the 1970s, not during the war; furthermore, in their thirty years of marriage, she had listened countless times to Casañas talk about the war in general and about July 19 in particular, and often about his comrades back then, but, to the best of her recollection, Marco's name did not crop up in his stories.

This was the only thing I learned in that abortive interview. Some days later, Casañas' wife telephoned to say that she had inquired about Marco with her husband's brother, Rogeli, who was two years younger, but that, like her, he had not heard his brother mention Marco's name in his stories of the war. At the time, I had read all, or almost all the interviews given by Casañas and consulted the historians who had interviewed him when he still had his memory; Marco made no appearance, no-one had heard Casañas speak of him, just as Casañas was not mentioned in the war stories Marco had written and which had been published while Casañas remembered enough to confirm or deny them. I realised that this was likely an example of the way in which Marco usurped other people's pasts, or inserted himself into them: chances are that Marco was not at the Sant Andreu barracks on July 19, and in order to "prove" that he was, he sought corroboration from an authentic witness who, as in the case of his friend Casañas, was no longer in a position to refute his story.

Marco's July 19 epic was undoubtedly a fiction, but did he have an uncle Anastasio, and was he who Marco said he was? Had he fought in the war in Majorca and in Huesca, and had Marco been with him? It was impossible to know, or at least I was unable to confirm it: during my research I searched for his uncle Anastasio on the internet, in libraries, periodicals and archives, and while there was no reason to doubt his existence, I could find no documentary evidence that he was an anarchist, nor a friend or acquaintance of Durruti, nor a former Republican soldier. This fruitless search, however, is not enough to dismiss the possibility that Uncle Anastasio was all of these things, or some of them, nor that Marco had been with him during the Battle of Majorca, or fought with him on the Huesca front, though at the time Marco would have been little more than a child. His memories of both incidents are vague, confused and generic, as was apparent to the members of Ateneu Llibertari Estel Negre—the Black Star Libertarian association of Majorca—who, in late February 2004, a year before Marco was unmasked, invited our man to give a talk about his experiences of the invasion. Many of those in attendance came away with the impression that Marco had not set foot in Majorca in 1936, since he scarcely gave any concrete details of what happened there. This, too, doesn't prove that our man didn't take part in the operation; after all, he was trying to remember something from almost sixty years earlier, and such a long period can blur and erase everything. Furthermore, I mentioned earlier the chaotic and unplanned nature of the Majorca operation, and the fact that some of those who participated were mere boys, something that explains why many reliable historians find it easier to accept the notion that Marco travelled to Majorca at fifteen than the notion that he fought on the Segre front at seventeen and was elevated to the rank of warrant officer.

Did Marco truly fight on the Segre front? As I have said, compared to the details he gives of his time in Majorca and Huesca, those of his time in Segre are much more plentiful and precise, or that was my first impression. This impression began to crumble when I discovered that, right up to the moment when his deception was unmasked, various historians had spoken to Marco to glean information about the battles fought there, and not only did their questions elicit nothing, or almost nothing by way of answer but, like the members, or some of the members, of Estel Negre in Majorca, they left with the unsettling impression that Marco had not lived through the events in question. For my part, knowing Marco (or the form and the purposes of Marco's fictions), I would bet that the episode with the legendary "Quico" Sabaté is a lie from beginning to end. There is no doubt that Sabaté did indeed fight on the Segre front at the end of the war; but that is where the truth ends (at least I believe so). In fact, Marco never spoke to me about his supposed meeting with the guerrillero, perhaps because he was afraid that, at this point in our relationship, or my knowledge of him, I would not believe him. The entire incident, it hardly needs saying, is characteristic of Marco's novelistic imagination, just like the high-flown and sentimental tone of his letter to the editor of *El País* ("Quico spilled every last drop of his blood and much more besides to win men greater freedom and to transform society"); and the goal of the text is no different from that of Marco's other fabrications: in it, he appears to be defending the figure of the indomitable anarchist when in fact he is vindicating himself as a comrade of the indomitable anarchist. It was also an opportune moment; the letter was sent to *El País* in January 2000, shortly before the great craze for so-called historical memory in Spain, so that his connection to a hero of the anti-fascist resistance might burnish Marco with some of that heroism and furnish him with moral and political capital.

Lastly, what can be said about the wound caused by the exploding shell which, according to Marco's account, sent him back from the front lines at Segre and forced him to endure an itinerant convalescence at various field hospitals behind the lines before returning to Barcelona, where he spent months recovering? In this case, the incident seemed to me suspicious, if not implausible from the outset (and not simply because of the dubious vagueness of Marco's account). Firstly, there is no mention of it in any of his biographies, even the most exhaustive—the one he dictated to Pons Prades in 1978, the one dictated to Jordi Bassa in 2002—and this detail seemed inexplicable, because a war wound is too important to leave out, especially in stories intended to vindicate the military past of the protagonist. Secondly, almost everyone I managed to interview who knew Marco as a young man—including his first wife's only daughter, her sister and brother-in-law—knew or believed they knew that Marco had fought during the war, and yet none of them had ever heard of him returning injured from the front. Thirdly, the injury itself: was it likely that a wound from an exploding shell could leave not the slightest scar, yet render the victim semi-conscious and forced to recuperate for such a long period? In an attempt to answer this question, I spoke to doctors and consulted medical books—both contemporary and of the period—and concluded that, if the injury were real, it could only have been caused by the rupture of an internal organ, almost certainly the stomach, which would leave no scar and could be caused by a powerful explosion near the victim. But I also concluded that it was very unlikely anyone could survive such an injury at the time and in the conditions Marco claimed: if he didn't die of an internal haemorrhage or peritonitis, the patient would have required an operation, something Marco himself insists was not performed and which, had it been performed, would have left a scar; moreover, such a procedure would have been exceedingly complex in the chaos and confusion of the front lines during the final weeks of the war in Catalonia. To recover from an injury of this nature without surgery would have been almost a miracle, and I do not believe in miracles.

This, in more or less these exact words, I explained to Marco one day on the veranda of his house. It was in September 2013, we had spent hours discussing details of his life, and, after a bitter argument, a dispirited, reluctant Marco eventually accepted that perhaps he had not returned from the war wounded. In that moment I realised that, assuming our man had fought on the front lines, and had come home during the winter of 1939, at some point in the retrospective process of forging a glorious biography for himself, he decided that the idea of *not* going into exile after the war, of remaining in Barcelona, did not square with his hero's journey, even though he stayed in Barcelona or claims he stayed in Barcelona motivated by the fearless aim of joining the armed underground resistance and certainly not, as with most Republican soldiers, motivated by the prosaic, jaded, spontaneous aim of going unnoticed, avoiding reprisals and surviving defeat. No: the heroic fictional character Marco created needed a very good reason for not choosing the path of exile, and the best his creator could come up with was a serious war wound.

So, did Marco fight in the war? Or was it all lies from beginning to end? The latter is what I thought for a long time and, although I do not believe in miracles, it took a miracle to convince me I was wrong.

A miracle, or what seemed to me a miracle. Or almost. What happened was that, one day, I stumbled on the photocopy of a news item published in *La Vanguardia* on September 29, 1938, at which point Marco said he had been on the Segre front; my assistant in Barcelona, Xavier González Torán, brought it to me in my office one afternoon in April 2013. The article gave an account of two acts of "civic-military confraternity," two celebrations in two different loca-

ACTOS DE CONFRATERNIDAD CIVICO-MILITAR

En una villa de Cataluña celebróse un festival, organizado por la primera compañía telefónica del Batallón de Transmisiones del Ejército del Este.

La señorita Pepita Bonet, en representación de las mujeres antifascistas de la población, hizo entrega, al jefe de la citada compañía, capitán don Mario Fusero, de un espléndido banderín. En correcta formación, y a los acordes de los himnos nacional y catalán, desfiló la primera compañía telefónica, acompañada de la población.

En el Ayuntamiento, la banda de música del XVIII C. E. ejecutó varias piezas de su escogido repertorio. Acto seguido, hubo audición de sardanas y vermut de honor.

Por la tarde, con gran asistencia de público, se celebró un lucido baile, amenizado por la orquestina de dicho cuerpo.

Por la noche actuó la banda del XVIII C. E., y también los artistas Cecilia Gubert, Rosa Llopis, Emilio Vendrell y Manuel Abad, que deleitaron a la concurrencia.

Asistieron a dichos actos, el comandante del Batallón de Transmisiones, don Santiago Herrera; jefes y comisarios del XVIII C. E. y otras autoridades militares, así como el Ayuntamiento y representaciones político-sindicales.

—Con motivo de la clausura de fin de curso de la Escuela de Capacitación de Cabos de la 121 Brigada, ha tenido efecto un simpático acto al que asistieron, especialmente invitados, los niños y niñas de la población civil. Comenzó con un partido de fútbol, a cargo de una selección de dicha escuela y el equipo de Sanidad de la 120 Brigada.

Luego se sirvió una comida, con asistencia de todos los alumnos y los niños invitados. Una nota digna de mencionar es la presentación de un periódico mural confeccionado por los colegiales.

Como invitados, asistieron a este acto de confraternización, el jefe y el comisario, los cuales hicieron uso de la palabra, realzando la alta moral de los combatientes y su abnegación por la capacitación de los soldados.

Seguidamente, se dió lectura a la clasificación obtenida, siendo los cinco primeros los siguientes: Enrique Marco Batlle, tercer batallón, 85'33 puntos. Enrique Cabrellez, segundo batallón, 77'91 puntos; Ramón Benaiges, cuarto batallón, 72'84 puntos; Jaime Prat, segundo batallón, 68'14; Pedro Riera, segundo batallón, 67'88 puntos.

Por la tarde, se efectuó una emisión de música en discos, y por la noche, sesión cinematográfica.

Acts of Civic-Military Confraternity

In a villa in Catalonia, a festival was organised by the first radio company of the Signal Brigade of the Eastern Army.

Señorita Pepita Bonet, representing the anti-fascist women of the area, presented the leader of the aforementioned company, capitán don Mario Fusero, with a splendid pennant. To the strains of the National and Catalan anthems, the first radio company marched in strict formation, accompanied by the townspeople.

At the Town Hall, the band of the XVIII C.E. played various pieces from their select repertoire. Afterwards there was a recital of sardanas* and toasts were drunk.

In the afternoon, great crowds attended a dazzling ball, with music provided by the dance band of the same regiment.

In the evening the band of the XVIII C.E. performed with Cecilia Gubert, Rosa Llopis, Emilio Vendrell and Manuel Abad, which delighted the audience.

Present at the festival were don Santiago Herrera, the commandante of the Signal Brigade; commanders and officers of the XVIII C.E., other military personnel, the town council as well as political and union representatives.

—To celebrate the end of training at the Officers Training School of the 121st Brigade, a charming ceremony was held, to which the boys and girls from the local civilian population were specially invited. It began with a football match between teams from the field training school and the Medical Corps of the 120th Brigade.

Afterwards, there was a meal to which all the trainees and the children were invited. It is worth mentioning the presentation of a bulletin board, made by the schoolchildren.

The guests of honour at this act of confraternity, the commandant and the comisario, gave speeches highlighting the excellent morale of the troops and their selflessness in training the soldiers.

Later, the grades of the trainees were read out, of whom the top five were: Enrique Marco Batlle, third battalion, 85.33 points; Enrique Cabrellez, second battalion, 77.91 points; Ramón Benaiges, fourth battalion, 72.84 points; Jaime Prat, second battalion, 68.14; Pedro Riera, second battalion, 57.88 points.

In the afternoon, there was a broadcast of phonograph records, and in the evening a cinematographic presentation.

---

* Catalan circle dances

tions on the Republican front which, for obvious reasons in time of war, were not named: the first was a festival "organised by the first radio company of Communications Battalion of the Eastern Army"; the second was held "to mark the end of training at the Officers Field School of the 121st brigade." According to the anonymous reporter, this second party, which included the children of the town, began with a football match, followed by a meal peppered with speeches from the leader and the *comisario* of the brigade and concluded in the evening with movies and music. After the meal and the speeches, there was a reading of the full list of aspiring officers at the school. The news item gave the names, the battalions and the grades of the top five graduates; the first among them, I read, belonged to the third battalion and achieved a grade of 85.33. His name was Enric Marco Batlle.

I gave a start, and cried out. It was true: Marco had fought in the war, more than that he had fought, just as he claimed, with the 3rd Battalion of the 121st Brigade of the 26th Division—the former Durruti Column. It was true: Marco had been a corporal in the Republican army (indeed it was possible that he ended the war a sergeant; on the other hand it is sheer fantasy that he became a lieutenant, though Marco claimed as much in one of the numerous supposedly autobiographical texts he sent to the Amical de Mauthausen after his deception was unmasked in an attempt to prove that, even if he hadn't been in a Nazi concentration camp, he had nonetheless been a valiant fighter against fascism). It was true and it was unbelievable. As I read the article, I remembered the suspicion Marco's account had inspired in historians of the Battle of Segre, and I thought about the fragility of memory, about the war, and about Fabrice del Dongo and Pierre Bezukhov, the protagonists of *The Charterhouse of Parma* and *War and Peace*, who fought at the battles of Waterloo and Borodino yet barely realised what was happening around them, and would have been able to recount as little of these battles as Marco of the Battle of Segre. And once again I thought, every great lie is constructed from small truths, it is formed from them. But I also thought, in spite of the unexpected documented fact that had just appeared, the greater part of Marco's war exploits were a lie, another invention of his monstrous egotism and insatiable desire for fame. Now, much later, I still think the same thing: Marco was not at the Sant Andreu barracks on July 19, he did not fight with the Columna Roja at Huesca, he was not one of "Quico" Sabaté's guerrillas fighting in enemy territory, nor was he wounded at the Battle of Segre. This is what I think. Although I cannot be certain that Marco didn't travel to Majorca in the summer of 1936 with his uncle Anastasio, and I cannot be any more certain than the historians of the Battle of Segre were that Marco had never set foot on the front lines there. I think about this, and I think about the moment when I seemed about to peel away the last onion skin of Marco's heroic biography, the last layer of fiction clinging to his imaginary character: on the veranda of his kitchen I explained that I didn't believe he had travelled to Majorca with his uncle Anastasio, and asked him to admit the truth. Marco was sitting opposite me, elbows on the table, fingers interlaced; as I remember it now, this may have happened on the same day he admitted he didn't come home wounded from the war, perhaps shortly after that confession. On hearing my words, Marco buried his face in his hands in a gesture that, though melodramatic, did not seem melodramatic to me; then he pleaded: "Please, leave me something."

I leave him this.

10

What did Marco do after the war? Or what does he say he did?

As I have already related: when he arrived back in Barcelona from the Segre front in the winter of 1939, just as the war was ending, Marco sought refuge in his aunt Ramona's home, a porter's lodge the Republican authorities had given her husband, Uncle Anastasio, to compensate him as a disabled serviceman. The house was on the corner of Lepanto and Travessera de Gracia in the district of El Guinardó; though it had two floors, it was tiny: downstairs, in the porter's lodge itself, were a cramped kitchen and dining room in addition to a cubicle where the porter could sit to regulate the comings and goings of neighbours; upstairs, almost on the terrace of the building, were two bedrooms, also tiny. I have likewise explained that it was some time before Marco set foot outside. On the one hand, he says he needed to recuperate from his war wound, he had no papers, and no desire to regularise his legal position, since his dignity would not allow him to accept the Franco regime, and because reprisals against people like him (a warrant officer in the losing army who had also been a militant in the C.N.T.) could be very harsh; on the other hand, he was overcome, he says, by a mixture of fear, disgust and shame. For an idealistic young rebel who had come through the libertarian revolution, had fought in a war and was prepared to carry on fighting to overthrow the Franco regime, his disgust and shame were greater than his fear.

The porter's lodge was located next to the Lepanto barracks and, during the first weeks or months, Marco confined himself to spying on life from his window, according to one of the autobiographical or pseudo-autobiographical texts he sent to the Amical de Mauthausen after his imposture was uncovered. He spied on the military parades, spurred on by the strains of the victors' anthems and led by the pennants and the flags of Francoism that, only recently, he had seen fluttering against luminous morning skies on the far side of the trenches; he spied on the processions, the stations of the cross, the worship of the religious symbols abolished during the Second Republic, between lines of kneeling men and women wearing mantillas carrying tall burning candles, and spied on the legion of arms making the Roman salute amid the crowds thronging the streets; lastly, he spied on the comings and goings of people in a city, starved, prostituted and trampled by the twin tyrannies of the Church and the Falangists, economically and morally corrupt, debased and despoiled by the greed and arrogance of the victors, a city where, scarcely three years earlier, the people had taken up arms and crushed a military uprising, and this same proud people that, throughout the war, had fought for freedom with a courage and a dignity admired all over the world was now broken, servile, cowardly, destitute, a people of empty baskets and lowered heads, of petty crooks, collaborationists, delinquents, informants, blackmailers and masters of the black market, a people exiled in their own city, a city where Marco knew that he would drown because he could not accept the barbarous, abject, claustrophobic life the new regime wanted to impose, a city where, despite everything, he was determined to stay to fight for justice and dignity as he had always done, steadfast to the libertarian ideals of his youth.

This he did, or this is what he has always said he did. Hardly had he recovered from his war wound than he began to venture out and, to hide his clandestine activities behind an innocuous façade—and in passing help Aunt Ramona pay the bills—he quickly found a job in the workshop on calle París, at the corner of Viladomat. The owner, Felip Homs, an elderly Republican who needed an apprentice because his son was engaged in one of the endless military service programmes that the victors used to punish the vanquished soldiers, took on his new trainee without asking any questions or requesting any documents and, later, on discovering he had been an anti-fascist volunteer in the Republican army, congratulated him. Thus Marco began to build a life that was normal, or almost normal. Though he did his utmost to control himself, by nature the young man was impulsive, often reckless, incapable of meekly enduring the humiliations of the victors, with whom he became embroiled in constant confrontations. He went to the cinema as often as he could, but, so as not to have to stand, right arm extended in fascist salute, as the Falangist national anthem played before and after the film, he would go in after the movie had started and leave just before it ended. He was not alone in practising this minor form of defiance, and perhaps because of this, one day the film was unexpectedly stopped in mid-reel, the houselights came up and the first chords of "Cara al Sol" blared out, in order to force the audience to stand and salute. This ruse caught Marco unawares, sitting in the middle of the cinema, next to the aisle, but he did not move; he sat motionless, glued to his seat, while all around him, as the music boomed, the crowd rose to its feet, sprouting a forest of arms. Then, without taking his eyes off the blank screen, Marco felt a presence in the aisle next to him; before he turned, he knew it was an army officer. In fact, it was a sergeant. He stared at Marco. "Aren't you going to stand?" asked the sergeant. Marco held the man's gaze; as he did so he noticed that the music had stopped, the place was silent, all eyes were trained on them. "No," he replied. The sergeant glowered at him for a few seconds longer and then turned on his heel and left. As for Marco, he says that he did what he did that day without thinking; contradictorily, he also says that he did it for himself, to preserve his own dignity, but mostly for the others, to preserve the dignity of everyone.

According to Marco, such incidents were common at the time; by which I mean common for him. (Marco remembers another: one summer afternoon, in a train station, while he was in line to buy a ticket to the beach at Castelldefels, a handful of Falangists in red berets and blue shirts tried to elbow their way in front of him in the line; Marco resisted and they ended up coming to blows, he ran for his train, melted into the crowd, and spent his trip to the beach popping his head out the window at each station and watching as the bastards got out and searched for him among the alighting passengers.) It was at this point that Marco was arrested for the first time. One afternoon, a group of men came into Felip Homs' workshop asking for him. They asked for his papers, and since he did not have any, they handcuffed him and turned the place upside down; they found nothing, other than some of his writings, a handful of leaflets from the British Consulate and the B.B.C., of which he was the principal distributor in Barcelona, and a scrawl on the bathroom wall behind the toilet that read: "*Arriba España! Viva Franco!* When you're done, pull the chain and flush it away with the shit!"

They detained Marco and Felip Homs, took the cashbox and closed the workshop. There wasn't room for everyone in the strangers' car, so two of them hailed a taxi, bundled them in and gave an address on plaza Lesseps. Up until this point, Marco had assumed the men were police officers; now he realised his mistake: some days or weeks earlier, a group of Falangists had burst into his home, looking for him, and having searched the house in vain, informed his aunt Ramona that her nephew had to report to an address on plaza Lesseps, doubtless the very address where they were now headed. Marco confesses that, when he realised that his captors were Falangists and that they were taking him to one of the offices of the Falange, he felt terrified, or rather the terror he already felt escalated, and he decided to escape at the first opportunity. This presented itself almost immediately, at the junction of Travessera de Gracia and Mayor de Gracia, where a city police officer was directing traffic. As they reached the junction, Marco threw himself from the moving car, rushed over to the officer, yelling that he was being kidnapped; a group of bystanders crowded around them, and though the Falangists showed their badges and their *Movimiento Nacional* identity cards, the officer decided that this was a police matter and it was up to the police to resolve it.

The officer took Marco to the nearest *comisaría* on the calle Rosellón. The Falangists followed, and on the way they continued to threaten Marco with the beatings and punishments that awaited him when they got him alone. Fortunately for him, they never got him alone. The inspector at the police station told the Falangists that Marco was a prisoner and as such would be dealt with by the judicial system, and that he would take care of everything, including the indictment and the report, and thanked them for their cooperation. After the Falangists left, the inspector was silent for a moment, studying Marco; finally he asked how old he was. Marco answered; the inspector reminded him that he was only a boy and told him that, were he his son, he would have thrashed him for being a witless, brainless idiot. Having said this, he went out, leaving Marco in his office, and did not come back for several hours until he was sure the Falangists would have grown tired of waiting outside. "Beat it," the inspector said to Marco, pointing at the door, "and don't let me clap eyes on you again!"

He did not sleep at his aunt Ramona's house that night, Marco says, neither that night nor those that followed. Nor did he go back to Felip Homs' workshop. He was convinced that the Falangists were hunting him and, if he continued this normal life, or this semblance of a normal life, sooner or later they would catch him. And so he decided to escape. First he turned to an old comrade from the C.N.T., a member of the metalworkers' union he had met when he worked at the Ford factory before the war, who offered him a bolthole on the roof of a little house tucked away next to Vallcarca bridge. There Marco spent several nights, after which his comrade disappeared and Marco realised that the place was no longer safe. And so he began to move around, sleeping in deserted houses, in parks, in stairwells; he spent many nights on the benches of the plaza de Cataluña, and the rented chairs on the Rambla, and many mornings and afternoons aimlessly riding the trams from one end of the city to the other. In his writings and statements, Marco remembers this as a difficult time for him, but he also remembers, with satisfaction, that he felt proud of himself, that he was consoled and comforted by the thought that he had not given in to the institutionalised brutality of the victors, that he had not surrendered to terror and folly, and that he felt he was a symbol, because he was still standing, still had his decency, his honour, his self-esteem, just as in a sense the whole population was still standing.

In fact, he did much more than this. What I mean is that, from what he says, it wasn't enough for him to avoid the savage assaults of the *franquistas*; in his own fashion, with his limited means, he assaulted them. Marco cannot precisely place the incident: sometimes he seems to suggest that it happened shortly after his return from the front, perhaps in the spring of 1939; at other times, that it took place in the summer or autumn of 1941, shortly before he left Spain. The fact remains that one night, Aunt Ramona told him that his grandmother Isabel, his father's mother, had died, and he was expected the following day at the funeral, which was taking place in La Trinidad, the neighbourhood in which he had spent the best part of his childhood, where he had not set foot since the first days of the war. The vigil took place in the former Ateneo Republicano, transformed, after Franco's victory, into a parish centre. There, during the ceremony, he met up again with relatives, friends and acquaintances he hadn't seen in a long time, among them Antonio Fernández Vallet, the boy with whom, in the summer of 1938, Marco had enlisted to fight on the front line at Segre.

More than simply friends, Marco and Fernández Vallet were inseparable. They had spent their childhood sharing games, adventures, books; they also shared libertarian ideals, although Marco enrolled with the C.N.T. and Fernández Vallet with Juventudes Libertarias (Libertarian Youth). It is hardly surprising, then, that after the pleasure of meeting again and the sorrow of the funeral, Fernández Vallet would take Marco aside and show him a pamphlet in which an organisation called the U.J.A. (Union of Anti-fascist Youth) called for a struggle against the victors. Marco had not heard of the U.J.A., and so, brandishing the pamphlet, he asked Fernández Vallet who they were. His friend told him that the U.J.A. was an organisation of young resistance fighters, that it had just been formed, that he was a member of the group, that it had been born and was well established in Santa Coloma de Gramanet, but that there were also members in Sant Andreu, La Trinidad, La Prosperidad, Verdún, and various other working-class suburbs of Barcelona, that most of its members were of the same age and similar pasts to theirs, because many of them had fought in the Republican army, though not all of them were anarchists like them: there were also communists and socialists. Marco claims that at this point he interrupted his friend. He told him he wanted no truck with such an ideological muddle, nor did he like the idea of being in an organisation with communists, who had ruthlessly hunted people like him during the war and doomed the revolution to failure; he added that he no longer lived on the outskirts of Barcelona, but some distance away, in Barcelona itself. These were feeble, almost perfunctory, objections—Marco was worried at the thought of emerging from his isolation and transforming his personal rebellion into an organised struggle—and therefore Fernández Vallet effortlessly refuted them: he said simply that this was no time to repeat the divisions of the war, but to unite against a common enemy, and the fact that there wasn't a branch of the U.J.A. in Barcelona was not a hindrance, but an incentive for Marco to start one.

Again, according to Marco's account, he devoted most of his energy to this task in the weeks or months that followed. The first thing he did was recruit a group of boys like himself, as courageous, as selfless, as idealistic as he was, or almost: a certain Francesc Armenguer (from Les Franqueses), a certain Jordi Jardí (from Anglès), a certain Jorge Veí or Vehi or Pei, a certain Thomas or Tomàs, and also a certain García and a certain Pueyo, maybe one more person. The second thing he did was find a place where he and his comrades could meet; he found it almost immediately in a cafeteria, on the corner of calle Peligro and Torrente de la Olla in the Gracia district, where he managed to rent a space recently vacated by a cycling club, with a few forgotten trophies in display cabinets and on shelves. Here, he and the group began to meet and, with a minimum of equipment (a revolver, two pistols, a box of cartridges, a typewriter, several reams of white paper, a few sheets of carbon paper, a pair of scissors and two staplers) they set to work: they wrote, printed and distributed pamphlets calling for resistance throughout the city, they scrawled graffiti, now and again they threw a firecracker, constantly arguing over the best way to overthrow the regime. This didn't last long, a few uncertain weeks at most, because the enthusiasm of these idealistic boys did not make up for their innocence, their complete lack of experience and their utter ignorance of the rules and procedures of clandestine struggle. One afternoon, Marco found himself waiting for a contact near the monument to Jacint Verdaguer at the intersection of Avenida Diagonal and Paseo de San Juan; this was a safety precaution, possibly the preliminary (Marco doesn't remember exactly, or says that he doesn't remember exactly) to a meeting with other members of the group. What he does remember is that his contact was late, and only appeared when Marco was beginning to think that he should leave because something had clearly gone wrong. Flustered and frantic, the contact told him that something had indeed gone wrong: police had arrested the secretary of the U.J.A. that morning, they'd found lists of names and addresses, a handful of members were now in custody and the police operation was still going on, he needed to get to safety. Before the contact had even finished speaking, Marco set off at a run, heading for the headquarters on calle Peligro and Torrente de la Olla. There, he found two of his comrades and gave them the news, helped them to hurriedly gather their belongings, and raced out of the coffee bar without looking back.

This was the end of the U.J.A. Marco never met up with his comrades in the group again; nor, obviously, with Fernández Vallet and the people in Santa Coloma, who, from snippets of news in the following weeks, he discovered had all been arrested, convicted, and given harsh sentences. Marco drew two conclusions from the demise of the U.J.A. (or so he says): the first is that it was suicidal to become part of a clandestine organisation, at least at that moment, and that in future he would confront Francoism alone; the second was that he could not confront Francoism alone, that his situation was desperate and that, with no home, no work, no friends and the police hot on his heels, the best thing he could do—perhaps the only thing he could do—was to leave Spain.

At this point, Marco's story diverges; or rather the discovery of his imposture obliged Marco to diverge. Before the Marco scandal broke, the story he told was essentially as follows:

Determined to go into exile in France and there continue his struggle against fascism, in the autumn of 1941 Marco got in touch with a cousin who was doing military service and who had friends and acquaintances working on the docks (in another version, this happened not in the autumn of 1941, but in the winter of 1942). After some negotiations, Pepín, for this was the cousin's name, managed, by bribing a customs guard, to have Marco taken aboard a merchant ship that plied the route between Barcelona and Marseilles (in another version, it was not the customs officer, but the captain of the ship himself that Pepín bribed). Marco made the journey as a stowaway. In theory, a member of the C.N.T. would be waiting for him in Marseilles; in practice, no-one was waiting for him and, while searching for his contact in the dive bars along the port, he was arrested by officers of Pétain, the elderly French Marshal the Nazis had appointed to lead the nominal government of the country's unoccupied zone (in another version, he names the C.N.T. member who had been supposed to meet him in Marseilles—a man called García—and insists that he wasn't arrested at the port but as part of a police inspection). After various interrogations, Pétain's police officers handed Marco over to the Gestapo, who held him in Marseilles for a month before sending him to Metz, where he was imprisoned in a convent and later sent on to Flossenbürg concentration camp (in another version he doesn't mention being handed over to the Gestapo and claims that, before being sent to Flossenbürg, he was held in Kiel, the capital of Schleswig-Holstein, the northernmost state in Germany). It was here, in Flossenbürg (or in Kiel), according to this first account, that Marco's German adventure began.

The second account—that is to say, the account that Marco gave after the scandal broke in May 2005—is simpler, has fewer variations, and if the beginning is similar to the first, the ending is very different, if not diametrically opposed; essentially, it is as follows:

Determined to go into exile in France and there continue his struggle against fascism, in the autumn of 1941 Marco got in touch with a cousin who was doing military service and who had friends and acquaintances working on the docks. After some negotiations, Pepín, for this was the cousin's name, managed to speak to a customs officer who offered to talk to the captain working the Barcelona–Marseilles route who, for a considerable sum of money, was supposed to allow Marco to travel as a stowaway on his merchant ship. Marco and Pepín met with the customs officer several times in a bar called Choco-Chiqui near the plaza del Pino, but, when they had raised the necessary money—a thousand pesetas, a fortune at that time—the customs officer claimed that the risks had increased, that the captain had misgivings and, in order to allay them, he needed twice the agreed amount. Although he knew he could never raise such a sum, Marco started looking. He was desperate. One day, while reading the newspaper, he saw another solution (or glimpsed it): an offer of work in Germany. The offer was attractive from every angle, including the financial, since it offered the possibility of buying a house in Spain in exchange for three years' work in Germany, but this didn't matter to Marco: all that mattered to him was getting out of Spain. It's also true that, although the work was being offered by a German company (the Deutsche Werke Werft), the offer was the result of an accord between

Spain and Germany, between Franco and Hitler, and was intended as a contribution to the war effort of the country attempting to impose fascism across Europe by fire and sword, but this didn't matter to Marco either: all that mattered to him was getting out of Spain. And so that very day he presented himself at the Barcelona offices of the Deutsche Werke Werft on calle Diputación (or possibly Consejo de Ciento) and applied for a job. Shortly afterwards he found out that he had been given a post, and in late November or early December 1941 Marco set off on a train full of Spanish workers from Estación del Norte for Kiel, the capital of Schleswig-Holstein, the northernmost state in Germany. This, according to the second account, is how Marco's German adventure began.

So ends the tissue of lies.

11

And the truth? The truth, from what I discovered as I peeled away layers of onion skin from Marco's biography, is that this tissue of lies was naturally moulded around truths.

It is true that, when he arrived in Barcelona, Marco sought shelter in the house or rather the porter's lodge of his aunt Ramona, that this was located on the corner of Lepanto and Travessera de Gracia, and it was perhaps as Marco describes it; but it is not true that his aunt Ramona lived there alone: she shared the house with a girl four years Marco's senior, named Ana Beltrán Ribes. It is true that it was some time before Marco set foot outside, but it is a lie that he was wounded; he was doubtless shattered, demoralised and terrified as only those are who return from the front having lost a war, but he was not wounded. It is true that those like him, who had been a warrant officer in the Republican army, and a militant in the C.N.T. besides, had good reason to avoid the attention of the victors and to fear reprisals—at the very least, three years' military service, perhaps a penal battalion, perhaps prison or the death penalty—but it is not true that his dignity prevented him from regularising his legal status with the victors, nor that his disgust and his shame at the triumph of the Franco regime were greater than his fear: there isn't the slightest doubt that his fear was much greater. It is true that he got a job as a mechanic in the workshop of a man named Felip Homs, on the corner of calle París and Viladomat, but it is very unlikely that, having been a Republican, Homs would have congratulated Marco on being an anti-fascist volunteer in the Republican army: firstly, because after the war, no-one talked about the war, certainly not those who were defeated (the most important thing after a war is to forget the war); and secondly out of fear. It is possible that, like almost every young man in almost every age, Marco was by nature impulsive and reckless, and that like many working-class young men in Barcelona before and during the war he had been an impassioned anarchist with revolutionary ideals, but it is certain that, like all or almost all of the vanquished soldiers, he was profoundly changed by the horrors of the front and the desolation of defeat, making him entirely capable of enduring the humiliations of the victors without the slightest protest: just as professions of bravery belie the coward, the romantic tales Marco tells of his prodigious escapes and his heroic refusal to raise his arm and sing "Cara al Sol" and submit to the brutality of Falangists in blue shirts with pistols tucked in their belts makes one think of all the times that Marco imagined they might arrest him, all the times he was humiliated by the victors, all the times, in cinemas, in the streets, in the hovels of the regime, when he had no choice but to raise his arm and sing "Cara al Sol." It is true that in Barcelona immediately after the Civil War, any normal life was a semblance of normal life because—this, too, is true—the city was starved, prostituted and trampled by the twin tyrannies of the Church and the Falangists, economically and morally corrupt, debased and despoiled by the greed and arrogance of the victors, but it is a lie that Marco lived a clandestine existence rather than a normal life or a semblance of a normal life or what we have mysteriously agreed to call a normal life, and, though it is true that the same idealistic, impassioned people who, for three years, had fought for their freedom with a courage admired all over the world had been forcibly turned into a broken, servile, cowardly, destitute people, a people of empty baskets and lowered heads, of petty crooks, collaborationists, delinquents, informants, blackmailers and masters of the black market, but it is not true that, exiled in his inner world, our man felt alien to them: Marco may be many things, but he is no fool, and with what little sense he still had as he faced the complete collapse of the country he knew, he must have known that he was a part of it, that he was like the others, that, like the vast majority of the defeated, he too was accepting the barbarous, abject, claustrophobic life imposed by the victors, that he had surrendered to terror and folly, that he did not feel proud of his actions, and was consoled or comforted by nothing other than that which consoled and comforted the majority of the vanquished Republican soldiers who, like him, had neither the strength nor the heroic mettle to carry on the struggle, and who had not stayed in their country with the fearless aim of joining the armed underground resistance but with the prosaic, jaded, spontaneous aim of passing unnoticed so they might avoid reprisals and thereby try to survive this catastrophe. Lastly, it is true that Marco is a symbol of that moment in history; but it is not true that he is a symbol of exceptional decency and honour in defeat, but of everyday indecency and dishonour.

This is the truth. Or this is the truth about this period of Marco's life: a truth that proved to be almost the exact antithesis of the saccharine, dishonest tales of romantic adventures that Marco told, with himself in the starring role as a champion of freedom. It is the truth, but it is not the whole truth; it is, let us say, the essential truth (or what seems to me to be the essential truth), but here are other truths. I will proceed to sum them up.

As I have already said, on his return from the front, Marco did not find himself alone in Aunt Ramona's house: a girl named Ana Beltrán Ribes was living with her; I haven't said, on the other hand, that Ana (or Anita, as her family called her) had a baby and had just left her husband. I'm not at all clear why these two women were living together; in fact, neither Marco nor Anita's family is clear. All of them remember that, some years earlier, Anita had run away in order to marry, but some of them believe that, after she and her husband separated, Anita's parents, good Republican Catholics, wouldn't allow her to come home and this is why she sought refuge with Aunt Ramona; others, however, claim that, in spite of their Catholicism, and the fact that she had run away from home, Anita's parents took her back and that she ended up with Aunt Ramona simply because in Ramona's house there was no shortage of food in the last months of the war. As for Aunt Ramona, it's likely she knew Anita because she lived in the neighbourhood—she had lived there all her life, both with her parents and with her recently abandoned husband—and took pity on her, and also saw in the girl's distress or her hunger a means of easing her own widowhood and the loneliness she had felt since the death of Uncle Anastasio. Whatever the case, the fact remains that for several months Marco, Aunt Ramona, Anita and her baby lived in harmony: every morning Anita set off for the fabric merchant on the calle Caspe where she worked, Ramona took care of the shopping and kept the house tidy while Marco looked after the baby. The harmonious atmosphere broke down when Marco and Anita fell in love, or when Aunt Ramona discovered that Marco and Anita had fallen in love. Aunt Ramona may have been libertarian like her late husband, but she still had the traditional principles of a matriarch and didn't consider her nephew suited to a girl burdened with a child, and one who was four years older than him, and so she did everything in her power to get Marco to see sense and break up with Anita; Marco did not see sense, he did not break up with her, so Aunt Ramona decided to evict Anita, who went back to live with her parents.

Marco quickly followed her. Anita's parents lived in a single-storey house on calle Sicilia, near the junction with Córcega, next to a bar and a *pelota* court. They were a humble family and much loved in the neighbourhood: the father worked in a textile factory, as a scrap dealer and as barman in a *cooperativa* on calle Valencia, of which he became chairman; the mother was an orphan raised by nuns as a strict, traditional Catholic. Neither parent ever recovered from the death of their only son at the Battle of Ebro during the last days of the war, but it is possible that Marco's presence in the house helped them to cope with their loss. This may partly explain why the mother was prepared to ignore the strict moral code by which she had been raised and allow Marco and her daughter to live together under the same roof without being married, in their overcrowded house where two other daughters and a son-in-law also lived. This improper situation—improper at least according to the strict Catholic precepts of Anita's mother—didn't last long: Marco and Anita were married in church on August 10, 1941 (Anita's previous marriage proved to be no obstacle, since the Franco regime didn't recognise civil marriages performed during the Second Republic). The wedding took place in the church of the Sagrada Família; only Anita's family were in attendance, Marco's family were not present since by now he had fallen out with most of them, including his father and Aunt Ramona, from whom he had cut himself off. By now, Marco had a new family, Anita's family; or to be more precise, by now Marco had managed to captivate Anita's family, who considered him intelligent, cultivated, hardworking, practical, cheerful, entertaining and charming, a young man who was unfailingly affectionate to his wife, ever ready to help his parents-in-law, to advise and protect his sisters-in-law, to do a favour for anyone who needed it, an ideal husband, an ideal and unexpected substitute for the son and brother taken from them by the war (and a saviour to Anita, whom he rescued from the dual stigma of being a separated wife and a single mother). It was a close-knit family, they worked hard during the week and spent Sundays at the beach or in the mountains, or, more often, in the cooperative on the calle Valencia, where the father served behind the bar and the children played cards or chess and staged little plays, and where Marco stood out as a champion table tennis player, an occasional singer and a passionate reader of the books in the library. And so at this point, with the memory of war still blazing and everyone or almost everyone trying to put it out, trying to come to terms with the new situation, Marco was not a hero or a rebel or a resistance fighter, but he was likely a happy man, or what we have mysteriously agreed to call a happy man.

Or almost. Because—as Faulkner says—the past is never dead; it's not even past; the past is merely a dimension of the present. And for Marco, as for others in 1941, he could only extinguish the blazing past that was the war if he regularised his situation by accepting the fraudulent legitimacy of the victors. Did he? Did he attempt it? Marco has always said no, that self-respect prevented him and that for two years he lived on the margins of the law, but the fact is—as I have already warned—he lied about this, and if he hadn't regularised his situation, or at least attempted to do so, he wouldn't have been able to live the normal life or the semblance of a normal life he led at the time.

It was by chance that I discovered Marco lied to this degree; by chance or because chance afforded me another small miracle. A double miracle, this time. The first miracle: an announcement published on July 23, 1940, in *La Vanguardia* (actually, *La Vanguardia Española*, as the newspaper was called after the war); it reads, "The enlisted sailors below should report urgently to the office of the Comandancia Militar de Marina"; there follows a list of thirteen names, the second to last of

MARITIMAS

LLEGADA DE CARBON DEL NORTE. —
Han llegado a nuestro puerto los buques
«Zurriola» y «Ulla», procedentes de La Co-
ruña y Avilés, respectivamente, con carga-
mentos completos de carbón de aquellos
puertos.
    Los citados buques pasaron a descargar
el combustible de que han sido portadores
en el muelle de Poniente, paramento Sur,
el «Zurriola», y Norte el «Ulla».
    BUQUES MERCANTES SALIDOS.—Duran-
te los dos días últimos salieron de nuestro
puerto, con rumbo a los de sus respectivos
itinerarios, los buques siguientes: vapores
«Plus Ultra», «Melchuca», «Demir» (turco),
«Ulla», «Monte Amboto», vapor sueco «Sicilia» «Sac 4», «Mallorca», buque-tanque «Zo-
rroza», «Monte Castelo» y varios pailebotes
y motoveleros.
    PRESENTACION DE INSCRITOS EN LA
COMANDANCIA MILITAR DE MARINA. —
Deberán presentarse con toda urgencia, en
la oficina del detall de la Comandancia
Militar de Marina los inscritos de Marina
que a continuación se indican: Antonio Ca-
pilla Pons, Jaime Soler Arbo, José Rojo
Ibars Juan Noguera Sala, Antonio Galindo
Céspedes, Adolfo Artero Rabal, Manuel
Ponte Ruiz Juan Montoya Garrido, Antonio
Ferrer Angosto, Jaime Sirvent Sallas, Enrique Marco Batlló, Joaquín Monsonís Escu-
der y Joaquín Puig Aleu.
    CAMBIO DE ATRAQUE. — La motonave
postal «Dómine», que procedente de Buenos
Aires y escalas llegó la pasada semana a
nuestro puerto, según indicábamos en una
de nuestras últimas ediciones, ha pasado
a atracar de costado en el muelle de Bosch
y Alsina, donde procede a la descarga de
varios efectos que trajo de aquella proce-
dencia.

which—as you will already have guessed—is Enrique Marco Batlló [actually Batlle]. What does this mean? It means that a year and a half after Marco came home from the war, the military authorities had already sent numerous orders to his home, or what they believed was his home, insisting that he report to their offices for conscription: to sign up, undergo a medical examination and prepare for military service. And it means that, despite the orders for him to attend, Marco had not done so: the publication of this announcement was probably their last resort before declaring him a draft evader. Well, did they declare him a fugitive? Did Marco eventually report to the authorities or not?

I found the answer to both these questions in another notice, similar to the first, which also appeared in *La Vanguardia*, almost a year later, on April 2, 1941. This is the second minor miracle. "The office of the Comandancia Militar de Marina," the announcement reads, "requires that those enlisted sailors of the 1941 call-up named below immediately report to be issued with their *cartilla naval*"; there follows a list of four names, the penultimate of which—as you will also have guessed—is Enrique Marco Batlle. What does this second notice mean? It means that, although Marco had every reason not to report to the military authorities, after the first ultimatum he had clearly done so, and that the military authorities hadn't investigated his past as an anarchist and a Republican officer, or had investigated and found nothing, or had found out the truth and thought it irrelevant, because Marco wasn't sentenced to any of the punishments reserved for Republicans, and his conscription was in keeping with the process legally set down for all Spanish citizens. As such, given his age, Marco would have been called up to begin military service in 1941, and this second notice in *La Vanguardia*—this second ultimatum—proves that, his situation having been regularised, by April of that year, the military authorities had been sending requests to him for some time, demanding that he report to the Comandancia Militar de Marina to collect his *cartilla naval*, the military service card issued to those about to join the navy; it also proves that Marco had still not reported to the authorities, forcing them, for the second time, to issue this notice as a last resort before declaring him a fugitive.

This, I believe, is what can be gleaned from the two ultimatums published in *La Vanguardia*: that Marco was a reluctant conscript but not a draft evader.

I spoke to Marco as soon as I worked out the significance of the notices; confronted with the truth (or with his own lie), our man told me the truth, or a fundamental part of the truth. The truth is that one day early in 1940, Aunt Ramona showed up at Anita's parents' house, where he was now living, and handed him an official notice requiring him to report to the Comandancia Militar de Marina to be conscripted. Marco knew what this meant and, though he was hesitant and afraid, he decided to play it cool, assuming that the military would forget about him. They did not forget. In the weeks or months that followed, Marco received further notifications that were similar or identical, but certainly more insistent and more worrying, and in the end he decided it was better to take the risk of reporting to the authorities than being declared a draft evader or going into exile. The fact is that, one morning, Marco presented himself at the headquarters of the Comandancia Militar de Marina on the Rambla and, after a brief interview, emerged unscathed and enlisted, without being crushed by the weight of his onerous record as an anarchist and a Republican officer. How did Marco do it? Did he manage to hide his true past behind a fictitious past? If he failed to hide it, did he manage to persuade the military to attach no importance to his true past? What happened that morning at the headquarters of the Comandancia Militar de Marina? I do not know precisely—Marco doesn't remember, or says he doesn't remember—but I will offer a hypothesis that now seems to me irrefutable: Marco is essentially a conman, a shameless charlatan, a peerless trickster, and he managed to dupe the military authorities, to convince them that his past was blameless or inoffensive and that he was an inoffensive, not to say irreproachable, young man.

If my hypothesis is correct, it would have been an extraordinary ploy; but whether or not it is correct, the outcome was that, by regularising his situation, Marco managed to disperse the ominous clouds looming on the horizon. At least in the short term; in the medium term it wasn't so simple, for although he knew he wouldn't be subjected to reprisals from the victors, he also knew that at some point in 1941 he would be called up to do the fifteen-month military service required of him as a Spanish citizen. The prospect wasn't as distressing as prison or a penal battalion, but nor would it be pleasant, the proof being that the majority of young men of military age did everything they could to avoid it. Marco had always sided with the majority, and this time was no exception. He attempted to avoid military service: though he did comply with the second ultimatum published by the military authorities and reported to the Comandancia Militar de Marina to collect his *cartilla naval*, in the months that followed, as he waited, heart in his mouth, to be called up to join the navy, he searched for a way out of this dilemma.

In early autumn, he found it. Towards the end of August of that year, on the 21st to be exact, the Spanish and German governments signed the "Hispano-German Accord concerning the dispatch of Spanish workers to Germany," an agreement that had four principal objectives: to settle the debt of 480 Reichsmarks that Hitler was demanding of Franco for the help he had given during the Civil War; to provide cheap manpower for German industry to make up for the millions of young German men who, since 1939, had been called up and dispatched to the front lines of the World War; to strengthen the

ties between the German Reich and a Spanish regime that was fascinated by the Nazi successes in the first three years of war; and, *last and
also least*, to afford some relief to the faltering Spanish economy by
exporting those without jobs and thereby to alleviate the enormous
problem of unemployment.

In October, the Spanish government published the employment
requirements for Spanish workers in Germany, and Marco seized the
opportunity. From this point, his story, as we know it—from discovering the tempting job offer in the newspaper to his departure from
Barcelona in a train packed with Spanish workers, having visited the
offices of the Deutsche Werke Werft on calle Diputación or possibly calle del Consejo de Ciento—conforms, in the main, with the
truth. By which I mean this is the truth that Marco used to shore up
his lie. By which I mean things almost certainly happened more or
less as Marco recounted them in the second version of his departure
from Spain, with the exception of the fantasy that in 1941 he was
a resistance fighter with Franco's police hot on his heels who had
no other choice but to get out of Spain. Of course—let it be said in
passing—the idea of a draft evader like the character Marco describes
travelling to Germany as a volunteer worker is not only implausible,
but absurd (and it is unthinkable that it could have passed for the
truth): implausible because, in order to secure a contract, a worker's
papers had to be in order, and the Office of Statistics and Employment, attached to the National Delegation of Unions, the official
organisation where candidates were required to register before signing a contract with one of the German companies, would not have
accepted a draft evader without papers, certainly not for a job as cov-
eted as this; absurd because it's nonsensical to think that anyone with
even a token spirit of resistance or a trace of anti-fascist sentiment
would be prepared to travel to Germany and contribute to the war
effort of the country that was ravaging Europe and plunging it into
fascism (which is why what feeble opposition still existed within the
dictatorship did everything in its power to dissuade Spanish workers
from going). Does this mean that Marco had already ceased to be a
committed anarchist and become a committed fascist? No, though in
the wake of the Civil War, he wouldn't have been the first nor the last
to change sides overnight. The fact is that, before signing their con-

tracts, workers were routinely categorised according to their support for the regime, and many applicants made a virtue of having fought with Franco's forces or their passion for the cause, just as it is true that newspapers published numerous photographs of the first convoys leaving for Germany that are striking in their ideological zeal, featuring trains bedecked with huge swastikas and carriages of fervent workers leaning out the windows to give the fascist salute; but it is no less true that, beneath the deceitful veneer of propaganda, the reality was that the vast majority of these men were not leaving in order to help the Nazis win the war, but fleeing the poverty of Franco's Spain out of sheer necessity.

This was the case with Marco. Our man travelled to Germany with the primary aim of avoiding (or deferring) his military service, and the secondary goal of earning a living in a country that was winning the war. In theory, one of the fundamental conditions for being hired by a German company was having completed military service, or having been exempted from it; with Marco, for whatever reason, this didn't apply, or he succeeded in duping the Spanish authorities once again: in all likelihood the authorities considered him politically sympathetic or harmless, while the German companies were likely impressed by his youth, his energy and above all his skills as a mechanic (metalworkers being among their priorities), because the fact is that on November 27, 1941, a two-year contract with the Deutsche Werke Werft tucked under his arm, Marco boarded a train at Estación Norte in Barcelona, to join the first convoy of workers and begin his German adventure.

Was that all? In the first two years after the Civil War was Marco merely a politically innocuous young man, an anarchist hastily converted to fascism (there is not a single piece of information nor a single witness statement to corroborate such a conjecture)? Was he simply one of the vast majority of the defeated who accepted without protest the barbarous, abject, claustrophobic life imposed by the victors? Or was there a part of him that did not conform? Did he harbour, deep inside, some vestige of anti-fascist consciousness, some residual spirit of resistance or civic courage? Did Marco have any contact with anti-Franco groups after all? Could he have done so despite living a normal life, or the semblance of a normal life? Can I leave him something? Can I leave him the U.J.A.? Did Marco belong to the U.J.A. or have any contact with it?

The history of the U.J.A. is extraordinary. It is a tiny episode that remained buried in the mass grave of resistance to Franco for sixty years until 1997 when it was exhumed by two young local historians, Juanjo Gallardo and José María Martínez; even today, the story is little known. In late January 1939, with two months to go before the end of the Civil War, but some days after Barcelona fell into Franco's hands, a group of Catalan boys decided they would not accept defeat. Some had fought with the Republican army, many were militant members of Juventudes Libertarias, all were very young: the eldest was twenty-three, the youngest, fifteen, but most were seventeen or eighteen; they came from all walks of life: day labourers, glassworkers, farmhands, accountants, tailors, electricians, railway workers, grocery boys, bakers, shop assistants and even three schoolboys. The nucleus of the U.J.A. was based in Santa Coloma de Gramanet but the organisation later spread to Sant Andrià del Besós and had ambitions to expand to other suburbs of Barcelona, and to Barcelona itself. The word "organisation" may be an overstatement: though it did have a basic structure, with geographical divisions and section leaders, in reality the U.J.A. was just a gang of boys who met in their parents' houses and who, during its brief existence, with derisory means and dauntless courage, authored, printed and distributed pamphlets calling for revolution, struck a blow against a garrison of Italian fascists, planned acts of sabotage against infrastructure and robbed infamous supporters of Franco, redistributing the money to help anti-Franco families in dire financial straits. The U.J.A., however, was short lived: it ended on May 30, 1939, scarcely three months after it began. This was the day of the raid (during which, according to the summary later released to members, "a typewriter, five pistols, three rifles, a grenade and various munitions were seized"), and on January 2 of the following year, a military tribunal tried the twenty-one members of the organisation and a further seven people; with the exception of three, who had not yet turned seventeen and were referred to the juvenile courts, all of the others were convicted: five were sentenced to death (though only one was actually executed), eight to life imprisonment, two to twenty years in prison, four to fifteen years and two to six years. And so, while everyone—willingly or unwillingly—was saying Yes, there were people who said No, people who did not comply, who did not surrender, who did not meekly endure the opprobrium, the indecency and the humiliation that was the lot of the defeated. They were a tiny minority, but it existed. For almost six decades their names were forgotten, so it does not seem out of place to remember them here. Honour to the brave: Pedro Gómez Segado, Miquel Colás Tamborero, Julia Romera Yáñez, Joaquín Miguel Montes, Juan Ballesteros Román, Julio Meroño Martínez, Joaquim Campeny Pueyo, Manuel Campeny Pueyo, Fernando Villanueva, Manuel Abad Lara, Vicente Abad Lara, José González Catalán, Bernabé García Valero, Jesús Cárceles Tomás, Antonio Beltrán Gómez, Enric Vilella Trepat, Ernesto Sánchez Montes, Andreu Prats Mallarín, Antonio Asensio Forza, Miquel Planas Mateo and Antonio Fernández Vallet.

Was Marco one of those clandestine adolescent heroes? Did Marco belong to the U.J.A.? For many years, he claimed he did: insistently; he claimed as much to me, with the same insistence, and in fact this was one of the details of his past we argued about most heatedly during our encounters, and which it took me the most effort to clarify. It hardly needs saying that, knowing the normal life or the semblance of a normal life that Marco was leading during the brief existence of the U.J.A., his incomparable talent for lying, his passion for appropriating the heroic past of others, at first I did not believe a word; moreover, as I investigated, the evidence that he hadn't been a member of the U.J.A. became more conclusive. Why then did I come to think that Marco may have belonged to the U.J.A., or may have had some contact with the U.J.A.? There are two reasons: the first is that, almost twenty years before Juanjo Gallardo and José María Martínez unearthed the history of this precocious little anti-Franco group, Marco had already recounted his time with them, and indeed described it in some detail, in the first, brief account of his life published by Pons Prades in 1978; the second is Antonio Fernández Vallet. According to Marco, he had been a friend since childhood, a volunteer, like him, on the Segre front during the war, and his sponsor at the U.J.A.; meanwhile, according to the summary records of the trial, Vallet had been a member of the U.J.A., had held the role of Secretary for Propaganda and had been sentenced to fifteen years in gaol for it. Could Marco have told the story of Fernández Vallet and the U.J.A. at a time when no-one knew them or everyone had forgotten them, without being a member of the U.J.A.? Or was his membership in the U.J.A. the little truth Marco used to shore up the lies of his early post-war period—the little epic poem with which he tried to colour the pedestrian prose of his life—just as his time on the Segre front was the little truth he had used to shore up his lies about the war?

It was a tempting theory. However, the evidence suggesting that Marco was not a member of the U.J.A. gradually came to seem more solid, more conclusive. His name doesn't appear in the trial records of the military tribunal, this despite the fact that members of the U.J.A. had been interrogated and tortured with savage brutality—in one case, fatally—and it seems improbable that, in such circumstances, young men of seventeen or eighteen, to say nothing of boys of fifteen, would have held their tongue. Furthermore, none of the surviving members of the U.J.A. ever mentioned Marco in any of their numer-ous oral and written statements, whether in interviews or more or less fictionalised accounts, and none of them ever stated that the U.J.A., despite its initial intentions, ever extended beyond Santa Coloma and Sant Andreu, nor did the young historians who uncovered its history, who are prepared to stake their reputations on that fact that all of the members of the U.J.A. were arrested and tried by the military tribu-nal. All of this is common sense, especially when one considers that the U.J.A. was broken up while still at an embryonic stage and, with little infrastructure, scant means and few members, couldn't even dream of setting up a cell or a sector in the capital. Faced with this evidence, I tackled Marco repeatedly during our meetings, attempted to show him that his story didn't fit the available facts and implored him over and over, with the usual arguments, to tell me the truth (the most common argument, which also proved the most effective: if he didn't tell me the truth, Benito Bermejo would eventually find out). Until finally one morning in September 2013, while we were having coffee on a little square in Collblanc, having spent the morning in a vain search for Bartolomé Martínez, his first apprentice mechanic,

Marco gave in: in a tortuous and convoluted manner he finally admitted, almost as though it didn't matter, as though he weren't admitting it, that he had not been a member of the U.J.A.

What, then, is the truth? Did Marco have some connection with the U.J.A.? Or was it a complete fabrication? This is what I have now pieced together, or what I now imagine happened: Marco did know Fernández Vallet: they had been childhood friends in La Trinidad, they shared the same political ideals, they had met on the front lines or on the way to the front. Just after the war in Catalonia, when Fernández Vallet was involved in setting up the U.J.A., the two friends met again, perhaps in La Trinidad (but not, despite what Marco says, at his grandmother's funeral: according to the Barcelona public records, Marco's paternal grandmother, whose name was Isabel Casas, passed away on May 15, 1940, almost a year before the U.J.A. came into existence). Fernández Vallet talked to Marco about the U.J.A., probably showed him a leaflet; perhaps he suggested Marco join the group and Marco refused out of fear, out of caution or a mixture of both, or perhaps Fernández Vallet never made the suggestion and Marco had no need to refuse. What is certain is that this must have been all there was to it. Marco went back to his in-laws' house, to his wife, his child, his job in Felip Homs' workshop, to his normal life or his semblance of a normal life, and didn't think about the U.J.A. again until, days or weeks later, he chanced to hear that its members had been arrested. As for Fernández Vallet, in this version, he didn't refuse to give up Marco's name when he was interrogated, adding this act of bravery to his bravery in setting up the U.J.A.: Marco wasn't a member of the U.J.A., and therefore no-one could give him up. Whatever the case, years later, in the early 1950s, Marco knew that Fernández Vallet had been released from prison. At the time, Marco himself was going through a rough patch. It didn't occur to him that his old friend from la Trinidad might need his help; on the contrary, although he didn't dare meet up with him, for fear of being seen with a communist recently released from gaol, he sent someone to ask Fernández Vallet whether he could give Marco money. The request made no sense: Fernández Vallet was a pariah, he was ill and lacked resources; it was he who needed a hand. I don't know whether anyone gave it to him, but he and Marco never met again, and the former leader of the

U.J.A. died shortly afterwards. And when, in the late 1970s, Marco began to fashion for himself a past as a resistance fighter, he appropriated this episode and cast himself as a fictional militant in the U.J.A., its fictional brains and the leader of its fictional Barcelona cell.

This is the truth. This is what happened, or what I assume or imagine happened. Marco did not belong to the minority, but to the majority. He could have said No, but he said Yes; he surrendered, he resigned himself, he gave up, he accepted the barbarous, abject, claustrophobic life imposed by the victors. He wasn't proud of it, or at least as of a certain date he wasn't proud of it, nor is he proud of it now, and that is why he lied. Marco is not a symbol of exceptional decency and honour in defeat, but of everyday indecency and degradation. He is an ordinary man. This is no reason to reproach him, obviously, except that he attempted to pass himself off as a hero. He was not. No-one is obliged to be a hero. This is why heroes are heroes: this is why they are a tiny minority. The glory goes to Fernández Vallet and his comrades.

And so we come to Germany. We come to the smouldering heart of
Marco's deception: I don't know whether it is his worst (or his best),
but it is the lie that made him famous, the one that led to his unmask-
ing. From the moment he first began fashioning a fictitious past for
himself as an anti-fascist resistance fighter and a victim of the Nazi
camps, Marco told the fabricated story of his deportation on countless occasions, in countless different versions and with countless different anecdotes, details and hues; it would be absurd, and probably
impossible, to attempt to summarise all of them, but neither absurd
nor impossible to recount the two on which Marco's deception was
based, those from which the sham of his time as a prisoner in Flossenbürg blossomed like a tree.

I have already mentioned them on several occasions, because they
contain the essence of Marco's German lie. Both are fake biographies
of Marco, the most extensive published about him; they appear in
two of only a small handful of books—at least at the time they were
published—on the subject of Spanish prisoners of the Nazi camps;
both include various fabricated biographies of camp members: the
first, published in 1978, the work of a prolific libertarian writer and
contemporary of Marco named Pons Prades, was written in Spanish
and entitled *The Kommandant's Pigs* (the book was written in collaboration with a communist survivor of the camps, Maríano Constante);
the second, published in 2002, the work of a young Catalan reporter
named Jordi Bassa, is written in Catalan and entitled *A Memoir of
Hell* (this book was a collaboration with a young photographer, Jordi
Ribó). The two biographies are similar: both begin with the heroic

and dishonest version of Marco's Civil War adventures and his departure from Spain, and both, to shore up a lie, mix lies with truth, but the two also differ, and not simply in specific details. Pons Prades' biography is narrated by Marco and was published when our man had not yet been to Flossenbürg and knew very little about the Nazi camps and when many Spanish survivors of the camps were still alive, and so Marco lies tactfully and concisely; on the other hand, Bassa's biography, written in the third person, was published when there were few Spanish survivors of the Nazi camps and when Marco, who by now was a member of the Amical de Mauthausen, had visited Flossenbürg, and had read up on concentration camps in general and on Flossenbürg in particular, believed that there were no remaining survivors of Flossenbürg, and so he lies liberally and easily.

"I spent very little time in Flossenbürg," Marco prudently begins his lie in Pons Prades' text, "and since I was transferred from one place to another and was kept in solitary confinement, I could not make contact with anyone." As the story gradually moves away from Flossenbürg, he throws caution to the wind, or almost, and here begins the epic, the local colour, the discreet heroic attributions and even a certain degree of patriotism, this last being a rare quality in Marco: "I was finally able to breathe a little," Marco continues, "in the satellite camp of Neumünster, near Hamburg, where we suffered terrible air raids by the British, dropping phosphorous bombs, in which hundreds of thousands of Germans died. Since no-one really knew whether these bombs had a delayed effect, we, the prisoners of the various camps around the port, were the first people to be sent in to dig through the rubble and pile human remains onto trucks. It was here I met another Spaniard, he was from Andalucía. We were the only Spanish prisoners in Neumünster, but we simply joined an international resistance organisation set up by the French and the Latvians, in which there were also Belgians, Poles, Italians and Germans (those imprisoned during the early days of the Nazi regime, in 1933, '34 and '35). The Poles were the youngest, since their older compatriots had been so badly beaten that they resigned themselves to death with startling apathy. This is something I never observed among the Spanish. Well, in general, because some of them also succumbed to despair."

Up to this point in Marco's story (or Marco's story as repro-
duced or re-created by Pons Prades), the lie is made up entirely of
lies; from this point on, there are also truths: "Just when I thought
they would not bother me any more, the Gestapo came one day and
took me to the prison in Kiel, and that was when the trouble started
again. I believed—and I really mean this—that my hour had come. I
spent eight months in complete isolation and learned German thanks
to the light—which burned twenty-four hours a day—and a bilingual Protestant Bible in Latin and German. It was in Kiel that we
found out the Franco regime had sent several groups of Falangists
and *Requetés*—Carlist militiamen—to Nazi Germany who agreed to
go into prisons and concentration camps to act as informants. During one of the first interrogations the Gestapo subjected me to in
Kiel, two such Spaniards appeared and openly accused me of being
one of the leaders of the resistance movement in Neumünster. One
was a Catalan, the other was from Valladolid. The name of the first
man was—*is*, because he is still alive and living in Martorell—Jaume
Poch, he was from Ponts, Lérida; the other was called José Rebollo.
The first was a *Requeté*, the second a Falangist. Because of their testimony I was brought before a military tribunal charged with conspiring against the Third Reich. Next to me was a Brazilian, a merchant
seaman named Lacerda da Silva, who had been arrested in Hamburg
when Brazil declared war on Germany. He was a cheerful lad. I was
sentenced to ten years' hard labour, a sentence I only partly served
since, in May 1945, Canadians from the North American army liberated Kiel and I regained my freedom."

Truth and lies: it is true that Marco was imprisoned in Kiel gaol,
that he spent some time in solitary confinement, and that he learned
some German, possibly from a bilingual Bible, but it is not true that
he had been a *deportado*—in fact he was a volunteer worker—or that
he was sent to Kiel prison from Neumünster—in fact he was sent from
Kiel itself, from the camp built for volunteer workers in Wattembeck
by the Deutsche Werke Werft—or that he was in solitary confinement for eight months—in fact he was in solitary for barely five days.
It is true that he was arrested based on accusations by two Spaniards
named Jaume Poch and José Robledo (not Rebollo), but it is a lie that
he was charged with conspiring against the Third Reich for organis-

ing a resistance movement in Neumünster concentration camp—in fact he was accused of high treason, but only for badmouthing the Nazis and praising the Soviets to his co-workers at the Deutsche Werke Werft; it is also a lie that he was sentenced to ten years' hard labour—in fact he was acquitted of all charges levelled against him. It may be true that he met a Brazilian sailor named Lacerda or Lacerta or Lacerte da Silva. His account of his departure from Germany at the end of the war and his return to Spain is sheer fantasy: "I was issued with a safe-conduct pass to get back to France, where I was sent to a rest home. When I left there, in 1946, I once again joined the clandestine struggle in Spain." The account by Pons Prades (or the account that Pons Prades attributes to Marco) concludes with a fireworks display of the special effects characteristic of Marco's fictions: a sentimental Roman Candle, a psychological one and finally an epic flare; all blanks, obviously, all false. "One of the things that saved me while I was in solitary confinement in Kiel," says Marco, "was listening to the cries of the gulls and the voices of the warders' children playing in the courtyard outside. I told myself: while gulls still glide over the sea and children still play, all is not lost. Since I was young, the after effects of my time in the camp quickly disappeared. But one thing that marked me for many years, when I was out in the street and I would focus on the pace of someone walking in front of me, was that I felt compelled to fall into step. The other thing that saved me was immediately plunging back into the fray. The underground resistance in the confederate militia in Spain in the late 1940s was thrilling. But that is another story."

Bassa's account is longer and more detailed than that of Pons Prades; it is also, to a great degree, more clearly false, more lacking in truth. According to this account, Marco was not deported to Flossenbürg from France as claimed in the false account of Pons Prades, but to Kiel, where he was sentenced to forced labour in the city's dockyards and where, without wasting a minute, he set up a clandestine information network and organised acts of sabotage (all of which is equally false). The differences between the two accounts of Marco's time in Kiel are not substantive, but anecdotal: in Bassa's version, for example, there is greater emphasis on Marco's courage and dignity as he endured the interrogations of the Gestapo after his imprisonment, the fictitious eight months of solitary confinement in Pons Prades' version become nine months, and the fictitious sentence of hard labour handed down by the military tribunal becomes a no-less-fictitious sentence of deportation to a concentration camp. It is here that fundamental differences between the two accounts emerge: while in Pons Prades' version, Marco dispatched his time in Flossenbürg with a single oblique sentence, Bassa's version runs to several pages, larded with sentimental heroic fantasies. Below, I have translated these pages from the Catalan, preserving the third person narration, with minimal changes, cuts and interruptions, beginning with the melodramatic scene when, one night in the dead of winter, in an unknown railway station, Marco is waiting for the train that is to take him to the concentration camp:

"It was cold, very cold. He did not know what day it was. The nine months of solitary confinement had left him disoriented and he had lost all track of time. It must have been January or February, because it was not long since the Germans had celebrated New Year. Trembling and constipated, he felt alone, utterly alone. He was surrounded by dozens of people who, like him, were waiting for a train. But really he was alone. The train arrived and the soldiers forced them to climb into the wagons. As he was about to board, Enric realised that there was no room, but hardly had he made a move to descend than the soldiers brutally shoved him. He was pressed against two other prisoners, face to face, breath to breath, skin to skin . . . They were packed in like animals. The doors were closed and the train pulled away. Soon, the smell became unbearable. The stench of urine and the defecations of the weakest prisoners was so pervasive that many vomited. It was all pitifully repellent. And so it remained for the two days and two nights. It was a long journey of stops and starts. The train would come to a halt to allow military convoys to pass, and inside the wagons, everyone hoped that they had finally reached their destination and the doors would open. But no. The train would start up again and the torture continued.

"When, inside the wagons, they heard the noise of the train coming to a complete stop and the engine being shut off, Enric peered through a crack in the slats and saw the name of the station: Flossenbürg. The doors were opened, allowing the icy air to rush into the wagons, which triggered much jostling. Everyone wanted to breathe fresh air, and elbowed those around them for a breath of this long-awaited purity. Pushed by their fellow travellers, the prisoners closest to the doors tumbled out and many were trampled. It was grotesque. Screams and whimpers. Moans and curses. They were like a herd of wild beasts set loose, a human tide surging forward until, suddenly, the course of the tide was reversed: the SS officers on the platform began to bludgeon those who had fallen, while dogs attacked anything that moved. Immediately, people scrambled to climb back into the wagons. The jostling between those trying to get out and those trying to get back in prompted more falls. And the SS were everywhere. Punches, kicks, whips, bites.

"*Raus! Raus! Aufrichten! Aufrichten scheibe dür!* [Out! Out! On your feet! On your feet . . . !]

"*Raus! Raus! Im reihe! Im reihe!* [Out! Out! Line up! Line up!]— roared one of the SS officers while the dogs barked as though they were rabid. Many people died right there, because they were so weak that, with four blows, the SS officers finished them off. Terrified, Enric began to march, in groups of five, in the direction indicated by the SS. Everything was covered in snow and, enfeebled by the darkness of the wagons, the prisoners' eyes found it difficult to adjust and focus on their surroundings. It was a relief that the sun had set because, if it had not, the glare would have been blinding.

"When they reached the concentration camp, they were forced to remove all their clothing before entering the cold showers. They were pushed inside by SS officers, whose thirst for violence seemed insatiable. Some of those who had travelled in the wagon were brutally beaten simply because they did not understand German.

"*Achtung! Da links! Da links!* [Attention! Left turn! Left turn!]

"Orders were constantly barked and anyone who did not understand was hit with a rifle butt which, according to the soldier's humour, could be followed by a rain of blows. Some were fatally wounded in these absurd beatings. Enric immediately realised that, if he was to survive, he had to be careful to stay as far as possible from the SS officers and instantly obey every order. A moment of inattention could cost you your life. This was when he understood that this was his fate. His punishment was Flossenbürg."

It is a classic scene: the arrival of prisoners at the concentration camps. There are hundreds, perhaps thousands of survivors' stories; they have been tirelessly re-created on film and in literature too. Marco reinvented the scene no less tirelessly in his conferences, his articles and his interviews. On January 27, 2005, for example, on the sixtieth anniversary of the liberation of Auschwitz by the Soviet troops, during a solemn ceremony at which, for the first time, the Spanish parliament paid tribute to the victims of the Holocaust and the almost nine thousand Spanish Republicans deported to the Nazi camps, Marco gave the following account: "When we reached the concentration camps in those hideous cattle trucks, we were stripped of our clothes and all our belongings were taken, not simply out of greed, but to leave us utterly naked, powerless: wedding rings, brace-lets, photographs. Alone, helpless, left with nothing. Nothing that might remind you of the outside world, nothing that might remind you of the tenderness of a loved one, that might help you to go on living in the hope that you might feel it again. We were ordinary people, like you, but they stripped us, set their dogs on us, dazzled us with their searchlights, screamed at us in German *Links-Rechts!* [Left-Right!]. We could not understand anything, and failing to understand an order could cost you your life."

It was all a lie, of course. Marco had not experienced what he said he had experienced, but by 2005, he had been the president of the Amical de Mauthausen for two years and was the only survivor to speak in Parliament that day. The photographs of the event are unequivocal: Marco's speech was greeted by astonished silence, many of those present were profoundly moved, including children and grandchildren of camp survivors; some people wept.

"The first barracks to which he was assigned was number eigh-teen"—Bassa's account continues, or Marco's account as rendered in Bassa's prose—"and having spent three days in quarantine, he was sent to the quarries, the harshest work detail in the camp. No-one survived there for more than six months, so there was a constant rotation of labourers. Many prisoners collapsed from exhaustion and were summarily shot by the soldiers. And since no-one was allowed to pick them up or bury them, they had to load the bodies onto the hopper wagons leaving the quarry. As they reached the rim of the quarry, the SS officers separated those wagons destined for the granite silos from those headed for the furnaces. It was here that Enric understood Hitler's ultimate objective: to create a superior race by making those who were excluded inferior. The Nazis wanted to create a subspecies, a race of slaves forever condemned to submit to the Aryans. He could see it clearly, because they were succeeding: all the prisoners suffered from a profound, crippling depression that led them to suicide or to apathy, which resulted in their summary execution. Enric had never seen anything like it: shattered people willingly choosing death because they were weary of dying every day when they awoke. Surrounded by desolation and anguish, he focused his energies on his conscience as a political prisoner, a resistance fighter. If he accepted the role of victim, he would be carried off by despair like so many other prisoners.

"After three months working in the quarries, he received orders to join the group devoted to repairing the fuselage of aeroplanes. The Gestapo reports detailing his skills as a mechanic earned him this transfer. His *kapo* was a German named Anton. Screaming and beatings were commonplace, but Anton took no pleasure in them. In fact, his was a special group and required careful handling. Moreover, his transfer coincided with first warnings from the infirmary, highlighting the disproportionate mortality at Flossenbürg. The crematorium could not deal with them all, and productivity was much lower than orders from Berlin would have desired. The immediate result was that the SS officers relented a little on the absurd executions, killing only those they considered rebellious or malingering. Even so, the bodies hanging in the courtyard continued to provide the backdrop to the daily routine. They were not taken down until the purple flush of the first days had turned greenish."

Hanging bodies. Another classic trope of Nazi horror Marco liked to exploit in his fantasies. In an article published in June 2005 in *El País*, for example, he gave the following account: "In our last Christmas in the camp, in 1944, we requested permission to put up a

Christmas tree, and on December 24, they hanged four Polish men from the illuminated tree." That's it.

"Pietr, a bitter, brutal Latvian," continues Bassa, or Marco as voiced by Bassa, "was the *kapo* in Enric's barracks. He always carried a club and he loved to administer punishment beatings, twenty-five strokes to the first person who gave him the slightest excuse. And no-one stood up for anyone. There were almost two hundred men in a barracks designed for fifty, but Enric felt very alone. There was no-one from Catalonia, and everyone was fighting to survive. He did not give up and managed to strike up conversations with a Frenchman, some Czechs, brave men who shared his spirit of resistance. It was impossible to count on the Russians, since they were exterminated in their hundreds as soon as they arrived in the camp. The Poles were gruff, abrasive loners and the Jews suffered more or less the same fate as the Russians: they did not last long.

"Gradually, he managed to convince the Czechs and the French to help him collect small snippets from the newspapers they found when working with commandos outside the camp. The objective was to gather what little information they could about the war and maintain contact with the world outside the camp. And the network set to work. The next step consisted of stealing small quantities of coal in order to extend the hours during which they could fuel the barrack stoves, and at this point they began to connect with prisoners who worked as secretaries in the transfer offices. In this manner some of their own were able to avoid being sent to the final infirmary (where prisoners were executed by being injected with petrol), by arranging for documents to be mislaid or names changed. They were risking their lives, but by this point the SS were not interested in such details. They were so convinced that the prisoners were inferior that they believed it impossible that any of them should be intelligent. Consequently, 'political' surveillance was somewhat relaxed.

"This is not something that Enric merely thought, it is something he suffered personally. One day, while he was playing chess with another prisoner, an SS officer wanted to challenge him. Obviously, Marco agreed, but within a few moves he had already captured the officer's queen and checkmate was imminent. The officer flew into a rage and dashed the pieces to the ground and rolled up his sleeves. He wanted to arm wrestle. And obviously, he won. Not simply because Enric made no real effort, knowing that his life was at stake, but also because an SS officer was ten times stronger than any starving, emaciated prisoner. The situation did not escalate, but the conclusion Enric drew from this episode was that the German soldiers were convinced of their superiority and, when anyone or anything upset their plans, they resorted to violence in order to assert their supremacy. Enric saw violence as a last resort, while they saw it as the ultimate proof of their power. They would always win."

Not always. Sometimes Marco's incredible courage and audacity not only frustrated the plans of the SS but, since they were no match for the heroic dignity of the Spanish prisoner, succeeded in defeating them. The story about the chess game is merely one example; it is also one of the greatest hits in Marco's repertoire. The version given by Bassa is relatively restrained; the one broadcast on Catalan public television in 2004 is more elaborate (and rather different). It combined an oral account by Marco, moved almost to the point of tears by his invented memories, while offering a dramatic re-creation of the memorable (and memorably false) episode: the static footage of Marco against a black background was intercut with a travelling shot of a chessboard, the sombre chess pieces framed against the desolate background of a Nazi camp or a setting designed to mimic a Nazi camp, accompanied by a poignant, emotion-laden soundtrack. "That day," Marco says in the report, "I was not so much playing chess with a friend, as teaching him to play, when I saw a shadow fall across the chessboard. I looked up and saw an SS officer, who kicked my comrade off his stool, pounded his fist on the table and ordered me to carry on playing. He wanted to best me, to prove once more that he was better than we were, better than I was; after all, who was I? A pathetic wretch, worse still, a Spaniard, a Latino, a Dago. And I played that game. And then I realised that, if I had to play the SS officer, I had to beat him and accept the consequences. And one by one I began capturing his pieces, he was no match for me. Then, at the end, I deliberately left him with only his king. I checkmated him, knocked over his king, though I was well aware what this might cost me. But this was the moment chosen for me, this was my moment, there was no way anyone could take it from me, and I believed that, whatever happened, I was once again a human being. That day, I reclaimed my dignity. I won the battle of Stalingrad."

Nor was this the only one, of course: in his heroic struggles against the Nazis—who invariably crumpled, crushed by his fearlessness and his generosity of spirit—he won many more battles. Here is one last example, also from a television report, before I return to Bassa's story. It is taken from a programme broadcast on the Galician version of the History Channel; the set-up is less mawkish than the chess match, the background music less saccharine and Marco's words are illustrated with images of genuine prisoners in genuine Nazi camps, but the protagonist's performance is just as overblown (the gravelly voice, the solemn, noble gestures, the eyes moist with emotion), the moral of the tale just as didactic and self-aggrandising and, needless to say, the story just as false. "How did I come to save my life," Marco asks himself as he begins his story, "when someone else, someone perhaps with less reason to lose his or have it taken from him (if reason exists to justify taking another's life), could not? What really happened on the day an exemplary punishment was ordered because several lads from my barracks who worked outside the camp had been missing for a few hours? What happened when the SS officer came to select one man out of twenty-five to be executed and when, overcome by fear, I saw him approach and knew he was coming for me? When he came to me, he stopped, raised his forefinger and pointed. He did not say a word. All I know is that I raised my head and gave him the most appealing look I have ever given anyone. All I know is that he went on staring at me seriously; his lips barely moved, but he said: *Der Spanier anderer Tag.* The Spaniard another day. And he left."

It took no more than a look from a noble and courageous man to intimidate an executioner. Pure kitsch. Pure Marco.

"They would always win"—is what Bassa says the Nazis were thinking, or what Bassa says that Marco thought the Nazis were thinking during his fictitious stay in Flossenbürg; and he goes on: "Like the day somebody relieved himself outside the barracks and one of the soldiers noticed. The prisoners were told to fall in and asked who had done so. No-one said anything, and as punishment, the prisoners were forced to strip and stand all night on the *Appellplatz* [the main square in the camp]. In mid-winter. By the following morning, a dozen prisoners had frozen to death. This was how they demonstrated their power. And they could do so whenever they chose. Any moment was a good one to kill these inferior creatures.

"Suffering and death pervaded every corner of the camp, and gradually consumed the soul of every prisoner. Enric was no exception. He was strong, and he had had solid political education, but in the camp, he was nothing. Torment and fear proved difficult enemies to defeat when they nightly besieged you in a darkness filled with the sobs of prisoners mourning friends and relatives who had died that day. A fear that sometimes made men lose their heads, as on the day the prisoners were led to a disinfection chamber. This is what the SS officers said but, obviously, everyone assumed it was the gas chamber. No-one had ever seen it, but everyone had heard the stories, and some had lost friends to it. Naked, they were locked inside and the steam was turned on. Many prisoners began to scream, to fall on the floor, to beat their heads against the walls. Enric panicked, thinking that the gas was already beginning to kill the weakest. But after a few seconds he realised that they were not dying, fear had triggered panic attacks and even epileptic fits. And the panic was contagious. It began with two prisoners, then three, five, ten . . . Until even the prisoners next to him began to lose their minds. He slapped each of them twice. And at least those closest to him began to calm down. That morning, he got a closer look at death than he had on the day when, with the assembled prisoners in the camp, he watched as twenty-five Czechs who had attempted to escape were hanged. But midday came, and then afternoon, and eventually the night. And with it, dreams, an escape that freed his soul if only for a few short hours.

"And the nights gave way to days, to weeks, to months and years. Until, on April 22, 1945, the U.S. Third Army arrived at Flossenbürg. Enric, who was hiding in the underground heating ducts, did not come out until he heard the whoops of joy. He had hidden because, knowing [as everyone else knew] that the Allies had crossed into Germany, he was afraid that the SS would execute the prisoners out of anger, or to ensure there would be no witnesses. But the Germans fled like rats before the Allies reached the village of Flossenbürg. On the following day, April 23, chaos reigned in the camp. The infirmary was filled with the dying, the barracks saw scenes of fighting and arguments, some prisoners had managed to get hold of guns . . . There were still German police patrols in the village to ensure the prisoners did not leave the camp. The Allies had liberated them, and then they had left. No-one knew what to do or where to go. And, surprisingly, after a few days new prisoners arrived at the camp. These prisoners had not been sent by the Nazi regime, they were displaced people sent there by Allied Forces who did not know what to do with them. In the confusion of the days that followed, the joy that followed the liberation turned bitter, especially for Enric, who was the only Catalan in the camp, the only stateless person no-one claimed."

This, then, is the essence of Bassa's account, which in turn constitutes the essence of the fiction Marco invented about his internment in Flossenbürg. The rest of Bassa's tale is a brief epilogue in which Marco returns to mixing lies and truths and in which he recounts his supposed return to Kiel, after his liberation from Flossenbürg, where he went back to working in the dockyards, his supposed return to Barcelona in 1946, his supposed links to underground anti-Franco movements during the dictatorship and his indisputable links, after the fall of the dictatorship, with the C.N.T., FaPaC, and with the Amical de Mauthausen, for which, a gratified Bassa concludes, in 2001, the Catalan government awarded Marco its highest civilian decoration, the Creu de Sant Jordi. Honour to the heroes!

This is the lie. But what of the truth? What really happened during the period Marco spent in Germany in the early 1940s? Is it possible to reconstruct the most controversial section of his biography? The answer is yes: for the most part.

Marco set off for his new life as an emigrant on November 27, 1941, from Estación del Norte in Barcelona, with the first convoy of Catalan volunteer workers leaving for Germany. The train was crowded with men, some of them adults, most of them young men, though few as young as Marco, who had barely turned twenty; each had an envelope with his name, his number, his train ticket, his seat reservation and a food coupon, in addition to a hunk of bread, some tinned food and a change of winter clothes; each wore an armband bearing the Spanish flag, and carried his personal passport and a sheet of instructions he was to observe during the journey. It lasted several days. At various stations, the train would stop; here they were given coffee and a roll, and they were allowed to get out and stretch their legs and visit the toilets, but not leave the station, and when they arrived in Metz, in northwest France, they were assigned to different trains headed for different destinations, and the French police who had escorted the convoy since it crossed the Spanish border were replaced by the German police (or this is what Marco remembers). Many years later, shooting a scene for Santi Fillol and Lucas Vermal's film *Ich bin Enric Marco* at this same station, Marco would wonder aloud, with the pensive and melodramatic air of someone seeking out his distant past but unable to find it, as though so many years later he could not understand why he had left Spain as a volunteer worker: "I would like to know where I was heading. And what I was hoping to achieve." In fact, the answers to these two questions are no mystery, and Marco knew them better than anyone: he was heading for Kiel, in northeast Germany, having been hired by a German company as part of a Spanish-German accord enabling Franco to repay his debt to Hitler for aid during the Civil War and to help him win the world war and impose fascism throughout Europe; he was hoping to avoid military service and to earn a much better living than he could have in Spain at the time. It is that simple. It is that easy.

Marco arrived in Kiel in early December. Like the rest of the Spanish workers, he was not billeted in Kiel itself, but in an encampment of wooden barracks some twenty-five kilometres away in Wattenbek, in the district of Bordesholm. Here he lived for three months, travelling into Kiel every day and returning every night. The city had been one of the principal German naval bases since the mid-nineteenth century, and the Deutsche Werke Werft, the company that employed Marco, had specialised in building merchant ships until the Nazis came to power and they began to specialise in building warships, submarines and various other military vessels. Marco worked on the docks as a mechanic, specifically in a unit dedicated to repairing and servicing the engines of torpedo boats; his job mostly involved checking the engines (dismantling cylinder heads, grinding valves, replacing piston rings), but also in manufacturing precision parts for the propeller shafts of torpedo boats. This was a rather specialised task, and one to which he was assigned because he was a conscientious and diligent worker. Not all of his co-workers were so diligent, in fact most of his co-workers were not, at least according to Marco, who considered himself better than they were, or who thought that, compared to him, they were plebs, a crowd of idle, illiterate, alcoholic morons. Marco prided himself, not only on being better than they, but on working in a section predominantly staffed by free Germans together with a number of French and Belgians, some of whom were prisoners of war. Marco claims that he organised a resistance cell with them, but there is not the slightest evidence that this is true. He also claims that he personally engaged in acts of sabotage, something that, according to him, he could do without running any risks, by failing to clean the rag he used to grind the valve and the valve seat of the three 20-cylinder Mercedes-Benz engines that powered each torpedo boat; but there is no proof that this is true either. There is, however, evidence, incontrovertible evidence, that Marco was arrested by the German police, that he spent several months in prison and that he was brought to trial.

All of these facts are contained in the charges against Marco brought by the Hanseatic High Tribunal in Hamburg. In it, we can read that our man was arrested on March 2, 1942, scarcely three months after arriving in Germany, and taken to the Gestapo gaol on Blumenstrasse in Kiel. For Marco himself, however, it all began several days before his arrest, when he was alerted by one of his colleagues. His name was Bruno Shankowitz, a German, and Marco had become friendly with him and his wife, Kathy, who had invited him to spend Christmas with them (Marco, ever the ladies' man, insinuated that he had, or could have had, an affair with Kathy, or that Kathy was infatuated with him; he also claims that he had several other affairs while in Kiel). One morning, while he was working, Bruno asked him whether he was a communist; surprised, Marco said no and inquired why he had asked. Because there's a rumour going around that you're a communist, said Bruno; then he advised him: Be careful what you say and who you say it to. It was sound advice, but Marco barely had time to follow it. Hours or days later he was arrested at his barracks in Wattenbek. According to the judicial record, Marco was held for five days before being remanded in custody; according to Marco, these five days were spent in a crowded cell with many other prisoners like him (among them a Brazilian sailor named Lacerda or Lacerta or Lacerte da Silva), sleeping on straw strewn over hard concrete and being repeatedly interrogated. Marco says (and I think we have to believe him) that this was the most difficult point of his life, that he was panicked, that he was mistreated, that he did not know what would become of him, and that he remembers being permanently sodden: with water, with urine, with vomit; but he also says other things that I do not think we have to believe, or that we do not have to believe wholeheartedly, like the fact that he faced up to his interrogators and that he presented himself to them as a freedom fighter.

According to the record, Marco was transferred to Kiel gaol on March 11, where he was held pending his trial until October of that year. We know nothing of what happened during those six months other than the account Marco began to give after his imposture was discovered, almost always with the intention of proving that all the lies he had told about his internment in Flossenbürg were a legitimate, educational and well-intentioned displacement, albeit a little embroidered, of the punishments he had suffered in Kiel prison, and not the bastard child of a *ménage à trois* between his need to be a protagonist, his imagination and his reading. Nevertheless, in a long letter to the editor of the *Diari de Sant Cugat* in January 2006, in response to a letter from a certain señora Ballester, published in the same newspaper, Marco offered some concrete details about his imprisonment which, though slathered in the usual pottage of heroism, victimhood and self-justification, occasionally have a distinct flavour of truth.

"Shaved, disinfected, daubed with some caustic, foul-smelling ointment," Marco writes in a Catalan full of rhetorical flourishes which I have taken the liberty of correcting or tempering in this translation, "I was confined to a cell on the second floor [of Kiel gaol], the last cell on the left, next to the drain where urine and excrement were emptied and where we filled our water jugs. In the cell there was no running water, no toilet and no flush mechanism, only a small stone washbasin against the wall that was barely large enough to fit my cupped hands when I washed my face, and which, on tiptoe, I could just reach to wash my arse. A bucket with no lid in which to shit and piss, and a handful of newspaper clippings to wipe myself, for which I will always be grateful, less for their hygienic purpose than because the pictures kept me connected to the outside world. A bed that was barely fifty centimetres wide, screwed to the wall by two hinges, with two folding legs so that it could be raised by a chain and stowed against the wall. It was important to save space in order to use the work bench. It was strictly forbidden to keep the bed lowered during the day. A straw mattress scarcely the thickness of two fingers. The remainder of the furnishings consisted of a box containing an aluminium plate and spoon, a comb—I never understood the purpose of this—and a bilingual book of prayers and psalms, in German set in gothic type, and in Latin, which, fortunately, I could understand. A large card bearing my name, misspelled as always—they assumed Marco was a first name rather than a surname—and significant details: 'Solitary confinement, indefinite sentence.' [. . .] Days of backbreaking work from morning to night, from Monday to midday on Sunday, with no possibility of being excused or exempted. Every morning, after coffee, the Wacht-meister brought me a box of metal objects from the foundry that I was to smooth using files and other tools given to us with the day's work. Metres upon metres of thick hemp rope that had to be separated into fibres. The dust from the hemp parched the nose and throat and irri-tated the eyes, but the most difficult thing was stripping electrical wiring with your bare hands to collect the copper from the cables the Germans ripped from the cities they conquered. Nine months in these conditions, Señora Ballester," Marco concludes, "nine months locked up in that cell."

It was not nine months, but seven, but that hardly matters now. Here and there, in this version and various other accounts and state-ments made after the scandal broke, our man gave many other details, real and fictitious, about his incarceration. Details about the revolting food he was given, about the beatings he received, about his repeated detention in punishment cells, about the despair that often threat-ened to overwhelm him and the remedies he used to combat it: with his infallible nose for melodrama, Marco told Pons Prades—as I have already recounted—that, listening in his cell to the cries of the gulls and the voices of the warders' children playing in the courtyard out-side, he said to himself: "While there are gulls gliding over the sea and children playing, all is not lost"; on the other hand, there is a story that Marco did not tell Pons Prades, one that surpasses this in its sentimentality; one that, though often repeated and alluded to in Bassa's biography, I have not yet recounted. According to Marco, while in prison he was allowed to write letters from time to time, let-ters that he wrote but which never reached their destination because they were kept by the authorities; he was compelled to write letters in German, but his German was so rudimentary and his gaolers gave him so little time to write, that he was forced to devise a system if he was to say everything he had to say: the system involved pricking his finger with a needle, mixing the blood with saliva, and using the resulting mixture as ink and the needle as a pen to write drafts of his letters in the margins of the newspaper articles he used as toilet paper; in this way, when the time came, when he was finally given paper and pen and a few scant minutes in which to write, he had only to make a clean copy of these bloodstained drafts.

Knowing Marco (and even without knowing him), this harrowing story is difficult to credit; what is true is that, like most of Marco's lies, it contains a sliver of truth: it is true that our man wrote at least one letter while in prison, and it is true that he wrote it in German, just as it is true that it never reached its destination because Marco's gaolers never sent it. I know this because the letter was found in the Schleswig-Holstein state archives and I am holding it in my hands. It is addressed to his wife—who had been informed by Spanish authorities that her husband was in prison—and is dated Kiel Prison, September 1, 1942, by which time Marco has already spent six months in custody and knows the serious charges levelled against him; the writer's German grammar is flawed, and his handwriting often illegible. Below, I have transcribed the letter in its entirety, chiefly because the intended reader is less its notional recipient than the writer's very real censors and well expresses Marco's desperate desire to ingratiate himself with them (Marco lies, flatters the Germans and even gives his own name and those of his relatives in German, or in his made-up German), in a display of obsequiousness that may partly explain the outcome of his trial. The translation, by Carlos Pérez Ricart, attempts to preserve the limitations of Marco's pidgin German:

My darling [name illegible, probably "Anni," meaning Anita],

I send kisses from far away with the hope of my happy
return to your side. I know that you do not understand
one word of German, I understand little. But, writing in
other language is not permitted and next week, Wednesday
exactly, my trial begins after seven months of investigation
where I defended myself against accusation of communist
and other lies said against me. My lawyer told me already I
will be found innocent. There is no guilt in me. They think
I was a red volunteer, but it is proved this is a lie.

A man accused me of being communist volunteer and
other madness that makes sense. These crazy things have
provoked seven months in prison and much silence, because
I know not many words of German and people are not kind
to me at work hour because they think I am red.

My imprisonment is a test for the Germans . . .
[illegible] But now everything will be resolved because I will
leave the gaol, we will get back our money and our little
[illegible, a child's name, probably "Toni," Anita's biologi-
cal and Marco's adoptive son] will have his father by his side
again. We will have tranquillity. I will demand justice from
my enemies and the recovery of salary for the seven months
spent in prison.

I know very well how much you have suffered but all
that is almost over and soon we will be together. In all this
time not one day has passed when I did not think about you,
nor one moment without kissing my wedding ring. It is all
I have left; everything else is kept by the prison. But you
know how much love I have. I have resisted seven months in
prison for you.

I have been thinking that it would be good for you to
come here. [Child's name, illegible, probably "Toni" again]
could come here too and love the German land more than
our own country. Perhaps here there is not the blue sky and
the dazzling sun of our country, but the men here have these
things [the blue sky and the dazzling sun] in their soul. Yes,
we could come and live here because we are like the Germans: careful and with open hearts. Here I have learned to
love them.

In fact, this is something I thought about before and
this is why I started looking for a house. I wanted to surprise
you with the news, but this trial has ruined everything. Now
is the time to resume those plans. I earn enough money in
my job and in only a few months after my release you could
come to the city.

I hope that all our relatives are well. Give my regards to
aunt Kathe and uncles Richard and Francisco.

My darling, I send all my love to you and to our son.
Your Heinrich

(I do not write more because my German is still bad)

Judging by what he told his wife, Marco was optimistic about the outcome of his trial; but perhaps he simply wanted to seem so, or wanted
the Germans to believe he was: the truth is that, several days before
the court hearing, when he must have known the charges against him,
he had no real reason to be optimistic. In the charges filed by the
prosecutor, a certain Doktor Stegemann, on July 18, 1942, Marco
is accused of a grave crime: "Systematically planning actions—of
high treason—with intent to change the constitution of the Reich
by force" (in German: *das hochverrätische Unternehmen, mit Gewalt die
Verfassung des Reichs zu ändern vorbereitet zu haben*). Specifically, the
prosecutor claimed that Marco was a communist and had been a volunteer in the Republican army during the Civil War, and accused him
of disseminating propaganda among the Spanish workers. There is no
need to pay much heed to the accusation that Marco was a communist; in such matters, the German authorities used the term broadly,
making no distinction between communists and anarchists: as far as
they were concerned, both were *Rotspanier*—Spanish Reds. As to the
charge of disseminating propaganda, the prosecutor based this on
the testimony of Jaime Poch-Torres and José Robledo Canales, two
of Marco's Spanish co-workers who had heard him boast about having fought against Franco, criticising Hitler and the Nazi party, and
predicting that the Russians would defeat the Germans and revel-
ling at this thought, since—according to what Marco said, or what
Poch-Torres and Robledo Canales said that Marco said—he would
be able to go back to his country "and fight for inevitable, indispen-
sible communism in Spain." It is true that none of this seems to be of
great import, certainly it was no more than a number of injudicious
remarks made in the presence of the wrong people; but there can be
no doubt that the crime of high treason—or "promoting the ideals of
International Communism and thereby imperilling Germany," to use
the phrase in the prosecutor's report—was very serious, all the more
so in Nazi Germany, and especially in Nazi Germany in the fourth
year of the war. So serious that the most lenient sentence Marco could
expect was to be sent to a concentration camp.

But the fact is that he was acquitted. How do we explain this verdict? I don't know. In his ruling, the presiding magistrate explained
it by stating that Marco was not dangerous and based his ruling on

the retractions of Poch-Torres and Robledo Canales, who insisted
that Marco had not attempted to convert them to communism (he
was, they said, simply a young man trying to impress them), and on
the testimony of Marco's immediate boss, who exonerated him of any
acts of sabotage and praised him as an excellent worker. The problem
is working out how the magistrate came to a finding so favourable to
Marco, and so at odds with the unequivocal initial view of the prosecutor, and indeed an order from the RSHA—the Reich Main Security Office—issued two years earlier on September 25, 1940, which
determined that communist veterans of the Spanish Civil War were
to be sent to concentration camps (though it is true that this order was
issued before the signing of the Hispano-German Agreement that
had brought Marco to Germany, and that it referred to prisoners of
war; it is also true that the order was rescinded shortly afterwards,
in 1943, so that Spanish communists could be used as manpower in
the war effort); let me put it another way: it goes without saying that
Marco was not a dangerous man, but countless utterly innocuous men
were condemned by the Nazi courts while Marco was not. Why did
his Spanish accusers recant? Why did the prosecutor himself recant,
why did he ultimately withdraw the charges? I don't know. In his letter to his wife, Marco mentions his defence lawyer, a midshipman
whom Marco freely admits did not understand a word of Spanish,
so communication between them was not easy. Nor can it have been
easy for Marco, with his faltering German, to write a statement to
the prosecutor rebutting the charges against him, still less to defend
himself before the magistrate when, one September morning, he was
transported from Kiel to Hamburg for the hearing. These linguistic difficulties must have made the proceedings somewhat confusing.
More so than was already the case. That said, let me reiterate that
Marco thrived in such circumstances, chaos and confusion were his
natural habitat, since this allows me both to highlight one of Marco's
essential traits and to offer a theory about his curious acquittal: Marco,
as I have said before, is essentially a conman, a shameless charlatan,
a peerless trickster, so it is impossible to dismiss the idea that, just
as he managed to dupe the French military authorities, convincing
them that his past was blameless or inoffensive and that he was an
inoffensive, not to say irreproachable, young man, he similarly duped

the Nazi judicial authorities, managing to persuade the German
magistrate that he did not represent the slightest threat to National
Socialism and as such deserved to be released. Whatever the case, on
October 7, 1942, the President of the District Court of the Hanseatic
High Tribunal signed a ruling rescinding Marco's incarceration.

Our man remained in Germany for several months after this, but
these are merely the epilogue to this crucial chapter in his biography.
In the ruling that brought an end to his trial, Marco was ordered to
"make himself available to the police for supplemental inquiries"
while a note in the margin ordered that a copy of the ruling be sent
to the "directorate of the Secret State Police [*Geheime Staatspolizei*,
the actual name of the Gestapo] in Kiel." This order is open to a
variety of interpretations, but Marco says that, although in theory he
was set free, in practice he was still a prisoner, and for several weeks
or perhaps months he was incarcerated, not in the prison in Kiel, but
back in the Gestapo barracks on Blumenstrasse, from where he
remembers two officers escorting him every morning to Kiel University library, where he spent hours classifying Spanish books and magazines. Marco also says that he clearly remembers that one afternoon,
without warning, he was driven to the lobby of the barracks and left
standing, with no explanation, with a duty officer who did not even
seem to notice him. And he says that, after he had been there for
some time, waiting for he knew not what or whom, he suddenly
noticed a number of familiar objects on the officer's desk—a passport
photograph, his expired permit as a Spanish volunteer worker, a few
other things—but he said nothing and carried on waiting. And he
says that at some point, by which time he had been waiting several
hours, the duty officer finally seemed to register his presence, looked
from him to the objects on the desk and back at him, then without
looking at his belongings he swept them to the floor and bellowed
"*Raus!*"

He says he hurriedly gathered up his belongings and raced out
of the barracks. He says that it was dark, that it was raining, that he
suddenly found himself alone, with no money and nowhere to go.
He says he searched for somewhere to shelter and was unfortunate

enough to find it in a park that turned out not to be a park, but a cemetery. He says that he does not remember where he slept that night, though he's almost certain it was out of doors, on the other hand he does remember going to seek help the following day at the only place where he knew anyone, the dockyards of the Deutsche Werke Werft, from which he had been evicted and where he was no longer permitted to work, but where he found a German who acted as an interpreter between the Spanish labourers and their German employers, a man, Marco remembers, or says he remembers, who had lived for some time in Argentina and had returned to Germany, lured by the promised prosperity of triumphant Nazism, someone with whom Marco was apparently on good terms, and may have been the same man who, according to the German court records, had acted as interpreter during his trial. Whoever he was, the man took pity on Marco, or so he claims, and managed to find him a job at Hagenuk, a telecommunications company, which meant he was provided with a roof over his head in a camp ground located in the factory. The memories that Marco retains of this period, or what he says he remembers, are scant and unhappy, because although his job was easier than that at the dockyards—here he built electronic components for rockets and aeroplanes—the atmosphere in the factory and in the camp was much more violent, given that, he says, it was full of dirty, brutal and desperate Lithuanians and Ukrainians.

Marco too was desperate, but he was desperate to return to Barcelona. Or so he says. And he says that, one day, the same providential interpreter who had secured him the job in Hagenuk suggested a way for him to return home: after a year spent in Germany, Spanish workers were entitled to return home for a one-month furlough on condition that they then returned to their post; Marco had not yet worked a full year, having spent most of his time in Germany in prison, but the interpreter assured him that he could arrange for Marco to join one of the convoys of workers returning to Spain on leave. Marco says that he accepted without a second thought, without considering what he would do when the time came for him to return to Germany and he failed to do so, without considering what he would do when, after he'd failed to return, the Spanish authorities demanded he complete his deferred military service, and of course without worrying about the fact that, in Spain, Franco was still imposing a reign of terror, without considering anything other than fleeing Germany and returning home, like those animals that can smell an imminent disaster in the air; in the summer of 1943, Marco had already intuited that a few short months later, on December 13, the city of Kiel would be destroyed in a rain of fire unleashed by hundreds of American bombers. Marco arrived in Germany when it looked set to win the war, and left Germany when it was certain to lose it. We do not yet know what sort of life our man led once back in Barcelona, but we know something much more important: at least up until this point, Marco always sided with the majority.

PART II

The Novelist of Himself

I

Marco was born in an asylum; his mother was insane. Is he mad too? Is this his secret, the conundrum that explains his personality? Is this why he always sides with the majority? Does this explain everything, or does it at least explain the essential? And if Marco truly is mad, what is the nature of his madness?

When the scandal broke, there were few who abstained from offering an opinion on his character: journalists, historians, philosophers, professors waded in; not to mention psychologists and psychiatrists. The diagnosis offered by the latter was unanimous and, to a certain extent, concurs with that of many of our man's acquaintances: Marco is a textbook narcissist. Obviously, narcissism is not a form of madness but rather a personality disorder, a simple psychological anomaly. It is characterised by blind, unwarranted faith in one's own greatness, a deep-seated need for admiration and a lack of empathy. The narcissist has an inflated sense of self-importance, he is shamelessly self-aggrandising, blows his own trumpet at the slightest pretext and, regardless of what he does, expects to be recognised as superior, unconditionally admired and revered. In addition to a tendency to arrogance and overconfidence, he cultivates fantasies of unlimited power and success and, though loath to put himself in another's shoes (or incapable of doing so), he ruthlessly exploits others because he believes that the rules that apply to them do not apply to him. He is an incorrigible charmer, a born manipulator, a leader determined to win over disciples, a man hungry for power and control and almost impervious to feelings of guilt. Is the narcissist, then, essentially a man in love with himself? Is the narcissist that psychologists speak of the same as the narcissist of popular wisdom? Or is he the Narcissus of myth? Who is the mythical Narcissus?

There are several versions; the most well known—and the finest—is the account given by Ovid in the third book of the *Metamorphoses*. It is a tragic story that begins with an act of violence: Cephissus, the river god, abducts and rapes the wave-blue water-nymph Liriope, a Naiad, and as the fruit of this violation she bears a son of dazzling beauty whom she names Narcissus. Liriope hurriedly goes to the blind seer Tiresias to ask whether her son will live to see old age; Tiresias' response is cryptic yet categorical: yes, "*si se non nouerit*"; meaning, yes, "if he does not know himself." The childhood of Narcissus passes without incident, despite the enigmatic prediction of the voice of destiny. During his adolescence, many youths and many girls desire Narcissus, but he does not reciprocate their love. One day, while hunting deer in the woods, he spies Echo, "she of the echoing voice, who cannot be silent when others have spoken, nor learn how to speak first herself"—and she too falls in love with him; unwavering in his coldness and his arrogance, Narcissus scorns her and, filled with shame, and overwhelmed with sorrow, Echo hides herself in the woods and curses he who has mocked so many men and women before her, "So may he himself love, and so may he fail to command what he loves!" And Nemesis, daughter of night and goddess of retribution, hears Echo's entreaty; her intercession seals Narcissus' fate. Coming to "an unclouded spring of silver-bright water" ringed by grass, Narcissus stretches out to rest and drink, but, when he seeks to slake his thirst in the pool, a different and insatiable thirst grows within him: "seized by the vision of his reflected form, he loves a bodiless dream, believing what is merely a shadow to be corporeal. He is astonished by himself, and hangs there motionless, with a fixed expression, like a statue carved from Parian marble." Echo's curse is fulfilled: burning with love for his image reflected in the water, Narcissus fails to command what he loves; and Tiresias' prophecy also comes true: when he sees himself, when he knows himself, Narcissus dies and his body is transformed into "a flower, with white petals surrounding a yellow heart": the narcissus.

So the Narcissus of myth is not the Narcissus of popular wisdom, but his antithesis. In Ovid's tale, Narcissus does not fall in love with himself, but with his reflected image; in Ovid's tale, Narcissus hates himself, is horrified by himself, scorns himself with all his might, and this is why when he sees himself he dies. The narcissist, through his self-aggrandisement, fashions delusions of grandeur and heroism, a flattering fantasy, a lie behind which he can shelter and take refuge, a fiction capable of hiding his reality, the sheer sordidness of his life or what he perceives as the sheer sordidness of his life, his mediocrity and his abjectness, the utter contempt he feels for himself. The narcissist has an insatiable need for the admiration of others to shore up his fantasy, just as he needs power and control so that no-one can demolish the magnificent façade he has created to hide behind. The narcissist lives in fear and misery, plagued by a crippling insecurity disguised as self-confidence (even arrogance or smugness), on the brink of madness, terrified by the bottomless void that exists, or that he senses, within him, enamoured of the flattering fiction he has created to forget his repellent reality, and so, he has made himself impervious not only to guilt, but to almost every emotion, which he strives to keep at bay for fear that he might be weakened or even destroyed.

Moreover, many psychologists claim that narcissism develops in childhood, born of violence or of profound injury—just as Narcissus is born of the initial violence Cephissus visits on Liriope—of some terrible trauma the child is incapable of processing, some humiliation, some devastating blow to his self-esteem, some premature experience of horror suffered within the bosom of the family. This may be true. What is certain is that fiction saves Narcissus, and that, if Marco in his own way is a narcissist, perhaps it was his lies that saved him: Marco was an orphan forcibly removed from his mother, a poor, mentally ill woman who had been abused by her husband; a boy who experienced a nomadic, loveless childhood; an adolescent inspired by a short-lived revolution and crushed by a horrifying war; a born loser who, at some point in his life, in an attempt to win the love and admiration he had never had, decided to invent his past, to reinvent himself, to rework his life into a glorious fiction that would hide the embarrassing, pedestrian reality. He proclaimed that he was not who he was—an utterly normal man, a member of the vast, silent, cowardly, grey, depressing majority who always say Yes—but an exceptional person, one of those singular individuals who always says No, or who says No when every-

one else says Yes, or when it is most crucial to say No: at the outbreak
of the Spanish Civil War, though he was hardly more than a child;
as an impassioned combatant against fascism in places of the greatest risk and stress; as an intrepid anarchist guerrilla operating behind
enemy lines during the war and, after the war, the first or one of the
first foolhardy resistants to oppose the victorious Franco regime; as
a political exile, a victim of and fighter against the Nazis, a champion
of liberty. These were Marco's lies. This was the fiction that perhaps
saved him, and which, as in the case of Narcissus, prevented him for
many years from knowing himself or from recognising himself for
who he was. Of course, if lies saved Marco, the truth I am telling in
this book will kill him. Because fiction saves, but reality kills.

2

What did Marco do on his return from Germany? What sort of life did he lead during the never-ending Spanish post-war period? Did he go back to Spain to resume a normal life, or the semblance of a normal life he had lived before travelling to Germany? Was this the point at which he began to lie about his past in order not to know himself, not to recognise himself, in order to save himself through fiction? Or was this the point when, having endured the terrors of the trenches of Segre, the ruins of vanquished Barcelona, the prison in Kiel, he mustered sufficient courage to exhume the political ideals buried since the victory of Franco and launch himself into the clandestine struggle for those ideals even as Franco's regime imposed its iron will upon the country?

According to most of those who knew him, and those who wrote about him—at least before the scandal broke—our man spent the post-war period as a tenacious opponent of the dictatorship in addition to being a tireless visitor to its prisons, police stations and dungeons; furthermore: for many people, Marco seemed to have embodied the innate rebelliousness of the Spanish (or at least the Catalans) and the passion for freedom that prevented them from meekly submitting to forty years of Franco's tyranny without a fight. Marco's own statements on the subject leave little room for doubt: in 1978, he told Pons Prades in *The Kommandant's Pigs* that, after his alleged stay in Flossenbürg in the mid-1940s, "I once again joined the clandestine struggle in Spain," and that what saved his life was "immediately plunging back into the [political] fray" (in case this wasn't clear enough, he adds that "the underground resistance in the confederate militia [meaning,

the anarchists] in Spain in the late 1940s was thrilling"); in 2002, in
A Memoir of Hell, he told Jordi Bassa that when he returned to Spain
in 1945, he "carried on the clandestine struggle until 1975"; then, in
May 2005, just as the Marco scandal was breaking, in an issue of the
history magazine *L'Avenç* devoted to the sixtieth anniversary of the
liberation of the Nazi camps, our man published an article recounting his fictional memories of the liberation of Flossenbürg in which
he claimed that he left Germany in 1945 to return to Barcelona, "to
do the only work [he] knew how to do: to live for life and to do so
fighting for freedom," and if this is still not clear enough, he added
that "the thirty years of clandestine struggle that followed were the
only way to pick up life where [he] had left off." Finally, in September
2001, when awarding Marco the Creu de Sant Jordi, its highest civil
decoration, the autonomous Catalan government specifically cited
among his virtues his years of struggle against the Franco regime.

The phrases that I am quoting are curious. On the one hand,
it's obvious that our man is attempting to evoke a past as a staunch
anti-Franco resistant; on the other hand, they are as nebulous and
vague as all his references to his political commitment during the dictatorship: Marco uses the word "struggle," he uses the word "clandestine," he uses various other abstract terms, but he never mentions
what precisely this struggle entailed, which specific organisation, or
party or underground movement he belonged to, nor the specific
names of those who joined him in the "clandestine struggle." It is
true that the biographical and auto-biographical accounts of Marco's
life focused chiefly on his time in the Nazi camps, while his struggle
against Francoism was mentioned only in passing, perhaps because
that was not the point at issue, or more likely because it was taken
for granted, as though it were impossible that a Spaniard like Marco
would not have opposed the dictatorship. It is also true that, on occasion, Marco did reference a specific event: in January 2006, for example, he wrote an (unpublished) letter to the editor of *La Vanguardia* in
which he mentions a supposed confrontation, initially verbal and later
physical, with Luis de Galinsoga, a Franco sympathiser who edited
the newspaper during the 1950s, famous for uttering a thoroughly
stupid phrase that caused a scandal and eventually cost him his job:
"All Catalans are shit"; and in March 1988, in an article published

in the newspaper *Avui*, Marco presented himself as one of the only people who, one morning fourteen years earlier, gathered outside the gates of the prison of Modelo de Barcelona waiting for the remains of Salvador Puig Antich, a young anarchist executed by garrotte during the dying days of the Franco regime by order of a military tribunal. But even in these rare cases (and assuming they can genuinely be considered acts of resistance), everything in Marco's account is vague and insipid, from the way in which he presents the events to the precise role he played in them. This nebulous collection of vague stories has led many of Marco's friends and acquaintances to see the post-war period as the most shadowy and mysterious part of his life.

Is this true?

Absolutely not. Here, as so often within and without Marco's life, what is mysterious is the desire to see a mystery where there is none. In fact, it's much more difficult to piece together Marco's life before his return from Germany than afterwards, not least because there are numerous living witnesses to this latter period who are in a position to corroborate or contest, to complement or clarify Marco's claims, which partly explains his reticence and his evasiveness. There is no mystery, there are no shadows: for more than thirty years, from his return from Germany in 1943 until the death of Franco in 1975, or to be more precise, until the early years of democracy, Marco was not active in any political party or trade union, he had no dealings with the clandestine struggle, nor did he oppose the Franco regime in any way. He was not a frequent guest of its prisons or police stations, he was never arrested for his political beliefs nor did he encounter any problems with the authorities—or at least no real or remotely serious problems. Before now, Marco had always sided with the majority, and through the years of the Franco regime he continued to side with the vast majority of Spaniards who, willingly or otherwise, meekly accepted the dictatorship and whose deafening silence in no small part explains why it lasted forty years. It is that simple. It is that easy. Once again, this is no reason to reproach Marco; no-one, as I have said before, is obliged to be a hero; or to put it another way, it would be as facile as it would be unjust to reproach Marco for the fact that, like the vast majority of his compatriots, he didn't have the courage to defy a dictatorship capable of jailing, torturing and executing dissidents. No: there can be no reproach. None, but for the fact that, many years later, he sought to occupy a place in the past he had not earned, attempting to persuade people that throughout the Franco regime he had belonged to the tiny, valiant minority who said No, rather than to the millions of fanatics, rogues, cowards, the indifferent masses who said Yes.

And so, during the post-war period, Marco lived a normal life or a semblance of a normal life or what we have mysteriously agreed to call a normal life, but this does not mean that his actual biography is uninteresting; quite the reverse, it is much more interesting than the trashy legend of intrepid adventures that he attempted to palm off as his real life.

On his return from Germany, Marco moved back into his in-laws' overcrowded house at Sicilia 354 with his wife, his son, his wife's sisters and a brother-in-law. In the eyes of this humble, tight-knit, sprawling family that worked hard during the week and spent weekends at the beach, in the mountains, or in the cooperative on calle Valencia, he once again became the intelligent, cultivated, hardworking, practical, cheerful, entertaining and charming young man who was unfailingly affectionate to his wife, ever ready to help his parents-in-law, to advise and protect his sisters-in-law, to do a favour for anyone who needed it; but now his heightened prestige as a traveller and a man of the world turned him into something akin to the leader or the centre of the clan. He returned to work in Felip Homs' car repair garage on París near the corner of Viladomat, opposite the Industrial School, and there were only two problems that troubled the happy and prosperous future his innate optimism sketched out before him. One: he was in Barcelona on leave and was scheduled to return to Kiel when his leave was over, something he had no wish to do. Two: if he arranged not to return to Kiel, he would have to fulfil the military service that he had avoided precisely by going to Kiel.

He did not go back to Kiel, he stayed in Barcelona and he did not do his military service. How did he manage to shirk both his civil obligations in Germany and his military obligations in Spain? I don't know. It's true that, in the late summer and autumn of 1943, with the course of the war marching inexorably towards Hitler's defeat, the Spanish authorities reached the conclusion that sending workers to Germany had been a bad deal and one that should be cancelled as soon as possible, so it is likely they made little fuss if one of the workers didn't return to his post. On the other hand, while Marco was in Germany, the Spanish military authorities had written to him, demanding that he fulfil his outstanding obligations, but his family replied that he was in Germany as a voluntary worker—a fact confirmed by the Ministry for Foreign Affairs—so the military had no reason to know that Marco was now back in Barcelona and therefore no reason to contact him. This may be what happened: perhaps everyone forgot about Marco, or ceased to care about him; perhaps Marco duped everyone yet again; perhaps it was a fortuitous combination of all three. Whatever the case, our man doesn't remember, or says that he doesn't remember. What is certain is that, in the midst of this double or triple misunderstanding, Marco, a master of confusion, eluded the twin swords hanging over him, and the future opened up before him.

On June 25, 1947, Marco's first daughter, Ana María, was born. At the time, though he didn't know it, he was preparing to embark on a new life. By now he had left Felip Homs' workshop and, having spent some time working in a furniture factory and later as a mechanic (mostly repairing and overhauling taxis, trucks and cars), he got a job as a travelling salesman with a car parts company called Comercial Anónima Blanch. It was a very different job to any he had done previously; it was also much better, or that, at least, is how he and the family saw things: he would leave home in a suit and tie and, between his salary and his commission, he was earning a lot of money, certainly much more than he had earned in any of his previous jobs. For Marco, this new position did not simply represent a financial gain, but also an advancement in his prestige and a more varied and intense social life. Marco's circle of friends changed and he began to drink and to go out at night. His wife quickly noticed he was no longer the affectionate, attentive husband he had been, and began to feel that he was strange and distant. Anita confided her fears to her sister Montserrat, eight years her junior, and one evening, her sister suggested they follow Marco.

Sixty-four years later, now more than eighty years old, Montserrat Beltrán still clearly remembers what happened that evening, and related the story to me in her apartment in Ciudad Badía, on the outskirts of Barcelona. She and Anita had posted themselves outside the offices of Comercial Anónima Blanch and saw Marco emerge with two colleagues. They didn't approach them directly, but followed the trio at a distance for some time, losing sight of them when they came to calle Sepúlveda. Confused, they decided it was best simply to wait, confident that Marco couldn't have gone far and would reappear sooner or later. So it proved. After a while, Marco emerged from a nearby building. He wasn't alone. He was accompanied not by his co-workers, but by two women who were walking arm in arm with him. The sisters instantly realised that the building Marco was leaving was a brothel and these two women were prostitutes. Montserrat says that, in a flash, before she could do anything to stop her, her sister rushed over to Marco, pushed between him and the women, grabbed his arm and said: "I can take your arm too, can't I?"

In the years that followed, Anita often repeated that part of the story. She and her family tried to forget the incident, putting it down to the dubious company he was keeping and the demands of his new job, but that proved impossible. At least it was impossible to ignore that Marco had fundamentally changed, he was no longer the perfect husband, son-in-law and brother-in-law he had been. In fact, from this point, things went from bad to worse. In 1949, Marco attempted to emigrate to Argentina with his family, though in the end he abandoned the project, possibly because he couldn't get the necessary documents to leave the country. Shortly afterwards, he was accused of theft and the police came to the house looking for him. Failing to find him there, the officers took his father-in-law to the police station where he had to make a statement. Marco made a statement that day or perhaps the following day and managed to wriggle out of trouble almost unscathed, with just a promise not to reoffend and to report to the police station once a fortnight. The Beltrán family were shocked, but even so they didn't ask Marco for an explanation, or they were satisfied with whatever vague excuses he offered. However, some days or weeks later, Marco was back at the police station, and this time he wasn't as lucky: he was held for several nights at the Modelo prison and came out with his head shaved, a stigma the Francoist police sometimes used to humiliate common criminals. The wedding of his wife's only remaining unmarried sister, Paquita, was a few days later. Marco attended the ceremony, but the following day, with no explanation or word to anyone, he left, never to return.

Marco's disappearance was a complete catastrophe for the Beltrán family; his wife sank into depression. It would be seven years before they had word of Marco again. A friend of his turned up at the Beltráns' door one day to say that Marco was sorry for what had happened and that he was prepared to help his wife and children. From that point, Marco began to pay some of the family expenses, such as the school fees of his daughter, Ana María; from time to time he would pick her up outside the school gates, and sometimes he would give her a present or a little money, as he did her brother Toni. This, however, was the extent of his relationship with his first family. Anita and her children were all too aware that Marco had erected an almost impenetrable barrier between them and his new life, about which they knew nothing; his children telephoned him at his new home now and again, but they had to introduce themselves as his godchildren. In the early 1960s, Anita asked him for money to put a down payment on an apartment in Badalona, and Marco gave it to her. In 1968, he walked his daughter down the aisle. In 1969, he became godfather to his first grandson. In 1974, having just given birth to her third child, Ana María called him at home and he told her that his telephone was being tapped by the police and not to call again. She didn't call again. Once again, she and her brother stopped seeing him.

Almost twenty years passed, during which they heard about Marco only in the newspapers, on the radio and the television. One day, Ana María went to see him at the offices of FaPaC, the confederation of school parents' associations of which Marco was now vice-chairman. She found him and they had coffee together. This is how she discovered that her father was living in Sant Cugat, that he had remarried and had two daughters, meaning that she had two half-sisters. In September 1999, Marco's first child and his only son, Toni, died, but the

news of his death didn't reach him until much later, when he accidentally bumped into one of his sisters-in-law while strolling along the
Rambla. The years that followed saw Marco's meteoric rise to media
stardom, something the Beltrán family watched with growing unease:
his wife, Anita, couldn't understand why Marco claimed to have been
in a concentration camp when she knew he had never set foot in one;
Ana María's children, Marco's grandchildren, didn't understand why
he kept his first family a secret; his daughter, Ana María, pretended
that she understood in order to pacify her mother and her children,
but in fact she didn't understand at all. And when the scandal broke
and the whole world discovered that Marco was an impostor, Ana
María felt both pity and shame for her father. It was only at this point
that she wanted to meet her half-sisters. Marco didn't object to intro-
ducing them, perhaps because he knew he couldn't prevent them from
meeting sooner or later (or simply because the scandal had broken
down his defences). First, though, he had to tell his current wife and
daughters the truth: that he had been married in the 1940s and that
he had another family—a wife, a daughter and several grandchildren.
This was how Ana María Marco came to meet Elizabeth and Ona
Marco, who were her half-sisters though they were young enough
to be her daughters, and this was how Marco came to divorce Anita,
who in the intervening half-century had not remarried nor had any
known partners. Anita died in January 2012. Ana María is still alive.
She is a passionate, cheerful, staunchly Catholic woman; her father
abandoned her when she was three years old, but it is impossible to
get her to say a single word against him.

3

During the many months I spent researching this book that I'd been so reluctant to write, quite a few strange things occurred, or at least they seemed strange to me when they occurred.

I cannot relate them all; I'll recount one of them.

For most of his life, Marco had earned his living as a mechanic, and from the mid-Fifties until the early 1980s, especially during the period when he was living with his second wife, María Belver, he owned, as part of a cooperative, a number of garages in the Collblanc district of L'Hospitalet, a city just south of Barcelona. The most longstanding of these was called Auto-Taller Cataluña, but when I visited it with my wife, Mercè, one afternoon in late July 2013, it had changed its name and was now called Taller Viñals.

I met the owner, David Viñals, in the tiny office at the back of the tiny premises. Sitting in front of an ancient computer, Viñals looked buried under a vast pile of invoices, papers and box files. He remembered the previous mechanic very well, not simply because he remembered buying the repair shop, or negotiating the purchase, but because, much later, he heard talk of the scandal. However, communications between them had been occasional and practical, he told me and, gesturing wearily around at the humming computer and the chaos of the office, said that right now he was snowed under but, come September, he would try to dig out contact details for someone who might have worked with Marco. I thanked him and said I would call in September. He seemed reluctant to see me go empty-handed, and just as I was leaving he added:

"Like I said, I didn't have much to do with him, but I thought he seemed like a decent man. I remember him telling me that he was selling the shop because he was giving up working as a mechanic so he could teach at university." He looked at me, half expecting to be disillusioned. "That was another lie, wasn't it?"

I had to tell him that it was. As we stepped outside again, my wife couldn't contain herself:

"I'm not surprised Marco invented an adventurous life for himself," she snorted. "With his imagination, if he hadn't, he wouldn't have survived twenty years holed up in that tiny workshop. He would have gone insane."

In September, I called Viñals. He told me he'd found an address and telephone number for a man named Toni or Antoni, who had been an apprentice mechanic in Marco's garage; he was now working in one of the Llasax garages on Carretera Real in Sant Just Desvern. "He told me he doesn't want to talk about it," Viñals warned, "so if I were you, I wouldn't try phoning: go and see him, that way at least maybe he'll hear you out." I did as he suggested, but I didn't go alone; on the pretext that I didn't know how to work the car's GPS, my son came with me.

The garage was just outside Barcelona on the road to Sant Feliu de Llobregat. I parked outside the gates and Raül waited for me in the car while I went into the garage—a vast space, with high ceilings and a concrete floor, that seemed to be a hive of activity, with people bustling between glass-walled offices and mechanics with grease-blackened hands rootling in the entrails of dilapidated cars. I inquired with one of the office workers and, after fifteen minutes and a minor misunderstanding—there was a mechanic named Antoni working at the garage, but he wasn't the man I was looking for—I finally spoke to him, a guy in his late fifties, perhaps sixty, who answered to the name Antonio rather than Antoni, and whom I remember as being gaunt with pale eyes. I introduced myself, I told him that I was a writer, that I was writing a book about Enric Marco; I said that, from what I'd heard, he had known Marco.

"I know him," the man said. "But I don't want to talk about him."

"It will only take five minutes," I said. "It's only a couple of questions. You can set the conditions; if you don't want your name in the book, it won't be there."

"I told you, I don't want to talk about Marco."

I persisted. I told him that I also knew Marco, that I was writing the book with his authorisation and his collaboration, and taking my mobile from my pocket, I added that, if he wanted to check, he could call him. The man stonewalled:

"I'm not going to talk about Marco."

I was about to ask him why, but I sensed that this would annoy him and that it was futile to insist. It wasn't the first time a witness had refused to talk to me about a book I was working on, but it was the first time it had happened face to face; and it was the first time while writing this book. I slipped my mobile back into my pocket and sighed.

"Sorry to have bothered you," I said.

With a curt smile, the man shook my proffered hand.

"You didn't bother me," he said.

"What did he say?" Raül asked as I sat behind the steering wheel.

"Nothing," I said.

"What do you mean, nothing? He wouldn't talk to you?"

Raül laughed.

"You're the best, *papi.*"

Still incredulous, I started the car and, as we headed back to Barcelona through the maze of roundabouts and motorways, I told my son what had happened.

"I don't think this guy is trying to protect Marco," I hazarded. "If he was, he would have taken my phone and called to check that I was telling the truth. This guy's no friend of Marco's, he doesn't like him, they obviously didn't get along. That's why he didn't want to talk."

"Bullshit," said Raül. "If they didn't get along, he'd be itching to talk: to fuck him over, to get his revenge. The reason he doesn't want to talk is probably completely the reverse."

"The reverse?"

"Not because they didn't get along, but because they *did*. Got along really well, I mean. This guy was young when he knew Marco, yeah?"

"I assume so, he was Marco's apprentice. He would have known him in the Sixties or the Seventies, certainly not before."

"If he was a kid, maybe he believed all the lies that Marco came out with, and now he's found out it was all lies, he's so angry that he doesn't even want to hear his name mentioned. After all, that's how lots of people must have felt. All things considered, it's probably better that he didn't want to talk: if he had, he'd probably have come out with some bullshit; by staying silent, he remains a mystery. And in a novel, mystery is better than bullshit, don't you think?"

Raül was right, of course, but this isn't an ordinary novel, it's a novel without fiction, a true story, and in a book like that, truthful bullshit is a thousand times better than a fictional mystery. Besides, Raül was wrong: this man had not gotten along well with Marco, at least not always, or at least their relationship ended on a sour note. In fact, as I later learned, his name was Antonio Ferrer Belver, and he was the nephew of María Belver, the woman to whom Marco had been married for several decades in the mid-twentieth century. Ferrer had indeed started out as an apprentice at Auto-Taller Cataluña, but in the late 1970s, when Marco got rid of the workshop, he was unhappy about the business, or unhappy about how it was managed. To this we can add a second, perhaps definitive, reason for his anger: in the mid-1970s, Marco had also gotten rid of María Belver, just as in the early 1950s he had gotten rid of Anita Beltrán, dumped her for a girl more than twenty years his junior. His desertion forever turned the Belver family against Marco, which explains why none of them (or none of those I tried to contact) was willing to talk. Not even Marco's former apprentice.

The embarrassing incident with María Belver's nephew brought back all the worries and uncertainties that had haunted me after my encounter with Benito Bermejo in Madrid, when the historian had floated the theory that Marco was a police informant during the period when he was an anarchist leader, and when Bermejo told me that he had abandoned or postponed the idea of writing a book about Marco because of his qualms of conscience: once again I began to wonder whether the book I was planning to write was not only impossible, but foolhardy; I began to wonder whether my goal of writing the true life of Marco was moral, whether I had the right to interfere in the lives of Marco and his family to expose his story (this story which meant poking a finger in everyone's eye, this story in which everyone came off badly), whether I had the right to do so and whether it was right to do so, even if Marco had given his permission and was collaborating with me.

In the ensuing days, I frequently thought of the two analogous and contrasting stories told by the French writer Emmanuel Carrère, author of *The Adversary*, a novel without fiction, or true story, that tells of an impostor named Jean-Claude Romand, who eventually murdered his wife, his two young children and parents so they wouldn't find out about his deception.

The protagonist of the first story is the American writer Truman Capote. In 1960, at the age of thirty-six, Capote decided to write a true story or novel without fiction that would also be his masterpiece. To do so, he chose a chance subject (or perhaps it was chance that chose him): the murder of a farming family in Kansas, in the so-called American heartland, by two complete strangers. Capote went to Kansas and settled in the little town where the crime had been committed; after a few weeks the killers were arrested: they were two young men named Dick Hickock and Perry Smith. Capote went to visit them in prison, he befriended them, and for the next five years, during which the prisoners were tried and sentenced to death, he became the most important person in their lives. The last two years of his relationship with them were harrowing. Owing to a variety of appeals, the executions were deferred several times. In the meantime, Capote assured his two friends, his characters, that he was doing everything in his power to save them, including hiring the finest attorneys; but at the same time, the writer knew that the deaths of the two accused was the best possible ending to the story, the finishing touch required for his masterpiece, and so he secretly prayed for this ending and went so far as to light candles to the Virgin so it might come to pass.

In the end, Dick and Perry were hanged; Capote attended the hangings and was the last person to hug them before they climbed the scaffold. The literary fruit of his moral aberration was *In Cold Blood*, a masterpiece. Carrère implies that, with it, Capote saved himself as a writer but damned himself as a human being, and the long process of self-destruction through alcoholism, snobbery and spite that followed its publication was the price the author paid for his moral turpitude.

The protagonist of the second story is the British writer Charles Dickens; the incident must have happened—Carrère does not specify—in 1849, while *David Copperfield* was being serialised in monthly instalments. In the first pages of the novel, a secondary character appears named Miss Mowcher, who, from all available evidence—she is depicted as scheming, envious and sycophantic, in addition to being a dwarf—is evil personified, and so, since there is nothing readers of fiction enjoy more than a villain, and since Dickens was by then a writer with a considerable readership, all of England was licking its lips in anticipation of the lady's future misdeeds. Then something unexpected happened. One morning, Dickens received a letter in which a provincial lady bitterly complained that, because of her physical resemblance to Miss Mowcher—the writer of the letter was also a dwarf—the people in her village had begun to mistrust her, they muttered as she passed and sent her anonymous threats; all in all, the lady concluded her letter, she was a good woman, but because of him and of Miss Mowcher her life had become a living hell.

We know how most writers would have responded to the lady's letter: they would not have responded at all; or, if so, their response would have been: the problem the lady had raised was not his, but that of those people who confuse reality with fiction and who cruelly and foolishly identify fictional characters with real people. Dickens' response was very different: he changed the character, he changed the plot of his novel, he changed everything: the book clamoured impatiently for more of Miss Mowcher's misdeeds, everything had been plotted to accommodate them, but in the following instalment, Dickens transformed his wicked witch into a good-hearted woman who, beneath her unfortunate appearance, was an angel. It is possible that, as he himself admits, Carrère is somewhat idealising Dickens' motives; it is possible that he is overstating Miss Mowcher's importance in the novel. The fact remains that *David Copperfield* was a resounding success, another masterpiece by Dickens, and that in it the writer saved himself not only as a writer, but as a human being.

This is not the only conclusion that Carrère draws from the two balanced and contrasting stories I have just related; nor the one that most interests me. Carrère says that, when he began writing *The Adversary*, he wanted to imitate *In Cold Blood*, the Flaubertian impersonal detachment of the book, Capote's decision to tell the story of Dick Hickock and Perry Smith while erasing his role in it, erasing his perverse friendship with them and the moral dilemmas that plagued him while the events were taking place; but in the end, Carrère says, he decided not to do so: he decided to tell the story without erasing himself from it, not in the third person, but in the first person, revealing his moral qualms and his relationship with the murderous impostor. And he concludes, "I think it is not an exaggeration to say that that decision saved my life."

Is Carrère right? Did he save himself both as a person and as a writer—*The Adversary* is also a masterpiece—by including himself in the story of Jean-Claude Romand's monstrous deception? Would I save myself, as a writer and as a human being—being unable to take Dickens' approach since I could not change or embellish Marco's story—by not writing in the third person as Capote had, but in the first person, without erasing the doubts and the moral dilemmas I faced while writing it, exactly as Carrère had? Though brilliant and comforting, was Carrère's argument not false, not to say self-serving? Was it not simply a way of buying moral legitimacy so he could allow himself to do with Jean-Claude Romand what Capote had done with Dick Hickock and Perry Smith and what I was trying to do with Enric Marco, and what is more to do so with a clear conscience and with no damage to myself? Was it enough to acknowledge one's own immorality for it to disappear or be transformed into decency? Should one not simply accept, in all honesty, that in order to write *In Cold Blood* or *The Adversary*, it was necessary to lay oneself open to a certain moral aberration and thereby to damn oneself? Was I prepared to damn myself in exchange for writing a masterpiece, always supposing I was capable of writing a masterpiece? In short, was it possible to write a book about Enric Marco without selling my soul to the devil?

4

It was Marco's best kept secret, perhaps because, of all his offences, it was the most shameful: in the early 1950s, Marco was a guest of Franco's prisons, not as a political activist, but as a common criminal.

It is something I discovered by chance, not because Marco told me. I found out thanks to Ignasi de Gispert, a labour lawyer who, in the late Sixties and early Seventies, was one of a group of middle-class Catalan boys obsessed with Marco, who was not known as Marco at the time, but as Batlle, Enric Batlle. To the rebellious sons of well-heeled families who were just discovering the world, Batlle represented the epitome of the cultivated, revolutionary anti-Francoist, working-class man. One day in late 1975 or early 1976, shortly after the death of Franco, De Gispert had a telephone call from María Belver, who was still Marco's wife at the time, telling him that our man was being held at Modelo prison and needed his help. De Gispert, who had just graduated as a lawyer, immediately rushed to Modelo prison. There, Marco gave him a rambling, confused story about having been arrested for political reasons while trying to carry out a bureaucratic transaction, and that they had tortured, or attempted to torture him, but De Gispert had a hunch that Batlle was trying to hoodwink him. His hunch was confirmed when he went to the court and discovered that an arrest warrant had indeed been issued against Marco for robbery with violence on the Rambla; fortunately, the offence had been committed in the late Forties or early Fifties and therefore was subject to the statute of limitations, and so, having spent a few nights in gaol, Marco was a free man. Eager to justify the episode, Marco told De Gispert that it had all been a misunderstanding: he had often told De

Gispert and his young friends that years ago, in order to avoid being pursued by the secret police, he had taken on the identity of a dead man named Enric Marco; from this unfortunate incident he had just learned that the aforesaid Enric Marco was a common criminal, and the actual perpetrator of the crime for which he had been arrested.

Obviously, De Gispert did not believe a word that Marco said, because by this time, they had been friends for some years and the young lawyer knew something of his friend's failings. But the question is: How did Marco come to be a thief in the early 1950s? What turned the man the Beltrán family knew as the perfect husband, father, son- and brother-in-law into a common criminal?

The seeds of the change in Marco, as the Beltráns suspected, began with his job at Comercial Anónima Blanch. Here, our man dis-covered a very different life, the nomadic life of the commercial trav-eller: men in suits and ties who eat lunch and dinner at restaurants, bistros and taverns, go out drinking every night, spend their salaries gambling and frequenting high-class brothels. One night, in one such locale (a place known as Ca la tia Antonia, or Aunt Antonia's house), Marco slept with a girl named Marina. Two days later he slept with her again, and after two weeks he realised he was in love with her. The girl stopped charging him for her services, but Marco paid the brothel madam so that she slept only—or almost only—with him. Although he was earning a lot of money, he was spending more than he earned and so, in order to supplement his income and carry on living this lifestyle, he began selling the samples he carried, which were the company property. At the same time, his marriage was deteriorating. As I related earlier, one afternoon, his wife caught him coming out of a brothel with two prostitutes and exposed his double life. Some days later, his bosses at Comercial Anónima Blanch discovered that he was cheating the company and began an investigation, deciding to suspend him without pay until the matter was cleared up. Marco found himself with no job, but since he didn't dare admit as much to his family, he was still forced to leave the house every morning and spend hours and hours wandering around the city in his suit and tie, with his despair and his travelling salesman's bag, and come back at night or in the early hours as though he had spent the day working.

It was at this point that he began to commit small crimes. On one occasion, he stole jewellery from the house of a creditor who had not paid him. On another, he tried unsuccessfully to prise open a client's safe. These are the two offences Marco remembers, or is prepared to admit (or that he remembered and was prepared to admit when he discovered that, thanks to De Gispert, I had found out the truth), but it's likely that there were more. His victims reported him and he had to suffer the humiliation of having the police visit his house, having to go to the police station and explain what had happened, to give back the jewellery and agree to report to the police station regularly. This is what happened the first time he was arrested; the second time, he was sent directly to jail. He was released shamefaced and shaven-headed. For a few days, he endured the glares of people who, until recently, had thought him the perfect husband, the perfect father, son- and brother-in-law. But the morning after the wedding of his only unmarried sister-in-law, he could bear it no more, and he left for good.

The weeks that followed must have been agonising. Knowing Marco, it's likely that his decision to abandon his family was thought through, that he planned his departure to some extent; it's possible that his plans may even have included Marina, the prostitute he'd been more or less supporting financially who had brought him to this point. Whatever the intention, all of Marco's plans failed, and he suddenly found himself with no family, no job and no home. He spent the days wandering the streets and at night he slept on the benches along the Rambla and the plaza de Cataluña among prostitutes, beggars and thieves. When he failed to report to the police station, he was declared a fugitive from justice and added to the list of common criminals to be detained and arrested. (Parenthesis: this, incidentally, explains a number of things including the arrest in late 1975 or early 1976, when De Gispert had to get him out of prison; the fact that during the post-war period he didn't register anywhere under his real name, until he eventually took advantage of De Gispert's intervention to regularise his position; the fact that many years later he could claim without lying—or without believing that he was lying—that throughout the post-war period he had lived a clandestine life being hounded by the Francoist police.) It seems likely that he committed other crimes during this period, but I don't know exactly what he did or how far he went, and I would almost rather not know. What is clear is that he hit rock bottom.

This terrible time cannot have lasted long: a few months at most. He was saved from the pit by a man named Peiró, who knew Marco vaguely, but clearly respected him because, as soon as he discovered the situation Marco was in (or as soon as Marco told him), one day when they met by chance, he invited him home and told him he could probably find him work. Peiró lived with his family on calle Campoamor in L'Hospitalet—a district that, at the time, was growing at a dizzying rate because of the flood of migrants arriving from southern Spain—and one of his brothers, Paco, offered to let Marco refurbish two army trucks he kept in a lock-up garage. It was a trifling job, one for which Paco didn't propose to pay him, but Marco accepted without a second thought.

This was the beginning of a new life. At first, Marco slept at Peiró's house and every day went to work at the garage at 144 calle General Sanjurjo (now calle Martí i Julià) in Colblanc, a neighbouring district in L'Hospitalet. Later, however, he moved into the garage, where, in exchange for his work, the Peiró family brought food and let him sleep in the cab of an old Hansa-Lloyd. According to those familiar with it, the garage was a hovel, a leaky pigsty; as for the Hansa-Lloyd, it was not so much a car as a pile of scrap metal. Nothing about his surroundings inspired optimism, but Marco didn't let himself be beaten down. He worked hard—morning, noon and night, Saturdays and Sundays included—and within a short time he had not only restored Paco Peiró's two trucks but, with the family's permission, he had turned the lock-up into a working garage where he serviced and repaired cars, trucks and taxis for the Peiró family and for other people in the neighbourhood. Having more than enough work and not enough time and manpower, Marco hired an apprentice, and then another, both poor boys from immigrant families whom he paid little and taught much, because by now our man was a skilled mechanic with many years' experience. Marco treated his apprentices well and they respected him: they called him Enrique, but they believed his surname was Durruti, like the legendary anarchist leader, and although at the time Marco never talked about war or politics, they assumed (because he allowed them to assume, or encouraged them to assume) that he had some sort of connection with clandestine organisations and the police were after him. They considered him a highly intelligent boss and a silver-tongued devil capable of selling shampoo to a bald man; but they also considered him to be generous and loyal, except when it came to women: on that score, they knew that their boss was merciless.

Marco spent three or four years holed up in the Peirós' garage. After that, in order to work more efficiently, he rented a workshop, or part of a workshop on calle Montseny, and later still he opened his own repair shop: Talleres Collblanc. By now, he was living with María Belver, an Andalusian girl he met in a bar near the Peirós' lock-up where he often went for breakfast or for dinner. When he took her to visit the garage, she convinced him to leave this hovel and found him a room to rent with a husband and wife who lived nearby on Ronda de la Torrassa. Later, he rented an apartment at 57–59 calle Oriente, a cheerful little street filled with shops, studios and bars; it was here that he lived with María, who divided her time between taking care of Marco and working privately as a seamstress. (Second parenthesis: María sewed for the Puig Antich family, the parents of the famous anarchist executed by Franco in 1974, and Marco sometimes went to pick her up at their house; this was Marco's only connection to Puig Antich, not that this stopped him from portraying himself as a close friend in an article published in 1988, when being a close friend of Puig Antich was almost synonymous with being an anti-Franco resistant.) In moving from Anita Beltrán to María Belver, Marco did not simply swap wives, he swapped families or rather he swapped clans; the Catalan and Catalan-speaking, staunchly Catholic, poor, well-mannered Beltráns were replaced by the Andalusian, Spanish-speaking, agnostic, dirt-poor, rambunctious Belvers as María's many relatives poured into L'Hospitalet from Almería, fleeing the poverty of the south. In spite of their many differences, the Beltráns and the Belvers shared a common trait, their limited education, and so Marco, an indiscriminate reader, a shameless charlatan, a man who could boast about leaving Spain and living in Germany, sparkled among the Belvers as he had sparkled among the Beltráns, becoming the centre of attention, becoming the leader and the patriarch to whom everyone listened. This, at least, is how he felt, and how those who attended the Belver clan get-togethers felt.

Marco was also admired and respected in the Collblanc neighbourhood. Everyone knew him as Enrique the mechanic, a cheerful joker who was always ready to do a favour for anyone in need. This was a prosperous period for Marco: Talleres Collblanc expanded to become Auto-Taller Cataluña and moved to larger premises at a better location on Travessera de Les Corts, near the Barça stadium; this economic upturn made it possible for him to get in touch with his first wife and his children, to help them out financially, though he kept them secret and at arm's length, and it also allowed him to get a mortgage on an apartment on Calafell beach, where he went during summers and on various weekends. (Third and final parenthesis: like all of the other properties he owned or rented, Marco put the apartment in the name of María Belver because, although no-one in his circle was aware of it, he still appeared on the police lists of wanted criminals.) Marco, however, was not the only one to prosper; his prosperity in the 1960s was mirrored by the whole of Spain, a country that, in the midst of the grey, sheep-like silence imposed by Franco's regime, was beginning to enjoy unprecedented comfort even as it struggled to forget the atrocities and the poverty of the Civil War and the post-war period. It is likely that Marco was struggling to forget as well, longing to free himself of the past. Not only the collective past, but also his personal past: the orphaned child, the homeless libertarian teenager, the soldier defeated in war, the broken, disheartened loser, the collaborator with Franco and with the Nazis, the prisoner in a German gaol, the unscrupulous salesman, the absent husband and father and the common criminal. But we know it's impossible to leave behind the past. The past is never dead—as Faulkner says—it's not even past, it is merely an aspect of the present. Something that, in the late Sixties or early Seventies, Marco, like the rest of the country, was beginning to realise.

5

When the scandal broke, countless allegations were levelled against Marco; some claims were made in his defence. The main allegation was untenable, as was the principal claim in his defence.

The main allegation scarcely needs to be refuted. It argues that Marco's deception provided the perfect fuel for revisionists—i.e., those who maintain that the Nazis weren't truly evil, that Auschwitz wasn't an industrialised slaughterhouse, that the almost six million Jews massacred are an invention by Zionist propagandists. In Spain, almost everyone who commented on Marco's case raised this argument; a chastened Marco even raised it himself, believing that the worst or the only real damage caused by his deception was to embolden revisionists. In fact, long before he was unmasked, Marco was already insisting that his foremost crusade as president of the Amical de Mauthausen—giving talks and conference speeches, writing articles, organising tours and events, creating libraries and archives—was to wage war against the legion of Holocaust deniers, here and elsewhere, who were threatening to erase from memory the victims of the worst crime in human history.

This is arrant nonsense. The horrors committed by the Nazis are among the most well known and best documented in modern history, and by the early twenty-first century are repudiated only by a handful of idiots who are easily identified and about as dangerous as those who insist that the earth is flat or that man did not land on the moon. Such people do not need fuel: they spontaneously combust. Moreover, as far as I am aware, revisionists have attempted to use Marco's case to their advantage only once. In March 2009, at the high court in Barcelona during the trial of Óscar Panadero—the owner of the Kali Book-shop charged with leading a neo-Nazi movement and of selling books denying the Holocaust—Panadero refused to answer a question from the barrister representing the Amical de Mauthausen on the pretext that Marco had been president of the organisation; it was an absurd pretext; as absurd as if he had refused to answer a lawyer because it was raining or because the sun was shining; as absurd as believing that doubt can be cast on the crimes committed by the Nazis simply because one person who claimed to have been a victim of those crimes had not actually been a victim; as absurd as believing that doubt can be cast on the destruction of New York's Twin Towers simply because Tania Head, a former president of the World Trade Center Survivors' Network, was an impostor who was not even in New York on 9/11. In reality, these days, the furore over Holocaust denial is dead, or at least dying (as it was in 2005 when Marco's scandal erupted): to claim that it is still alive betrays an ignorance of the realities of the Holocaust and the debate surrounding it; or, as in the case of Marco and many of those who battle against Holocaust denial, a desire to exaggerate the struggle by conjuring a powerful illusory enemy.

The principal claim made in Marco's defence when the scandal broke is equally incoherent, though slightly more sophisticated. There is a logic to this sophistication: Marco's wrongdoing is so fla-grant that any serious plea in his defence would seem to be the pre-serve of cynics, sophists, non-conformist conformists, or particularly audacious (or perhaps foolhardy) minds. It is true, goes this argu-ment, that Marco was never a prisoner in Flossenbürg and that he is a liar; but he is a liar who told the truth: his small lie served to dissemi-nate the great truth of Nazi crimes and as such is not blameworthy, or not as blameworthy as others. It goes without saying that, when the scandal broke, this was one of the principal claims advanced by Marco himself. Nonetheless it is worth remembering that the claim was made not only by Marco, out of desperation, but by intelligent men like Claudio Magris, who felt no such desperation.

The claim, as I have said, is untenable, although it requires more effort to refute than the first. First and foremost because it presents at least two problems that are interrelated. The first is momentous, but can be briefly stated: is it morally acceptable to lie? On this, thinkers throughout history have divided into two broad camps: relativists and absolutists. Contrary to what one might suppose, since thought tends inexorably towards the absolute, most are relativists. Some, like Plato (who in *The Republic* talks about "*gennaion pseudos*": a noble lie), or like Voltaire (who, in a letter to his friend Nicolas-Claude Thieriot in 1736, wrote: "Lying is only a vice when it harms; when it does good, it is a very great virtue"), argue that a lie is not always morally wrong and is sometimes necessary, or that whether a lie is good or evil depends on the good or evil consequences it produces: if the result of the lie is good, the lie is good; if the result is evil, the lie is evil. Absolutists, on the other hand, argue that a lie is morally wrong in itself, irrespective of its consequences, because it constitutes a lack of respect for the other and is, essentially, a form of violence, or as Montaigne puts it, a crime. But even Montaigne, who abhorred lying and considered the truth to be "the first and most perfect degree of excellence," in his essay "A Trait of Certain Ambassadors"—perhaps echoing Plato's "noble lies"—nevertheless defends "*mensonges officieux*," diplomatic or altruistic lies told for the benefit of others.

As far as I am aware, only Immanuel Kant takes the absolutist principle of truthfulness to its logical conclusion and, in a dispute with Benjamin Constant in 1797, argued that the prohibition admits no exceptions. Kant addressed a famous example: imagine that a friend seeks refuge in my house because he is being pursued by a murderer; suppose that the murderer calls at the door and asks whether or not my friend is in the house; in this situation, Kant affirms, my moral duty, as in any other situation, is not to lie but to tell the truth: my duty is not to tell the murderer that my friend is not in the house in an attempt to avoid him forcing his way in and killing him, but to admit that he is here, even at the risk that the man will enter and kill him. This is Kant's position, and he has no lack of arguments to support it; the most important arising from the categorical imperative, according to which one should act only according to that maxim whereby one can, at the same time, will that it should become a universal law. Applied to the previous example, this would mean that, while in the short term my lie might result in the small good of saving my friend's life, nevertheless since society is founded on mutual trust, in the long term it would result in a greater evil by fostering absolute chaos. The logic is unimpeachable, though few people—even among Kantians—seem inclined to agree with Kant. In fact, there is no shortage of people who consider his view lunacy, or attribute it to the depredations on his mental faculties wrought by his sixty-three years; there are even some who consider it a joke by the philosopher. It is possible that Kant's commendable reasoning admirably demonstrates that logic tends towards the absurd. Commenting on the debate, De Quincey, in an essay on "Casuistry," rails ". . . by all the codes of law received throughout Europe, he who acted upon Kant's principle would be held *a particeps criminis*—an accomplice before the fact." I would be interested in the opinions of Kant's friends on the subject.

Be that as it may, whether or not they were aware of Kant, Marco's defenders scorn the philosopher and claim that Marco's were noble lies, as Plato calls them, or altruistic lies, in the words of Montaigne; in short, they assert, as Marco himself does, that, yes, he was an impostor, but, because no historical falsehood passed his lips, his fictions helped to communicate the reality of twentieth-century barbarism *urbi et orbi* and as such his were good lies, inasmuch as the consequences were good. So then—and this is where the second problem arises—is it true that no historical falsehood passed Marco's lips? What I mean is, leaving aside for a moment the reasons that led Marco to lie; let's suppose for a moment that his lies were altruistic and didactic and well intentioned, that Marco did not lie in order to be a hero, to be loved and admired, to hide the fundamental abjectness and mediocrity of his life behind a flattering fantasy constructed of delusions of grandeur. Let's focus on the consequences of his lies, not their cause. In which case the question is: did Marco's lies tell the truth? Or, to put it another way: did Marco tell the truth about history (the history of the Nazi camps and, more generally, the history of the war and the post-war period in Spain) even if he invented his place in it and the role that he played?

Absolutely not. Though he did his best to thoroughly research his lies, reading history books and immersing himself in the written and oral accounts of survivors, Marco often included mistakes or inaccuracies, such that his stories are invariably a mixture of truth and lies, which is the most sophisticated form of lying. It's true that, in relating his own experience, Marco deliberately combines actual data with fabrications, while in recounting the collective experience (which frames and seeks to provide a veneer of truth to his personal experience), he does so accidentally, out of ignorance or carelessness, but the result is the same. I've already given numerous examples of how Marco embeds lies into his personal experience, and I could give several examples of how he does so when recounting the collective experience; here is just one, which is as concrete as it is conspicuous. In his account of the liberation of Flossenbürg published in May 2005 in the historical review *L'Avenç*, Marco states that there was a gas chamber in the camp, as there was in other concentration camps; I don't know how many times he mentioned this in his talks and his conference speeches, but it is false: there was no gas chamber in Flossenbürg.

This sort of factual error is much more important than it might appear, because a single fabricated "fact" turns a true story into a fiction, and just as a single germ can result in an epidemic, that "fact" can contaminate all the stories that follow with fiction. But that isn't the key point. The key point is that Marco's account would have been a complete fiction even if, hypothetically, he had flawlessly researched his subject and his stories didn't contain even the slightest factual error. First and foremost because all of his stories are based on a crucial earlier lie: his time in a Nazi camp, and his actions during the Civil War and afterwards. And, secondly, because even if all the factual data Marco presented were true, his approach is pure kitsch, in other words a lie; or to be more precise, because Marco is pure kitsch.

What is kitsch? First and foremost, it is an artistic term that implies a debasement—or at least a significant devaluation—of genuine art; but it is also a negation of everything that is unacceptable in human existence, by veiling it behind a façade of sentimentalism, superficial beauty and affected virtue. Kitsch, in short, is a narcissistic lie that hides the truth of horror and death: in the same way that aesthetic kitsch is an aesthetic lie—art that is in fact false art—so historical kitsch is a historical lie—history that is in fact false history. This is why the novelistic and garish past that Marco propagated in his stories of Flossenbürg and of the war and the post-war period in Spain are pure lies (or pure kitsch); narratives larded with sentiment, with theatrical effects and melodramatic moments, unsparing in their bad taste but oblivious to the complexity and the ambiguity of truth, starring a papier-mâché hero capable of coolly maintaining his dignity when faced with a Nazi brute, or a Falangist brute, willing to beat the former in a chess match despite knowing it could cost him his life, or to remain seated when the latter orders him to stand, salute and sing "Cara al Sol." Just as the established entertainment industry feeds on aesthetic kitsch, which offers the consumer the illusion of appreciating genuine art while sparing him the effort such appreciation requires, together with the intellectual and moral risks that it entails, so the modern industry of memory needs to feed on historical kitsch, which offers the consumer the illusion of understanding genuine history while sparing him the effort, but most of all, the ironies, the contradictions, the anxieties, the shames, the terror, the nausea, the giddiness, the disillusionment that such understanding entails. Few in Spain have rivalled Marco in providing sickly toxic kitsch (the "poisonous sentimental fodder seasoned with historical good conscience" I wrote about in "I am Enric Marco") of such purity and profusion, and this may explain the enormous success of his stories. Kitsch is the spontaneous style of the narcissist, the tool he uses in his assiduous attempt to hide reality so as not to know or recognise it, so as not to know or recognise himself. Marco was a peerless producer of kitsch and, therefore, falsehoods constantly passed his lips; historical falsehoods, but also aesthetic and moral falsehoods. Hermann Broch observed that kitsch presupposes "a determinate attitude in life since kitsch could not, in fact, either emerge or prosper without the existence of the kitsch-man." Marco embodies this individual better than anyone. This is why he is pure kitsch.

6

In order to hide the reality of himself (or to hide himself), Marco reinvented himself many times throughout his life, but twice in particular. The first time, in the mid-Fifties, he did so because he had no choice: he changed his job, his city, his wife, his family, even his name; he ceased to be a travelling salesman and went back to working as a mechanic, abandoned Barcelona for L'Hospitalet, abandoned Anita Beltrán and the Beltrán family for María Belver and the Belver family, ceased to be Enrique Marco and became Enrique Durruti, or Enrique the mechanic. Marco's second great reinvention came in the mid-Seventies, shortly after the death of Franco when the way was opening up for democracy, but this reinvention was deliberate and, more importantly, it was more successful. The fundamental reason for this is that Marco discovered the power of the past: he discovered that the past is never dead, and that at least his past and that of his country was not even past, and he discovered that he who controls the past, controls the present and the future; consequently, in addition to once again changing all the things he had changed in his first great reinvention (his job, his city, his wife, his family and even his name), he decided he would also change his past.

It began a decade earlier. Let's say 1967 or 1968. At that time, not only was his life different, the country itself was very different. Spain had left behind the starving, stifling, Nationalist, Catholic, economic self-sufficiency of the immediate post-war period and—from an economic standpoint at least—life in the country had improved almost as much as Marco's own life: Francoism, however, seemed more entrenched than ever, the savage repression of dissidents of the

early years had relaxed somewhat, allowing for the rise of a burgeon-
ing opposition comprised mainly of workers and non-conformist students. In the summer of 1967, or perhaps it was 1968, Marco met
two of these students. Their names were Ferran Salsas and Mercè
Boada and they were engaged. Both were at university studying
medicine, both had just turned twenty, both hailed from the middle
classes—the great silent majority who, willingly or unwillingly, said
Yes to Franco and who, at home, never talked about politics or the
Civil War. Though Salsas and Boada had never been members of a
clandestine organisation or a union, they were seething with social
anxieties, they were loosely anti-Franco, they felt the pull of politics
(Salsas in particular) and, armed with the idealism and rebelliousness
of their twenty years, they were eager to create or to help create a
better country than the one in which they believed their parents had
resigned themselves to living.

They were fascinated by Marco. He was almost thirty years their
senior and not only did he become their friend and mentor, he also
became their idol, their hero, almost their guru. They had never
met anyone like him. In their eyes, Marco personified the best of
their country's vanished past, and the best of its future; he was the
epitome of the cultivated worker and the professional revolutionary.
His real name, he told them, was not Enric Marco but Enric Batlle:
Marco was merely an alias he was forced to use to elude the Francoist police who had ruthlessly hounded him for his political activism,
and who had arrested, jailed and tortured him on countless previous occasions—especially comisario Creix, the most fearsome police
officer in Barcelona. Marco also talked to them about his libertarian activism, his relationship with Buenaventura Durruti, his exploits
during the Civil War, his political exile in France after the war, his
time in Nazi jails for his indomitable resistance and a thousand other
things, although he never mentioned that he had been in a Nazi concentration camp—perhaps at the time the Nazi camps did not yet
have the terrible prestige they would come to have later, or perhaps
because Marco didn't yet know that almost nine thousand Spaniards
had spent time in the camps. It goes without saying that he never gave
precise details about his clandestine activities—certainly not about his
current clandestine activities—but Salsas and Boada imagined that he

withheld this information for their protection, in order not to impli-
cate them, and they were convinced that, after visiting him at the
garage, or having a coffee with him at the Bar San Juan a short distance from the workshop on Travessera de Les Corts, or lunch or dinner with him and María Belver in their apartment on calle Oriente,
Marco would shrug off his mechanic's disguise, and plunge into the
treacherous, perilous, shadowy world of anti-Francoists, a world of
strikes, acts of sabotage, graffiti, mimeographed pamphlets and secret
meetings in smoke-filled basements.

Marco was best man at Salsas and Boada's wedding. This was in
1969. By this time, there were more students who considered Marco
to be not just their *maître à penser* but their *magister vitae*. Perhaps he
was a catalyst in their revolt against their families, against their social
class, against the state of their country under the dictatorship, as
though, unbeknownst to him, Marco had become an artist capable of
exposing—through his experiences both real and invented, through
the understanding gleaned from his autodidact's reading, with his
overwhelming oratory, or through his mere existence—the historical,
political and social lies that had, until now, deceived them, or that
they had allowed to deceive them. In Marco's house, for example, a
number of these scions of the law-abiding Catalan bourgeoisie experienced the revelation of a hitherto unknown reality: during Christmas and New Year celebrations in the Belver family, where Marco was
the undisputed master of ceremonies, in the midst of the hullabaloo
of screaming and swearing and unimaginable delight, some realised
that these penniless immigrants from southern Spain who had been
flooding into Catalonia since the Fifties were completely changing
the face of the country, that they were much more complex than they
had imagined. This revelation doubtless persuaded some to take up
social and political activism.

Between 1967 and 1972, while studying medicine, Boada and Salsas earned their living through an academy they had set up to prepare
secondary school students for university entrance exams. In the early
days, they held classes in their home, later at the Academia Mallorca,
at 460 calle Mallorca, and eventually at the Academia Almi on calle
Valencia, near the Sagrada Família market where they rented a few
classrooms. Salsas and Boada taught there from 7 p.m. to 10 p.m.

every evening and also employed other teachers, like Quim Salina, an elderly Republican butcher who had a stall in the Sagrada Família market and was an authority on art history, or Ignasi de Gispert, a lad from a good background who was active in the banned Spanish Socialist Workers' Party, who would later become a close friend of Salsas and Boada and also of Marco and who, in late 1975 or early 1976, having just earned his law degree, would secure Marco's release from prison where he was being held for a crime committed twenty years earlier. Our man also began to teach classes at this informal academy. Occasional rather than regular, they were wide-ranging master classes in which Marco talked a little about whatever he liked, history, the Civil War, his experience during the war and in exile, politics in general, and also about himself. His occasional classes at Salsas and Boada's academy, together with the coffees or the drinks that followed, were enough for Marco to mesmerise the most committed and the most politicised of his students, and acquire a group of admirers who were as loyal and as dazzled as Salsas and Boada—by his illusory past, his fictitious clandestine present, his silver tongue and his charisma, or what everyone took to be his charisma.

Marco may have been dazzled by himself, by his own ability to dazzle. Because over the course of these years he made a number of discoveries that would prove decisive to his future. Marco had always known, or had long known, that he needed an audience, that he needed to be admired, to be a star; now he discovered, perhaps to his astonishment, doubtless to his deep personal satisfaction, that he could make himself heard, respected and admired not only by poor, uneducated families like the Beltráns and the Belvers, or displaced farmhands like his co-workers in the barracks in Kiel, or his apprentices at Peirós' garage and his own workshops, but also by intelligent, educated young men from wealthy, or at least middle-class, families, not to mention by pretty young girls, the sort of people who, he surmised, would rule the country in the future. And he also discovered, with the same pleasure, that he was capable of leading them, and that his talents as a charmer, as an actor, his eloquence and his imagination or his ability to weave imagination with reality meant that these young people considered him not simply an exceptional person, but a genuine hero. Above all he discovered, now Francoism was crumbling or beginning to crumble, that his past as an anarchist and a Republican, about which he had said nothing for decades since it was dangerous to talk about, might become his staunchest asset, provided that he could learn to use it to his advantage, provided that he could work out how to manipulate it, transforming cowardice into bravery, mediocrity and corruption into virtue and heroism and, more generally, transforming the succession of Yes's in his life into a series of No's; in other words, provided that, in order not to recognise himself, like Narcissus, and not to allow others to know or recognise him, he managed to hide reality behind fiction, his true life behind a false life, the genuine history of his country behind a kitsch version of history. It was at this point he realised that, if he was going to falsify personal experience, he needed a deep understanding of the collective experience, and he made a pivotal decision: enrolling at university to study history.

A curious document survives from this period, from April 4, 1970, to be precise. A day earlier, Josep Carner, perhaps the finest Catalan poet of the twentieth century, had returned to Barcelona after three decades in exile. It was a major event. *La Vanguardia* (which was still called *La Vanguardia Española* since Franco was not yet dead) put two large photographs on its front page: the first foregrounds Carner, elderly, dignified, gaunt, doffing his hat, having come back to his homeland to die, or before he died; in the second, he's barely visible, because he is getting into a car, surrounded by a cheering crowd. But on one of the inside pages, there is another photograph of the great poet. He is wearing his hat, his back is to the camera, and he looks as though he is just getting out of the car; once again, he's surrounded by a group of people, though it is smaller, or seems smaller, and they aren't applauding now but trying to touch or even to hug him. And there, in the foreground, is Marco, beaming, unmistakable, animated, wearing his mechanic's overalls. He is touching the poet's face with the fingers of one hand, as though he were one of the family, as though he knew him, or at least was a trusted friend, but the truth is that he doesn't know him from Adam, he has barely even read his work; nor does he know anyone who knows him. In fact, he went to greet him with María Belver, who neither speaks nor reads Catalan and doesn't even know who Carner is. But what Marco *does* know is

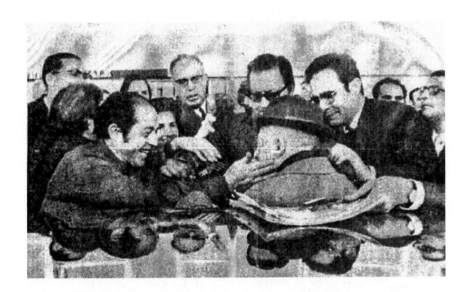

what will make the news, because he has just begun to develop his supreme talent for hogging the limelight, a narcissistic syndrome that will stay with him for the rest of his life. You might call it an addiction to being in the media. One might even call it *mediopathy*.

Marco's assumption was correct. Some of the middle-class students he bewitched in the late Sixties and early Seventies did end up in important positions in the country. Such was the case with Ferran Salsas who, having flirted with the idea of becoming seriously involved in clandestine politics, and even the armed struggle during the death throes of the Franco regime (the result of Marco's influence, according to his wife, or the image he had of Marco), held positions of responsibility in the Unified Socialist Party of Catalonia (P.S.U.C.) and did much notable work in the field of psychiatry before dying in 1987 at the age of forty-one. By this time, his wife, Mercè Boada, was on her way to becoming what she is today: one of the leading specialists in neurodegenerative diseases in Spain. As for Ignasi de Gispert, he has long worked as a labour lawyer in the judicial service of the Workers Trade Union of Catalonia (U.S.O.C.). However, neither they, nor any of the other middle-class kids in Marco's entourage of admirers, went on to play a role as important as Marco himself played in later years.

Having decided to study history, in 1973 our man enrolled in an access course at a university for mature students. He was still living with María Belver, but while he was attending classes here, he would meet the woman who was to be his third and last wife. We have already met her: Dani, Danielle Olivera. Besides being much younger than Marco, Dani was charming, pretty, well-educated, and half-French, and at the time was preparing to take a degree in Catalan language and literature. They immediately fell in love and began to date, and in the three years that followed, Marco divided his time between Dani and María. I don't know any intimate details of their romance, and if I did I wouldn't relate them; suffice to say it was a long, convoluted affair, not least because of the deviousness of Marco and the misgivings of Dani, who was reluctant to see Marco end a twenty-year marriage to a woman who was utterly devoted to him. In order to seduce Dani, Marco used every well-oiled weapon in his arsenal, in particular the one guaranteed to sap the resistance of this young anti-Franco activist: his fictitious political activism.

At least two notable testimonies to his one-sided battle still exist. They are two texts typed by Marco, one in Spanish, the other in Catalan, the first untitled, the second, echoing Verlaine, entitled "From My Prisons"; both are signed from the Modelo prison in Barcelona, one bears the false, handwritten date "September 1974," the other is undated, although both were written during Marco's courtship of Dani and were doubtless inspired by his brief spell in the Modelo in late 1975 or early 1976 for petty offences rather than political crimes. Despite this fact, both purport to be accounts of the incarceration of a political prisoner and, replete with the melodramatic, sentimental flourishes typical of Marco's biographical writings, relate the fictional experiences of this character and his prison comrades, along with the author's thoughts. The first of these texts modestly presents itself as "jottings from a dungeon, with no more proof than the true wound of lived experience. I fear that even writing a clean draft it will lose its thick, filthy atmosphere. It does not smell of heroism, but of the sweat of suffering and of damp, of dirt and disinfectant." With no less modesty, the second text begins by listing the now classic injustices that posterity visits on anonymous heroes (not mentioning anyone in particular) and the disdain this inspires in those same anonymous heroes (not mentioning anyone in particular), given they are indifferent to future honours as well as any form of worldly recognition (I'm still not mentioning anyone in particular, but I'm starting to get a little nervous), and concerned merely with squaring their actions with their own conscience (of course, my love, I'm talking about me! Who else? I was starting to think you were an idiot). Marco writes: "All those who suffer or lose their lives while engaged in a conscientious struggle or an act of desperate rebellion eventually secure a privileged place in the memory of the people or in history yet unwritten. Whether they are considered misguided or martyrs, the satisfaction of knowing they have done their duty compensates for everything."

Well, not everything. At least not in Marco's case; particularly not in his case. In the course of these two biographical texts cunningly crafted with the sole intention of winning the heart of a woman, she is mentioned only once ("I think of you, of your tender eyes that gaze in wonder upon life. I do not yet know what will come of this, but the memories of you will help me through the nights here"), but what is true is that Marco, who by this time was a peerless seducer, achieved his objective, and in 1976, he left María Belver in L'Hospitalet and went to live with Dani Olivera in Sant Cugat. By now, Franco was dead and Marco had spent a year dividing his time between María and Dani, between his garage on Travessera de Les Corts and the History faculty at the Autonomous University near Sant Cugat, where students waited with feverish excitement for Franco's death and where Marco, with his need to play a starring role, his way with words, his energy and his gifts for persuasion, was beginning to get himself noticed in classes and meetings. One day in late February that year, when Franco had been dead for three months but the shift from dictatorship to democracy had not yet begun, a classmate gave Marco a leaflet announcing a meeting intended to relaunch the C.N.T.

Marco was in a daze. The C.N.T., the cradle of Buenaventura Durruti, of his uncle Anastasio, of his own father, his ideological home in his homeless teenage years, the foremost union during the Second Republic, the communal hero of the anarchist uprising that gripped Barcelona during the first days of the war, the great revolutionary organisation razed and destroyed during the Franco regime, was suddenly rising from the ashes. An elated Marco realised that, now Franco was dead, anything was possible. The following day, the same classmate told him that the meeting was to take place on Sunday the 29th, in the parish of Sant Medir in the district of Sants, and gave instructions on how to get there without revealing the existence of the meeting. At about 9:00 a.m. on the appointed day, Marco arrived in Sants and tried to do what he had been told but, when he noticed gangs of people hanging around plazas that were normally deserted early on Sunday morning, and shady men in trenchcoats whispering directions on every corner of the labyrinthine streets, he felt as though unwittingly and unwillingly he had stumbled into a Marx Brothers movie, into a scene where everyone is heading for a secret meeting that everyone knows is not a secret.

The meeting began at 10:00 a.m. and it was historic. For the first time since the Civil War, representatives of the two exiled branches of the C.N.T. (the Paris-based Frente Libertario and the C.N.T.-A.I.T. from Toulouse) were meeting in Catalonia with various libertarian groups and factions from within the country. The hall was jammed; according to estimates, 1,500 people were present. Over the course of five hours, a series of measures was passed, intended to reconstitute and relaunch the union; the final speech brought a lump to the throats of many: this was the first time in forty years that the C.N.T. had held such a meeting in Spain, the chairman reminded them. "So it is important," he added, "that we not conclude this session of the Catalan National Assembly without fondly remembering all those comrades who lost their lives in the struggle for freedom, in social battles, in the trenches, and facing the firing squad. We pay tribute to each and every one, from the first to the last libertarian executed by the dictatorship, Salvador Puig Antich."

In the long years of the Franco regime, Marco did not join the C.N.T. in the struggle for freedom or in its social battles. He did not meet with the union (or with any other competing union, party, group or faction) either in exile or in Spain. In fact, Marco—as I have said—hadn't heard a word from the C.N.T. for almost four decades, nor had he wanted to hear from them. And yet, within a few months of this foundational meeting at Sant Medir, our man became secretary general of the Catalonia branch of the union and within two years he was Secretary General of the C.N.T. in Spain. How could this have happened? How did Marco manage to hoist himself to the top of this legendary organisation in such a short space of time? How did he become the leader of what had been, and still was, much more than a union, an organization that many people hoped—or feared—would regain the social and political pre-eminence it had enjoyed before Franco? And, above all, how could he have done it given who he was—someone who had spent forty years giving the union in particular and the anti-Franco movement in general a very wide berth, someone who had spent more than half of his fifty years holed up in a car repair workshop?

I'm not at all sure how Marco managed such an unexpected and meteoric rise, but what I am completely sure about is that only someone like him could have done it.

7

To return to Claudio Magris, or to the title of Claudio Magris' article about Marco, "The liar who tells the truth"; to go back to Vargas Llosa who insists that all novels tell a truth by telling a lie—a moral or literary truth through a factual or historical lie—and who, in his own article about Marco, claims that our man is a brilliant storyteller, welcoming him to the guild of novelists: Are Magris and Vargas Llosa seeking to absolve Marco as some have accused them? Is Marco a novelist, and are his lies and truths not historical but novelistic? And if Marco is a novelist, what kind of novelist is he? It's impossible to attempt to answer such a question without first answering an underlying two-pronged question: Is a novel a lie? Is a fiction a lie?

From Plato to Bertrand Russell, a whole school of Western thought has accused writers of fiction of straying from the truth, of propagating falsehoods, which is why Plato banishes them from his ideal Republic. Of course, a falsehood is not a lie—a lie is worse—but, fed up with being considered enemies of the truth, and perhaps fed up with the lies told in the name of truth, many artists, at least since Oscar Wilde, have defiantly embraced their standing as liars: in "The Decay of Lying," Wilde asserts that "Lying, the telling of beautiful untrue things, is the proper aim of Art," while Orson Welles, at the end of *F for Fake*, says: "What we professional liars hope to serve is truth. I'm afraid the pompous word for that is 'art.'" Picasso himself said it: "Art is a lie, a lie that helps us to see the truth." So, when Vargas Llosa gives the title "The Truth of Lies" to an essay that is actually a theory of the novel—perhaps echoing an autobiographical story of Louis Aragon, "Le mentir-vrai," which is also in its way a theory of the novel—he is simply joining a large and illustrious tradition of dissidents. Whatever the case, this multi-faceted and cheerfully paradoxical expression has prompted many criticisms, some a little simplistic. "Only through a novel is it possible to arrive at the truth," says Stendhal, and no-one, or almost no-one, doubts the fact that fiction offers a truth: a truth that is timorous, profound, ambiguous, contradictory, ironic and elusive, a truth that isn't factual but moral, not concrete but universal, not historical or journalistic but literary or artistic. Many simply reject the idea that fictions are lies. Their arguments can be summarised in two points. Firstly: unlike lies, the facts that occur in a fiction are not verifiable and therefore it is not possible to prove whether they are true or false. Secondly: unlike lies, fictions make no attempt to fool anyone. On the face of it, both arguments seem convincing; in fact neither of them is. We know that Don Quixote and Emma Bovary did not exist (or at least that they didn't exist as they appear in *Don Quixote* and *Madame Bovary*), and, at least in theory, this can be verified by data documenting that no-one like Don Quixote lived in Spain in the sixteenth century just as no-one like Emma Bovary lived in France in the nineteenth century. Cervantes and Flaubert, therefore, are advancing a falsehood; but not just that, they are fooling us, they are deliberately using all the wiles and talents of charlatans to get us to believe that people who never existed actually existed and things that never happened actually happened. Two thousand four hundred years ago, Gorgias, quoted by Plutarch, said it better than anyone: "tragedy [meaning fiction] is a deception, wherein he who deceives is more *honest* than he who does not deceive, and he who is deceived is *wiser* than he who is not deceived." I stress the word "honest": the moral duty of the fiction writer is to deceive in order to construct the timorous, ambiguous, elusive truth of fiction; I stress the word "wiser": the intellectual duty of the reader or the spectator is to allow himself to be deceived, in order to capture the profound contradictory, ironic truth that the author has fashioned for him. Fiction is a lie, therefore, a deception, but, at heart, reveals itself to be a particular variant of Plato's "noble lies" or Montaigne's "altruistic lies"; it is a lie or a deception that, in a novel, does not seek to harm the reader who, only through believing this lie or deception, can attain a particular truth: the truth of literature.

Is this the nature of Marco's lies? Is Marco actually a storyteller? Vargas Llosa's article is entitled "Monstrous Genius" because the Peruvian novelist feels that Marco has a sort of monstrous genius as a novelist. He makes it clear that Marco works like a novelist and that, in a certain sense, the result of his work is identical to that of the novelist; also he intuits that the urge that prompts Marco to invent and the origin of his lies are the same as those of a novelist.

His intuition is correct. Literature is a socially acceptable form of narcissism. Like the mythical Narcissus, like the real Marco, the novelist is utterly unsatisfied with life, not only his own life, but life in general, and this is why he refashions it according to his desires, through words, in fiction. For Narcissus, for Marco, for the novelist, reality kills and fiction saves, because more often than not fiction is a way of disguising reality, a way of protecting oneself from it or curing oneself of it. Like Marco, the novelist invents a fictional, hypothetical life, in order to hide his real life and live a different one, to process the humiliations and the horrors and the inadequacies of real life and turn them into fiction, to hide them, in a sense to avoid knowing or recognising himself; just like Narcissus, he must avoid knowing himself if he wishes to live to old age, in accordance with the prophecy blind Tiresias makes to his mother Liriope. Like Marco, the novelist doesn't create his fiction out of nothing: he creates it from his own experience; like Marco, the novelist knows that pure fiction doesn't exist and that, if it did exist, it wouldn't be remotely interesting, and no-one would believe it, because reality is the fuel that drives fiction: and so, like Marco, the novelist creates fiction by painting and distorting historical or biographical truth, by mixing truth and lies, what actually happened with what he wished had happened, or what would have seemed interesting or fascinating if it had happened. Like Marco, who studied history, listened carefully to its central figures and assimilated their stories, the novelist knows he needs a foundation for his lies and this is why he researches thoroughly, so that he can thoroughly reinvent reality. Marco, moreover, has all the qualities required of a novelist: energy, fantasy, imagination, memory and, more than anything, a love of words; almost more so for the written than the spoken word, which to the novelist is merely a substitute for the written word: from the first, Marco has not only been an indiscriminate reader, he has also been a compulsive writer, author of countless stories, poems, articles, biographical fragments, manifestos, reports and letters of every kind that clutter his archives and have been sent to countless people and institutions. Vargas Llosa is right: Marco is a genius because he succeeded for many years at what great novelists only partly achieve in their novels, and even then only for as long as it takes to read them; that is to say, he deceived thousands and thousands of people, making them believe he was someone he wasn't, that what is actually a lie is in fact the truth. But Marco's genius, of course, is only partial. Unlike great novelists, who in exchange for a factual lie deliver a profound, disturbing, elusive, irreplaceable moral and universal truth, Marco delivers only a sickly, insincere, mawkishly sentimental story that from the historical or moral point of view is pure kitsch; unlike Marco, great novelists make it possible, through their paradoxical truth fashioned from lies—a truth that doesn't hide reality, but reveals it—to know and recognise the real, to know ourselves and recognise ourselves, to gaze into the reflecting waters of Narcissus without dying. So, if Marco is a genius, is he also monstrous? And if so, why?

The answer is obvious: because the rules of a novel are different from the rules of life. In novels, it is not only acceptable to lie, it is obligatory: the factual lie is the path to literary truth (and this is why Gorgias says that he who deceives is more honest than he who does not deceive); in life, on the other hand, as in history or in journalism, lying is "an accursed vice," to quote Montaigne, a baseness and an act of violence, a lack of respect and a violation of the first rule of human coexistence. The result of mixing a truth with a lie is always a lie, except in novels, where it is a truth. Marco deliberately confused fiction and life: he should have mixed truth and lies in the former, not the latter; he should have written a novel. Perhaps if he had written a novel he would not have done as he did. Perhaps he is a frustrated novelist. Or perhaps he is not, and perhaps he couldn't settle for writing a novel and instead turned his life into a novel. This is why he seems monstrous: because he didn't accept who he was and had the audacity and the effrontery to invent himself out of lies; because lies are a bad thing in life, whereas they are a good thing in novels. All novels, except for those without fiction, the true stories. All novels other than this one.

8

The question was: How is it possible that Marco was president of the C.N.T. during the transition from dictatorship to democracy? How is it possible that, in a few short months after the death of Franco, a man who, during the regime, hadn't had any contact either with the C.N.T. or any anti-Franco movements, a man who had spent forty years not lifting a finger to bring down Franco or to improve the working conditions of labourers, became secretary general of the Catalonia chapter of the C.N.T. and, a couple of years later, of the C.N.T. throughout Spain? How is it possible, at such a decisive moment, for such a man to take control of a decisive organisation, an anarchist or anarcho-syndicalist union that had been banned for forty years under Franco, that had dominated the unions before the dictatorship and aspired to do so again? The answer to these complex questions is very simple: because he was the ideal person to do so.

When Franco died, anarchism in Spain was broadly divided into two large blocks: those in exile, and those who had remained in Spain. The largest and most powerful section of the exiles, based in the French city of Toulouse, was comprised of veteran anarchists who had fought during the Civil War and had been exiled from Spain for forty years; almost inevitably, all or most of them had a utopian idea of Spain, an antiquated notion of political struggle and an inherited concept of the union, of which they considered themselves the standard bearers. The anarchists who stayed in the country, on the other hand, many of whom had been part of the anti-Franco struggle, were much younger working men with an altogether more realistic vision of the social and political complexities of contemporary Spain. These were the anarcho-syndicalists. Among them were also what might be called counter-culturalists, heirs to the subversive spirit of May '68, with its joyful emphasis on anti-authoritarianism, personal growth through drugs, sexual liberation and alternative lifestyles. (There was a C.N.T. splinter group among the exiles as well, though they were not particularly relevant: called *Frente Libert-ario*, based in Paris.)

In short, between the exiled veterans and the young anarchists in Spain there was a generational and ideological rift, just as between the young anarcho-syndicalists and the young counter-culturalists there was an ideological gulf that was also a cultural (and often class) rift. As if this were not enough, to add to these twin rifts within the C.N.T., there were three others. The first was between the purists and the *posibilistas** or realists: the purists advocated a return to the fundamental values of anarchism before the Civil War, in other words they would have no truck with politics and negotiations like other unions; the *posibilistas* or realists, on the other hand, advocated concrete improvements for workers even at the cost of renouncing principles which, moreover, they considered obsolete or impractical. The second rift separated those who considered the C.N.T. to be merely a union, responsible for fighting for the rights and welfare of workers, and those who considered it to be a libertarian movement whose aim should be a popular anarchist revolution. The third rift separated those who advocated violence from those who rejected it. There may have been other rifts, but it hardly matters. What is important is that, to many C.N.T. militants in 1977–78, Marco could easily seem the ideal leader, the only one capable of bridging these unbridgeable gulfs, or at least some of them, and as such the only man capable of resolving the contradictions at the heart of the anarchist union. The astonishing thing is that, in a sense, he may have been.

Marco resolved the fundamental contradiction of the C.N.T. because, in 1976, having just turned fifty-two, he filled the most obvious gap in the union brought about by four decades of Franco:

---

* *posibilistas.* The name relates to Libertarian Possibilism (*posibilismo libertario*), a political current in the twentieth-century Spanish anarchist movement.

the lack of activists of intermediate age. He was neither as old as the exiled veterans nor as young as those who stayed in Spain. Unlike the veterans, Marco understood the country's realities, including employment; unlike the young activists in Spain, Marco had fought in the Civil War and had a command of the language and culture of the C.N.T. during both the war and the pre-war period. It's true that the exiled C.N.T. members, who had never met him, distrusted Marco, but it's also true that they distrusted anyone outside their circle and they distrusted the young activists even more than they did Marco. It's true that Marco was more than thirty years older than most of the activists in Spain, but it's also true that he connected with their dishevelled, dynamic energy and that, thanks to his friendships with Salsas, Boada et al., he knew them well and knew how to charm and to lead them; it's equally true that, from his physical appearance, his energy and his manner, he might easily have been mistaken for one of them, or at least he passed unnoticed. Marco possessed the best characteristics of the young, their strength and their understanding of the country, and he contrived the best traits of the veterans, a past of epic feats of war and anti-Franco resistance: this is one of the reasons he embroidered his war record, adding heroic incidents like his fictional relationship with "Quico" Sabater—to the young activists, a figure almost as mythic as Durruti or Che Guevara—and this is how he later managed to pass for an anti-Franco resistant, especially among the young. In April 1978, when he was proclaimed secretary general of the C.N.T. in Spain, the magazine *Triunfo*, the most important magazine of the Spanish left at the time, presented him as an activist who, during the Franco regime, had been involved "in every clandestine struggle and in the confederal organisation," while in his memoirs, José Ribas, the editor of *Ajoblanco*, the most popular magazine among young libertarians at the time, wrote that Marco was known among his comrades "for having suffered in the dungeons of Francoism." All of these things stood in Marco's favour as a potential leader of the C.N.T. He also benefited from the fact that he was a member of the metalworkers union, which experienced greater growth in Catalonia than any other union in the years after Franco's death. This may have proved to be a decisive advantage, alongside the fact that as a member of a cooperative—this was the legal status of his garage—he could spend more time working for the union than most of his comrades. There were a number of personal qualities in his favour, too: his powerful speeches, his frenetic activism, his extraordinary gifts as a performer and his lack of any serious political convictions—in fact, Marco's only real goal was to be in the limelight, thereby satisfying his *mediopathy*, his need to be loved and admired and his desire to play the leading role—which meant he was capable of saying something one day and the opposite the very next, telling each side exactly what they wanted to hear.

But there is something more, and perhaps more important. The transition from dictatorship to democracy in Spain was basically a muddle, a theoretical impossibility that became a practical reality largely thanks to chance, the conciliatory nature of the majority, and the unifying talent of a few, most notably Adolfo Suárez, the fundamental architect of the change, who was able to take advantage of the confusion to get his own way, which meant putting himself forward as prime minister, but also destroying the Franco regime and building a democracy. Within the sprawling chaos of political change, the re-creation of the C.N.T. was perhaps an even greater upheaval. On the one hand, after decades of dictatorship, the early years of democracy saw an explosion in libertarianism and a fashion for anarchism and the counter-culture, particularly among the young, influenced by the post-'68 anti-authoritarian movements of the West: in the eye of this storm, Marco continued to be part of the majority. On the other hand, the C.N.T., having been stripped and gutted and all but destroyed by Franco, now threw open its doors to fill the void, which quickly turned it into a curious jumble of multifarious inclinations, collectives and ideologies; the aforementioned José Ribas lists them as follows: "Ecologists, university students, homosexuals, feminists, cooperativists, anti-psychiatric collectives, prisoners' groups (C.O.P.E.L., the Committee of Spanish Prisoners in Struggle), communards [. . .], members of F.A.I. (Iberian Anarchist Federation), members of councils, anarcho-communists, libertarian communists, extremists, radicals more or less advocating violence, dropouts, Trotskyites, members of the Spanish Revolutionary Workers Party, the Organisation of the Communist Left, the Christian Liberation Movement, Leninist infiltrators, revolutionary spontaneists, naturists, and even disguised

Christians." Anyone missing from this list? Yes: there is no mention of police officers or informers, who were so numerous they could have easily created their own internal faction. Enough said. The fact remains that this utter chaos was the perfect terrain for opportunists, people with an insatiable need to be in the limelight, and that in the midst of the colossal double-muddle of political transition and the reconstruction of the C.N.T., no-one was more likely to flourish than a professional conman, a shameless charlatan and schemer like Marco, a past master of creating confusion and navigating within it.

And that is what he did. And, like Adolfo Suárez, he could get his own way, getting himself noticed but also transforming the C.N.T. into what some people in 1977 hoped (or feared) it might once again become after forty years: the largest union in the country. This was not easy to achieve. The traditional philosophy of Spanish anarchism was obsolete, its long-standing theoretical apolitical stance was anachronistic and its direct action strategy woefully inefficient, especially compared to the other more modern and skilled left-wing unions. But if the C.N.T. could adapt its approach and its theories to the realities of the country and could resolve the contradictions tearing it apart, adding the lure and the potential of the youthful counter-culture movement to the prestigious legend of the old union, who knows what might happen; ultimately, it would be much more difficult to move from dictatorship to democracy in the space of a year, yet Suárez achieved this. To say nothing of the fact that, at least at the beginning of political transition, the government didn't seem to mind the reappearance of the C.N.T.; on the contrary, as far as they were concerned, the anarchist union would serve as a counterbalance to the fearsome power of the large left-wing unions, particularly the communist-leaning Workers' Commissions, but also the socialist-leaning U.G.T. Whatever the case, in the second half of the Seventies, many supporters of anarchism believed that if anyone could unite the union, reconcile its disagreements and get it in shape, that man was Enric Marco; for his part, Marco made the most of this belief, and of the glorious confusion that reigned, to burst into the limelight as leader of the C.N.T.

.   .   .

Perhaps the first point at which people decided that Marco was the ideal candidate to lead the union was on July 2, 1977, eighteen months after the inaugural meeting in Sant Medir, six weeks after the legalisation of the C.N.T. and just over a fortnight after the first free democratic elections. By now, Marco was secretary general of the Catalonia chapter of the C.N.T.; by now, he had changed his name: he was no longer Enrique Marco—as he had been for most of his life—or Enrique Durruti—as his apprentice mechanics at Peirós' garage called him, or as he told them he was called—nor Enric Batlle—as Salsas, Boada and their friends called him, or as he told them he was called—he was Enrique Marcos. He had changed his name so that no-one would confuse him with Enrique Marco Nadal, an elderly libertarian leader and a notable resistant against the Franco regime who, with a number of other left-wing union leaders in the early Sixties, had made a pact with the dictatorship and was ostracised by his comrades as a collaborationist (whereas, in the early twenty-first century, when Marco Nadal was dead and people had forgotten his alleged collaboration but not his unquestionable anti-Franco militancy, Marco made no attempt to avoid this confusion; rather the reverse). July 2 was the first meeting of the C.N.T. since its legalisation, by far the largest since the Civil War. It was a Saturday afternoon, and more than one hundred thousand men and women gathered in Monjuic park in Barcelona. On YouTube, you can watch a short but eloquent film of the event.

The first minutes of the film capture the celebratory atmosphere of vindication and offer a panorama of the vast crowds that attended; in the background you can hear "A las barricadas," the anthem of the C.N.T. Then the music stops and the meeting itself begins, with shots of the speakers and the crowd listening and cheering. Suddenly, Marco appears, sitting on the speakers' platform, and from that moment, his starring role in the film never falters: he chairs the meeting, making speeches, chanting slogans and getting the audience to chant with him ("*Sí, sí, libertad; sí, sí, libertad; amnistía total*"), he introduces the other speakers, he is constantly moving around the stage, chatting to comrades, standing next to or behind them, gripped by a feverish enthusiasm.

The slogans are strange. Years after Marco's scandal broke and our man became the great impostor and the great pariah, a historian of the anarchist movement noted that the Spanish libertarian tradition did not involve chanting slogans, and Marco's behaviour at the Montjuic meeting should have marked him out as an interloper who didn't understand the ethos of anarchism. I'm not convinced. Although it's true that the anarchist tradition did not involve slogans, and therefore it's possible that the chanting of the crowds offended the ears of the veteran activists and the exiled leaders, for the young activists, by far the majority, who knew nothing or very little about the anarchist tradition and were used to chanting such slogans on protest marches against the dictatorship, Marco's gesture was unlikely to ring false. At worst (or at best), both young and old might have seen it as a way of bringing historic anarchism into the present, updating the form without betraying its spirit.

In fact, this is what many of the activists thought about Marco's performance that day; and not just the young anarchists, but members of the communist and socialist unions who had come to Montjuic more out of curiosity than any ideological affinity. Many of them also felt that the exiled leaders surrounding Marco on the stage looked like mummies or zombies, resurrecting ancient heroes thundering preposterous Civil War speeches. José Pierats, the editor of *Solidaridad Obrera*, the official organ of the C.N.T., seemingly unaware that a large majority of the Catalan people and the entire anti-Franco movement had long been demanding autonomous status for Catalonia, mocked Catalan aspirations for self-government before demanding "free municipalities," a concept no-one really understood. For her part, Federica Montseny, eternal embodiment of libertarian orthodoxy, and *de facto* leader (if not *de jure* proprietor) of the C.N.T., was oblivious or pretended to be oblivious to the jubilation of the vast majority of Spanish people who, only two weeks earlier, had had the opportunity to vote in free elections after forty years of dictatorship. She referred to the elections only to disparage the money it had cost to organise them and to say that "the price per kilo for a member of parliament seems very high," a statement theoretically compatible with her radical apolitical stance but, in practice, opportunistic-seeming, even cynical, at least to her more circumspect colleagues; after all, "the Lioness"—as she was known—had taken a

position with the Ministry of Health of the Second Republic during the Civil War. In contrast to these bombastic speeches, aloof to
everyday concerns and beholden to an archaic ideology, and whose
language, tone and manner hailed from a bygone age, Marco's speech
seemed to many of the young and the not-so-young activists in attendance to be clear, forceful, candid, effective, firmly rooted in reality.

Less than a year later, Marco would catapult to the position of
secretary general of the C.N.T. for all of Spain. Although he always
tried to get along with the various factions in the union, from the start
he relied on the most reasonable, competent and ambitious sector,
the young domestic anarcho-syndicalists, who, as it turned out, were
those who respected him and perhaps most needed him. For this reason, the policies in his mandate were also fairly reasonable, though not
his manner of implementing them. Despite his activism in the C.N.T.
as a teenager, Marco didn't have the first idea how a union worked
or how to improve its organisation; and though he had a vague and
very general notion of its goals, he didn't know how these might be
achieved or how he should proceed. However, though Marco might
have been ignorant, he wasn't stupid and so he employed two complementary strategies to disguise this yawning gap in his knowledge.
The first was to understate; the second, to exaggerate. On the union
committee, Marco was surrounded by intellectuals and ideologues, or
those who claimed or aspired to be, and therefore he never claimed
to be an intellectual or an ideologue but a man of action. He barely
contributed to discussions about ideas and strategies; he carefully and
shrewdly listened to everyone waiting until, through conviction or
from sheer exhaustion, all the positions had been laid out and agreement had been reached, at which point, with his gift for oratory and
his authority as secretary general, he would simply restate the agreed
position and ratify the decision. In this way, not only did he learn
from the discussion and hide the fact that he held no serious position
on anything, or almost anything, that his only goal was his desire to
continue in his current role or secure a better one; it also won him the
admiration of his fellow members, particularly the intellectuals and
the ideologues, who interpreted his reluctance to contribute to the
debates as a sign of humble diffidence of a simple worker hardened
by resistance to the dictatorship, and more especially as proof of his

innate perspicacity that led him to rise above the debate, and adopt the role of arbiter, thereby facilitating outcomes that were acceptable to all.

This was the first concealment tactic. The second was no less sophisticated, though it was more fitting to his temperament; in particular it played to his reputation as a man of action, since it involved launching himself wholeheartedly into the fray. Marco never stopped: in addition to continuing his work at the garage and studying at the university, Marco went everywhere as secretary general of the union, talked to everyone, attended every meeting, party, commemoration and funeral, ensured he was at the forefront of every struggle, every strike, every demonstration and if necessary, of every confrontation with the police or the authorities. This unthinking restlessness made it difficult, if not impossible, to work with him; it also made his own work impossible, or very difficult: rather than solving problems, he postponed them, or transformed them into different problems, such that they continued to mount up in an ever growing chaos. Marco also used the dust clouds raised by his constant hyperactivity to conceal his political ineptitude and, more importantly, to ensure he was in the limelight, gradually becoming famous, indeed a celebrity in the union, a man people stopped in the street, someone everyone wanted to talk to, everyone respected for his entirely genuine fight for the rights and the dignity of workers, and more especially for his past as an indefatigable Republican hero and an opponent of the Franco regime, a past that was fictitious, or at the very least heavily embroidered, but one that Marco proudly wore like a sergeant's stripes, a military medal, or a saint's halo, as the ultimate source of authority, one that he only flaunted when it was absolutely necessary and when no-one could contradict or challenge it. (On the other hand, he barely mentioned his no-less-fictitious past as a prisoner of Flossenbürg: in part, because he had only just begun to construct it, but mostly because it was unlikely to be useful or afford him any influence over his comrades. It should be remembered that, at the time, even the left-wing did not consider the Second World War, the Holocaust and the Nazi camps relevant to Spanish history.) Marco was more than happy, he was exultant. Not only had he begun a new life, but this new life was better than he could ever have imagined. And although his ruse meant that he had to present himself to the media as a simple mechanic—"To aspire to something more would feel like hogging the limelight, something I would find embarrassing," he declared in an interview with the weekly magazine *Por Favor* in 1978—he knew that he was much more than that: by now, he was giving speeches to rapt crowds, he was a respected and admired leader, he was the promising secretary general of one of the largest unions in the country, he had won the heart of the young, beautiful, educated woman he loved and had gone to live with her in Sant Cugat, and they had just had their first daughter, Elizabeth (the second, Ona, would be born six years later, in 1984). What more could he wish for?

In early 1978, as the number of those joining continued to grow at the same dizzying rate it had since the C.N.T. was legalised, many people believed that it would become the second or third largest union in the country; it's quite possible that many, including Marco, still thought so in mid-April when, at a meeting in Madrid, our man was elected secretary general of the C.N.T. throughout Spain. After all, the union seemed to have united around a sensible programme of reforms and around its new leader, about whom Juan Gómez Casas—outgoing secretary general and later a bitter enemy of Marco—declared was "dynamism personified, he is brave and intelligent and, in short, he is the man this organisation needed." Marco had reached the summit, and so had the C.N.T. From there, it was downhill for both.

The C.N.T.'s self-destruction didn't come about because of the contradictions within it, but because of mistakes it made which made those same contradictions irreconcilable. The first, and perhaps the most important, was a miscalculation. In 1977, in the midst of the euphoria surrounding the rise of the union, the young anarcho-syndicalists who supported Marco proposed arranging a conference that would redefine the organisation, correct the anachronisms and the inefficiency of many of its approaches, adapting them to the modern world; it was a perfectly reasonable idea, especially considering that the last congress had taken place in 1936. But among the talking points, the young anarcho-syndicalists made the

rash (or naive) mistake of including a review of the role played by
the exiled leaders during the forty years of the Franco regime, and
insisting that Federica Montseny personally write a report explaining what had happened during this period: Marco and his friends
did not anticipate that the exiled veterans would take the proposal as
they did: as a slap in the face, a threat or a snub by a bunch of
ungrateful brats who, after the veterans had heroically held aloft the
banner of freedom during the brutal years of the dictatorship, pre-
sumed to judge their behaviour and to settle scores. This tactical
error unleashed a fury within the organisation.

But what eventually tipped the balance was the Scala affair. It happened on January 15, 1978, when Marco was still secretary general of
the Catalonia chapter of the C.N.T. The union had organised a protest in Barcelona against the Moncloa Pact, an agreement proposed
by the government of Adolfo Suárez and signed three months earlier
by the main political parties, unions and business associations, eager
to allay the social unrest in the country and to establish a process
for regulating the economy during the transition from dictatorship
to democracy; the protest was a success: some ten thousand people
took part. But, towards midday, after Marco had brought the demonstration to a close on the plaza de España and the crowds had dispersed, four Molotov cocktails exploded in the Scala nightclub. Four
workers died in the blaze. Although two victims were members of the
C.N.T., suspicion for the attacks immediately focused on the union
and its entourage, and also (at least within the union itself) on police
infiltrators acting on orders of the government, who were seeking to
discredit the only major union opposed to the process of the political
transition because they considered it to be contrary to workers' interests. Although the two theories were contradictory, both proved to be
accurate. In December 1980, a court convicted six people with con-
nections to the C.N.T. for the Scala bombing, but two years later, a
police informant named Joaquín Gambín was also convicted of insti-
gating and organising the attack. There can be no doubt that the government was interested in discrediting or even destroying the C.N.T.,
but it is impossible to rule out the idea that the most traditionalist,
inflexible factions within the organisation—notably the exiled veterans who didn't want to be investigated by their comrades at the next

congress and were seeking to regain complete control—had sought to radicalise the union by resorting to violence, thereby distancing the C.N.T. from the realist, *posibilista* path it had been following until then, and side-lining Marco and the young anarcho-syndicalists. The goals of the government and of the extremists within the union were compatible, and both achieved their aims.

The Scala affair proved fatal to the C.N.T. This unexpected flare-up of violence frightened off many anarchist sympathisers: the massive influx of members came to a grinding halt, and many members decided to leave; also the fashion for libertarianism more or less faded. This frantic retreat was a victory for the government, which succeeded in stigmatising the C.N.T. in the media, associating it and the libertarian movements with mindless radicalism and with terrorism at a moment when terrorism—particularly from the Basque separatists, E.T.A.—was responsible for countless deaths; but it was also a failure for the C.N.T., which proved incapable of contesting the government strategy, and allowed the contradictions it had heretofore kept under control to flare up. The Scala affair split the union down the middle. On one side, the young anarcho-syndicalists who supported Marco demanded that the union roundly condemn the use of violence, though they didn't rule out helping the C.N.T. activists caught up in the attack, or denouncing police infiltration and government-orchestrated attempts to discredit anarchism; on the other side were the exiled veterans and the young, radicalised counter-culturalists, who flirted with violence or let it be thought they flirted with violence, and were prepared to condemn the government, but were not prepared to condemn violence in the abstract or the Scala attack in particular, just as they committed to unfailingly support the suspects accused of committing it. In principle, this was an ideological battle: the young anarcho-syndicalists were realists, reformers, possibilists and opposed to violence; the veteran exiles and the young counter-culturalists, on the other hand, were purists, idealists, radicals and, at the very least, had not resolved the eternal debate about the necessity and the legitimacy of using violence. In the end, it resulted in an all-out power struggle, duly disguised as a debate over principle, that left the union preoccupied with internal troubles and completely cut it off from the concerns of workers.

It was a fight to the death and one that the exiled purists—who had never truly relinquished control of the union—were destined to win. Faced with the congress proposed by the young anarcho-syndicalists, the exiles drew up a plan to purge the union of their adversaries who might otherwise compel them to give an account of their actions during the dictatorship, take control of the congress and, with it, take power. The first thing they did was to demonise the young anarcho-syndicalists, accusing them of being revisionists, collaborators, reformers and heterodox Marxists; the second was to expel as many of them as possible from the union; the third was to resort to insult, intimidation and violence. Realising that the young anarcho-syndicalists on whose support he had thus far relied were about to be expelled from the union, Marco distanced himself from them and attempted to mediate between the two factions and put himself forward as a sort of intermediate option, a third way, warning that if things did not change, the C.N.T. was headed for disaster: "A process of disintegration and collapse has taken effect in the C.N.T.," he wrote on March 5, 1979, in *Solid-aridad Obrera*, "one that, if it is not stopped now, will destroy us to the benefit of our common enemies: capital and the state [. . .] Either we act quickly, or it will be too late. The struggle for control of the C.N.T. will result in there being nothing left to control, and that in short order."

This was no exaggeration. It must have been a difficult period for him, yet at the same time it must have been intense and thrilling, a glorious period in its way, or at least a period that produced one of the most glorious moments in his life, or one of the moments whose glory he most exploited. It happened on the evening of September 28, 1979, in the centre of Barcelona, where a number of anarchists had chained themselves together and blocked traffic on calle Pelayo, calling for an amnesty for the accused in the Scala affair; Marco happened to be there and, as the protest was being dispersed, he was beaten and arrested by the police. In his statement, our hero insisted that he had done nothing more than remonstrate with the officers beating the protestors who were chained together; for their part, the officers testified that Marco had not remonstrated about anything, but had called them "murderers, bastards, sons of bitches, etcetera" while they attempted to unchain the protestors: this, they claimed,

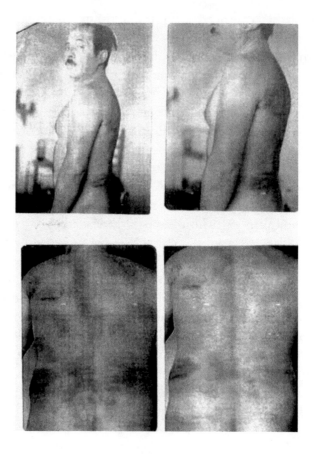

was why they arrested him. In any case, Marco was released that same evening, and lost no time having photographs taken—two in profile, and two from the back—showing the bruises left by police truncheons and rifle butts on his back and his ribs, photographs that, from this moment on, he always carried with him. For Marco, they were crucial. There are witness statements from the period when he was leader of the C.N.T. that attest that our man was capable of acts of bravery when confronted by the authorities or by police who were still Francoist or unable to shake off their Francoist mentality and behaviour, but Marco immediately realised that no witness statement was a match for these photographs. At last, he had succeeded in becoming the man who, for years, he had dreamed of being or imagined being, certainly the man he had always claimed to be, the man many people believed him to be. These photographs were the proof. Clear and unequivocal, in black and white. Now, he too was a victim of the Franco regime—or what remained of it. He too was a resistance fighter. He too was a hero.

Marco managed to arrive at the C.N.T. congress as national secretary general and leave having been all but expelled. "I was treated better at the police station," he declared at the time in the libertarian magazine *Bicicleta*. Once again, he was not exaggerating, or at least not much. The congress took place in early December 1979 at the Casa de Campo in Madrid, and it was a pitched battle—the ultimate or penultimate battle in the ultimate or penultimate war between anarchists—during which members witnessed everything, from tricks and procedural irregularities, to shouts, insults, threats, beatings and people brandishing guns. Predictably, the young anarcho-syndicalists, most of whom had left the party or been expelled, were defeated, as was Marco: he could not be a consensus candidate or an intermediate alternative, and though he stood for re-election, he was far from garnering the votes required to remain in office. With the indestructible Federica Montseny controlling remotely from Toulouse, the veteran exiles, who had never trusted Marco, swept all before them and succeeded in imposing their agenda, and their candidate, José Buendía.

The rest of the story is also sad, or perhaps sadder, both for Marco and for the C.N.T., more so perhaps for the C.N.T. In the two years that followed, our man clung to his reputation and his role as a union leader in an attempt to regain his influence within the C.N.T., or within the trade union movement. Hardly had the congress at Casa del Campo ended than he founded the C.C.T. (Confederación Catalana del Trabajo), allied to the C.N.T., and with others who had lost at the congress, attempted to challenge the results, but he succeeded only in getting himself expelled from the union in April 1980 for "his blatant attempts to foment splits within the Confederación," declared the Organising Secretary of the C.N.T. in *Solidaridad Obrera* in June, and for colluding with the government in undermining the reputation of the union and seeking to destroy it, according to the Coordination Secretariat in a denunciation in late May, also quoted in *Solidaridad Obrera*. These slanderous rumours accusing him of being a traitor, an infiltrator and a collaborationist—the result of the bitter clashes and the paranoid infighting within the C.N.T. at the time—have haunted Marco to this day, but, shortly after they began to circulate, he abandoned all hope of returning to a senior role in trade union- ism. His decision came in 1984, when his old comrades, the young anarcho-syndicalists who had been defeated at the Madrid congress with him, formed the C.N.T.–Valencia Congress in conjunction with various other C.N.T. splinter groups and, doubtless remembering that Marco had distanced himself from them when they most needed him, they distanced themselves from him.

Marco was left alone: this ends his career as a trade unionist. It is true that, by this time, the union that had played such an impor- tant role in his life was also beginning to wane. In 1989, after a court decision determined they could no longer use the initials C.N.T., the young anarcho-syndicalists—by now, no longer young—renamed themselves the C.G.T. (Confederación General del Trabajo), which is now the third largest union in Spain, while the C.N.T. has long since been reduced to an irrelevancy. As for Marco, in the early Eighties, he gradually disappeared from the newspapers and retreated to his private life, to his wife and daughters and his degree in history, which he completed during this time; meanwhile, he carried on working in his garage, though not for long since, in 1986, he reached retirement age. It is possible that he was a little bruised by his turbulent time in the C.N.T., a union he joined in a moment of euphoric chaos and left at a moment of dismal chaos, whose leadership he took up when it seemed the union was destined for success and abandoned when it was nose-diving towards abject failure. But it is undeniable that, though he had tasted bitter gall, his time in the spotlight, where he was heeded, respected, admired and recognised as a leader, meant that Marco could no longer live without the attention. And so, still possessed of a boundless, youthful energy at the age of sixty-four or sixty-five, he immediately set about looking for some way to return to that kind of life.

It did not take him long to find it.

9

In my article "I am Enric Marco," I compared Marco to Don Quixote because both are formidable liars who "cannot reconcile themselves to the greyness of their real lives and so invent and live out a fictitious heroic life." The comparison still seems valid to me, but I now believe there are many other reasons to make it.

Don Quixote is the story of a simple nobleman named Alonso Quixano who, shortly before his fiftieth birthday, having led a mediocre, tedious, unfulfilling existence holed up in a one-horse town in la Mancha, decides to throw everything to the devil and reinvent himself as a knight-errant, setting off to live the life of a hero, an idealistic life brimming with courage, honour and love; Marco's is a similar story: a simple mechanic named Enrique Marco, shortly after his fiftieth birthday, having led a mostly mediocre, tedious, unfulfilling existence holed up in a car repair shop in Barcelona, decides to throw everything to the devil and reinvent himself as a civic hero, setting off to live an idealistic life brimming with courage, honour and love. But there is more. Alonso Quixano is a narcissist, who invents Don Quixote so as not to know himself or to recognise himself, so as to conceal, behind the epic grandeur of Don Quixote, the crass pettiness of his past life and the shame it inspires in him, so that, through Don Quixote, he can lead the noble-minded, tumultuous life he never lived; in Marco's case, his narcissism led him to invent first Enrique Durruti, or Enric Batlle, or Enrique Marcos, implacable working-class libertarian and tireless opponent of Franco, then later Enric Marco, former prisoner of Flossenbürg concentration camp, president of the Amical de Mauthausen, and tireless opponent of the

Nazis, so as to hide behind this heroic mask the mediocrity of his past life and the shame it inspires in him, so that, through Enrique Durruti, or Enric Batlle, or Enrique Marcos and later through Enric Marco, he can lead the great, noble-minded, tumultuous life he never lived. Shortly before his fiftieth birthday, Alonso Quixano gave up the prosaic name Alonso Quixano and adopted the poetic Don Quixote de la Mancha, he abandoned the quotidian affections of his house-keeper and his niece for the dazzling, unattainable love of Dulcinea, he left the bland routines of home for the appetising uncertainties of the byways and taverns of Spain, and left his pitiful life as a nobleman for the adventurous life of a knight-errant; likewise, shortly after his fiftieth birthday, Marco gave up the name Marco and adopted the name Marcos, he abandoned an ageing, uneducated immigrant from Andalucía for a young, educated, elegant half-French girl, he left a working-class suburb of Barcelona for a middle-class suburb, and cast aside the tedious life of a mechanic for the thrilling life of a union leader and champion of political freedom, social justice and historical memory.

More? Like Marco, Don Quixote is hungry for fame and glory, anxious that his exploits should be graven in the memory of the world, eager that men and women should talk about him, love and admire him, consider him an exceptional and heroic individual; like Marco, Don Quixote is a *mediopath*, addicted to being in the limelight. He is also a compulsive reader and, like Marco, has many of the funda-mental qualities of a writer or novelist: energy, fantasy, imagination, memory and a love of words; it is even possible that, like Marco, he is a frustrated novelist: if Alonso Quixano had written a book of chival-ric deeds, perhaps he would never have been Don Quixote, because he would have invested his incomparable talents as a storyteller in his fiction and, through it, vicariously led the life he wished to live, just as the real Marco might perhaps not have created the fictional Marco if he had dreamed up his adventures and lived them vicariously by writing fiction. Above all, Alonso Quixano is an actor: from the age of fifty almost until his death, he plays the role of Don Quixote, just as, from the age of fifty to this day, the true Marco has been playing the fictional Marco. This is central. What defines Don Quixote, just as it defines Marco, is not that he confuses dreams with reality, fiction with reality, or lies with truth, but the fact that he wants to make his dreams a reality, transform lies into truth and fiction into reality. What is extraordinary is that both succeed: one of the things that distinguishes Part One of *Don Quixote* from Part Two is that in Part One, Don Quixote imagines the adventures that happen to him, mistaking windmills for giants and taverns for castles, while in the second volume, the adventures truly happen, or so he believes, winning the hearts of pretty maidens, being shipwrecked, hearing enchanted heads speak and jousting in single combat with other knights-errant; similarly, particularly in the late Seventies, when he was secretary general of the C.N.T., Marco finally got to live the life he imagined, he became a working-class leader, confronting the police and being beaten by them, spending at least a few hours in a police cell for political—or politically related—reasons. But there can be no doubt that though first and foremost an actor, Alonso Quixano was not play-acting the role of Don Quixote; he *was* Don Quixote: he was so deeply immersed in the role that he believed himself to be the character he portrayed, so much so that it would have been impossible to persuade him that he was not Don Quixote but Alonso Quixano. The same was true of Marco, and it's partly for this reason that, after the scandal broke and his deception was unmasked, he did not acknowledge his mistake, did not stay silent, did not know or recognise himself for who he was but refused to accept his true identity and actively defended himself in the press, on the radio, on television and on film. He rushed to defend his imaginary I, the heroic I people were trying to kill, and he tried desperately to shore up the existence of this teetering fictional character with elements of his real past.

Thus Marco is Don Quixote, or a particular version of Don Quixote. In a certain sense—as my son pointed out when he met him—he is a better, more accomplished Don Quixote than the Don himself because, unlike Don Quixote, who has almost no past, Marco has a past and moreover knows that the past is never dead, it is merely an aspect of the present and—as Faulkner says—it's not even past; as a result, as well as reinventing his present, Marco reinvented his past (or reinvented his present by reinventing his past). And he is a better, more accomplished Don Quixote than the Don himself because he succeeds where Don Quixote fails: while Alonso Quixano never succeeded in fooling anyone, everyone knew he was just a poor fool who believed himself to be a gallant hero, Marco convinced everyone that the fictional Marco was the real Marco and that he was a civilian hero. Having said this, some will object that, despite the similarities between Marco and Don Quixote, there is a decisive difference that separates them: Don Quixote is mad, while Marco is not. I don't think this objection is watertight. It's true that Don Quixote is utterly mad, but it's equally true that he is completely sane, and, after a fashion, this is also true of Marco: just as Don Quixote talks gibberish only when speaking about the knight-errant, Marco talks gibberish only when speaking about his exploits as an anti-fascist hero. Marco, too, has a collection of chivalric books: they are his own past.

One last thing. Earlier, I said that perhaps Don Quixote and Marco are frustrated novelists and that, if they had written down their dreams, they might not have tried to live them; I also said, or implied, that Don Quixote and Marco do not seek to turn reality into fiction, but fiction into reality: not to write a novel, but to live it. The two hypotheses are not incompatible, but the latter seems to me much more convincing than the former.

Don Quixote and Marco are not frustrated novelists, they are their own novelists; they would never have been content to write their dreams: they want to play the starring role in them. At the age of fifty, Don Quixote and Marco rebel against their natural destiny, which is, having reached the pinnacle of their lives, to be satisfied with the lives they have lived and to prepare for death; they refuse to acquiesce, refuse to resign themselves, refuse to surrender, they want to carry on living, they want to live more, to experience all that they always dreamed of but never lived. They are prepared to do anything to achieve this; and "anything" means anything: including duping the whole world, persuading everyone that they are the great Don Quixote and the great Enric Marco. Between truth and life, they choose life: if lying brings life and truth kills, they choose lying; if fiction saves and reality kills, they choose fiction. Even if choosing fiction means refusing to acknowledge that there are things one can do in novels but not in life, because the rules of novels and the rules of life

are different; even if choosing lies means flouting one of the basic
principles of our morality and lapsing into Montaigne's "accursed
vice," into a baseness, an aggression, a lack of respect and a violation
of the first rule of human coexistence which requires that we tell the
truth. Like the bird in T. S. Eliot's poem, Nietzsche observed that
humankind cannot bear very much reality and that often truth is inju-
rious to life; this is why he despised our petty, petit-bourgeois morality, the narrow-minded ethics of respectable people who respect the
truth or believe that the truth is respectable, and praised the great lies
that sustain life. Insensible to remorse and to bad conscience, Marco
and Don Quixote seem like Nietzschean heroes: neither immoral nor
amoral but extra-moral. Are they? Is this the unexpected and spectacular means by which Marco transforms himself into a hero? Is Marco
a moral or an extra-moral hero, like Lucifer, a rebel railing not simply against the strictures of bourgeois morality, but the strictures of
reality? Is this how, having spent his life saying Yes and siding with
the majority, Marco finally, unexpectedly said No and sided with the
minority?

I would like to say yes. I say: yes, but only in part. Marco invented
a past for himself (or embellished it or gilded it) at a moment when,
all around him in Spain, almost everyone was embellishing, or gild-
ing, or inventing a past; Marco reinvented his life at a moment when
the entire country was reinventing itself. This is what happened during the transition from dictatorship to democracy in Spain. With
Franco dead, almost everyone began to construct a past to better face
the present and prepare for the future. Politicians, intellectuals and
journalists of the first, second and third rank did it, but also people
from all walks of life, left-wingers and right-wingers, eager to prove
that they had always been democrats, that during the Franco regime
they had been clandestine opponents, *official pariahs*, silent resistants,
dormant or active anti-Francoists. Not everyone lied with the same
skill, shamelessness and insistence, obviously, and few succeeded in
inventing a whole new identity; the majority were content to titivate
or embellish their past (or to finally lift the veil on a private life fear-
fully concealed or opportunistically hidden until now). But whatever
they did, they did so with no moral qualms, or few moral qualms,
knowing that everyone around them was doing much the same thing

and therefore everyone accepted it or tolerated it, certainly no-one was interested in delving into anyone's past because everyone had something to hide: in short, in the mid-Seventies, the whole country was carrying the burden of forty years of dictatorship during which almost no-one had said No and almost everyone had said Yes, a regime with which almost everyone had collaborated by choice or by force and from which almost everyone had profited, a reality that they tried to hide or mask or embellish just as Marco hid or masked or embellished his. The country invented a fictitious individual and collective past, a noble and heroic past in which very few people in Spain had supported Franco, in which most had been resistance fighters or anti-Franco dissidents including those who had never lifted a finger against the regime or those who had worked side by side with it.

This is the reality: at least during the years of transition between dictatorship and democracy, Spain as a country was as narcissistic as Marco; it's also true, therefore, that democracy in Spain was built on a lie, whether an enormous collective lie or a long series of individual lies. Could it have been built any other way? Can democracy be built on truth? Could the whole country honestly have recognised itself for what it was, in the horror, the shame, the cowardice and the mediocrity of its past, and forged ahead regardless? Could it have recognised or known itself, like Narcissus, and yet not died of an excess of reality like Narcissus? Or was this great collective lie one of Plato's noble lies, one of Montaigne's altruistic lies, one of Nietzsche's vital lies? I don't know. What I do know is that, during those years, Marco's lies about his past were not the exception but the rule, that he did no more than take to extremes what was a common practice at the time: when the scandal broke, Marco couldn't defend himself by saying this, but he must surely have considered it. I also know that, though no-one dared to take their deception as far as Marco took his, perhaps because no-one had sufficient energy, talent and ambition, in this, our man—in part, at least in part—sided with the majority.

10

Marco is utterly incapable of keeping still. In the mid-Eighties, after he had been pushed out of the C.N.T. and realised he had no future as a union leader, our man became a director of FaPaC, a progressive organisation that brought together most of the state school parents' associations in Catalonia. Marco had joined the C.N.T. at a moment of great political mobilisation after the death of Franco, when people, excited by the promise of the new democracy, were rushing to join trade unions and political parties; Marco joined FaPaC at a moment of great political demobilisation that resulted from a general disillusionment with democracy or the workings of democracy (or simply the stabilisation of democracy), when people were deserting political and trade union activism in favour of returning to their own lives, or taking shelter in the community activism of organisations. Marco joined the C.N.T. at the kind of moment of crisis and confusion, not to say chaos, in which he thrives like no-one else; the point at which he joined FaPaC wasn't very different.

At the time—this took place in 1987—the second left-wing Spanish government in forty years was preparing a general educational law, the so-called L.O.G.S.E., which many socialists considered not very socialist, because they felt it benefited private schools to the detriment of state schools. This disagreement triggered protests and demonstrations. It also triggered the fall of the directors of FaPaC, who were socialist, as was the left-wing government; or perhaps the leaders of FaPaC were simply pro-socialist or were accused of being pro-socialist, certainly they were accused of collaborating with the socialist government or not being sufficiently combative in opposing the socialist government's law. What is certain is that, at the Annual General Meeting of FaPaC at Cocheras de Sants, in Barcelona, there was a revolt against the leadership, which, after only a few months—at an Extraordinary General Meeting at the Centro Cívico de La Sedeta in Barcelona—resulted in the socialist or pro-socialist board being replaced by a communist or pro-communist board, an understandable change of political direction since this was a grass-roots movement that had immediately been taken over by the communist party. Marco attended both meetings as a representative of his daughter Elizabeth's school (Ona, who was two at the time, wasn't yet in school) and although he was not communist or pro-communist and was not among the leaders of the revolt, he was there during its gestation, spurred it on, and manipulated events such that, in the midst of this confused mutiny, he managed to get himself elected to the board. He would not leave the board until thirteen years later, when he was forced to step down because his daughters were no longer of school age and he could no longer play a role in FaPaC. At this revolutionary or post-revolutionary E.G.M. in La Sedeta, dozens of others were also elected to serve the board, most of whom would gradually give up their posts. Marco did the reverse; gradually, through hard work and perseverance, he made himself indispensable and quickly rose to become vice-president and FaPaC delegate for Barcelona.

This was the post he held when my sister Blanca met him in the late Eighties, when she joined the board of FaPaC. And so, when I seriously began work on this book after years of hesitant fumblings, I asked Blanca to talk to me about Marco again. I say "again," because she had already spoken to me about him shortly after the scandal broke, at the dinner I'd organised at my house with my wife, my son, and two colleagues from the university—Anna María García and Xavier Pla—but since that day we'd barely spoken on the subject. Now I asked if we could go back to it, there was no hurry, and one Saturday afternoon in early February 2013, while we were having a beer in a bar near my mother's house in Gerona, we talked about Marco. Though Raül wasn't there because he was running in La Devesa park, my wife Mercè, who from the outset had shown as much interest in Marco as Raül, was present; unlike Raül, Mercè hadn't personally met Marco, though she could easily have encountered him—in the late Seventies when she was active in the C.N.T. as a pretty young libertarian fascinated by elderly libertarians like Marco. As for my sister Blanca, she is a woman of iron, who survived two brutal separations, a motley crew of lovers and two potentially fatal illnesses—hepatitis C and ulcerative colitis—that resulted in a series of painful, life-threatening operations and long stays in the hospital.

"For about ten years, I was constantly in touch with him," Blanca began that afternoon. The three of us were sitting around a table on the terrace of the bar: on either side of us were groups of people chatting and sipping aperitifs and, in front of us, on the plaza Pau Casals, young parents and their children were playing on the swings and enjoying the dazzling winter sunshine; the Chinese family who managed the bar bustled about serving customers. "Constantly. And we got along well, to be honest," Blanca continued. "Especially after I was appointed vice-president and Gerona delegate for FaPaC, the same position Marco held in Barcelona; his opposite number, if you like. After that, we saw each other regularly and talked on the phone almost every day. People can say what they like, but I always thought he was amazing, he had an extraordinary energy, he was entertaining, funny, charming. He was forever telling jokes. He tried to charm everyone, especially the women. I've always liked men who like women, but I've never met one who liked them as much as Marco. Though what Marco really liked was to be the centre of attention."

"Yes," I interrupted, "Marco is fond of the limelight."

"Fond of it? No, he's obsessed with it." Blanca laughed. She took a sip of her beer and said, "He had a lot of power within FaPaC. Don't get me wrong, it wasn't handed to him on a silver platter: those of us with positions on the board worked there in our spare time, because we were all volunteers so we had to earn a living elsewhere; not Marco, he was a volunteer too, but he had retired and could give a hundred per cent of his time to the organisation. He was never president, though it seemed like he was because he was the only one with an office in the FaPaC building and even a parking space at the Ministry of Education, the only one with a direct line to the Counsellor, he talked to her all the time. Besides, he took care of the day-to-day running of FaPaC, he was the manager and the president's right-hand man. Actually, I think that for outsiders who had dealings with FaPaC

but weren't members, Marco *was* FaPaC. Not for those in the organisation, obviously. We thought of him more as a bit of a rogue, a
colourful character; and I'm not saying he wasn't, but that doesn't
mean he didn't have power or didn't play an important role in FaPaC.
That's the way I see it. Although, if you're going to write about this,
you should talk to other people who worked with him at FaPaC."

"I'd love to," I said.

"If you like, I can talk to a couple of people who were members
of the board at the time. I'll suggest we get together and you can
join us."

"That sounds great," I said. "Tell me something else: did Marco
talk much about his past? I mean . . ."

"All the time," Blanca interrupted me, "about his time as a soldier
during the Civil War, about being an anti-Franco resistance fighter,
about his time as head of the C.N.T., about his past as a prisoner in a
Nazi concentration camp and I don't know what else. It was the basis
of his authority, his way of getting attention, of asserting himself, of
shutting other people up, or trying to at least, and he used it whenever
necessary. Wasn't it around this time that he started giving talks in
schools about the Nazis?"

"I think so," I said, "I think it was around the time when he was
about to leave FaPaC but hadn't yet joined the Amical de Mauthausen."

"He was a charmer," said Blanca, "and he charmed a lot of people.
He portrayed himself as a hero, and there were people who thought he
was. I think at some point he became untouchable, and not just within
FaPaC. He got along well with politicians and leaders. The members
of the Generalitat adored him, and he loved them; I remember he
used to say to me 'Listen, Blanquita, even though they're right-wing
and we have different points of view, we still have to get along with
them.' You get the idea: he wasn't a radical, he was a reasonable guy
and reasonably effective, which, now that I think of it, seems pretty
strange given he was the most disorganised and unsystematic person
I've ever met in my life. I don't know. When the scandal broke, I
heard a lot of people say they'd seen it coming, they sensed Marco
was a phoney, they'd never believed him, but I think that's garbage:
the truth is that Marco fooled everybody, and everyone swallowed
it hook, line and sinker. Or almost everyone. Obviously there were

some things that jumped out at you: the fact that he was desperate to hog the limelight as you put it; but it's not as though Marco even tried to hide that. Not that he could have, even if he'd wanted to."

Then Blanca recounted an anecdote. I don't remember the exact date she said it happened, but I remember the place: the corner of calle Pelayo, in the centre of Barcelona, where a protest march was about to set off protesting against L.O.G.S.E., the education reform bill that the left-wing government had been debating for several years and finally ratified in October 1990. The demonstration had been organised by a collection of various educational groups, including FaPaC, and before it got started, the leaders of those organisations were discussing precisely where they and the politicians and the union leaders joining them should be on the march. They argued about it for a while. By the time they reached a decision, Blanca and her colleagues from FaPaC realised Marco was no longer with them, and started looking for him in the crowd, shouting his name. Finally they found him: he had paid no attention to the decision and was calmly standing at the front of the crowd, clutching the banner meant to lead the march as though afraid someone else would take the privileged position he wasn't prepared to give up for anything.

Blanca ended the story with a loud laugh. I smiled and thought about Raül's comment, "He's the fucking master!"

Mercè's expression was inscrutable. "Poor guy," she said.

"That's not the way everyone sees him," I said, eager to contrast her view with ours, or at least to get her to talk. Then, remembering the meal we'd organised at home when the scandal first broke, and the judgement passed on him by Anna María García, I added, "In fact most people think he's despicable."

"Well I still think he's a poor bastard," said Mercè.

"I don't remember him as being despicable," Blanca admitted, "and I bet no-one in FaPaC thinks of him like that. I'm not saying that what he did wasn't despicable, but *he* wasn't despicable. At least during the time I knew him, he never did any harm to anyone. He wasn't out for money, and he wasn't a social climber. He just wanted to be famous. But, I don't know, whenever there was a workers' dispute at FaPaC he always sided with the workers. Someone despicable wouldn't do that." She picked up her almost-empty glass of beer, and as she raised it to her lips for a final sip, she looked at me and said, "Now that I think of it, you know the word he used most often?" She drained the glass. "Truthfully," she said. She laughed again. "Truthfully," she said again, "I always associate that word with him."

I realised Blanca was right, but I didn't say so. I said:

"Me, I associate him with Don Quixote. Raül did too when he first met him. Marco is like Don Quixote because he lived a grey, boring life until he decided to invent a new identity, a new life, to turn himself into a hero, to live it up and experience all the things he hadn't been able to experience until then. More or less what Don Quixote did."

"And who exactly did Marco hurt by doing that?" asked Mercè.

"Marco would ask the same question," I answered. "He says everyone lies and at least his lies were truthful. He claims he never said anything false, which is false. He says he lied for a noble cause. That kind of thing."

"Lying isn't a crime," said Mercè.

"Sometimes it is," I said. "But nobody likes to be lied to."

"True," Mercè admitted. "Look, I can understand that the people who were fooled by him are angry, after all he took them for a ride; I can even understand that most people are a little angry, because he fooled everyone. What I don't understand is why he gets attacked so relentlessly when this country is full of bastards who have murdered, robbed and done all sorts of disgusting things, and nobody seems to go after them: in fact, people kiss their asses."

It was almost 2:00 p.m. By now, Raül would be at my mother's house, showered and ready for lunch, as would my mother, but despite this I went up to the bar and ordered another round of beers. Back at the table, as I was handing Blanca her drink, she said:

"I was just saying to Mercè that Marco would love to know that we're talking about him, but I'm not so sure he'd want to know that she thinks he's a poor bastard."

"And I was saying that I don't care what Marco thinks," said Mercè. "As far as I'm concerned, he's still a poor bastard."

"Wait till you meet him," I said.

"Yes," said Blanca, "wait till you meet him."

Truthfully, Blanca was right: the word Marco most often uses is "truthfully." Not "true," not "truly" but "truthfully." Truthfully this, truthfully that, truthfully the other. I knew it from the first time I talked to Marco, that day Santi Fillol introduced me to him in Sant Cugat, or perhaps when Raül started recording him in my office as he told me his life story, but I only knew that I knew when my sister said it. In a number of radio and television recordings, as he recounts his fictitious experience in Flossenbürg, Marco uses this word several times in the space of a few minutes, sometimes even a few seconds, as though stuck on it. Especially during his years with the Amical de Mauthausen, the years when he took on the role of hero and champion of so-called historical memory, Marco presented himself as an evangelist of the hidden or forgotten or unheeded truth of the horrors of the twentieth century and its victims. Truthfully, evangelists of truth are not to be trusted. Truthfully, just as an insistence on bravery betrays the coward, an insistence on truth betrays the liar. Truthfully. All insistence is a form of concealment or deception. A form of narcissism. A form of kitsch.

A month and a half after our conversation about Marco on the terrace of the bar in Gerona, Blanca organised a dinner with the two friends from FaPaC she'd told me about that afternoon. The dinner was at La Troballa, a restaurant near my office in Gracia that I often went to at the time. When I arrived, the three of them were already waiting for me in the inner courtyard.

Blanca introduced me to her friends. The woman was Montse Cardona, she was small and lively, about the same age as my sister, forty-five; Joan Amézaga was a man in his sixties with white hair and a white beard, and steel-rimmed glasses. Before leaving my office, I'd looked him up on the internet: he was married with two children and for eight years he had been mayor of Tàrrega, a small town in Lérida; since the early Eighties, he'd been a member or a supporter of the Socialist Party and was involved in local politics. As for Montse, my sister had told me she was a social worker, that she lived with her father and her son in Agramunt, a town in Lérida even smaller than Tàrrega, and that she was a militant, or had been for many years, a member of left-wing parties so extreme that Amézaga and my sister cheerfully made fun of her, or perhaps they were mocking the idea that Montse could be a militant. Whatever the case, as soon as I sat down it was obvious the three were happy to see each other again.

It took no effort from me to steer the conversation to Marco. In fact, as soon as his name was mentioned, the three of them immediately seized on the subject, and while I listened to their jumbled conversation about Marco's talent as a people person, his need to charm, to be loved and admired and heeded, about his vanity and his energy and his hyperactivity, his ability to always say precisely what people wanted to hear, his ability to avoid conflict and to sidestep confrontation with anyone, I wondered whether they were talking about Marco because my sister had told them I was interested, whether they talked about Marco every time they met up, whether these meetings were simply an excuse to talk about Marco, or, on the contrary, maybe Marco was an excuse for them to continue meeting up, the secret thread that had kept their friendship alive since the three of them had left FaPaC. I quickly understood why my sister had suggested I talk to them; as she herself had said at the bar in Gerona, her concept of Marco, or Marco's role within FaPaC, was very different from theirs: none of them had taken Marco particularly seriously, and all three saw him as rather a comic character—which contrasted with the absolute seriousness with which he was regarded by members of the C.N.T. and the Amical de Mauthausen—but whereas Blanca thought Marco had played a decisive role in FaPaC, Amézaga and Montse thought not, or not so much.

"Enric was vice-president of FaPaC," Amézaga reminded me. The waiter had brought the first course but I was so focused on the conversation that I don't remember what we ordered, nor did I write it on the pad where I take notes. I do remember that they'd already slaked their thirst with beer and had moved on to wine, and that I didn't drink beer or wine. "Vice-president and delegate for Barcelona. While the two of us," he gestured to Montse and himself, "were simply the representatives for Lérida on the board."

"And I was vice-president and delegate for Gerona," said Blanca. "But, since Marco was the most visible face of FaPaC, and in all the papers, everyone assumed he was president."

"And he would have loved to have been president," said Amézaga.

"Are you sure?" said Blanca.

"Absolutely," said Amézaga. "And he would have been a logical choice, given that he dedicated more time to the organisation and did the most work. After all, he was retired so he had nothing else to do. The problem was he didn't have the stature to be president; the stature or the ability or the skillset, nothing: one day he'd say one thing and the next day he'd tell you the complete opposite. The fact is, his opinion didn't matter, in FaPaC or outside it. You know what Enric's like," he added, turning to me. "He's pure chaos."

"That's true," said Montse. "One of the things I noticed about Enric was his chaotic ideology. He was supposed to be an anarchist, but he would suddenly come out with proposals that were neoliberal, or ultra-liberal. He had no clear criteria, he didn't even really know what he wanted, he accepted all sorts of crazy things from the administration, he could come out with completely unexpected ideas."

"Of course," said Amézaga, "that's why he never opposed anyone or got into an argument with anyone; when things got heated, he shut up. He could talk and talk and talk, but no-one knew what he was saying, or he wasn't really saying anything. He wasn't even a good manager."

"I'm not sure I agree with that," said Blanca. "I think he managed reasonably well. Not as well as the rest of us, obviously, but . . ."

The three burst out laughing. I couldn't join them because I was simultaneously eating and taking notes.

"No, but seriously," Blanca said, "I was saying to my brother the other day, Enric *was* FaPaC, he handled the day-to-day administration, the president and the administrator did nothing without consulting him, he worked all hours, he was constantly talking on the phone to the Minister of Education. Did you know he had a parking space at the Ministry?"

"No," said Amézaga.

"No," said Montse, "but it doesn't surprise me."

"Me neither," said Amézaga. "But I don't see the contradiction, Blanca: OK, so it's true that Enric had power, that for many people he was the face of FaPaC, that he had a finger in every pie; you'd know better than we would, you saw him and spoke to him much more often than we did. But whether Enric's opinion was respected and heeded and followed within FaPaC is a different matter, and the fact is, his opinion meant nothing. You remember the C.E.A.P.A. meetings?"

The question was rhetorical, and the three immediately began talking about the meetings of the Confederación Española de Asociaciones de Padres de Alumnos held every year in Madrid; all three

had attended on various occasions together with other members of
FaPaC, including Marco. No-one allowed Marco to get a word in
during the two or three days that the meeting lasted and if, by some
miracle, he managed to say something, no-one paid any heed. I interrupted their laughing to ask Amézaga how Marco had come to be at
FaPaC, and how he had managed to hold such an important post for
so many years.

"It pains me to say it, *hombre,* but the truth is you don't need to
be Pericles to be a board member at FaPaC," he said, and Blanca and
Montse burst out laughing again. "It's a lot stranger that he managed
to be secretary general of the C.N.T., don't you think?"

"Couldn't agree more," said Montse.

"Though, obviously, given the state of the C.N.T. back then . . ."
Amézaga needled.

"Couldn't agree less!" Montse interrupted him.

This time, all three of them laughed and I noted that we had
become the centre of attention on the terrace of La Troballa.

"But while we're on the subject," Amézaga continued, too cheerful or too engrossed in the conversation to notice the looks trained
on us, "do you know how Enric ended up on the board of FaPaC?"

I said I did, or at least I thought I did. We talked about the meeting at Cocheras de Sants and the E.G.M. at La Sedeta in the late
Eighties where Marco was elected to the board of FaPaC. Amézaga
told me he had been at both meetings, and didn't contradict my version of events.

"It was like the storming of the Winter Palace," he said. "And
when you storm the Winter Palace, anything can happen, including
someone like Enric ending up on the board."

Amézaga's explanation was so categorical that for a moment,
everyone around the table fell silent. They made the most of this to
drink their wine, while I finished off my main course, or maybe it was
dessert.

"An angel passing," said Montse.

Before any of them could react, I asked Montse and Amézaga
the question I had asked Blanca a month earlier: whether Marco had
talked a lot about his past. Their response was the same: all the time.

"But none of us even questioned whether or not he was telling the truth, if that's what you're asking," said Amézaga. "We all thought it was Enric's business, end of story. Isn't that right, Blanquita?"

Blanca didn't have time to answer; Montse cut in.

"I never believed the stories Enric told," she said.

"OK," I said, remembering one of Blanca's objections, "but everyone says that now, now they know he was lying."

"OK," Montse echoed, shrugging her shoulders, "but that's what I thought back then. You can believe me or not, but it's true. Listen," she went on, "back then I had a lot of dealings with old left-wing militants, people who had fought in the Civil War, people who had been in the resistance. And Marco wasn't like them."

"In what way?" I said.

"He just wasn't," said Montse. "He had too much energy, he was too quick to tell his little war stories, too quick to talk about everything. The real veterans didn't talk much; they were reserved, they were older, they didn't revel in past defeats. But Marco never stopped talking. I'm not saying I didn't find his war stories entertaining, because I did, I found them very entertaining. But I took them with a grain of salt; that's what Joan used to say, when you listen to Enric, it's like listening to someone telling you the story of a movie. That's how I saw it: he was like a guy who told stories from the movies to keep us entertained. And he did, my God did he entertain us. But it was nothing more than that. Besides, like I said, politically he was a strange animal: he was supposed to have been a left-wing militant, but he didn't talk like a left-wing militant, and certainly not like a leader of the C.N.T."

"I saw him as a bit of a phoney," said Amézaga. "A survivor. A hustler, a con artist who's had to look out for himself ever since he was a kid and knows just how to do it. I hate cheap psychology (and even expensive psychology), but I've always gotten the impression that Enric was the sort of guy who was bullied as a child and as a teenager and grew up with such a terrible lack of affection that he's tried to make up for it any way he can."

"He needed people to love him," Montse agreed, "he needed to be loved and admired. He couldn't stand being ignored."

At this point, Blanca reminded them of the incident she had mentioned to me, which they had also witnessed, when they lost Marco while preparing for a protest march in Barcelona and, having looked for him everywhere, found him clutching the banner at the head of the march, panicked at the thought that he might not be in the limelight. They laughed again, loud and long this time, and in that moment I realised that, like Blanca, they laughed about Marco affectionately.

"That's what I was trying to say the other day," Blanca said when I pointed this out to them, "Enric could always get people to love him."

"We all loved him," Montse agreed. "How could you not? He was charming, he was funny, he was affectionate, he told great stories. He's like a child, you end up forgiving him no matter what he does."

"What Montse is saying sounds weird, I know, but it's true," said Amézaga, trying to catch my eye as I took notes. "Let me put it plainly, Javier. As far as I'm concerned, in telling the lies he told, Marco committed a mortal sin, but if he came through that door right now, I'd be delighted to see him, I'd give him a hug and invite him to dinner; whereas someone else might commit a venial sin and I wouldn't want to set eyes on him again. I remember the day the scandal broke. If it had been anyone else who had done what he did, I would have thought, 'Evil scumbag, how could he make up that stuff.' But with Enric, I thought, 'Fucking hell, what a mess. How is he going to wriggle out of this one?' Just like that. Of course, to be brutally honest, I wasn't really that surprised. Not that I suspected the stuff about the concentration camp was a lie, but I wasn't surprised that it was. Not coming from him. Everything suddenly slotted into place, it almost seemed normal. But that's how I reacted; I can understand why other people reacted differently. I remember, not long after his deception was unmasked, I met a young guy who had gone with Marco to a meeting or a conference or something like that, and really admired him. This guy stopped me in the street, heart-broken, and told me he couldn't believe it: 'I can't get it out of my head,' he said."

"I remember that day too," said Blanca. "I remember I called him up at home and said, 'What the hell is going on, Enric?' And he said, 'Listen, *chica*, I screwed up, but I can explain everything.'"

"I had the same reaction," said Montse. "I didn't actually phone him, but it didn't seem all that strange to me. I know you'll say it's easy to say that in hindsight, but I always thought something like that might happen, I sensed it, I was always afraid of how Enric might end up. It's not just that I didn't believe what he said, it's that, I don't know, he was overblown, larger than life, he was in a position he had no business being in, he had risen too far, like a balloon that might explode at any moment. I felt bad, to be honest. And I felt bad about the way he left FaPaC. I don't know about you guys, but I didn't get the impression that he left because his daughters had grown up and he no longer had a role there, but because people were fed up with him, they didn't love him anymore."

No-one chimed in with Montse's observation, perhaps because Amézaga pointed out that we were the only people left on the terrace of La Troballa. Blanca insisted on paying for dinner, and as we left the restaurant, the four of us wandered back towards my office. Only then did Amézaga nod to my notepad and ask whether I was thinking about writing a book about Marco; Blanca and Montse didn't hear him, because they had walked on ahead. I told Amézaga that I was.

"Well, don't publish it while he's still alive," he said.

"Don't worry," I said, to calm him, "Marco knows I'm going to tell the truth; that was the deal we made. And he knows that I can't rehabilitate him. Even if I wanted to, I couldn't."

"That's not what I meant," Amézaga said. "Knowing Enric, I don't think he'd want you to redeem him, among other reasons because I'm sure he's realised that he damned himself all on his own. No. He doesn't want you to rehabilitate him, he wants you to write a whole book about him, preferably a big thick book. That would make him happy and, frankly, I don't think he deserves that happiness."

Amézaga fell silent and I remembered the words Anna María García had said to me three years earlier: "The best thing to do about Marco is forget him," she had said. "That would be the worst punishment for such a monstrous egotist."

Amézaga spoke again. "Although, now I think about it, maybe that's not true: on the one hand Enric probably wants you to write the book, and on the other he's afraid you will and thinks your book will be the final verdict, the last nail in his coffin."

On the corner of the street where my office is located, there was an Irish pub. Blanca and Montse suggested they go in; Amézaga agreed, and I said my goodbyes. I felt a pang of jealousy, I don't know whether it was because of the drinking session they were about to embark on or because I imagined that, even though I was no longer there (or precisely because of it), they would keep talking about Marco. Before leaving, I asked them a stupid question, one I'd never asked anybody though I'd wanted to for a long time: I asked whether they believed Marco was an ordinary man or an extraordinary man. The three of them chorused:

"Extraordinary!"

I went up to my office; I didn't need to jot down their reply on my notepad.

PART III

The Flight of Icarus

I

When was the first time? When did Marco first say he had been a prisoner at Flossenbürg? Where did he say it? To whom did he say it? I don't know precisely; nor do I think that even Marco knows. All indications, however, are that it must have happened around 1977.

At the time, Marco was fifty-six and had already been lying about his past for some considerable time, or at least embellishing it or embroidering it, mixing lies with truth. Franco was two years dead and the country was completely reinventing itself; as was Marco: he had furnished himself with a personal history as an anti-Franco resistance fighter, had changed his name, his wife, his home, his city, and almost his job since, though he was still a mechanic, he was principally a trade union leader at the C.N.T. Marco was studying history at the Autonomous University, and one day he came across a book entitled *La deportación*, published in 1969 by Ediciones Petronio. It was a translation of a French text offering an overview of the Nazi camps. The book contained a chapter on the subject of Flossenbürg; in this chapter, there were various photographs of the camp: photos of the barracks and the watchtowers, of prisoners working in the quarry, of the cremation furnace, of Reichsführer-SS Heinrich Himmler visiting the facilities. One of these pictures caught Marco's attention. It depicted a monument on which were engraved the number and the nationalities of prisoners who died in the camp; Marco noticed that among them were people from most European countries, and more especially, Spaniards, but very few: fourteen, to be exact. This information was inaccurate—which is important in the context of history with a capital H, but in our story matters little. What is important is that, when he saw the photograph, Marco, with the infallible sense of a compulsive liar, knew instinctively that the tiny number of

Spaniards who died made it possible for him to fabricate a stay in a lesser-known concentration camp he had never heard of, with only the remotest possibility that anyone could contradict him; after all, at the time, Marco knew very little about the Nazi camps, but he knew three things that were crucial to his deception: firstly, most people in Spain knew even less about the subject than he did; secondly, very few Spaniards had been in the Nazi camps; thirdly, the vast majority of these had been in Mauthausen. Years later, Marco assured me that, as soon as he saw this photograph, he decided to pass himself off as a prisoner of Flossenbürg to bear witness to the memory of the four-teen dead Spaniards whom nobody now remembered. Bullshit: Marco decided to pass himself off as a prisoner of Flossenbürg because he couldn't resist the temptation to add a new chapter to the story of the anti-fascist resistance fighter he'd been crafting for years.

He added it immediately. As I said: I don't know to whom he told this first lie, whether to his wife, whom he had just won over and with whom he was living in Sant Cugat, to his comrades in the C.N.T., or to his friends at the university, whom he had also suc-ceeded in charming; what I do know is that, that same year, two men who were jointly writing a book about Spanish Republicans who had been sent to the Nazi camps heard that Marco had been among them and went to visit him. From a documentary or historiographical point of view, at least, the subject was virgin territory (or almost: in the same year the novelist Montserrat Roig wrote a long article on the subject, though this was limited to Catalan prisoners); the two men in question were Maríano Constante and Eduardo Pons Prades. Con-stante was a communist and a survivor of Mauthausen concentration camp; Pons Prades was an anarchist and a prolific writer, and our man knew him because he was a member of the union of liberal profes-sions within the C.N.T. It was to Pons Prades that Marco told his story. He did so with his usual skill, intermingling his real and his fictitious past, but most importantly he did so cautiously, because he'd had neither sufficient time nor interest to manufacture a biography as a camp prisoner, something that was of little value in Spain at the time, and consequently he couldn't lie safely with convincing details; in fact, in his account to Pons Prades, Marco devoted only a single sentence to his time in the camp, a diabolically effective sentence, admittedly, formulated as a safeguard or a loophole in the event that he was challenged by witnesses: "I spent very little time in Flossenbürg, and since I was transferred from one place to another and was kept in solitary confinement, I could not make contact with anyone." The remainder of the story, which is also brief, we already know: it recounts his fictitious membership in the U.J.A. after the Civil War, his fictitious furtive departure from Spain, his fictitious incarceration in Marseille and his fictitious time in a subcamp of Flossenbürg; also his exploits during the Civil War and his time in Kiel prison, both true—true but glossed with a veneer of the heroism and sentimentality Marco favoured in such cases.

The book by Constante and Pons Prades was published in 1978 and in the same year, Pons Prades included an abridged version of Marco's story, with some variations, in a pioneering article that appeared in the magazine *Tiempo de Historia* about the Spanish Republicans imprisoned in Nazi camps. Marco wasn't very happy with either of these versions, not because they didn't correspond to the story he'd told Pons Prades, but probably because he immediately realised they were wrong. He had managed to elbow his way into the photograph, but it was a blurred, washed-out photograph. During this period of collective metamorphosis, everyone in Spain understood the power of the past, Marco better than anyone, but he had just recycled part of his true past—his time as a volunteer worker in Kiel in the 1940s—without having the information to construct a solid fictional past. It's clear that at this point in his life, Marco was ashamed of having been a volunteer worker in Hitler's Germany, but he must have wondered whether the experience might be of genuine use—particularly the episode of his arrest and imprisonment—beyond the anecdotal use he had made of it in the two published accounts of his time in Germany. In these, Marco had linked his fictional time in Flossenbürg with his genuine time in Kiel prison without giving it much thought. Now he must have been wondering whether it would be easier to fabricate a connection, make it more convincing, whether he could shore up his time in Kiel. Could he? What evidence was there of his presence in Nazi Germany? The important thing was to be able to control this hidden part of his past, he must have thought; afterwards he could decide what to do with it.

This hypothetical reasoning (or something like it) would explain why, on April 12 of that year, Marco wrote to the Spanish consul in Kiel requesting information about his time in Germany thirty-five years earlier. The letter is postmarked Barcelona and bears the seal and the letterhead of the C.N.T. To give greater impetus to his request, Marco signed it as secretary general, C.N.T. Spain; in fact that was not his title—he would be elected to the post precisely ten days later—at the time he was merely secretary general of the Catalonia chapter of the C.N.T. The letter reads:

To the attention of the Spanish Consul,

We would like to request information about Enrique Marco Batlle, a Spanish national, who was stationed in the Deutsche Werke camp in Kiel, located in Bordesholm.

He was arrested by the Gestapo in Kiel on March 7, 1942.

Remanded to Kiel prison, but does not remember the precise date.

Charged with conspiring against the Third Reich.

Tried by a Court Martial, date unknown.

Transferred to a Gestapo prison, about which he remembers only that it was located on Blumenstrasse.

Transferred to Flensburg or Flossenbürg camp.

Liberated by British Forces in 1945.

All documentation for the period having disappeared, as it pertains to this person, we would be grateful if you could take an interest in the matter and provide us with such documentation and proofs as attest to the abovementioned facts.

By the same token, we would be grateful if you could furnish us with an address for Bruno and Kathy Shankowitz, residents of Ellerbeck, Kiel.

We remain, señor, yours faithfully,
For the Secretariat of the National Committee
Secretary General, Enrique Marco Batlle

P.S. During this same period, he was listed as missing by the International Red Cross.

To judge from the letter, Marco's fears about his fictional status as a camp prisoner were justified, as was his worry that he had been inaccurate. He doesn't even seem to know that it was the Americans, not the British, who liberated Flossenbürg, nor even how Flossenbürg is spelled (so hesitates between it and Flensburg, a town near Kiel). I would highlight three other details in the letters: Marco did not forget Bruno and Kathy Shankowitz, his friends and guardian angels in Kiel; he signs himself Marco, the name he went by in Germany, rather than Marcos, the name he went by when he signed this letter and while he was leader of the C.N.T.; Marco seems to be attempting to rectify the story of his time in Germany, or at least explore the possibility, perhaps so as to make the story more consistent and not to have to hide the fact that he was a voluntary worker: who knows whether Marco was trying to change the story of his time in Germany to that of the many Spaniards who, like him, went there willingly, but, unlike him, ended up in a Nazi camp against their will. Who knows.

Marco's letter received no response. Marco forgot about it; his post as secretary general of the C.N.T. during a period marked by great hopes, abrupt reversals and fierce internal struggles kept him sufficiently occupied such that he didn't have time to concern himself with anything other than his work at the union. He didn't think about the matter again (or there is no evidence that he thought about it) until four years later, when the transition from dictatorship to democracy was almost over, the C.N.T. had splintered into a thousand pieces, he had been expelled from the union and was languishing in one of the factions created by the schism, uncertain about his future and eager to find somewhere to invest that perpetual uncertainty, somewhere that might provide relief for his mediopathy. In March 1982, Marco wrote again to the Spanish consul in Kiel; this time he did so as a private individual, without the seal and the letterhead of the C.N.T., addressing it from his home in Sant Cugat. Marco enclosed a copy of his original letter, reiterated his request for information, justifying it by saying "I am motivated by no other intention than to document this period of my life which remains, even to me, somewhat mysterious." Regretfully, he adds, "The lives of public figures are subject to certain constraints and in my case I find myself obliged to prove the how and wherefore of these events."

This time, Marco was more fortunate: and at the end of the following month, he received a letter from the Consul General of Spain in Hamburg. It was dated April 21, 1982, and in it the diplomat, Eduardo Junco, informed him that the first letter had never been received since there was no consulate in Kiel and the second had arrived only thanks to the Prussian diligence of the German postal service; he also informed Marco that he had initiated proceedings to obtain the requested information. He was unable to obtain much. Although the Spanish diplomat wrote to Marco several times over the following year, the only thing he managed to discover was that at the Missing Persons service of the West German Red Cross, there was no record of him. In mid-1983, the letters stopped; perhaps the consul realised it was a vain search; perhaps Marco grew tired of asking him to continue. The fact is that, some time later, Marco found a position at FaPaC and lost all interest in researching his true past in Kiel and using his fictitious past as a prisoner in Flossenbürg.

His interest was not rekindled until fifteen years later, in the late Nineties. By this time, Marco knew that his days as vice-president of FaPaC were numbered—in principle, one could only remain a member of FaPaC while one had children of school age, and his elder daughter had already left school, and the younger was about to—so he realised that he would have to look for a new occupation suited to his energy levels and his requirements. It was at this point that he remembered the Amical de Mauthausen, the association that represented almost all the prisoners of the Nazi camps in Spain. Marco had known of the existence of the Amical for many years, but only now did he think of approaching them. He had felt no need to do so before, being busy with other responsibilities; nor could he have done so, in part because there were too many survivors likely to uncover his deception and in part because he hadn't yet crafted a character plausible enough to risk meeting with genuine survivors of the camps. Having decided that now was the time to join Amical, since the number of survivors was steadily declining, and those who remained were now very old, Marco set about the serious work of constructing his character. The first thing he needed to do was control his true past in Germany, so his first effort, in late 1998, was to write again to the General Consul in Hamburg. The consul wrote back, referring Marco to the consular head of social services, José Pellicer, and so the two entered into correspondence as they sought out any traces of our man in Germany; Marco's implicit aim being to rewrite his time in the country, his explicit aim to claim compensation as a victim of the Nazis.

Not content with this, however, in early 1999, during the Christmas holidays, Marco travelled to Germany with his wife and visited Kiel. It was a disappointing visit, at least from what he told Pellicer in a letter written shortly after his return and dated January 7. In it, Marco says that he searched for the places he remembered in Kiel—the barracks in Bordesholm, the shipyards of the Deutsche Werke Werft, the prison and the university library—but everything had disappeared or had become unrecognisable, all save the former Gestapo gaol, which was now a police station; of his time in the city in the 1940s, there was no trace, nor of his arrest and trial; at the prison, he was told that all documents had been transferred to the Schleswig-Holstein state archive. Marco concluded his letter by asking Pellicer to continue his research, and this he did; for his part, Marco continued to fashion an identity as a former camp prisoner. An interesting document emerges in April 1999. On the 25th, *La Vanguardia* published a letter to the editor entitled "Life Is beautiful? Not always," signed Enric Marco. The letter begins with the disagreeable impression made on our man by *Life Is Beautiful*, a sweet film about life in the Nazi camps for which actor Roberto Benigni won an Oscar that same year. "It is a feeling of rejection that I cannot quite describe," Marco wrote, "although I have to admit that, in my case, I managed to survive thanks to the conviction that life is vital, regardless of circumstances, that you have to imagine that life is beautiful, to leap, to soar above the barbed wire where there is no real possibility of escape." Immediately after this, in a terse paragraph, Marco gives an account of the punishments he suffered and those he witnessed in his fictitious experience as a camp prisoner, and concludes with a hymn to himself and a hymn to life not unlike that in Benigni's film: "I still feel the pride of refusing to be annihilated, at having won the game, at still being alive, and feeling that, in spite of everything, life is beautiful. Everyone's life. Yes, it is true, I felt an uncomfortable queasiness, one that might seem irrational in someone whose experience so closely mirrors the film. Perhaps I should go and see it again when my stomach stops churning." There can be no doubt: Marco was publicly submitting his application for admission to the Amical de Mauthausen with all attendant honours; he was also quickly fashioning his new character.

Nothing was of greater help to him than his knowledge of Flossenbürg. His first visit to the village was in the spring of that year with his wife, with whom he had planned a holiday in Prague. While he was planning, or perhaps after they had arrived in Prague, Marco mentioned to Dani that Flossenbürg—the place where he had told her he had been a prisoner of the Nazis for several years—was not far from the Czech capital, and suggested they visit the camp, or what remained of it. Unlike his trip to Kiel, his visit to Flossenbürg was a success, though he had visited the former in search of his true past, and was visiting the latter in search of a fictitious past. By this time, the memorial site had already existed for several decades, but an institution tasked with administering the memorial had not yet been created—it was founded shortly afterwards, in late 1999—and the only resource in the village was an information office at the Town Hall. Marco and his wife were given a rapturous welcome; the reception was justified: although former prisoners of various nationalities visited the camp every year, this was the first time those in the information office had met a former prisoner from Spain.

On their first trip to Flossenbürg, Marco visited the remains of the concentration camp with his wife—the SS Headquarters, the *Appellplatz*, the camp kitchen, the laundry, the *Platz der Nationen*, the crematorium—and took home all the information leaflets he could find. On his return to Barcelona, he set about reading them, or rather assimilating them, together with all the information he could track down on the camp prisoners in general, and the experience of the Spanish in particular. He quickly realised he had hit the jackpot. He discovered that, in Spain at that time, there were almost no serious studies about the camps, certainly not about Flossenbürg, a minor camp that was all but forgotten, particularly in Spain where nobody,

or almost nobody, had even heard of it. He discovered that his deception would have been much trickier if he had chosen one of the
well-known camps like Dachau or Buchenwald, and almost impossible if he had settled on Mauthausen, which had held the majority
of the almost nine thousand Spaniards sent to the Nazi camps; Flossenbürg, by contrast, had seen very few Spaniards, and he could find
no evidence of any that had survived the camp and were still alive,
meaning that no-one in Spain could dispute his story (to say nothing
of the fact that, unlike Mauthausen, where most of the Spaniards were
housed together and knew one another, Flossenbürg had numerous, widely dispersed subcamps, and the prisoners had little contact
with each other). And although he quickly learned that his deception would have been much easier had he been a Jew and claimed to
have been sent there from Germany rather than from France—the
transportation of Jews had left little paperwork compared to that of
non-Jews and, unlike those from within Germany, deportations from
France were reasonably well documented—he also discovered that
a number of Flossenbürg prisoners appeared in the archives under
incorrect names and many had not even been listed in the arrival register. Twenty-five years earlier, Marco had successfully passed himself
off as an anti-Francoist agitator in a famously anti-Franco union with
no shortage of members who had been anti-Franco resistance fighters, so why should he not be able to pass himself off as a former prisoner in a little-known Nazi camp among the few, ever-diminishing,
increasingly elderly Spaniards who had been interned in Nazi camps?
Besides, why would anyone attempt to unmask him? What purpose
would it serve? What for?

A few months after his first visit to Flossenbürg, Marco went back
there to attend one of the reunions of former prisoners which had
periodically taken place since 1995; in this particular year, it was held
on June 26. After this, Marco became a diligent visitor to these gath-
erings. It would have been at one of the first reunions he attended
that he met Johannes Ibel, and something happened that Ibel would
not forget.

Ibel is a historian. He had taken a position at Flossenbürg in early

2000, shortly after the Flossenbürg Memorial Foundation began operating in the former SS headquarters; his job consisted of establishing a database of all information of every prisoner who had passed through the camp, a task that was to take him five years. From his first visit, Marco had been eager to establish documentary evidence of his presence at the camp and, like any former prisoner who made the request, he had been given photocopies of the pages from the registers in which his name was likely to appear—in his case, those pages where the Nazis had noted the names of Spanish prisoners—with the caveat that it was possible his name would not figure, since the lists were incomplete. On the day Ibel met him, Marco showed him a photocopy of one of the pages and indicated a name. There I am, he said, that's me. Ibel looked. He was accustomed to the handwriting of Nazi officials at Flossenbürg and immediately noted the information: the entry Marco had indicated was prisoner number 6448, a Spaniard whose first name was Enric, but whose surname was not Marco but Moné. Ibel pointed this out; Marco insisted and launched into a garbled explanation about the workings of the clandestine struggle, the need to use false names to confuse and disorient the enemy. There is no doubt, he said, pointing to the photocopy again. That's me. Ibel studied the entry: it stated that the Spaniard was from Figueras, had been admitted to the main camp on February 23, 1944, and transferred to the Beneschau subcamp on March 3 of that year, at which point the historian remembered (or he may have remembered it later) that neither of these dates tallied with those Marco had given him, or those he remembered Marco giving him, but he didn't want to argue. He said simply: If you say this is you, it must be you. There's no doubt, Marco said again. It's me. And then he asked Ibel to issue him with a certificate stating that he had been Flossenbürg prisoner number 6448. Ibel was bewildered. I can't do that, he said. Why not? asked Marco. Because we cannot be certain that you were that person, said Ibel, then gestured to the photocopy and added, we can give you another copy of the register, but not a certificate stating that you were a prisoner here. Marco cannot have been particularly satisfied with this response, but he must also have realised that it would be unwise to pursue the discussion. He did not pursue it.

The incident had no negative repercussions, and from that

moment, everywhere he went, our man misappropriated the camp
number of Enric Moné, whose actual name was Enric Moner; everywhere but Flossenbürg, obviously. Despite the fact that his behaviour had briefly aroused the suspicions of Ibel—who also concluded
from Marco's responses to his questions about the last days of the
camp, that he was merely repeating hearsay—Marco continued to be
invited to survivors' reunions by the foundation. He attended every
year, or almost every year, alone or with his wife or with Spanish
friends or acquaintances, laid flowers on the stone commemorating
the Spaniards who had died, acted as a guide for visitors, or gave talks
about his experience in the camp at nearby schools. The Foundation treated him as just another survivor, and he acted like one. He
even managed to strike up a friendship of sorts with other survivors,
as, for example, with Gianfranco Mariconti—an elderly Italian par-
tisan who had fought against the fascists during the Second World
War and, after his arrest in 1944, spent the last year of the war in
Flossenbürg—with whom he corresponded; the two men met up on a
number of occasions unrelated to the commemorations in Germany
and in Italy, alone or with their wives. All of these things allowed
him to identify with the camp, with the survivors of the camp, with
himself as a survivor of the camp. The identification was radical and
complete: to understand Marco it is important to understand that, in
a sense, Marco did not pretend to be a camp survivor, or at least after
a certain point he was no longer pretending, at a certain point Marco
became a camp survivor just as, at a certain point, Alonso Quixano
became Don Quixote.

I am looking at a photograph of one of the annual reunions of former
prisoners of Flossenbürg. The picture shows all the survivors who
were still alive when the reunion took place, or all the survivors
who were still alive and could or wished to attend. It's a colour photograph, the atmosphere is summery—everyone is wearing short-
sleeved shirts and light jackets—probably taken in July, since that
was when the reunions were held, I don't know which year, but it
must be between 2000 and 2004, when Marco was attending. I don't
know whether all the survivors present are in the picture, because it

is poorly framed and looks as though people sitting to the right may have been cropped out. Most are men, though there are four women (Flossenbürg was originally a camp reserved for men, but towards the end, women comprised almost a third of the prisoners); one of the men, on the far right of the photograph, is wearing a prisoner's uniform; unsurprisingly, all of them are old or very old. Marco is there, right in the middle of the photograph, where he will be most visible—the second row down, sixth from the left. He's wearing a blue, short-sleeved shirt and dark trousers, his hands are clasped, his fingers interlaced, his thick moustache and his thinning hair are dyed black; he's staring at the camera, and although the image is blurred, in his eyes and on the lips hidden by his moustache, it is just possible to make out a smile. He looks calm, relaxed, happy to be where he is, among his former comrades in captivity. If you didn't know he was not one of them, nothing would give it away. In fact, he is one of them.

2

In May 2005, when the scandal about Marco broke, many people wondered how our man could have duped so many people for so long with such a monstrous lie. Like any question, or at least like any complex question, there is not one answer but many; here I will list seven of them.

The first, unsurprisingly, is that Marco is not only a superlative conman, a shameless charlatan, a peerless trickster and an exceptional storyteller, but also a phenomenal performer, a "magnificent actor" as Vargas Llosa calls him, capable of completely immersing himself in his character: just as, at a certain point in the Seventies, Marco stopped playing a former anti-Franco resistance fighter and *became* a former anti-Franco resistance fighter, at a certain point in the early years of the twenty-first century, Marco stopped playing a former prisoner of the Nazis and became a former prisoner of the Nazis.

The second answer is that the more monstrous the lie, the more believable it is to most people. This is the very basis of political totalitarianism, and no-one has described it better than a genius of totalitarianism: Adolf Hitler. "The masses," Hitler argues in *Mein Kampf*, "more readily fall victim to the big lie than the small lie, since they themselves often tell small lies in little matters but would be ashamed to resort to large-scale falsehoods. It would never come into their heads to fabricate colossal untruths, and they would not believe that others could have the impudence to distort the truth so infamously." Given that an emphasis on truth betrays the liar, I hardly need to point out that, in the passage quoted above, Hitler isn't arguing in favour of the "big lie," but denouncing it in the name of truth.

The third answer is no less important than the previous two, but it is less evident. It has sometimes been implied that the Marco affair could only have happened in Spain, a country with a complex, flawed ability to assimilate its recent past, one where there were few victims of the Nazis compared to other European countries (among other reasons because it didn't take part in the Second World War, or did so only as a German ally), where even in the early twenty-first century there were few reliable studies about Spanish victims of the Nazi genocide and where the Holocaust doesn't have a major role in the collective memory, or what we usually call the collective memory. I too believed that these things were true, or at least plausible, which is why in my article "I am Enric Marco," I wrote that one of the things that made Marco's case possible was "our relative ignorance of the recent past generally and of Nazism in particular," and continued, "although Marco promoted himself as a remedy for this national failing, in fact he was the finest proof of its existence."

This isn't false but, at least at first glance, it isn't remotely certain either. Because the truth is that, from the very moment the Second World War ended, there were many people of many different nationalities who claimed to have been in the Nazi camps when they hadn't been, or people who embellished or embroidered or exaggerated the reality of their time in the Nazi camps, perhaps because, as Germaine Tillion says, the madness of the camps fostered such fantasies. Norman Finkelstein offers two more tangible reasons for the phenomenon: "Because enduring the camps became a crown of martyrdom, many Jews who spent the war elsewhere represented themselves as camp survivors. Another strong motive behind this misrepresentation, was material. The post-war German government provided compensation to Jews who had been in ghettos or camps. Many Jews fabricated their pasts to meet this eligibility requirement." Only some of these impostors attained the notoriety of Marco, obviously, but a few of them surpassed him, or almost did so. Among them is Jerzy Kosinski, whose fabricated memories as a child victim of the Holocaust, titled *The Painted Bird*, was hailed in 1965 as one of the greatest denunciations of Nazism and became a fundamental text on the subject of the Holocaust—it won many prizes, was translated into countless languages and became recommended reading in schools. Or the case of Binjamin Wilkomirski, who became famous in 1995 when he published *Fragments: Memories of a Childhood, 1939–1948*, in which he narrates as real his fictional internment in Auschwitz and Majdanek. Or that of Herman Rosenblat, who, in a false memoir entitled *Angel at the Fence*, recounts how as a child in a Nazi camp he had struck up a friendship with a girl who gave him food, a girl he met again many years later in an improbable coincidence, and to whom he was still married when the book was published in 2008. Or the case of Misha Defonseca, a Belgian woman who in 1997 published *Misha: A Mémoire of the Holocaust Years*, in which she relates that in 1941, when she was just six years old, her parents were arrested as Jews and sent to a concentration camp and that she spent the next four years wandering through Germany, Poland, Ukraine, Romania and Yugoslavia before returning to Belgium via Italy and France, when the reality is that she was not Jewish and never left Belgium during the war years. The list of great impostors could be longer: for twenty years Deli Strummer gave talks in the United States about her experience in the Nazi camps until, in 2000, it was discovered that she had significantly distorted the truth about her past during the war; Martin Zaidenstadt, having been a prosperous businessman, spent his retirement offering his services as a guide and begging for money from visitors to Dachau, claiming he had been a prisoner there. All of these people are or were Jews, or claimed to be. This fact is not incidental. As Marco himself could have attested when he began to research his character as a camp prisoner, the Holocaust—the vast, systematic extermination of millions of Jews—and the "Deportation"—the imprisonment in the camps, use of slave labour and murder of hundreds of thousands of non-Jews—are very different things; it isn't always easy to distinguish between them, because the two sometimes overlap or interconnect, but the fact is that the Holocaust left much less of a paper trail than the Deportation, particularly in eastern Europe, where millions of people were exterminated, sometimes without leaving any paper trail. One can only conclude that Jewish impostors had fewer difficulties than non-Jews, and from this that the best-known impostors were Jews. It's true that in many European countries, particularly in eastern Europe, Marco's task would have been much more difficult; even in France, where many more were deported to the camps than in Spain, where survivors were grouped into associations immediately after the war, where the status of *déporté* required passing a series of tests and where deportees were entitled to claim a pension and enjoyed certain privileges. To be fair: all, or almost all European countries—and indeed the vast majority of countries in general—have a complex, flawed ability to assimilate their recent past, because no country can boast of a past without war, without violence, without a shameful episode, and because, like Marco, countries do everything in their power to avoid knowing or recognising themselves for what they are; so it is perhaps not true that Marco's case could only have happened in Spain. Perhaps. But, without wishing to pander to traditional Spanish masochism, it should be recognised that, largely because of the forty years of dictatorship that followed the Civil War, Spain was a more fertile ground than almost any European country to produce Marco's case, the proof being that in 2004, only months before he unmasked Marco, Benito Bermejo exposed Antonio Pastor Martínez, another false Spanish *deportado* who acquired almost the same level of notoriety. As far as I am aware, nowhere else in Europe experienced two such similar cases.

This is the third answer, the third reason why Marco was able to dupe so many people for so long: Spain's historic delay in attaining democracy and our general indifference to the most bitter period of recent European history.

The fourth response is that, if you study the case carefully, Marco didn't fool all that many people—only those who were easily fooled or wanted to be fooled—and certainly didn't fool them for very long. Marco publicly declared he had been a prisoner of the camps in 1978, in the books by Pons Prades and Mariano Constante, but until 1999, when he made his first visit to Flossenbürg and became a member of the Amical de Mauthausen, his character as a *deportado* showed few signs of life, and even these were private and infrequent, almost secret, as though the character were dormant. This means that, at least in his role as a fake prisoner of the camps, Marco didn't fool people for thirty years, as is usually claimed, but for only six: from 1999 until the scandal broke. As for the number of people he fooled, there can be no doubt that it was large, but most were schoolchildren, while the vast majority of people, including journalists, teachers, historians and politicians had no idea, or only the most superficial notion of the Deportation, and didn't have the data to refute Marco's deception, nor did they take the trouble to verify whether what he said was true. He did not, however, fool genuine survivors of the camps, or not all of them: we don't know the opinion of the real prisoners of Flossenbürg—who met him on only a handful of occasions where linguistic barriers proved useful in protecting his deception—but we do know that a number of Spanish deportees had their suspicions, that they discussed their suspicions before he was exposed, that Marco managed to spend as little time with them as possible and had a talent for avoiding them. We also know that he didn't have anything to do with the larger Spanish associations—the Amical Francesa and the F.E.D.I.P. (Spanish Federation of Deportados and Political Prisoners)—which were based in France because after the Second World War the majority of Spaniards who had been in the camps remained in France, just as we know that by the time he joined the Amical de Mauthausen, there were very few survivors, most of whom were in poor health. I don't wish to be misinterpreted: nothing could be further from my intention than to play down Marco's deception, which is extraordinary; as everywhere in this book, or almost everywhere, so in this very paragraph, I am simply trying to be even-handed.

The fifth response partly explains why Marco wasn't unmasked by any of the genuine survivors who suspected him. "Public impostors are surrounded by a sort of curious protective silence," writes the psychiatrist Carlos Castilla del Pino. "There are almost always those who know about the imposture but dare not reveal it. The obscure reasons for this silence can sometimes mean that the deception carries on for years. The complicity is not always self-serving, and those involved are not accomplices in the strict sense of the word." The question is, what were the obscure reasons for the silence of Marco's unwitting accomplices? I will venture two explanations. The first is obvious: in recent decades there has been a "sacralisation of the Holocaust" (the phrase is from Peter Novick); this, combined with a gradual eclipse of the witnesses to the Holocaust, has led to a sacralisation of the witnesses to the Holocaust, who have ceased to be victims and become heroes or secular saints, and no-one likes to be a wet blanket, to go around poking people in the eye, certainly not in the case of a heroic, sacralised witness to the Holocaust while dancing at the permanent funereal celebration of the Holocaust. The second explanation is no less obvious: although it may seem improbable that there were other cases of imposture among Spanish camp survivors (other than Marco and Pastor), it isn't remotely improbable that some of those who came together through the Amical de Mauthausen might have succumbed to the temptation of embellishing or embroidering their pasts, and that none of them would wish to cast the first stone.

We have come to the sixth response. This relates to the afore-mentioned sacralisation of the Holocaust, or simply the sacralisation of the witnesses. In "I am Enric Marco," I argued that in our time the witness is afforded such inordinate respect that none dare question his authority, and the spineless capitulation in the face of this intellectual blackmail facilitated Marco's deceit. The article was published in *El País* in December 2009; exactly a year later, in December 2010, when I thought I had definitively given up on the idea of writing about Marco and was in the middle of writing a book that had nothing to do with him, I published another article in the same newspaper, one entitled "The Blackmail of the Witness," and there is little doubt that I was thinking about Marco when I wrote it. It reads: "It never fails: in any discussion about recent history, every time there is a discrepancy between the historian's version and that of the witness, some witness pulls out the unassailable argument: 'What would you know about it? You weren't there!' The person who was there—the witness—possesses the truth; the one who comes later—the historian—has only fragments, echoes and shadows of the truth. Elie Wiesel, a survivor of both Auschwitz and Buchenwald, puts it thus: for him, any survivor of the Nazi concentration camps 'has more to say than all historians combined about what happened' because 'Only those who were there know what it was; the others will never know.'" This, to my mind, isn't an argument, it is the blackmail of the witness.

I found the quote by Wiesel in a much-needed plea in favour of history published by Santós Julia in the magazine *Claves* (No. 207). Much-needed, because memory is threatening to replace history in an era saturated with memory. This is bad news. Memory and history are notionally opposites: memory is individual, partial and subjective; history is collective and aspires to be comprehensive and objective. Memory and history are also complementary: history gives sense to memory; memory is a tool, an ingredient, a part of history. But memory is not history. Elie Wiesel has a point, but he's only half right: the survivors of the camps are the only ones who know the truth, the unimaginable horror of that diabolical experience, but that does not mean that they understand the experience; in fact, preoccupied with their own struggle for survival, they may be in the worst possible position to understand it. In *War and Peace*, Tolstoy writes, "he who plays a part in a historic event never understands its significance." In Book Eleven of the novel, Pierre Bezukhov goes to fight at the Battle of Borodino; he sets off in search of the glories he has read about in books, but finds only utter chaos, or, as Isaiah Berlin puts it, "only the ordinary confusion of individual human beings haphazardly attending to this or that human want [. . .] a succession of 'accidents' whose origins and consequences are, by and large, untraceable and unpredictable." Thirty years before *War and Peace*, Stendhal described a similar scene: in the first pages of *The Charterhouse of Parma*, Fabrizio del Dongo, a fervent admirer of Napoleon, takes part in the battle of Waterloo, but, like Bezukhov at Borodino, he understands nothing, or understands only that war is utter chaos and not "that noble and universal uplifting of souls athirst for glory which he had imagined it to be from Napoleon's proclamations!" The testimonies of Bezukhov and del Dongo contain a profound truth: that for those caught up in it, war is a tale full of sound and fury, signifying nothing. But the truth of Bezukhov and del Dongo is not the whole truth; it is precisely because he didn't fight at Borodino or at Waterloo that the historian can silence the sound, appease the fury, situate Borodino and Waterloo within the context of the Napoleonic wars, and the Napoleonic wars within the context of nineteenth-century history, or history more generally, and in doing so, give the tale meaning. Unless he or she is particularly ingenuous (or particularly arrogant), the historian doesn't claim to attain absolute truth, which is the sum of an infinite number of fractional truths, and consequently unattainable; but unless he or she is particularly irresponsible (or particularly lazy), the historian knows that he or she has a duty to come as close as possible to this perfect truth, and a greater chance of doing so than anyone else.

A historian is not a judge, but the ways in which they work are similar; like the judge, the historian studies documents, corroborates evidence, connects facts, questions witnesses; like the judge, the historian pronounces a verdict. The verdict isn't definitive—it can be appealed, revised, refuted—but it is a verdict. It is issued by the judge, or the historian, not the witness. Witnesses aren't always right; their truth depends on memory, and memory is fragile and often self-serving. We don't always remember accurately, we aren't always capable of distinguishing memory from imagination, we don't necessarily remember what happened, but instead what we previously remembered as having happened, or what other witnesses have said happened, or simply what it suits us to remember. Obviously, witnesses aren't to blame for this (or not always): after all, they alone can answer to their memories; the historian, on the other hand, must answer to the truth. And being answerable to the truth, the historian cannot tolerate the blackmail of the witness; when necessary, he or she should have the courage to reject the witness's claim to truth. In an era of memory, history should belong to historians.

The seventh and last response: in our era of memory, when, more even than memory, what triumphs in Spain is the industry of memory, people wanted to listen to the lies the champion of memory had to tell. Once again, Marco was on the side of the majority.

3

Marco first approached the Amical de Mauthausen after one of his early visits to Flossenbürg. At the time, the Amical had its headquarters in an attic room at 312 calle Aragón, in the district of Ensanche. Marco introduced himself as a former *deportado* eager to work with the association; I don't know to whom he spoke that first day, but it seems clear that no-one was particularly interested and he got the impression they were giving him the runaround. Some time later, Marco visited again, with no better results. Our man was then vice-president of FaPaC, and some weeks or months after his second frustrating visit to the attic office on calle Aragón, one of his colleagues at FaPaC told him that a member of the Amical had been asking about him and wanted to meet him. The colleague was Frédéric Lloret, a biology teacher; the person from the Amical was Rosa Torán, a history teacher who was, or would soon be, a member of the board of Amical. She is also an important character in this story.

Marco and Torán met at a lunch organised by Lloret, during which Torán talked to Marco about Amical, told him that her uncle had died in Mauthausen and that she had only recently begun to get involved in the organisation and take an interest in the Deportation. Marco talked to her at length about his experience as a prisoner in Flossenbürg, told her he had given talks on the subject at various schools and gave her a photocopy of a letter he had just sent to an Italian friend from Flossenbürg. The letter was genuine: the friend was Gianfranco Mariconti, whom Marco had just met while attending his first reunion of former prisoners at the camp. Five years later, shortly before the scandal broke, Torán published the letter in a book titled *The Nazi Concentration Camps: Words Against Forgetting.* Marco begins the letter to his (genuine) new friend and (fictitious) former fellow prisoner with a description of the difference between the camp as he had known it—or had not known it—and how it looked now: "It's not easy to recognise the camp as it is today. There is just enough left to avoid mistaking it for a park or the gardens of the industrial estate that nowadays covers a large part of the old foundations of the barracks." Towards the end of the letter he writes that, at the age of seventy-eight, his anger and hatred should have burned out, but implies that this is not the case, and concludes with one of the slogans that he would endlessly repeat during his years at Amical, duly emphasised using capital letters: "Forgive, YES; forget, NO."

At his next visit to the Amical everything changed, though this was not thanks to Rosa Torán but to Josep Zamora, who was secretary general of the organisation at the time. Zamora wasn't a deportee, he was the son of a deportee, but he had fought in the Civil War and later in the French Resistance, and had been a member of the Amical since the Eighties. The Amical de Mauthausen literally lived off the past—here the past wasn't the past but the present or an aspect of the present—so, although Marco and Zamora didn't know each other, they began exchanging stories from their past, discovered they had fought with the same unit during the war (26th Division, the former Durruti Column) and hit it off. Marco immediately applied to be a member of Amical. To validate his admission, over the following days he provided written answers to the questionnaire; his answers are an almost perfect mixture of truth and lies: he gave his date of birth as April 14, 1921, the symbolic date of the proclamation of the Segunda República, rather than April 12, 1921, his actual birthdate; he declared that he had been a prisoner in Kiel gaol, which was true, and in Flossenbürg concentration camp, which was false; he declared that his prison number was 623-23, which may well have been true, though I haven't been able to confirm it, and that his camp number was 6448, which was false (the number itself was real: he usurped it from Enric Moner); he declared that he had been admitted to Kiel prison on March 6, 1942, which was true, and to Flossenbürg on December 18, 1942, which was false; he also declared that he had been released on April 23, 1945, which was of course false (though it was also symbolic, in its way, being the date of the liberation of Flossenbürg). One of the last questions on the form related to the reason or reasons for which he had been brought to trial; Marco gave one true ("High Treason") and one false ("Conspiracy against the Third Reich"). At the bottom of the questionnaire, the prospective member had to list the documents or photocopies of documents attached as evidence of his status as a *deportado;* Marco wrote: "Court Martial ruling, certificate prison entry, document from KL Flossenbürg."

This is what Marco said he was appending, but this wasn't what he actually appended, or not exactly. He attached a document from the prosecutor detailing his trial in Kiel from which it was clear that he had been arrested and had spent several months in prison, but he didn't attach the judge's ruling, which proved that he had been found not guilty and released. He attached the photocopy of the Flossenbürg camp register bearing the handwritten name Enric Moner which could have been read as Enric Marco (or so Marco hoped), the same photocopy with which, in the archives of Flossenbürg Memorial, he'd tried to get Johannes Ibel to certify that he had been a prisoner in the camp. And he attached another document. It was dated June 25, 1999, and, especially to anyone who knew no German, it looked like an official certificate attesting that Marco had been a prisoner in Flossenbürg concentration camp, because it consisted of a list of thirty-two names of citizens of fourteen countries, among them Marco's, and a second page stapled to it bearing the seal of the Flossenbürg information office (in case there might be any doubt, at the bottom of the page, Marco himself wrote "Survivor located"); the truth is that the document merely certified that he had attended the reunions for former prisoners at the memorial site, and it hadn't been issued by Flossenbürg information office, but by an organisation within the Bavarian Ministry for Education. As such, none of the documents Marco provided as proof of his time at Flossenbürg camp proved that he had been a prisoner there. So, either no-one at the Amical de Mauthausen could read German, or no-one actually read the documents, or whoever read them found them convincing, or didn't find them convincing but didn't want to be a wet blanket or go around poking people in the eye and capitulated to the prestige or the subornment or the blackmail of the witness, dared not say No and opted to say nothing. If this last hypothesis is correct—and it isn't impossible—it's likely that whoever allowed Marco in did not immediately regret their actions.

Because, when he joined the Amical de Mauthausen, Marco seemed to be precisely the man Spanish *deportados* needed, just as twenty-five years earlier, when he joined the C.N.T., he had seemed to be precisely the man Spanish anarchists needed. And just as with the C.N.T. and with FaPaC, Marco joined the Amical at a moment of crisis. The organisation had been founded in 1962 with the support of the Amicale association in France, and until 1978 it remained illegal. Its chief purpose was facilitating contact between *deportados* and their families, providing information, legal assistance and, later, financial aid; by 1999, however, this model seemed to have run its course, because the last survivors were beginning to pass away, or were so old that they were no longer in a position to manage the association, meaning that it had to be completely restructured to avoid dying with them. The restructuring had already begun by the time Marco arrived, although everyone acknowledges that he did more than anyone else to consolidate the change. He was charming, tireless and extremely generous with his time—indeed he began to invest all his time in the association. The most important thing, however, was that despite being a *deportado* he had the youth and energy that the survivors at the Amical were lacking. Furthermore, he wasn't as sparing in his words as they were, or as most of them were, nor as reluctant to talk about his experience in the camps; on the contrary, he was delighted to do it, and knew how to do it, or at least knew how to dazzle people with his vivid stories. As a result, when he spoke publicly, Marco was much more convincing than the real survivors of the camps, the proof being that when he did talks with them, he outshone them, he became the man who moved and thrilled audiences, the focus of any conference. The reality is that, wherever he was, Marco couldn't bear not being the centre of attention. On November 15, 2002, a plenary session of the Catalan parliament paid tribute to Republicans exiled after the Civil War; representatives of all parties addressed the session, but none of the fourteen Republicans chose to speak, except for Marco, who appeared as a survivor of the Nazi camps and who, at the end, as the chamber echoed with cheers and applause, made his own contribution, with a roar that made the head-lines of every newspaper the following day: "*¡Viva la República!*"

It took Marco only a few short months to prove that he could play an important role in revitalising the Amical de Mauthausen. The year 2001 was the tenth anniversary of the death of Montserrat Roig, a writer with strong ties to the organisation since, in 1977, she'd writ-ten the first book about Catalan prisoners of the Nazi camps. The board decided to honour her with a series of events, including an homage at the Palau de la Música. For Amical, this was an ambitious project, especially given its parlous finances and the frailty of many of its leaders; this perhaps explains why, in April of that year, a num-ber of younger directors were co-opted to the board, among them Marco, who was appointed secretary for international relations. His dynamism and his tireless dedication did much to contribute to the success of the events, as did the close ties he'd cultivated with the political leaders in the Catalan parliament during his time as vice-president of FaPaC. These ties explain why, two months before the homage to Montserrat Roig, the Catalan government honoured Marco with the Creu de Sant Jordi, its highest civilian decoration, for a lifetime of generous and selfless commitment, even in adversity, to safeguarding the dignity and welfare of the country: not only for "his loyalty to the libertarian tradition of the Catalan workers' move-ment, as evidenced by a long career as an activist culminating in his time as secretary general of the Catalan chapter of the C.N.T.," according to the official citation extolling his virtues, or for "his con-stant striving for the betterment of public education," but also for his struggle against the Franco regime and against the Nazis, "which led to his arrest by the Gestapo and his internment in a concentration camp." This was the greatest moment in Marco's life to date, mark-ing the public consecration in Catalonia of the character he had cre-ated. Can it really be a surprise, then, if many members of the Amical saw Marco as a blessing sent from heaven to lift them out of decades of poverty with his prestige as a civic hero and his miraculous youthfulness?

While he reinforced his power at Amical, Marco continued to

put the finishing touches on his character. It must have been about this time that he told his story to a young journalist named Jordi Bassa, who was preparing a book about Catalan prisoners of the Nazi camps; he had done this with Pons Prades twenty-five years earlier, but Jordi Bassa's book, published the following year as *A Memoir of Hell*, was unlike that of Pons Prades, at least as far as Marco was concerned. By the time he spoke to Bassa, our man had already visited Flossenbürg and had conscientiously researched and created—or was creating—his character as a survivor of the Deportation, and so, rather than glossing over his time in Flossenbürg as he'd done with Pons Prades, now he spoke about it at length, describing the camps, inventing anecdotes and stories, evoking mood and atmosphere, giving details, dates, places and characters; in short he fashioned a much more convincing story than the one he'd told to Pons Prades, like a novelist who, with time and effort, has learned his craft, expanded his sources and thoroughly mastered them.

During this period, Marco made a visit to Flossenbürg with his wife and a group of colleagues from Amical, among them Rosa Torán. There were seven or eight of them, and they made the trip by minibus. When they arrived at the camp, Marco was greeted by the staff at the memorial site, including the director, Jörg Skriebeleit, as just another former prisoner; he took part in a tribute paid by young people to the former prisoners who, of course, also treated him as one of their own. Before or after the ceremony, Marco and his companions from the Amical laid flowers on the stone commemorating the Spaniards who had died in Flossenbürg and visited the site while our man recalled his time there: my barracks were just here, the camp kitchen was there and over there the mess hall, inspection took place every morning here on the *Appellplatz*, over there I was beaten, over there they murdered what's-his-name. Rosa Torán remembers three things about the trip. The first is that, at a certain point, Marco and his wife headed off to the village because they were apparently meeting with Gianfranco Mariconti, Marco's fake camp comrade and real friend, and they returned early from the meeting: according to Marco's wife, who had met Gianfranco on previous occasions, the Italian didn't show up. The second thing Torán remembers is that, out of curiosity, while visiting the Memorial archives, she asked to see Marco's admission slip. She doesn't remember exactly who she asked, but she remembers that the person in question explained the difficulties of finding documentary evidence for the presence of all the prisoners in the camp, mentioned the database that Johannes Ibel was working on and told her that, when the camp was liberated, the Americans had taken away all the documentation on site which was now stored at the National Archives in Washington, where for some time they'd been drawing up alphabetical lists of the names that appeared in the camp registers and were sending them via microfiche; she told Torán that, so far, the lists had only gotten as far as the letter F or possibly G, but certainly not as far as M for Marco, so it was impossible to know whether Marco's name was on the list or not; the person also told Torán that there was no guarantee Marco's name would appear, since it was likely that not all prisoners were on the list. Torán doesn't remember Marco or anyone else showing her the photocopied page of the register bearing the name Enric Moner which Marco had vainly tried to convince Johannes Ibel was his alias, his name in the resistance, a name that might have been mistaken for Marco, or which Marco hoped might be mistaken for his, which was why he had attached the photocopied page to his application for membership to the Amical de Mauthausen. The third thing Torán remembers about the trip was the first to occur and was the most important, or seems to me the most important: during the drive to Flossenbürg, she heard Marco's wife confessing, "Every time we come to Flossenbürg, I suffer, because Enric doesn't sleep for days before the trip."

Finally, on April 6, 2003, at a meeting in Sant Boi de Llobregat—the town outside Barcelona where his mother had spent thirty-five years in a sanatorium—Marco was elected president of the Amical de Mauthausen. He succeeded Joan Escuer, a former inmate of Dachau who had been president of the organisation for ten years. Escuer, by then, was almost ninety years old and in failing health, and Torán remembers that, one afternoon, shortly before the meeting at Sant Boi, he invited her and Marco to his house to ask them to see to the continuity of the Amical and he urged Marco to take over as president, because, he said, he had total confidence in him and believed he had the qualities needed to modernise the association. The scene is plausible; it's also likely that, if the members of the Amical were privately asked now about the period of Marco's presidency, most of them would say it was the best in the history of the association. This wasn't entirely due to Marco, of course: his presidency coincided with the rise of so-called historical memory in Spain, with a period of enormous interest in the recent past and in the remembrance and vindication of its victims; it also coincided with a radical change in the Amical board of directors, which opened itself up to younger members, among them Rosa Torán, who was appointed one of its vice-presidents. However, it would be cruel, and indeed false, to deny that Marco played a decisive role in the revival of the association.

Revitalised and thriving, the Amical de Mauthausen reached its apogee during Marco's presidency. Just as he had been at the C.N.T. and at FaPaC, Marco was a shambolic manager who hid his confusion and administrative incompetence behind a flurry of frenzied activity, ceaseless chatter and countless working hours; nevertheless, under his aegis, the Amical went from being an association that did little more than unite and advise former Spanish *deportados* and their families to one that also served as a centre documenting and disseminating their memories and their histories: during these years, the Amical reached out to other, similar organisations, catalogued its considerable archives, its library of books and periodicals, hired new staff, organised trips and conferences, secured substantial grants from government and signed important agreements with it, and was able to give up the attic office on calle Aragón and move to more spacious offices in a building on calle Sils, in the historic quarter of Barcelona. These and other changes also meant that, in a short time, the Amical de Mauthausen went from being virtually unknown to becoming ubiquitous and influential, at least in Catalonia.

Marco played a decisive role in this change. He was the most visible face, the very embodiment of Amical, not simply because he was president or because, being retired, he devoted himself to the organisation body and soul as he had done with the C.N.T. and FaPaC, but because he gave talks anywhere and everywhere: at universities, cultural centres, retirement homes, prisons, adult learning centres and sundry associations, and particularly at secondary schools. In

2002, Joan Escuer had signed an agreement with the Catalan government which agreed to finance or jointly finance some twenty-five
talks a year, which members of the Amical were to give at Catalan
educational institutions; Marco reviewed and expanded this agreement every year, and became the principal and almost only speaker.
After the scandal broke it was often said that our man made money
from these conferences; this is garbage: leaving aside the fact that the
Catalan government paid the princely sum of between €76 and €80
each for these talks—monies paid directly into the coffers of Amical,
which in turn covered only travel expenses—Marco didn't give these
talks for the money, but for a variety of reasons, chief among which is
that he wanted to be Don Quixote rather than Alonso Quixano; that
is to say, he wanted every schoolchild in Catalonia to love and admire
him, he wanted them all to think him a hero.

He almost succeeded in his quest. He enjoyed giving these talks
so much that, as he spoke, he grew younger, as though they weren't
speeches but blood transfusions. Marco presented himself in these
talks with the same mixture of lies and truth ("My name is Enric
Marco, and I was born on April 14, 1921, exactly ten years before
the proclamation of the Second Republic") and then launched into
his tale, continuing and enhancing this mixture of lies as he blended
almost a century of his country's history with his own story, the story
of a man who was a personification or a symbol or a digest of his
country's history, a man who had been everywhere and met everyone
(Buenaventura Durruti and Josephine Baker and "Quico" Sabater and
Salvador Puig Antich), and who, from the age of fifteen, had spent
his life fighting for freedom, solidarity and social justice, the story
of a tireless activist who had fought to defend the Second Republic,
fought against fascism, confronted the Franco regime and even the
Nazis and had refused to be broken by the war, by the concentration
camps, by the Francoist police, who had suffered all manner of punishment without ever ceasing his fight for a better world, the story of
a veteran of every war, or every just war, who, in old age, had resolved
to tell his story so that the things he'd witnessed and experienced
would never happen again, so that the youth of Spain might be spared
what he'd suffered, and what others were suffering all around the
world, in Palestine, in Iraq, in Kosovo, in Guantanamo Bay, in Sierra

Leone, and this was why it was crucial that the youth of Spain should be just and free and honour the memory of the victims and above all be loyal to the past—"Forgive, YES; forget, NO"—to their own past and that of others. This was why, when he concluded his talk, he often urged them to go and see their parents and their grandparents, to talk to them, to tell them that the time had come to end the silence and the concealment, to demand that they face the truth, the shame and indignities that they and their country were hiding, that the time had come for them to know themselves or recognise themselves for who they were, because first and foremost one must be true to oneself and to one's own past, however difficult and terrible, shameful and humiliating it might be.

This or something like it is what Marco would say to the schoolchildren (and often to adults), because his talks weren't simply about history and politics, they were, or at least to him they were, moral lessons: by evoking the memorable occasion when he refused to get to his feet and sing "Cara al Sol" in a Barcelona cinema despite the blue-shirted Falangist with the pistol in his belt, or the even more memorable episode when he risked his life by winning a chess match against a ruthless SS officer in Flossenbürg, Marco was telling them or trying to tell them that a man may be humiliated, brutalised, treated like an animal, yet, in a moment of madness and supreme courage, he can reclaim his dignity, though it should cost him his life, and such moments were within the reach of everyone, and that it is these moments that define and save us; in reliving his long years as a pitiless adversary of dictatorship, hiding in the shadows, organising the clandestine struggle, running from the Francoist police who were constantly at his heels, Marco was telling these schoolchildren or trying to tell them that the human animal can survive the most terrible ordeals and the most harrowing conditions if he can retain his freedom, his dignity and his solidarity. Marco invariably told stories taken from his own invented experience, always used himself as an example, and in doing so earned the palpable admiration of his young audience and the covert reinforcement of the character he'd created, embedding the character within him as deeply as Alonso Quixano embedded Don Quixote.

The talks were a spectacular success. Over the years, the Amical de Mauthausen received dozens of letters from teachers, pupils and managers of educational institutions effusively thanking Marco for giving the talk, for his generosity, his humanity, for everything. One such letter is signed by a history teacher named Sofía Castillo García, from the Abat Oliva de Ripoll, and addressed to all the members of the Amical de Mauthausen; it is dated May 28, 2002, before Marco became president, and it reads:

To whom it may concern:

> You are to be congratulated that you have people of the stature of Enric Marco in your association.
> Yesterday, he gave a magnificent talk to our students. A lesson in history, but more importantly in humanity and courage and the defence of freedom.
> May we continue to enjoy his talks for many years to come.
> You may count on the History Department here, and on me personally for anything you might need.

> Yours faithfully

The letter I have just transcribed (or rather translated from Catalan) is noteworthy; the one that follows will give you goosebumps. It is written by a schoolboy whose name I have omitted and whose age I don't know; I know only that he lives or lived in Anglès, a town near Gerona, and that he dated his letter June 12, 2002. It reads:

Señor Enric:

> I am writing to let you know that your visit to our school—for which I would personally like to thank you—moved many people enough for them to change their minds about principles and concepts. On a personal level, I would also like to thank you because you gave me much

to think about. I have problems at home, but thanks to you I have realised that we often unthinkingly exaggerate our everyday problems.

Sometimes, the problems I have mentioned made me think of committing suicide. Now I believe it is the worst mistake I could make. The other day, after your talk, I was thinking: here I am, with trivial problems, thinking of taking my own life, and here is this man who has had to struggle to survive.

All this has meant that I have changed the way I look at the world. I do not pay as much attention to things that once seemed very important to me, and already I have noticed that I feel better. I think people should only worry about things that really matter. Perhaps this was not the conclusion you were hoping to communicate in your talk, but I believe that, for me, it was worth it.

Once again: thank you.

Yours sincerely.

But it was the media that finally turned Marco into a hero, a champion of so-called historical memory, a bona fide rock star. Marco had long been a mediopath, but now his mediopathy sky-rocketed because, though it was an illness, for Marco it was also a drug: the more you take, the more you need.

In the years that saw the apotheosis of so-called historical memory, Marco had all he could wish for. Aside from the talks here, there and everywhere, our hero seemed to be constantly on television, on the radio, in the newspapers recounting his experiences as a prisoner of the camps, almost always to the soundtrack of Roberto Benigni's *Life Is Beautiful*, or Steven Spielberg's *Schindler's List*. Journalists loved him, they went crazy for him, they fought to interview him. It's not surprising. The other prisoners or exiles or veterans of the Second Republic, the other stars of so-called historical memory, were mostly elderly and frail, their memories were failing, interviewing them was a chore: you had to wheedle information, coax their stories from them, constantly repeat questions, even pause the interview to give them time to go to the bathroom, to stop coughing or to find the thread of what they were saying. Marco was the complete opposite. Journalists were immediately impressed by his physical appearance, he was nothing like the geriatrics they were used to but a man who looked much younger than his eighty-odd years, with his powerful, senatorial profile, his black hair, his luxuriant moustache, his piercing eyes, his gravelly voice and his silver tongue. It was this last that was crucial: Marco remembered everything and recounted everything, he poured forth a torrent of words, a blend of colourful anecdotes, heroic, harrowing or heartbreaking stories, poignant and edifying reflections on the solidarity and honour a human being is capable of in the most terrible circumstances, each illustrated with examples from his personal experience and told with such narrative structure and coherence that, as they left, the journalists often felt—especially when compared to the stories of other survivors—that Marco had done their work for them, that far from being the subject for a short press or television interview, here was a man who merited an entire book or a documentary. Furthermore, Marco appealed to their vanity: interviewing this extraordinary character, this veteran of every war, or every just war, the journalists saw themselves as fearless investigators unearthing a forgotten chapter of the past about which no-one dared to speak, the most interesting, the most noble, the most furtive chapter of their country's past, and in doing so they felt as though they were righting a miscarriage of justice and, through Marco, paying homage to all the victims who had been silenced, not only by Franco but by the democracy that followed the Franco regime. Marco triggered such a dependency among journalists, or at least Catalan journalists, that they even included him in a television programme about Ravensbrück, a concentration camp for women only. "The thing is, he's also a historian," the researchers might have claimed if anyone had asked what the hell Marco was doing on the programme; the less dishonest might admit: "Look, the truth is that he's such a wonderful storyteller, so evocative, so effective, that we wanted to have him on."

It was the media who ultimately turned Marco—in Catalonia, though not just in Catalonia—into a rock star, a champion of so-called historical memory, a character who was known and recognised, a genuine hero, the epitome of all the virtues of a country that, thanks to him and a handful of others like him, was finally reclaiming the memory of anti-Francoism and anti-fascism that Spanish democracy had brushed aside and bringing them to the fore after a long silence. It isn't surprising, in fact was inevitable, that Marco would also become an apostle of the truth, in particular of historical truth. It was one of the fundamental themes he talked about in his interviews and his writings, in his endless talks to teenagers and adults. Marco believed that the country was living a lie and blamed this on the way the transition from dictatorship to democracy had been managed. The Transition, he believed, had been founded on a lie and on a Pact of Forgetting: in order to build a democracy, the country, incapable of knowing or recognising itself and ensuring justice, had decided to forget the horrors of Civil War and dictatorship, with the result that it was a false democracy founded on a false reconciliation, because it was built on lies, injustice and amnesia, on the sacrifice of victims and the sacrifice of truth, since the guilty parties during the Civil War and the dictatorship had not been punished nor their victims compensated. In short: "Forgive, YES; forget, NO." This is why Marco continued to say the things he did. For example, in an article published on June 8, 2003, in *La Vanguardia* about the survivors of Mauthausen—not only had he never been a prisoner there, but he hadn't even claimed to be a prisoner—he said: "We [camp survivors] have never had any public acknowledgement from the Spanish state, beyond a memorial plaque or a wreath: they need to recognise the reasons for our struggle, which were no less than freedom itself. [. . .] It is clear to me that we are the price paid for the Transition: this country founded its reconciliation on a pact of forgetting." And this is why, on December 18, 2002, just before he was elected president of the Amical de Mauthausen, Marco signed a manifesto at the Museum of Catalan History calling for the recovery of so-called historical memory and the creation of a Truth Commission that would compel the country to finally face up to its recent past.

The paradox, however, is specious, because the emphasis on truth betrays the liar: in his denunciation of a country that hid the truth in order not to know itself or recognise itself, and his defence of the memory of the *deportados*, or simply of so-called historical memory, Marco, who had spent his life hiding the truth so as not to know or recognise himself, finally found a cause equal to his ambitions, the cause that would turn him into a popular hero and put the finishing touches on his plan to hide the truth about himself and his own past. The anarchist leader who made up for his lack of policy with his frenetic hyperactivity and the charming, funny, but rather insignificant old man at FaPaC were far behind him now; at Amical, or during the time he spent at Amical, Marco attained a different, superior stature. At an institution that literally lived off the past, because the past not only imbued everything with meaning but was its principal asset, its principal source of prestige and its principal instrument of power, an institution where no-one had a past to rival his, to say nothing of his youth, his energy and his gift with words, an institution that had made heroes of victims, Marco felt he was untouchable, he abandoned the wariness that had thus far informed his deception and lapsed into a vice that had thus far eluded him: arrogance. Betrayed by his insatiable need to play the starring role, feeling that he was now beyond harm, convinced that he was the character he had completely internalised over the course of hundreds and hundreds of talks and public speeches, believing himself armour-plated by virtue of his social status, his political prestige and his aura of hero, martyr and secular saint, from time to time Marco could not resist launching into a subtle battle of egos with the elderly *deportados;* disparaging or looking down his nose at his co-workers at the Amical or his comrades in the cause, and, if the situation required, crushing them beneath the unassailable weight of his past as omnipresent demigod in the history of the country; inventing new anecdotes that were utterly implausible, such as his conquests and sexual adventures in Flossenbürg camp; or even daring to dramatise for television incidents that, until now, had been no more than a few discreet sentences in a book and used in public only in his talks with schoolchildren, like the life-and-death chess match with the SS officer. Now he had no fear of saying anything because he believed that, whatever he said, people would unquestioningly believe him; now he no longer listened to anyone around him because he no longer considered anyone around him to be his equal. Arrogance was his downfall; arrogance and, ironically, forgetting the past. Marco forgot that the past is never dead, it is only an aspect or a dimension of the present, that it's not even past, as Faulkner says;

it always returns but it doesn't always return to save, as, transformed into fiction, it had always or almost always saved him; sometimes, transformed into reality, it returns to kill. Because fiction saves and reality kills, or that's what Marco believed and what I believed, but the past sometimes saves and sometimes kills. And this time it killed him.

4

In the years when Marco was the public face of the Amical de Mauthausen, when he was transformed into a champion or a rock star
of historical memory, Spain was experiencing the apotheosis of so-
called historical memory; in fact it had reached its apotheosis all over
Europe, but few countries experienced it as intensely as Spain. Why?

The expression "historical memory" is ambiguous and deeply
confusing. At heart it entails a contradiction: as I wrote in "The Blackmail of the Witness," history and memory are opposites. "Memory is
individual, partial and subjective," I wrote, "history is collective and
aspires to be comprehensive and objective." No-one capitalised on
this insoluble antithesis better than Marco. Maurice Halbwachs, who
developed the concept of historical memory, says that it is "borrowed
memory," in which we remember not our personal experiences, but
those experienced by others and related to us; Marco practiced this
impossibility to the letter, fashioning his speeches from the memories
of others (which partly explains why, in his talks, he would casually
shift from "I" to "we"). Although in theory he did so to reclaim the
memory of the victims, in practice he simply laid bare the futility and
the lethal risks entailed in using this concept that is as absurd as it has
been successful. If this were not enough, in Spain, aside from being
an oxymoron the expression "historical memory" was a euphemism;
so-called historical memory was in fact the memory of the Republican victims of the Civil War and of the Franco regime, and recovering or vindicating it entailed demanding redress for these victims
and demanding truth and justice concerning the Civil War and the
Franco regime in order to finally move beyond this terrible past.

It was a perfectly just demand. Marco was both right and wrong: he was right when, in his speeches and his interviews, he said that Spanish democracy had been founded on a big collective lie; he was wrong when he said that it was founded on a pact of forgetting. It is a contradictory truth, or so it seems, but the truth often seems, or is, contradictory. Spanish democracy was founded on a big collective lie, or rather on a long series of little individual lies, because, as Marco knows better than anyone, during the transition from dictatorship to democracy, people constructed a fictitious past for themselves, lied about their true past, or embellished or embroidered it, the better to face the present and prepare for the future, eager to prove that they had always been democrats and, during the Franco regime, had been clandestine opponents, official pariahs, silent resistants, dormant or active anti-Francoists, all hoping to hide the fact that they had been apathetic, cowards or collaborators (and therefore, in this period of massive reinvention, Marco wasn't the exception but the rule). We don't know whether this was a necessary lie, one of Plato's noble lies, one of Montaigne's altruistic lies, one of Nietzsche's vital lies—one of the fictions that saves from the reality that kills—nor do we know whether democracy could have been established in any other way, whether it could have been built on truth with the whole country rec- ognising or knowing itself, without dying, like Narcissus, when faced with its own reflection. The only thing we know is that it was a lie and that it is there, at the source, at the origin of everything.

As for the pact of forgetting, it isn't so much a falsehood as a cliché; that is to say, a half-truth. It isn't true that during the Transi- tion, memory was deactivated and people forgot the war, the post-war period, or even its victims; on the contrary, although the expression "historical memory" wasn't in general circulation at the time, the recent past was very much the fashion, one that was particularly ben- eficial to Marco, and, at the age of fifty, allowed him to build a new life for himself. There was a great interest in history, or at least in that particular period of history: numerous books were published, numer- ous articles were written, films were made and conferences held about the Second Republic, the Civil War, the Republican exile, the Fran- coist courts-martial, the Francoist prisons, the anti-Franco guerrillas, the opposition to Franco and a thousand other subjects in an attempt to satiate the public's obsessive thirst for information about a period that had hitherto been hushed up or distorted by the dictatorship. In fact there was a pact of remembering, which explains why, during the Transition, all or almost all the political parties came together in order not to repeat the mistakes that, forty years earlier, had triggered the Civil War, and which also broadly explains how it was possible to make the death-defying leap from dictatorship to democracy with no war, no bloodshed and without unleashing a reckless conflict. This was an implicit pact that forbade using the recent past as a weapon in political debate; had that period been forgotten, such a pact would have been irrational: it worked precisely because everyone remembered all too well.

So, where is the truth in the half-truth that is the pact of forgetting? Aside from being a cliché, the pact of forgetting is another euphemism, a way of naming one of the principal failings of the Transition without naming it: it refers to the fact that there would be no thorough investigation into the recent past, no prosecution of the crimes of the dictatorship and no compensation for its victims. The first two of these could probably not have been done at the time without undermining the democracy, or that was believed by all or almost all the parties and all or almost all the people of Spain who chose not to pursue justice in exchange for building a democracy; as for the victims, it isn't true that nothing was done, but it is true that not everything that should have been done was done, whether from a moral, material or symbolic point of view. In this, Marco was also right: although he was not among them, the victims of the dictatorship were the price paid, or an important part of the price paid, for the Transition.

And so, strictly speaking, the great myth of the "silence of the Transition" is just that, a myth; in other words, a mixture of truth and lies; in other words, a lie. In fact, the silence came later, in the Eighties, when the right-wing that grew out of Francoism, now in opposition, still had no desire to talk about the past because it only stood to lose by doing so, and the socialist left, now in power, was no longer interested in doing so because it had nothing to gain. As for the rest of us, we were too busy enjoying our pristine, brand-new future as rich, civilised Europeans to concern ourselves with our sordid recent past as impoverished, fratricidal Spaniards. This is the reality: we didn't assimilate the past. This is what happened: the fashion for the past passed. At times, the past itself seemed to pass, or seemed to be past. But we know that, even if it seems so, the past is never dead, it cannot lapse, because—as Faulkner says—it's not even past.

And the past inevitably returned. In the second half of the Nineties, while throughout Europe the obsession with the cult of memory continued to thrive, in Spain the right won the elections and the left discovered the power of using the right's past during the Civil War and the Franco regime against them, since they were the heirs of Francoism and had never completely disaffiliated themselves. Something else happened at precisely the same time. A new generation of Spaniards was coming of age who, perhaps because they barely had an individual past or were barely conscious of it, had not been interested in their collective past, or not particularly: this was the moment they began to take an interest. These were the grandchildren of the Civil War, those who had no personal experience of war, and scarcely any memory of the Franco regime, but suddenly we discovered that the past is the present or a dimension of the present. The convergence of these two factors changed everything completely.

This was the beginning of the apotheosis.

In October 2000, a group of people who, three months later, would go on to found the Association for the Recovery of Historical Memory excavated the bodies of three Republicans murdered at the beginning of the Civil War and buried in a mass grave in El Bierzo, León. It wasn't the first time something of the kind had happened—in 1980, for example, a similar discovery took place in La Solana, Ciudad Real—but this incident garnered sufficient media attention to seem symbolic. In the years that followed, a movement began to emerge in Spain, particularly in Catalonia, Madrid and Andalucía, one that, in a short period, cultivated towns and cities with associations and foundations devoted to reviewing the past and vindicating the memory of the victims: in late 2003, there were some thirty organisations, but by late 2005, there were almost one hundred and sixty. These three years coincided with the three years when Marco was president of the Amical de Mauthausen and with the upsurge of so-called historical memory. During this period and in the three or four years that followed, mass graves were excavated, corpses exhumed and attempts were made to trace the *desaparecidos*—estimated at between 30,000 and 50,000 people. Conventions, memorials, assemblies and seminars were held, theses were written, countless novels and books about the recent past were published and numerous films and documentaries were released, projects were devised to collect testimonies while political and institutional initiatives of every kind were launched, the most important of which was the Law of Historical Memory, which was first proposed when the Socialists regained power in 2004, and whose full title says all that needs to be said: "Law to recognise and extend rights and to establish measures in favour of those who have been victims of political persecution or violence during the Civil War and the Dictatorship."

The past had returned. It had come back stronger than ever. There is a German word, *Vergangenheitsbewältigung*, which can be translated, or which the writer Patricio Pron has translated, as "the process of coming to terms with the past through its constant revision." It describes a process begun by the Germans in the late Sixties, a quarter of a century after the end of the Nazi regime, with the purpose of facing up to their Nazi past; in 2001, a quarter of a century after the death of Franco, all signs point to the fact that Spain was beginning a similar process. *The worst thing is to think / that you are right because you were right,* says the poet José Ángel Valente; it's possible that in the late Seventies, just after the dictatorship in Spain, investigating and prosecuting its crimes and even compensating its victims would have made democracy impossible, and therefore, in the immediate aftermath of Franco's death, it was as difficult for the Spanish to face up to the past, to recognise or know themselves and to see justice done as it was for the Germans in the immediate aftermath of the death of Hitler; but twenty-five years later, with democracy firmly rooted in the country, and the country firmly rooted within Europe, this was no longer the case, and the apotheosis of memory seemed to be a signal that Spain was about to repay its debt, the price it had paid for a bloodless transition from dictatorship to freedom: the symbols of Francoism that still lingered on the streets and the plazas would be eliminated, the dead would be buried with dignity, a record would be made of the *desaparecidos*, the victims of the Civil War and the dictatorship would be fully compensated.

All of these things were not simply reasonable, they were necessary. However, many of them later began to seem suspicious; even I, who believed all these things were necessary (or perhaps because I believed it) began to find them suspicious. The proof being that, on January 2, 2008, after the so-called Law of Historical Memory was finally passed and Judge Baltasar Garzón requested information about those who disappeared during the war and the post-war period, intending to open an investigation into the crimes committed during the Franco regime, I published an article in *El País* entitled "The Tyranny of Memory" in which, having suggested that we forbid the use of the expression "historical memory" and speaking out against the dangers of the abuse of memory, especially the analogous and much greater danger that memory might come to be substituted for history, I praised the objectives of the movement in support of victims; but then qualified:

> It is a very different matter for the government to enact a law in order to do something it should long since have done without needing to pass a law, especially a law that has no teeth and one which, to cap it all, the authorities now seem reluctant to enforce: I do not find it remotely acceptable to have the government legislating about history, let alone about memory—just as I would not find it acceptable if it began to legislate about literature—because history is made by historians, not politicians, and memory is made by each of us, and because a law of this kind is embarrassingly evocative of the methods of totalitarian states, which know that the best way to control the present is to control the past; but the law is there to be enforced and, once ratified, it should be immediately and rigorously enforced. Nor is it acceptable that a judge has been tasked with doing something that—as I have just said—the government should already have done: Adolfo Suárez could not have done it, had he tried, La Moncloa would have been bombed; Felipe González did not do it; nor

José María Aznar—it would have been good if he had, since it would have proved that the right had truly distanced itself from Francoism; and now since José Luis Rodríguez Zapatero is all bark and no bite and reluctant to enforce, it is a good thing that Judge Garzón is prodding him a little (he will go no further, Garzón knows that what he is proposing is impossible).

But there was something much more suspicious, and much more dangerous, and this was the fact that what had started out as a deep-seated need in the country had quickly become a passing fad. Perhaps no-one realised this sooner or more acutely than Sergio Gálvez Biescas, a member of the Department of Historical Memory at the Complutense University of Madrid: "At the intersection between associations, institutional initiatives and the work being carried out by investigators," Gálvez Biescas wrote in 2006, "the Recovery of the Historical Memory of the victims of Francoist oppression has entered a competitive market that has turned these elements into both a powerful marketing tool and an instrument of control of the present in the service of political interests." Interests, marketing, market, competitive: this was the transformation of historical memory into the industry of memory.

What is the industry of memory? A business. What does the business produce? A pale imitation, a devaluation, a prostitution of memory; and also a prostitution, a devaluation, a pale imitation of history, because in an era of memory, memory takes up much of history's space. To put it another way: the industry of memory is to genuine history what the entertainment industry is to genuine art; and just as aesthetic kitsch is the product of the entertainment industry, so historical kitsch is the product of the industry of memory. Historical kitsch; in other words: a historical lie.

Marco was the perfect embodiment of this kitsch. First and foremost because he himself was a walking lie; but also because he was a relentless supplier of kitsch, of "poisonous sentimental fodder seasoned with historical good conscience" that, as I wrote in the article "I am Enric Marco," fuelled Marco's discourse, a discourse with none of the shading, the ambiguity, the complexities, the gaps and fears and dizziness and contradictions and asperities and moral chiaroscuro of genuine memory and genuine history, a discourse devoid of the terrifying "grey zone" Primo Levi talked about, the mawkish, soothing, deceitful discourse that people wanted to hear. In December 2004, shortly before he unmasked Marco's deception, Benito Bermejo concluded an article written with Sandra Checa, in which they unmasked the fake *deportado* Antonio Pasto, with the ominous sentence: "Paradoxically, the celebration of memory may signify its downfall."

This is precisely what happened. I write this in mid-2014, when few people in Spain still remember so-called historical memory and when any mention of it, or what remains of it, occurs only very occasionally in newspapers, on radio or television. The fashion for the past passed yet again and, especially after the financial crash of 2008, the country ceased to worry about the past so it could focus its fears on the present, as though the past were a luxury it could no longer afford. The so-called Law of Historical Memory was quickly revealed for what it was: an inadequate law, indifferent to victims, conceived by Socialists less to put an end to the problem of the past than to keep it alive for as long as possible and use it against the right. In any case, it hardly matters, because it is some time since the law has been enforced, because there's no money to enforce it, according to the current right-wing government, and many of the associations that flourished in the previous decade only to become quickly entangled in byzantine arguments and impenetrable internal struggles have vanished or are rusting in dry dock, no funds, and perhaps no future, as happened to the Amical de Mauthausen. As for Judge Garzón, he truly believed it was possible to achieve his goal, but he was wrong: in February 2012, he was barred from the legal profession for eleven years and removed from the bench, in theory because he ordered wiretaps on an organisation paying off politicians within government, but more especially because he attempted to investigate the crimes committed under the Franco regime, because he'd made too many powerful enemies, and, ultimately, for sticking his nose where it did not belong. Meanwhile, the corpses of the dead still lie in mass graves and in ditches—the so-called Law of Historical Memory didn't handle the exhumations, it simply subsidised them, and the subsidies have dried up—the victims will not be fully compensated and this country will never break with its past if it doesn't make any effort to face it or stamp out the lie which was the root or the foundation of everything. Spain will never recognise or know itself for what it was, or in other words what it is, and we the Spanish will not have our *Vergangenheitsbewältigung*. Or at least not until the past comes around again. Except that when it comes back, it will already be too late, at least for the victims.

That is how things stand. The industry of memory proved fatal to memory, or that which we call memory and is little more than a craven euphemism. This may have been the last opportunity, and we missed it. Nothing is worse than thinking you can save yourself because you have saved yourself: perhaps fiction did save us for many years just as for many years it saved Marco and Don Quixote; but in the end only the truth can save us, just as in the end it saved Don Quixote, turning him back into Alonso Quixano, and perhaps it will save Marco, turning him back into the real Marco. Assuming we can hope for salvation, obviously: Cervantes saved Alonso Quixano and perhaps, without realising, or without recognising it, I am doing my utmost in this book to save Marco. The question is: Who will save the rest of us? Who, at least, will do their utmost to save us? The answer is: no-one.

5

Now we come to the man who, for many people, is the hidden villain of the story, the man who unmasked Enric Marco, our hero's Nemesis: now we come to Benito Bermejo. From the moment the Marco scandal erupted, people have said all manner of things about him, almost as much as they've said about Marco himself. There have been pronouncements from journalists, historians, politicians, trade unionists, writers, businessmen and workers more or less familiar with the industry of memory. Below are some of the things that have been said about him.

It has been said that Bermejo exposed Marco because for many people Marco embodied the movement for the recovery of so-called historical memory in Spain and that, in destroying Marco, Bermejo was attempting to destroy this movement. It has been said that he personally resented Marco and the Amical de Mauthausen and destroyed Marco in the hope of destroying the Amical. It has been said that he wanted to destroy the Amical because it was the largest Spanish association of *deportados* and was based in Barcelona and that he wanted to move it to Madrid and seize control of it. It has been said that he wanted to wrest control of the Amical to make it part of the Fundación Pablo Iglesias, which is part of the Spanish Socialist Workers' Party. It has been said, inversely, that Bermejo wanted to damage the Spanish Socialist Workers' Party and its secretary general, José Luis Rodríguez Zapatero, who was prime minister at the time. It has been said that he acted out of pure malice, or sheer opportunism, or an overwhelming desire to be in the limelight. It has been said—said in the throes of the scandal by no less a figure than Jaume Álvarez, a Mauthausen survivor and Marco's successor as president of Amical, and widely reprinted in the press—that Bermejo, who was born in Salamanca, exposed Marco as an act of revenge for the so-called Salamanca papers, a collection of documents confiscated from the Catalan government by Francoist forces in the last days of the Civil War and stored in an archive in Salamanca, documents that the left-wing Spanish government, after repeated appeals by Catalonia, had agreed to return in spite of fierce opposition from all right-wing parties, some of the left-wing, and by the City Hall and the University of Salamanca. It has been said that Bermejo is not actually a historian but an agent of Mossad, the Israeli secret service, or that he is a historian hired by Mossad or by the Spanish secret services on behalf of Mossad, in short that he is an individual paid by the Israeli government to punish Marco for a remark made in a speech given to the Spanish parliament on January 27, 2005, in the presence of the Israeli ambassador to Spain, as part of an homage to the victims of the Holocaust, a remark he had previously made in all or almost all of his countless talks: that concentration camps had not disappeared, but still existed in various parts of the world, including Palestine.

I'll stop there. Though I could carry on: many more things have been said about Bermejo, all or almost all as bizarre as those listed above. The reason is that Marco is a consummate storyteller, but he doesn't have a monopoly; in fact, what Marco did was simply exploit our incurable penchant for fiction, one all the more palpable given the damning evidence that we can hide behind it, and all the more useful given it allows us to shirk unpleasant responsibilities. Because it is extraordinary that no-one stated the obvious, that Bermejo is a serious historian and, as such, a sworn enemy of the industry of memory, just as a serious artist is the sworn enemy of the entertainment industry: on principle, both battle deceitful narcissism; both seek out knowledge—knowledge or self-knowledge, knowledge or acknowledgement of reality; both wage war on kitsch, or—it amounts to the same thing—lies. Bermejo didn't simply expose Marco's deception, he also exposed—or so felt many who sought to turn him into the villain—the culpable credulity and the lack of intellectual rigour of those who fell for Marco's deception.

· · ·

While he is a serious historian, Bermejo is also a marginal historian: a man who lives on the sidelines of the academic and university system. He isn't a professor at a university or institution, and at the time the scandal erupted, he hadn't even presented his doctoral thesis, an indispensable requirement for anyone wishing to pursue an academic career. In fact, he didn't pursue any form of career in academia, though he took his degree in history in Salamanca, the city where he had been born into a middle-class family. Perhaps there was something about the Spanish university system, with its intractable hierarchies, its frenzied in-breeding, its *cursus honorum*, encrusted with rhetorical rigidness and prudish pantomimes, that was anathema to the typically sober and reserved Castilian character of Bermejo, because he certainly never fit in; though to tell the truth, I doubt he tried very hard. Nonetheless, it's worth wondering why it was someone outside the groves of academe who dared to unmask Marco and give a poke in the eye to the industry of memory which had benefited so much from academia. Bermejo is a maverick: he doesn't give classes, he doesn't write for newspapers and, though he has a wife and two young daughters, he has no permanent post and earns his living in an ad hoc fashion. He lives in a modest apartment on calle García de Paredes in the district of Chamberí in Madrid.

Despite the fact that he didn't pursue an academic career, when he completed his history degree, Bermejo presented a thesis to the University of Salamanca on the subject of propaganda and the control of social communications in the early years of Francoism and, in 1987, thanks to a research grant, he moved to Madrid. It was in part thanks to another grant that he spent two years in Paris, doing research at the Sorbonne. It was in Paris, at the Librairie espagnole, 72 rue de Seine, that he first heard about Spanish *deportados* being imprisoned in the Nazi camps, many of whom knew the bookshop manager, Antonio Soriano; however, he only became truly interested in the subject in the early 1990s. At this point no academic historian had conducted serious research into the fate of the *deportados*; there had been books by writers and journalists like Pons Prades, Montserrat Roig or Antonio Vilanova, but none of them had the technical tools or the meth-

odological rigour of historiography. At the time, Bermejo had just
begun to work with the National University of Distance Learning
on a series of documentaries about the Spanish exiles of 1939, and, as
part of his exploration, got in touch with a number of *deportados*, with
two of the big exile associations—the French chapter of the Amical
and F.E.D.I.P. (Spanish Federation of *Deportados* and Political Prisoners)—and with the only organisation within Spain, the Amical de
Mauthausen. In the late Nineties, while researching a documentary
about Francesc Boix, the Spanish photographer of Mauthausen who
had given evidence at the Nuremberg trials, he began working more
closely with the Amical in Barcelona and found himself needing to
use its archive. He was allowed in, though this created friction with
the Amical and a number of its members, particularly Rosa Torán.
The film about Francesc Boix was broadcast on television in 2000;
two years later, Bermejo published a book based on his documentary.
By this time, he had personally known Marco for some months.

The first he'd heard of our hero was in late 2000, or perhaps early
2001. Margarida Sala, curator of the Museu d'Històrie de Catalunya
and member of Amical, mentioned him. She told Bermejo that one
of the members of Amical, a man named Enric Marco, was a survivor
of a Nazi camp and, more than a survivor, he was a historian. Bermejo was very interested by this news: firstly, because, although he'd
spent more than a decade gathering information about the *deportados*, speaking to them, delving into their lives, no-one had ever mentioned Marco's name; secondly because, although he knew a number
of French *deportados* who were both camp survivors and historians, he
knew of no-one in Spain who fulfilled both criteria. Later, searching
his memory, or going through his papers, Bermejo realised he'd been
mistaken: obviously, he was very familiar with Pons Prades' book
about the *deportados*, now it occurred to him that the Marco he'd read
about there, and perhaps in some other books, was the same man Sala
had been talking about.

Shortly afterwards, the two men met. It happened on November
6, 2001, at the Amical tribute in honour of Montserrat Roig at the
Palau de la Música in Barcelona. It was a brief encounter; at the end
of the tribute, Bermejo, having been invited by Rosa Torán, went over
to a table where the Amical were selling various books; Marco was

there, packing the books away. They introduced themselves. Marco's youthful appearance must have confused Bermejo, given everything he had read and heard, because he asked whether Marco was the son of the camp survivor; no, Marco replied, it was he who had been a prisoner in Flossenbürg. That was the extent of their conversation. The crowds and the commotion that followed the event made it impossible for them to carry on, or Marco made the most of the confusion to cut things short. Nevertheless, the brief exchange piqued Bermejo's curiosity. He knew that there had been very few Spaniards in Flossenbürg concentration camp, and until now all his attempts to locate one had proved futile (though he had managed to track down and interview a French survivor from the camp). Needless to say, this made Marco even more valuable to Bermejo as a witness.

The second encounter between the two men wasn't accidental, and the historian arrived well prepared. It took place in Mauthausen during the celebrations commemorating the liberation of the camp, which took place every year on the weekend following May 5. Bermejo, a regular visitor at such events (which were useful for his work, since they allowed him to meet with *deportados* and gather information), suggests it took place in 2001, but that is impossible since at that time he hadn't yet met Marco; it must have been in 2002, or perhaps even 2003. Bermejo was still intrigued by Marco, though his suspicions hadn't yet been aroused, despite the fact that the three accounts of Marco's life he'd read—in *The Kommandant's Pigs*, in the magazine *Tiempo de Historia*, and in *A Memoir of Hell* which had just been published—did not match up: Bermejo was well aware that it was typical for various accounts by a single survivor to contain discrepancies and attributed those he noted in Marco's accounts to errors made by the interviewers, Marco's failing memory, or a combination of both. That day at Mauthausen, Bermejo twice spoke to Marco about his experience in the Nazi camps. The first time was in the camp itself, 200 metres above the Danube, before the ceremony took place. Bermejo asked Marco about his dual status as camp survivor and historian; Marco offered a nebulous response, he was evasive, he said something vague about having studied history at the Autonomous University in Barcelona, said that he had worked with Josep Fontana and together they had set up a research team to explore the subject.

The second time they spoke was during lunch. They were now back in the city of Mauthausen and in the company of Rosa Torán—who may have gone to the camp with Marco or met with him there. The three chatted over a lunch organised by the descendants of the hundred or so Spaniards who had elected to stay on in Austria after the camp was liberated, and who met every year on the same date. There were some thirty or forty diners, most of them Austrian, but Bermejo engineered things so that he could sit opposite Marco; Rosa Torán was sitting next to Marco.

What happened over lunch proved very disconcerting for Bermejo. As he had planned—it may have been something he always did when he first met with a camp survivor—he asked Marco to talk about the time he had spent in Flossenbürg; Marco cut him off before he had even voiced his request: told him he didn't feel talking about the matter would lead anywhere, told him not to bother with such things, told him there were much more important subjects, then he immediately took a photograph from his wallet and showed it to Bermejo. It was a photograph of Marco himself, stripped to the waist, his back and his hips mottled with bruises; Bermejo did not know—he couldn't have known—that this was one of the photographs Marco had had taken on September 28, 1979, while secretary general of the C.N.T., after he'd been beaten by police attempting to break up an anarchist demonstration calling for amnesty for the accused in the Scala Affair; but more importantly it was documentary evidence that he, too, had been a victim, a resistance fighter, a hero. This is what you should be investigating, Marco peremptorily informed Bermejo. Not the other thing. There was a tense silence, or so Bermejo remembers; he also remembers that Torán, who was sitting on the other side of the table, seemed tense and uneasy. She looked worried. Marco's message was clear: don't go down this road; perhaps Marco hoped to present this as an academic suggestion—you should choose a different path: not the victims of the Nazis but those of the Franco regime—but Bermejo took it as a piece of personal advice, even a veiled threat. He was thunderstruck. He had often encountered camp survivors who didn't want to discuss their experiences, because they were still traumatised, because they wanted to forget, or because they found it painful to remember; Marco, however, was completely different: at the time he would have already been president of Amical, or at least a member of the board of directors, and for years now he had been giving talks, granting interviews, talking endlessly about his experiences in Flossenbürg. How was it possible that Marco was prepared to talk about the subject to anyone but him?

It would take Bermejo some time to clear up the matter. That afternoon in Mauthausen, he didn't ask Marco anything else about his past, but our man's behaviour had sowed the seeds of suspicion.

In the months that followed, his suspicions continued to multiply. In October 2003, there occurred a scene similar to the one I've just described, though it didn't take place in Mauthausen but in Almería, and the protagonists were not Marco and Bermejo but Marco and Sandra Checa, another straight-shooting historian interested in Spanish survivors of the Nazi camps. The incident took place at the funeral of Antonio Muñoz Zamora, an Amical member and survivor of Mauthausen; Checa, who had attended the service as a friend of Muñoz Zamora, told Bermejo about it in a phone call shortly afterwards.

Among the mourners, Checa told Bermejo, were Marco and Antonio Pastor Martínez, a phoney camp survivor they were trying to unmask at the time: Pastor had been at the funeral though he'd only been a vague acquaintance of the deceased; despite this, he said a few words during the service; Marco had been there as president of Amical. Checa told Bermejo that, at some point, she approached Marco, introduced herself as a historian, and said that she would be very interested in talking to him. Marco's response was identical or almost identical to the one he'd given Bermejo in Mauthausen: though he didn't show her the photograph of the bruises, he told her to forget the matter, that it would lead nowhere, that she should find a more interesting subject. This was the extent of her conversation with Marco, but not of her phone conversation with Bermejo. Among the veteran Republicans, camp survivors and friends of the deceased in attendance, she told Bermejo, was Santiago Carrillo—the almost nonagenarian former secretary general of the communist party forced from his post some twenty years earlier, a wily old fox with a gift for detecting impostors honed by decades of exile and Stalinist interference—and after the funeral, he made some sarcastic or ironic comment about Marco and Pastor. Only a few of those present overheard and Checa had forgotten or didn't remember exactly (or perhaps it was Bermejo who forgot or didn't remember exactly), but effectively he suggested that the two men were not to be trusted.

The third and last meeting between Bermejo and Marco occurred six months after the funeral of Muñoz Zamora. It took place in May 2004, again in Mauthausen, on the day commemorating the liberation of the camp, or to be more precise, on the eve of the commemoration, and not in Mauthausen itself, but in Ebensee, an *Aussenkommando* or subcamp or satellite camp eighty kilometres south of Mauthausen. By now, Bermejo had spent several years compiling information about Marco, comparing various sources and working out that Marco's account of his time in the camp made no sense, that it was riddled with contradictions and impossibilities; he didn't yet have definitive proof with which to categorically refute the story, but he was completely convinced, or almost completely convinced, that the president of the Amical was not who he claimed to be.

For some time, Bermejo had been asking questions about Marco, especially of those who'd had a direct relationship with him. Whether he spoke to former *deportados* or to veteran anarchists from the C.N.T., the response was always the same, or almost always the same: "I wouldn't stick my neck out for him," they said. "He's a shady character," they said. "There's something fishy about him," they said. "He's not trustworthy," they said. And even: "Maybe he's an infiltrator." I'm not sure whether Bermejo knew or was sufficiently conscious of the fact that such responses might be explained by the deep wounds inflicted during the brutal power struggles within the C.N.T. in the Seventies, in which Marco played an important role; nevertheless, to Bermejo, such unanimity seemed suspicious. He also thought it suspicious that Marco, whose official story claimed that he left Spain clandestinely and was imprisoned in Marseille before being deported to Flossenbürg, had never had any contact whatever with the French organisation the Amicale de Flossenbürg, where no-one knew anything about him. Nor did anyone at the Spanish Federation of *Deportados* and Political Prisoners (which also had a branch in France), something that seemed more than suspicious to Bermejo, who thought it almost impossible that a Spanish anarchist who had survived the Nazi camps would have no contact with the organisation.

Naturally, Bermejo had requested information from the Flossenbürg Memorial archives about Marco and been informed that there was no mention of a prisoner named Marco in the camp registers; moreover he still couldn't get his head around the patent contrast, not so much between the abundance and the epic, sentimental tone of Marco's stories compared to those of other camp survivors, but between Marco's loquacity in public and his categorical refusal to speak in private.

But what he found most suspicious and which, together with the foregoing, led him to the conclusion that Marco had invented his story, or a large part of his story, was: the more he studied Marco's various accounts and discovered points that were contradictory or even nonsensical, the more he realised these couldn't simply be attributed to Marco's poor memory or to errors made by journalists or writers who had set the stories down, and therefore Marco must be wilfully altering his life story. He began to glimpse the truth. He began to speculate that perhaps Marco *had* been in Germany in the Forties, not as a *deportado*, but as a volunteer worker, because his account of his route to Germany via France sounded very similar to that of Spanish volunteer workers—on at least two occasions, for example, Marco had mentioned Metz, the city from which such workers were reallocated—and because he knew that Marco was a metalworker and that one of the first volunteer convoys to leave Barcelona had been made up of metalworkers, most of whom ended up working in northern Germany, where Marco admitted he'd spent time in prison. Lastly, in early May 2004, when Bermejo was writing an article with Sandra Checa proving that the supposed Mauthausen *deportado* Antonio Pastor was actually an impostor, he had the conviction—though not the proof—that Marco, too, was an impostor.

It was at this point that he had his last encounter with Marco. It took place, as I said, at Ebensee, one of the subcamps of Mauthausen, set in a mountainous region where, late in the war, the Germans excavated a network of underground tunnels where they could set up armaments factories safe from Allied bombings. That day there was to be a small commemoration service at Ebensee prior to the main ceremony at Mauthausen camp the following day. Bermejo and Marco met in one of the tunnels beneath the subcamp. They talked. Marco was surrounded by a group of teenagers; he explained to Bermejo that they were students who had travelled from Barcelona thanks to the Amical and that he was acting as their guide. Then he talked to Bermejo about the activities of Amical, which were increasingly numerous and varied, and mentioned that the following year, the sixtieth anniversary of the liberation of Mauthausen, they hoped to bring an important person, perhaps a member or a representative of the government, to attend the commemoration. This was followed by a very brief exchange, every word of which is engraved in Bermejo's memory: "We're flying high," Marco told him, remarking on the success of the Amical under his leadership, "higher and higher." Bermejo commented: "Well, we must hope it doesn't turn out to be the flight of Icarus." Contrary to what he expected, Marco didn't seem annoyed by his ironic quip about Daedalus' reckless son, who because he wanted to fly close to the sun tumbled into the sea and lost his life, as Narcissus did contemplating his reflection in the pool. Before taking his leave with his students, Marco replied fervently, "Our Icaruses are old and increasingly feeble, but they are still here, still fighting." Bermejo remembers that he stressed the second syllable of the name *Icaro*, while Marco stressed the first syllable. In Spanish both pronunciations are correct.

The proof that Bermejo was lacking finally appeared early the following year. In fact it's possible to be more precise, because the historian noted the discovery in his diary: January 21. In less than a week, the Spanish parliament would for the first time commemorate International Holocaust Remembrance Day, and, also for the first time, welcome a representative of the Spanish survivors of the camps, a ceremony at which Marco was to give a speech; in just over three months, commemorations for the sixtieth anniversary of the liberation of Mauthausen would take place, and for the first time the Spanish prime minister would be in attendance and for the first time a speech would be given by a Spanish *deportado*, who, until the last minute, was to be Marco.

Bermejo didn't stumble on the evidence by accident. At some point it had occurred to him that he might find information about Marco in the archives of the Ministry for Foreign Affairs, which he had consulted on previous occasions, and when he visited the archive, he discovered that his hunch had been right. There was a file on Marco, no more than three pages but not a word was wasted. The file contained a request from the captaincy of the IV Región Militar, headquartered in Barcelona, stating that Marco had not reported for military service and asking the Ministry for Foreign Affairs to confirm whether, as his family insisted, Marco had travelled to Germany as a volunteer worker; the response from the Ministry for Foreign Affairs confirmed that the family was telling the truth, that Marco was currently in Germany, in Kiel to be exact, working for the Deutsche Werke Werft. In other words, the army was seeking information about a possible draft evader and the Ministry for Foreign Affairs replied that he was not a draft evader but a conscientious citizen who had travelled to Germany in accordance with the Hispano-German Accord signed by Franco and Hitler. There were only three pages, but they were enough to prove beyond all doubt that at least one fundamental part of Marco's story, in its many variants, was false; he had not left Spain clandestinely, he had not been arrested in France and sent to Germany, he was not a *deportado*. The document did not prove that Marco wasn't a survivor of Flossenbürg—there was still the possibility that, while in Germany, Marco had been arrested by the Nazis and sent to a concentration camp, as had happened to other volunteer workers—but it did prove that Marco had lied. There were only three pages, but they were enough to destroy Marco.

Bermejo's euphoria at his discovery must have been short-lived, because his next thought was "What now?" Despite what many later claimed, Bermejo felt no animus towards Marco, nor did he relish the idea of being a wet blanket, of poking people in the eye, certainly not an old man. The proof is that, a few short months earlier, he and Sandra Checa had had to wrestle with their scruples before publishing the article that exposed the deception of Antonio Pastor—they questioned whether it was justifiable to run the risk of destroying a man's reputation in exchange for re-establishing the historical truth, and what the likely consequences of such destruction would be; further proof is, in the end, they decided that in their article Pastor would not be identified by name, but only by his initials. What now? Bermejo asked himself. His provisional response was to call a number of trusted individuals and tell them what he'd found out about Marco. He told two camp survivors, Paco Aura and Francisco Batiste; he told Jordi Riera, the son of a *deportado* and a member of Amical; he may have told others. None of these people knew what to advise, and at least one of them said: do anything except do nothing.

In early February, specifically February 9 (again, according to Bermejo's diary), something strange occurred: Marco telephoned Bermejo at home. It was the first time he'd done such a thing. Marco didn't beat about the bush, he said he'd heard rumours that Bermejo was casting doubt on his past, specifically saying he was not a camp survivor. Bermejo did not deny the accusation, and Marco carried on: he said he respected Bermejo's work and understood his interest in reconstructing the past and seeking out documentary evidence to do so; he said he could understand how accounts of his experiences might have raised doubts with Bermejo or seemed shocking; he said, despite appearances, everything could be explained and, with time and goodwill, the whole issue could be resolved; he offered to answer all Bermejo's questions and to help him clear up any dubious or obscure points, or all the points he found dubious or obscure and felt it necessary to elucidate; and he said, since he often visited Madrid, he would call him and, if Bermejo wished, they could meet up in late February or early March so that he could sort out this misunderstanding. This, more or less, is what Marco said to Bermejo, or what Bermejo remembers that Marco said, more or less; but what Bermejo most remembers is he had the unmistakable feeling that beneath the surface of the conversation there were many invisible currents, countless subtexts, all intended to charm him, to inveigle him with a glimpse of the benefits that would ensue if the two of them could agree and the hassles that would result if they didn't agree, and it was at this point, Bermejo says, he realised the man playing for time on the other end of the line was a master manipulator. Despite this, the historian accepted Marco's proposal and, before hanging up, said that he would wait for his call.

Marco did not call Bermejo in February; nor did he call in March. One afternoon, Bermejo went to the headquarters of the Centre for Political and Constitutional Studies—an autonomous agency associated with the Ministry for the Presidency—at the request of a professor from the University of Complutense who was working there. The professor was Javier Moreno Luzón, and he'd asked to meet with Bermejo to discuss a number of events commemorating the Deportation which were to be held in May at the Círculo de Bellas Artes in Madrid; Moreno Luzón was responsible for coordinating the programme and had asked Bermejo for help. The two colleagues talked about the subject that had brought them together, but also about the events celebrating the sixtieth anniversary of the liberation of Mauthausen, which would take place shortly before, and which, it was rumoured, would be attended for the first time by the prime minister, at the request of the Centre for Political and Constitutional Studies. In the course of their conversation, they had been joined by José Álvarez Junco, the director of the Centre, who left at this point in order to make a phone call and came back with confirmation: Prime Minister Rodríguez Zapatero was still considering travelling to Mauthausen for the commemoration ceremony in May. Only then did Bermejo steel himself and announce that there was a problem. What problem? they asked. A problem with the president of the Amical de Mauthausen, he said. He explained the situation. When he had finished, Moreno Luzón announced that he would sideline Marco from the events at the Círculo de Bellas Artes; however none of the three had a clear idea of what other steps they could or should take, and decided to defer the matter.

The protagonists of the preceding scene don't remember precisely when it took place, but we can place it in late March. By this time, Bermejo had spent weeks waiting for Marco to call and say he was coming to Madrid so they could meet. He let two or three more weeks go by, then, tired of waiting, he tried to contact Marco by phone. He couldn't reach him. Eventually, he sent a message via fax to Amical. The message is dated April 15, and reads:

Enric:

In February you called me and suggested that we meet up during one of your visits to Madrid. At the time, you said that you would call me shortly and that the meeting could take place in "late February or early March" (those were your words). Those dates have come and gone and I have had no word from you. And the fact is that I would be very interested in meeting with you and hearing your story at first hand.

I hope it will be possible to arrange a meeting.
Thank your for your attention.

Warm regards.

A few days after sending the fax, Bermejo received a phone call from Marco. This time, the conversation was briefer. Marco began by apologising for not calling earlier, explaining that he had been unable to travel to Madrid because preparations for the celebrations to be held in Mauthausen in May had taken up all his time. He told him that the Amical was snowed under with work and as a result it would be impossible for him to see Bermejo, and they would have to postpone their meeting until after the anniversary of the liberation of Mauthausen, at which point, he guaranteed, he would call Bermejo and give an explanation that would allay all his doubts. Bermejo listened carefully and realised it was futile to argue, so he told Marco, if that was what he'd decided, so be it, but he didn't think it was the most advisable approach.

So ended the last conversation between Bermejo and Marco. Some days later it was announced that, for the first time, the Spanish prime minister, José Luis Rodríguez Zapatero, would travel to Mauthausen to celebrate the sixtieth anniversary of the liberation of the camp, and it was also announced that the camp survivor who would speak at the main event would be Enric Marco. Bermejo realised that this changed everything and that, if he stayed on the sidelines, looked the other way, and allowed the definitive crowning of Marco's imposture to go ahead, he would never forgive himself. All the qualms, scruples and hesitations that had left him paralysed until now suddenly evaporated. He telephoned Moreno Luzón and told him he wasn't prepared to be complicit in this farce, he wanted to communicate what he knew to the prime minister or to someone close to the prime minister. Moreno Luzón asked him to write a report and send it to him. Bermejo wrote it and sent it; he also sent copies to a member of the Fundación Pablo Iglesias, the foundation associated with the prime minister's political party, to a member of the Amical de Mauthausen, and to various historians. He felt relieved that he had done his duty. The anniversary of the liberation of Mauthausen was scarcely two weeks away, but Bermejo stopped worrying about it. Or almost.

6

I can be sure of one thing: while I was trying to discover the truth about Marco, I wasn't the only person to harbour doubts about this book that for so many years I didn't want to write; Marco had doubts too.

At the beginning of my investigation, relations between us were not good, in fact they were bad. I was to blame. When I stopped fighting against writing this book and agreed with Marco that he would tell me his whole story and, with my son's help, I would record him telling it, we began to see each other more regularly in my office in Gracia. Looking at the footage of those early interviews, I can see I am cold, tense, calculating, reticent, as though I couldn't overcome the repugnance I felt for Marco, or as though I didn't want to, or was afraid to. It isn't simply that I didn't trust him, that I didn't believe a word of his stories; what's worse is that it is patently obvious. Looking back, aside from being a tactical error, my attitude seems to me both hypocritical and ridiculous, the sanctimonious posturing of an inquisitor or a Sunday school teacher that on more than one occasion led me to demand that Marco acknowledge the damage his lies had done and express remorse. He always refused. As I've already said, Marco may be many things, but he isn't a fool, so he didn't always refuse to acknowledge that he had lied, and that this was a bad thing; sometimes—though only when he felt it appropriate, not when someone tried to compel him—he would acknowledge it, albeit half-heartedly and in passing, only to immediately bury the acknowledgement under a torrent of his usual justifications about the good that had resulted from his lies, and about the lies and the spite and the misrepresentations he had suffered because of his deception.

At the time—I'm talking about the spring of 2013—Marco was a wounded man, but also defiant and determined to vindicate himself, and I hadn't yet learned to deal with him; it's natural that initially we would collide. Unlike Truman Capote's approach with Dick Hickock and Perry Smith, the young murderers in *In Cold Blood*, I didn't immediately befriend Marco, in fact our working interviews more often seemed like pitched battles: I attacked, bombarding him with his contradictions, his scams and his ruses, and he counterattacked with all the weapons in his rhetorical arsenal, which were many and powerful. More than once, the interviews ended badly, with us parting at the door to my office almost without a goodbye or a handshake, and when this happened we wouldn't meet or call each other for some time. Then I would go back to my uncertainties, go back to thinking about Vargas Llosa and Claudio Magris who believed that perhaps it was impossible to know Marco's true story, go back to thinking about Fernando Arrabal, who believed that the liar has no story but, if he did, no-one would dare present it as a true story or a novel without fiction because it would be impossible to tell without lying; in short, I went back to thinking that I was writing the wrong book, or that it was impossible to write it, or that I shouldn't write it.

Fortunately, I spent much of that winter travelling. I spent time in Colombia, in Mexico, in Paris, in Brussels, in Trento, and I spent two weeks in Pordenone in northern Italy before settling in Berlin for spring and summer, enabling me to return to Barcelona fresh, full of energy, with no uncertainties but with lots of new ideas about Marco and an urge to talk to him. Naturally, I called him again. Sometimes Marco would answer immediately, but at other times he didn't answer, or took his time getting back to me, or got back to me to say that we couldn't meet, offering all sorts of excuses: he was busy, he wasn't feeling well, his wife and daughters didn't want him to see me because our interviews unsettled him. At such times, to persuade him to meet with me, I would tell the truth, or a half-truth; for example, I'd say that I was only passing through Barcelona and if we didn't meet now, it might be months before the next opportunity. My words always had an explosive effect: Marco would immediately change his mind

and insist that we meet at my office that very afternoon or the following day. This was how I came to realise that I wasn't the only one
with doubts, and that, as Joan Amézaga had sensed over our dinner
with my sister Blanca and Montse Cardona at La Troballa to discuss
Marco and FaPaC, our hero was wavering between vanity and fear:
on the one hand, he was flattered that I was writing a book about him,
on the other, he was afraid of what I would say in that book. This was
how things were, at least in the early stages of our relationship: Marco
both wanted and didn't want me to write about him and therefore he
wanted and didn't want to talk to me. Or to put it more clearly: Marco
wanted me to write the book that he would have wanted to read, the
book that he needed, the book that would finally rehabilitate him.

From the first, I had unequivocally warned Marco that I had no
intention of writing that book, nevertheless, at least in the beginning,
he tried to get me to write it, or at least he tried to control what I
would write. In theory, Marco not only agreed not to hinder my work,
he was prepared to help me with it; in practice, that wasn't the case.
In his house, Marco had an archive comprising hundreds of documents, personal papers and writings of every kind, but when I asked
him to let me study them, he flatly refused. He always turned up at my
office weighed down with folders stuffed with documents, but these
were carefully selected documents that favoured his version of events.
Sometimes I asked him for documents and he promised to bring them
to me but never did. At other times he'd bring documents and allow
me to scan them for a moment only to snatch them from my hands
and not allow me to photocopy them. Now and then he'd postpone
our meetings with no explanation, and on one occasion he showed up
with another person (a young filmmaker who floated the impractical
suggestion of filming us while we talked, for a documentary about
the process of writing my book or something of the kind), which put
paid to the meeting. Needless to say, Marco concealed information
from me, deceived me, lied to me, and whenever I caught him in a
lie, he'd instantly come up with some explanation and try to pass the
lie off as a mistake or a misunderstanding. He often suggested I meet
people he had known at different periods in his life who could tell me
about him, but he'd wait for weeks or months before giving me their
phone number or address and in the meantime call or write to them,

warning them that I would be in touch, letting them know my intentions and (at the very least, I imagine) attempting to manipulate them so that they'd say what he wanted them to say. He was cunning as a fox and slippery as an eel, and it didn't take me long to work out that he wasn't cooperating in order to help me, but merely pretending to help in order to keep a watchful eye, to control my movements, lead me through a maze of lies and thereby get me to write the book he imagined.

He didn't succeed, or I don't think he succeeded. And not because I prevented him, but because he could not succeed: it's impossible for anyone to write the book someone else has imagined; besides, my book could only be written based on truth, or based on facts that are as close as possible to truth; moreover it's impossible to hide a truth like Marco's if someone is determined to reveal it by any means. Marco is a masterful liar, but, while he was marshalling his lies, thirty, forty, fifty years ago, he could never have imagined that one day a writer would devote himself body and soul to dismantling them, so he didn't feel it necessary to safeguard them against such an improbable possibility. There is, perhaps, another explanation, or rather another hypothesis, for Marco's failure, which is that it wasn't a failure but a success; perhaps Marco realised not only that he couldn't hide the truth from me and get me to write the book that would rehabilitate him, but perhaps he also realised that the only way he might be rehabilitated was to tell me the truth.

I'm not sure there ever came a point when Marco reached that conclusion, but I know I made every effort to get him there. This effort began after I'd spent many months pestering him and fighting pitched battles with him, when I had overcome the repugnance I'd initially felt and abandoned the absurd façade of judge or prosecutor or inquisitor or Sunday School teacher, realising that my task was to peel away the lies of his past as one might peel away an onion skin, and that I could do so only by gaining his trust as Capote had done with Dick Hickock and Perry Smith. In this, Benito Bermejo—or rather the extremely long and deadly shadow cast by Benito Bermejo—proved very useful. I would say to Marco—without quite lying, but without quite telling him the truth—that Bermejo hadn't completely given up on his plans to write a book about him, and therefore the book I was writing had to be unassailable, because if it wasn't, Bermejo would make mincemeat of us, he would demolish us, eviscerate our version of events, and destroy us, him and me. I was on his side and Bermejo wasn't, I would tell him, so it was better to tell me the truth than leave it for Bermejo to unearth, since he would use it maliciously while I would use it for good. We have to come up with a completely true story, I insisted, irrefutable, candid, not just credible, a story that, even if it weren't entirely documented (that would be impossible), corresponded as closely as possible to what documentary evidence we did have, and therefore to the facts. This is what I told Marco: Bermejo was evil incarnate, and only I could keep him at bay, but in order to do so, I needed the truth.

So began a new and strange phase in my relationship with Marco. By this point, I was completely immersed in his life story, I'd heard him recount it from beginning to end, I'd read countless documents about him and spoken to numerous people who had known him. By tracking down documents that Marco himself had never seen, cross-referencing facts and dates, challenging witnesses, I'd discovered many of the truths hidden from Marco's public biography; more than that, by confronting him with blatant contradictions and obvious falsehoods, I'd succeeded in getting him to admit that some were true and others were lies. The most surprising thing (or what I found most surprising) was that the more lies I uncovered, the more I adapted to the sad, sordid reality he'd concealed behind this magnificent façade for so many years, the more I saw of the true villain hiding behind the fictional hero, the closer I felt to him, the more I pitied him, the more relaxed I felt in his company. I'm lying: I too attempted to conceal the truth. The truth is that there came a moment when I felt affection for this man, sometimes even a sort of admiration that even I didn't understand and which I found unsettling.

By the time this happened, Marco had already opened his archives to me and had even arranged for me to meet with his secret daughter, the fruit of his first (equally secret) marriage. By the time this happened, there remained only a few problematic points in his biography, or what we had euphemistically agreed to call problematic points: lies that Marco hadn't yet acknowledged were lies and which I wasn't prepared to accept as truth, among other reasons because nobody would accept them—beginning with Benito Bermejo. I remember sitting on the veranda of his house on the morning when the last of these points were discussed, heatedly as always (but there was no longer any tension or bitterness), I trying to get him to admit the truth and he doing his utmost to salvage his lie; that morning, after Marco had yielded on three of the points, or rather when we'd set them aside because I was convinced he'd given up and would eventually admit the truth (that he hadn't taken part in the assault on the Sant Andreu barracks on July 19, 1936, the day after the Civil War began; that he hadn't returned wounded from the front but had regularised his situation after the war and had never been involved in clandestine activities in the post-war period; that he had never been a member of the U.J.A. with Fernández Vallet and his comrades), I gave him the impression that the interview was over.

"Oh, I forgot," I said slyly as he was getting to his feet, his guard down, exhausted after several hours talking, or perhaps simply fed up with talking, "there's another problematic point. It's the last one."

He remained standing as he listened to my explanation, eyeing me with what interest he could still muster: I told him that I didn't believe he had participated in the Majorca landings with his uncle Anastasio and that, although I couldn't prove it was false, all indications suggested it was. When I'd finished reeling off the list, he slumped back into his chair, planted his elbows on the table, buried his face in his hands in a gesture that, though melodramatic, didn't seem so. I heard him whisper:

"Please, leave me something."

We met again two or three days later. That morning, I drove to Sant Cugat early to collect him, and we spent the day wandering the streets and alleyways where he'd spent his childhood and his adult years, through Collblanc, Gracia and El Guinardó, seeking out the streets and the houses where he'd lived, talking to neighbours who had known him and going over episodes from his life, and in the hours we spent together, Marco tacitly or explicitly acknowledged that all or almost all the problematic points I'd raised during our last encounter were not problematic points but truths that had been embellished or embroidered, or simple lies. I cannot say that this admission came as a surprise to me, because by now I was familiar with his strategies in

these duels we fought over his past: if the evidence I offered was conclusive (and sometimes when it wasn't), Marco eventually acknowledged the truth one way or another, though it might take hours or
days or weeks before he did so, because he needed to come up with an
honourable way out, an explanation for his earlier lie, an explanation
or a way out he usually found in the confusion, the uncertainty and
the ramblings brought about by old age and his conveniently failing
memory. In any event, when I pulled up outside his house in Sant
Cugat as night was falling, Marco, who must still have been thinking
about the lies he'd just admitted to, said to me with a mixture of sad-
ness and resignation:

"Truthfully, I feel as though I'm working against my own
interests."

I understood, and I hurriedly corrected him:

"No: you're acting against the interests of the false Enric Marco;
and in the interests of the real one." When Marco didn't say anything,
I clarified: "You're acting in your own interests just as Alonso Quixano is at the end of *Don Quixote* when he gives up being Quixote."

Marco looked at me curiously, perhaps worried.

"When he recovers his sanity, you mean?" he said.

"Exactly," I said: and in that moment I saw a boy who looked just
like him, bald and wrinkled with the same moustache, reading *Don
Quixote* to his alcoholic stepmother eighty years earlier, in a grubby
little room by the light of a paraffin lamp; "when he ceases to be the
false, heroic Don Quixote and returns to simply being the true Alonso
Quixano."

A frank laugh banished the worried look from Marco's face.

"The Good," he clarified, "Alonso Quixano the Good. I wonder
how many times you need to read that book in order to truly understand it."

I don't remember another word of that conversation, if indeed
there were any others. But what I do remember is that as I drove back
to Barcelona on the carretera La Rabassada, I felt for the first time
that Marco no longer wanted to hide behind a lie, that with me at
least he didn't feel the need to, that he wanted the truth and nothing
but the truth, as though he'd discovered that the prosaic, shameful,
authentic life story I planned to tell might be better or more useful

than the brilliant, poetic and false story he'd been telling, and I particularly remember that, as I crested the summit of El Tibidabo and drove down La Rabassada and watched as Barcelona appeared below, and beyond it the sea shimmering red in the sunset, I thought of that extraordinary passage at the end of Don Quixote where Cervantes has his pen speak ("For me alone was Don Quixote born, and I for him: it was his to act, mine to write; we two together make but one"), and for a fleeting second I felt I understood what Cervantes—or Cervantes' pen—was trying to say, and I had a sudden dizzying realisation: Marco had never wanted to dupe me, Marco had been testing me all this time to see whether or not I was worthy of his truth; I hadn't uncovered that truth, he had guided me to it. Over the space of almost a century Marco had fashioned the monumental lie that was his life not to deceive anyone, or not simply to deceive, but so that some future writer, with his help, might decipher it, recount it and share it with the world and, in the end, might have his computer speak as Cervantes does his pen ("For me alone was Enric Marco born, and I for him: it was his to act, mine to write; we two together make but one"), just as Alonso Quixano had created Don Quixote and had him perform his lunatic feats so that Cervantes might decipher them, recount them and share them with the world as though Don Quixote and his pen made but one. In short, I wasn't using Marco as Capote had used Dick Hickock and Perry Smith, it was Marco who was using me the way Alonso Quixano used Cervantes.

This thought came to me in a second, as the car coasted down La Rabassada. A second later, I tried to forget it.

7

It was perhaps the pinnacle of Enric Marco's public glory. It was Thursday, January 27, 2005. That morning, precisely sixty years after the liberation of Auschwitz by Soviet troops, the Spanish parliament commemorated International Holocaust Remembrance Day for the first time and paid tribute to the almost nine thousand Spanish Republicans who had been interned in the Nazi camps.

It was the solemn act of remembrance Marco and the *deportados* had long been calling for. It included a religious ceremony during which the Chief Rabbi of Madrid, before the standing congregation, said Kaddish, the Jewish prayer for the dead; six candles were lit in tribute to the six million Jews exterminated by the Nazis, half a million of them children, to the Gypsies and the Spaniards who died, to those who risked their lives to avoid the slaughter and to those who managed to survive it. "We have waited too long to honour them," said Manuel Marín, the President of the Congress of Deputies, "I regret that." He was referring to all the victims of the Nazis, but perhaps to the *deportados* in particular.

Marco spoke on their behalf. He did so standing, without referring to notes, because he'd given this speech a thousand times, he knew it by heart. He said, for example: "When we reached the concentration camps in those filthy cattle trucks, we were stripped of our clothes and all our belongings were taken, not simply out of greed, but to leave us completely naked, powerless: wedding rings, bracelets, photographs. Alone, helpless, left with nothing." He also said: "We were ordinary people, like you, but they stripped us, and their dogs bit us, they dazzled us with their searchlights, screamed at us in German

'Links-Rechts!' [Left-Right!]. We could not understand anything, and failing to understand an order could cost you your life." And also: "When the first selection came and the men were put on one side and the women and children on the other, the women formed a circle and protected their children with their bodies, their elbows, the only tools they had." And also: "We must remember those troubling times. Those nights in the barracks when there came a sudden howl, the cry of a wounded animal. A man who, by day, still had pride and dignity enough to hide his weakness, fell to pieces in the dead of night." And also: "Never again. Never again should we have to see women cradling their dead babies in their arms, their empty breasts unable to provide milk." And also: "The Amical de Mauthausen was founded in order to teach the Spanish who had no country. We did not end up in the camps by chance, but in defending things we believed were worth the struggle. We were defending equal rights, we were defending a Spain that, at the time, seemed open to progress." And, lastly: "Every year, when we march at Mauthausen, a voice from the stand announces: here come the Spanish Republicans, the foremost defenders of liberty and democracy in Europe. We had no luck during the war. We had no luck when we were liberated from the camps. We did not have a government that was prepared to help us, to take our tattered rags and offer us medical assistance. Nor a country to which we could return. The Jewish people, who suffered so much, were able to create their own homeland. We were not. The time has come for justice."

Marco's speech caused an extraordinary commotion. Newspapers, television and radio stations published or broadcast parts of it; some of those who heard him deliver the speech—relatives of camp survivors, journalists and high-level politicians—were moved to tears; others, like the Israeli ambassador, were incensed by a reference to his country in one of the customary points Marco made in his speeches: "We need an educational system that will teach history. There are modern concentration camps in Rwanda, in Sierra Leone, in Ethiopia, where children in their millions are dying. There were concentration camps in Kosovo. And it must be said aloud: unfortunately, they still exist in Guantanamo Bay, there can be no doubt they exist in Palestine, and in Iraq. How many times must we point it out?" No-one, in short, was left unmoved by Marco, who was carried from the Parliament in triumph, more than ever the champion or the hero or the rock star of so-called historical memory.

Despite this resounding success (or rather thanks to it), the following months were a tense period for Marco. In addition to continuing his dizzying whirl of talks and conferences, he devoted himself to organising the contribution of the Amical at the events for the sixtieth anniversary of the liberation of Mauthausen, to be celebrated, as always, in early May, but at which the Amical was to play a much more important role than ever: with the support of the French branch of Amical, they wanted to mount an exhibition entitled "Images and Memories"; they planned to bring a great number of people from all over Spain to Mauthausen for several days and they were canvassing for two symbolic gestures that would mark the history of the Deportation: for a Spanish camp survivor to speak at the inaugural ceremony on behalf of the *deportados*, and for a representative or a member of the Spanish government to attend the ceremonies in Mauthausen. All of this may have been beyond the organisational capacities of Amical, an organisation that, though rapidly expanding, was still small, but its president devoted himself to the challenge wholeheartedly, prepared, as always, to compensate for a shortage of resources with man hours. However, the tension Marco suffered in those final months wasn't because of future events, but of the past, which is never dead.

One afternoon in early February, shortly after Marco's triumphant speech to the Spanish parliament, one of his closest colleagues at Amical, a man named Enrique Urraca, took him aside when he arrived at the offices on calle Sils and told him he'd heard rumours that Bernito Bermejo was casting doubt on Marco's claim to be a camp survivor. Marco didn't even stop to talk to Urraca, he roundly dismissed the rumour, assuring Urraca that it was nothing but slander, that he and Bermejo had had a personal disagreement, that he should forget the matter entirely. That same evening, Marco telephoned Bermejo. The historian said he had found him out; Marco said things were not as they seemed, that he could explain everything, that he would be in Madrid sometime in the coming weeks and they would have an opportunity to meet and clear up the misunderstanding. Bermejo waited for Marco's call, but in the weeks that followed our man didn't go to Madrid, or if he went he didn't call Bermejo, nor did he offer an explanation and so, in mid-April, Marco received a fax from Bermejo urging him to explain himself as promised. Marco telephoned Bermejo again. He told him he could not go to Madrid, he told him that he was snowed under with work preparing for the commemoration ceremony at Mauthausen, he told him that he would not be able to see him or speak to him until he had emerged from the turmoil that he and the Amical were in, he told him to wait until then because at that point he would explain everything; Bermejo didn't argue with him or try to persuade him, he simply said he thought Marco was making a mistake.

Only weeks remained before the Mauthausen celebrations, and scarcely a few days before Marco's fate was sealed.

Enrique Urraca was not only one of Marco's closest co-workers at Amical, but virtually his private secretary. He wasn't a camp survivor but the nephew of a *deportado*. His uncle, Juan de Diego, had been a prisoner in Mauthausen, and Urraca considered him a hero, as he did his fellow-inmates. On the death of his uncle in 2003, Urraca joined the Amical de Mauthausen with the intention of keeping alive the memory of his uncle and his companions. Marco, who had been president of the organisation for only a month at the time, charmed him so completely that Urraca all but transferred the affection and admiration he'd felt for his uncle to Marco. This explains why, in early February 2005, shortly after the tribute to the *deportados* at the Spanish parliament, Urraca dared to tell Marco bluntly about the rumours circulating about him; it also explains how Marco could so easily persuade him the rumours were completely unfounded and he should forget about them.

Urraca knew Bermejo, who had had a connection with his uncle, though this wasn't how the rumours about Marco had reached him. However, in late April, when the celebrations at Mauthausen were about to take place and the historian finally decided to expose Marco, he settled on Urraca as the most suitable member of the Amical to be told the truth. I don't know why: perhaps because he had a good relationship with him and believed him to be a decent, idealistic man; perhaps because he knew Urraca was the closest person to Marco within Amical. What I do know is that on the evening of Friday, April 30, Bermejo telephoned Urraca; there were nine days left before the events at Mauthausen, and only two before the annual meeting of Amical. Bermejo told Urraca what he had discovered. Urraca replied that what he was saying was impossible. Bermejo told him about the document he'd found in the archives of the Ministry of Foreign Affairs, and then forwarded him the report he'd sent to the prime minister. When he'd read the report, Urraca had no choice but to accept that Bermejo was telling the truth. Then, Bermejo reminded him that, in a few days, Marco was scheduled to speak in the name of the *deportados* at the inaugural ceremony at Mauthausen and asked him a question: are you going to allow an impostor to speak in front of the Spanish prime minister and sully the memory of your uncle and of all the *deportados*?

When he replaced the receiver, Urraca was a broken man. He couldn't believe what he'd heard and read, he couldn't believe Marco had done what he did; and yet, he had to believe it. In an instant, his whole world had collapsed, or that was how it felt. He didn't know what to do. He was besieged by doubts. And then came Sunday, the day of the annual Amical meeting.

The Amical meeting that year was held on May 1 in Vilafranca del Penedès, a town some sixty kilometres from Barcelona. At first, everything suggested it would be a routine annual meeting: as every year, members would elect a new board of directors (Marco was elected president and charged with international relations, Torán vice-president and Urraca a member of the board); as every year, a small monument was erected to the memory of local *deportados*. It was during the unveiling of the monument that some members began to realise this wasn't going to be a run-of-the-mill meeting. While the ceremony was taking place, Torán was approached by the Amical delegate for Valencia, a historian named Blas Mínguez, who said he'd just spoken to Urraca who had told him he was in possession of a report that cast doubt on Marco's having been a camp survivor. Bewildered, Torán went to speak to Urraca; they were joined by other members of the board including Mínguez, who had just been elected. Urraca announced that what Mínguez had said was true, that he had the damning report at home, although at first he attributed it to the French branch of the Amical rather than to Bermejo, perhaps because he sensed the historian's difficult relationship with the Amical or with some of its members might discredit his findings. At the end of the meal, when the rest of the members were enjoying dessert, the members of the board held an urgent meeting to discuss the matter. Since they didn't wish to arouse suspicions, the meeting was brief; Marco himself was present and said only that Bermejo was conducting a personal vendetta against him and that the rumours he was spreading about his past were simply evidence of his antagonism towards the Amical and himself as president of the association. The other board members listened in dismay, probably not knowing what to think beyond the fact that, whether it proved true or false, it was essential that Bermejo's accusation be cleared up, so Torán asked Urraca to send her the report as soon as he got home.

Urraca took longer than expected to send the report, as though he still had doubts about how to proceed, but eventually he sent it, and that night Torán read it. From what Torán understood, Bermejo's report didn't imply that Marco had not been in Flossenbürg or another Nazi camp, but that he had lied and that, in 1941, he had arrived in Germany as a volunteer worker, not as a *deportado;* nevertheless the charges were sufficiently serious to require Marco to explain himself as soon as possible. Accordingly, first thing on Monday morning, Torán summoned the members of the board to the office on calle Sils as soon as possible. The meeting took place at 7:00 p.m. that same evening, and those who attended remember it as dramatic, not only because of the subject of the meeting, but because of the dramatic way in which Marco dealt with it. Though perhaps the appropriate word is not dramatic but melodramatic. As he spoke, Marco broke down, he seemed hysterical, desperate, capable of doing something desperate; in fact, some of those present felt he was suggesting that he could or would do something desperate, as a form of emotional blackmail, a way of asking them to shield him.

Marco spoke for some time, but he didn't offer a clear explanation, nor did he admit his deception. All he would say was it was true
that in 1941 he hadn't left Spain clandestinely, but as a volunteer
worker, because this was the only way he could think of to escape the
constant hounding by the Francoist police; he also said it was true
that he had been in Flossenbürg, though for a short time, only a few
days. As to the rest, he wondered aloud between racking sobs how he
could tell his family, his wife and daughters, how he could tell them
that not only had he lied about being a *deportado*, but that he had hidden the fact that he had another family, a wife and daughter about
whom he'd never said a word to them. This supplemental confession
had little—indeed, nothing whatever—to do with the subject under
discussion; nonetheless Marco decided to put it on the table, perhaps
to elicit as much sympathy as possible from the board.

Marco's blackmail was only partly successful. The board's first
decision was to request that Marco resign, and Torán, who had only
been elected vice-president the day before, became acting president.
Next, they agreed that, when the time came, they would write a statement outlining what had happened, but for the moment they had to
keep it secret at all costs, because not to do so would trigger a scandal
that would ruin the Mauthausen commemorations and the achieve-
ment represented by the fact that, for the first time, a Spanish prime
minister would attend the ceremonies and, also for the first time, a
Spanish camp survivor would address the international community.
Several of those present took it for granted that Marco wouldn't now
be the one to give the address at Mauthausen on behalf of the *deportados*, but in fact no decision was made, at least not explicitly, perhaps in
part because it wasn't yet certain that Marco had not been in a Nazi
camp; in fact, he wasn't even forbidden from travelling to Austria two
days hence to attend the meeting of the International Mauthausen
Committee, of which he was a member.

Marco accepted all the conditions imposed by the board without
protest and left the meeting. Things, however, did not end there: that
night and the following day, Torán and other members of the Amical
did everything they could, hurriedly and confusedly, to inform others
involved in the Mauthausen commemorations of what had happened
and to agree on a strategy. They telephoned camp survivors and rela-

tives of *deportados*, spoke to the prime minister's office, and perhaps the Spanish embassy in Vienna, and the following day organised an impromptu meeting with members of the Catalan government where it was decided that the most important thing was to salvage the events at Mauthausen and distance Marco from any involvement with them on the pretext that he was ill. Then, once it was all over, they would decide what to do.

On May 3, four days before the commemoration ceremony at Mauthausen, Marco and the treasurer of Amical, Jesús Ruiz, travelled to Vienna and on to Linz, a 25-minute drive from Mauthausen, where the International Mauthausen Committee, of which they were both members, was to meet the following day. They were joined on Wednesday morning by a third member of the Amical board, Blas Mínguez, the delegate for Valencia, who had driven to Linz; together they decided it was best if only Ruiz attended the meeting of the International Committee while Marco and Mínguez waited for him at the hotel. When he returned that evening, Ruiz told Marco that the news had already reached the committee—in fact it was Bermejo who had contacted them—and that evening, over dinner, Mínguez demanded that he tell them once and for all whether he had been in Flossenbürg or not; Marco admitted he had not, neither in Flossenbürg nor any other camp. At that point, Ruiz telephoned the offices of the Amical and it was decided Marco would return to Barcelona the following day.

On the morning of Thursday, May 5, our man landed at Barcelona airport on the first flight leaving Vienna. He would have arrived at Terminal B at about 10:30 a.m., because it was here, in front of Botero's colossal sculpture of a muscular black horse, that more than two hundred people had gathered to travel with the Amical to Vienna to take part in the Mauthausen commemorations. Inevitably, Marco bumped into them. The group was completely shocked. The Amical board members accompanying the group knew what had happened in Linz, but they didn't know that Marco had taken this particular flight back to Barcelona and had said that the president wouldn't be attending the ceremonies because he had fallen ill. Marco's sudden appearance created a commotion: people threw themselves at him, asked him what he was doing there, where he had come from, what had happened, why he wasn't going to Mauthausen with them. Marco brushed them off as best he could while Torán and other members of the board helped ward off curious bystanders. When he finally escaped, he walked away quickly, boorishly, without addressing a word to anyone.

There was a curious atmosphere on the flight to Vienna, there were rumours among the *deportados* that the board of Amical, jealous of Marco's prominence and eager to be rid of him, had plotted a coup and, just before the crowning moment of the great Mauthausen commemoration, had ousted its president.

On the morning of Saturday, May 7, Benito Bermejo flew from Madrid to Vienna. He was going to Mauthausen, as he did every year or almost every year around this time; but this time everything was different. He must have been worried, because no-one had told him what was happening at Amical; he believed that his report about Marco had had no effect and that, on Sunday, the great impostor would give a speech on behalf of the *deportados* in the presence of the Spanish prime minister and the crowds attending the inaugural ceremony. Just before he caught the plane, however, he bought a copy of *El País*, and, in a note about the Mauthausen celebrations, he read that Marco had flown back to Barcelona because he was indisposed; he felt relieved: he realised that his report had done some good and that things were being put right. When he arrived at Mauthausen, Bermejo encountered the delegation from the Amical who had already been there for two days and he realised that at least some of them were aware of the truth, though none would speak about it openly; though Bermejo may not have known it at the time, in the hectic days before the Mauthausen commemoration, the board of the Amical had organised a meeting to tell some of its members about Marco. On Saturday night, Bermejo had dinner with a group that included Anna María García, my colleague at the University of Gerona, the historian who, shortly after the Marco scandal broke, would advise me not to write about him ("The best thing to do about

Marco is forget him," she would say. "That would be the worst punishment for such a monstrous egotist"), and on the Sunday, he finally
attended the commemoration of the sixtieth anniversary of Mauthausen's liberation.

The event went off without incident. First there was a brief ceremony at the monument to the memory of the Spanish *deportados*,
which was attended by two or three hundred people including the
Spanish prime minister. Then came the main ceremony, attended by
several thousand people, at which the speakers included, among others, the Spanish prime minister and a Spanish camp survivor chosen
to replace Marco, Eusebi Pérez, who read the speech that Marco had
planned to read, which, despite what was later reported in the press,
had not been written by Marco: it had been jointly penned by the
board of the Amical to be read on behalf of all the Spanish camp
survivors. This is all that happened that day at Mauthausen. Nothing
more. Although some of those in attendance knew that the president
of the Amical had been exposed, and half-whispered rumours circu-
lated among knots of people, no-one officially unmasked Marco.

That night, Bermejo slept at the Weindlhof, a hotel perched on
the hill in Mauthausen. For the time being, at least, he felt satisfied: his
goal hadn't been to destroy Marco, but to prevent him speaking at the
Mauthausen commemorations and thereby avoid the sanctification
of his imposture and the humiliation of the *deportados*. On Monday,
Bermejo returned to Vienna; he had work to do in the Mauthausen
Memorial archives, and in the two days that followed he could forget
Marco. I don't know whether he managed to do so. On Wednesday
morning over breakfast, he received a text message from a friend suggesting that he buy a copy of *El País*, because there was an article
about him. On his way to the archives, Bermejo bought the newspaper at a kiosk on Graben almost on the corner of Bräunerstrasse. This
was how he discovered that the Marco scandal had broken. A couple
of hours later, the journalists started to call.

From May 5, when he hurriedly flew back from Austria and bumped
into the Amical group at the airport, until Monday, May 9, when the

group returned from Austria and the board of directors summoned him to an urgent meeting at the office on calle Sils, Marco spoke with no-one about what had happened: not to his wife, nor to his daughters, nor to any friend, co-worker or acquaintance. Four days that must have been agonising. I don't know what Marco did during this time, because he doesn't remember, or says he doesn't remember; nor does he remember what he was thinking. What follows, therefore, is pure hypothesis.

I have no doubt that, during those four days, Marco put his brain into overdrive in order to identify and evaluate the various consequences that the revelation of his deception might entail. In fact, he must have been thinking about this since the previous Sunday, at the meeting in Vilafranca del Penedès when he discovered that word had already spread among his co-directors of the board, or perhaps even since early February when Bermejo had told him what he'd discovered; it's even possible that he'd been working on it from the beginning, or almost the beginning: from the very moment when he began to pass himself off as a *deportado* and realised there was a possibility—however remote it might have seemed at the time—that someone would expose him. Of course, the first thing that must have occurred to him during those days of anxious waiting was that he could deny everything, or deny the greater part of the accusations. He had no choice but to acknowledge that in the Forties he had travelled to Germany as a volunteer worker, that much was clear, and therefore that he had lied about part of his life story, or distorted it; but although in Linz he had admitted to Mínguez and Ruiz, his colleagues from Amical, that he had never been an inmate in Flossenbürg, he could claim that he'd not said what he'd said, or that he'd said it but it was false, and he could go on claiming that he had been in Flossenbürg. To judge from what Bermejo had told him, and what he had written in his report, the historian couldn't prove that he had not been a prisoner in Flossenbürg; and, from what Marco himself knew, it would be difficult to prove: the archivists at the Flossenbürg Memorial were clear that not all prisoners appeared in the camp registers, and he could always claim to be one of those ghostly prisoners.

It wouldn't be easy to prove that he had not been in Flossenbürg, but nor would it be impossible. For a start, Marco had no idea how much Bermejo knew: he might know much more than he'd said he knew, he might have recounted only part of what he knew. But there was one thing Marco did know: Bermejo was a pitbull, and now that he'd sunk his teeth into Marco, he wouldn't let go. So, just as he had found a document that proved Marco had been a volunteer worker in Kiel, Bermejo might also find evidence that his German adventure had begun and ended in Kiel, and therefore he could not have been in Flossenbürg. Marco didn't know whether such evidence existed, but he knew that it might exist and that Bermejo or someone else might find it. Besides, although Bermejo hadn't been able to prove that his time in Flossenbürg was a fabrication, he'd discovered that Marco was not a *deportado*, that he'd lied, and that an important section of his past was false, he'd brought to light a part of Marco that had remained hidden until now and suddenly his persona was cracking, the anti-fascist hero, the rock star or champion of so-called historical memory was teetering and threatening to collapse because, regardless of the decision they arrived at, his co-directors at the Amical would insist that he make a statement acknowledging his deception. Of course, he could do something else: disappear, never go back to Amical, wait until everyone there had forgotten about him; there was even the possibility that no-one would unmask him, no-one would report that he'd been lying for years, because it was in no-one's interest to air a story that would be detrimental to everyone, and to the Amical first and foremost. As for Bermejo, perhaps he could talk to him in private, sound out his intentions and try to come to some sort of agreement.

It was a possibility. But not one that was in keeping with his character, or rather with the noble image he had of himself at the time, with the arrogance of Icarus, like the wings of feathers and wax that he'd fashioned from his triumphs as hero or champion of so-called historical memory. It wasn't a possibility that dovetailed with his character because it amounted to surrender, and what squared with his character was not to surrender but to defend himself; or rather: to attack.

Incredibly, this is what he did. Marco must have thought, with good reason, that what he was facing was a battle, that in battle the victor is the one who seizes the initiative and that, if he waited for Bermejo to uncover the whole truth about his time in Germany (not to mention the whole truth about everything), there would be no possible defence. The best thing was to preempt the historian, give his version of the story, acknowledge his lie, formulate the best arguments to justify it and thereby protect the rest of his story, shore up his persona so that the removal of a single piece of his history—however important the piece, and assuming it was necessary to remove it—wouldn't cause the whole persona to collapse as removing a single card from a house of cards can bring it down. He must have thought that his reputation was hard-won, that he wasn't just anybody, that he had genuinely been a union leader at the C.N.T., a civic leader at FaPaC, a peerless proponent of so-called historical memory at Amical, that he had been awarded the Creu de Sant Jordi and knew the leading lights in Catalan society, and so a minor flaw couldn't simply destroy his reputation overnight. He must have thought that, throughout his eighty-four years, he'd always landed on his feet, that he'd emerged unscathed from much more compromising situations than this, that he was a conman, a shameless charlatan, a peerless trickster, an incomparable talker who had succeeded in hoodwinking Franco's military authorities, the Nazi courts, countless journalists, historians and politicians, that he was Enric Marco and he would also get through this unscathed. He had more than enough energy and oratory to do so, he had more than enough arguments to charm and hoodwink everyone all over again.

More than enough. He hadn't lied, he had only slightly altered the truth, perhaps embellished it a little, nothing more. And even if he'd told a lie, even if he'd made a mistake, who could claim they had never told a lie? Who could say they had never made a mistake? Who was entitled to cast the first stone? Especially since, if he had lied, or altered or embellished the truth a little, he'd done it for a good cause, to publicise so-called historical memory, the horrors that, over a century, had destroyed both Spain and Europe; he'd made these things known to the young and the not so young, to the whole country, at a time when genuine survivors of the Nazi camps were too old and too frail to do so, he'd lied only to give a voice to the voiceless, to promote a message of justice, solidarity and memory. Who could blame him for that? Who could criticise him for placing himself at the heart of those horrors in order to lend greater truth, greater force, greater drama to his message? Besides, he too was a victim, a survivor, he too had suffered prison and persecution in Germany, everything he'd said was absolutely true, not just about the Nazi camps, given that he was a historian and had thoroughly researched the subject, but also about his personal history, given that he'd done nothing other than change the backdrop, recount what had happened in Kiel as though it had happened in Flossenbürg, what had happened in a Nazi jail as though it had happened in a concentration camp. Was this mistake—if it truly was a mistake—enough to wipe out all his achievements? Did his fighting during the Civil War, his militant anti-Francoism, his years of clandestine struggle, his trade union leadership, his fight for better state schools and his titanic work as head of the Amical count for nothing? Could this innocuous lie, always assuming it was innocuous and not a noble, altruistic lie, weigh more than all his virtues?

There were more than enough arguments; this is what Marco thought: that the weight of his arguments would be overwhelming, that everyone would forgive his mistake, that his reputation wouldn't suffer, or would suffer only briefly and barely perceptibly, that his persona would survive intact, or almost intact, and after a little time everything would go back to being as it had been, his colleagues would ask him to return as president of Amical, where he would once again fight for so-called historical memory. This is what he thought, or what Marco may have thought would happen if, instead of surrendering, he defended himself, or rather, went on the attack, if he seized the initiative; and so he did. Bermejo had attempted to destroy him, but had succeeded only in making him stronger. He had tried to make him go back to being Alonso Quixano, but he would carry on being Don Quixote. Reality had done its utmost to kill him, but fiction had once again saved him.

This was not what eventually happened, or not exactly. On Monday, May 9, shortly before 5:00 p.m. when the plane carrying the Spanish delegation from Vienna was due to land in Barcelona, the board of the Amical held a meeting at the headquarters on calle Sils. Marco was present. In the course of the meeting a text was written entitled "A Statement by Sr Enric Marco Batlle," which read:

In response to the stories that have been circulating about my past in recent days, I would like to acknowledge the following points:

1 I travelled to Germany as part of a convoy of Spanish volunteer workers in late 1941.
2 I was not interned in Flossenbürg camp, although I suffered prison while on remand, charged with conspiring against the Third Reich.
3 I returned to Spain in early 1943 after I was released.
4 I made public statements about my life story, including elements that distort reality, in 1978, long before my association with the Amical de Mauthausen in the past six years.
5 In consequence I have relinquished my responsibilities at the Amical and suspended all activity within the organisation.

The text was written with considerable thought: it contains two of the fundamental arguments Marco had prepared in his defence. Firstly, it doesn't mention "lies," simply that he'd "distorted" the truth; secondly, that though he hadn't been imprisoned by the Germans in Flossenbürg, he had been in Kiel, so he had fought against the Nazis, had been a victim of the Nazis, and therefore had a right to speak as a resistance fighter and a victim of the Nazis, and on behalf of the resistance fighters and the victims of the Nazis (such that, in recognising his lies, Marco slipped in another lie, that in Germany he'd been accused of "conspiring against the Third Reich," rather than "high treason," which was the actual charge against him). For the rest, the statement represented the security or the hope that Marco nurtured that his persona would remain intact and that, sooner or later, he would regain his privileged status within the Amical (and within society): the proof is that he didn't resign, he merely relinquished his responsibilities with the organisation; that he simply "suspended" his activities at Amical. The text was dated May 9 and signed by Marco.

The following morning, our man made photocopies of the statements and one by one he visited the Barcelona newsrooms of the principal Spanish newspapers, so that he could personally hand the statement to the editor. None of them was prepared to meet with him, so he had to leave the statement at reception with an explanatory note. Then he returned to his house in Sant Cugat and, having decided to put up a good fight, though he couldn't possibly imagine the sheer scale of the scandal, he waited for developments.

8

Yesterday, April 28, 2014, I spent the whole day fantasising an imaginary conversation with Marco; I'm transcribing it as I imagined it, word for word. For once in this book, it is not Marco, but I who am adding the fiction.

"Well, it's about time."

"What is?"

"It's about time you let me talk."

"You've spent the whole book talking. Remember you're the one who told me your life story; I'm simply repeating what you told me."

"That's a lie: you're doing much more than that. Don't take me for a fool."

"I'm not."

"Yes you are. You think I'm foolish and dangerous. That's why I only get to appear in your book in this way. In a bad light. In this fantasy of yours. When the book is nearly finished and almost everything has been said . . . If you think that making me appear like this will defuse what I have to say and ensure people don't take me seriously, you're wrong: you may be a fool, but not everyone else is. And speaking of your book: something you wrote a while ago interests me."

"I wrote a lot of things. Which one are you referring to?"

"The one where you say you're writing this book to save me."

"I didn't say that."

"Of course you said that."

"No. What I said is that there have been times, since I started writing this book, when I've had the impression or the suspicion that, without realising, or without recognising it, or without wanting to recognise it, I was trying to save you, and not to save you in the way you think I should save you, meaning rehabilitate you, but by confronting you with the truth."

"The same way that Cervantes saved Don Quixote, right?"

"Exactly."

"Yes, I know the tune. You've played it many times. In any case, don't forget I only asked you to defend me, not to save or rehabilitate me. I never asked for that. Never ever."

"Be careful; you know what I think about insistence, two *nevers* and one *ever* add up to at least one *always*."

"You're just a cynic. You're not writing this book to save me; you're writing it to line your pockets, to make yourself rich and famous, to be in the limelight, as you put it, so that people will love and admire you and consider you a great writer. I mean, I'm not saying you're writing it simply to alleviate your petit bourgeois neuroses and your complexes, but that's the main reason."

"A thief believes everybody steals. That said, I don't think there's anything wrong with writing for the various reasons you suggest."

"Nothing. As long as you admit it. As long as you don't tell yourself fairy tales."

"They're not fairy tales. At first I just wanted to understand you, but now, there are times when part of me isn't content with that; at least that's the impression I have. Now I sometimes hear a little voice that says, 'Why not try to save him? Why not try to save the great impostor, the great pariah, this extraordinary rogue who has condemned himself? Just because it's impossible? Because from the beginning this has been an impossible book? Why not make it a little more impossible? What have you got to lose? Besides, if literature cannot serve to save people, what purpose does it serve?'"

"You sound like you're going mad."

"Maybe I am, but you're to blame. In any case, whatever I do, I have to tell the truth here. That much is certain. And in telling it, maybe I'll help you recover your sanity, free you from being Don Quixote so you can go back to being Alonso Quixano. As for the rest, don't talk nonsense: how do you expect me to line my pockets with a book like this?"

"It's about me, isn't it? Can you think of a more fascinating subject than me?"

"No."

"Neither can I. Let's be honest, the one who isn't fascinating is you. You might be of some interest, but you're so dishonest, it's impossible."

"I don't follow."

"Of course you do. Look, what's impossible is that you've spent I don't know how many pages accusing me of lying and deceiving, of being a charlatan, of not wanting to know myself or recognise myself for who I am, and you still haven't said that you're doing exactly the same. Tell your readers the truth, then maybe they'll start to believe you."

"What precisely should I tell them?"

"Everything."

"For example?"

"For example, that you've benefitted as much as I have from the so-called industry of memory. And that you're just as much to blame for it as I am. Maybe more so."

"You'll have to explain that."

"What was the title of your novel?"

"Which novel?"

"What do you mean, which novel? You know perfectly well. The one that lifted you out of anonymity, the one that put you in the limelight, the one that made you rich and famous."

"It didn't make me rich or famous: it simply made it possible for me to earn a living as a writer. It was called *Soldiers of Salamis.*"

"That's the one. So, tell me, when was it published?"

"In 2001. February or March."

"And tell me, how many copies did it sell? How many people read it? And what is it about: it's about a journalist the same age as you, a grandson of the Civil War who starts out believing that the war is something as remote, as alien as the Battle of Salamis and in the end realises that this isn't true, that the past is never dead, that the past is the present or a dimension of the present, that the war is still alive and without it nothing can be explained; you could put it another way: it's about a journalist your age who thinks he is tracking down a fascist who saved the life of a Republican until he discovers that in fact it was the Republican who saved the life of the fascist, and in the end, he tracks down the Republican, who turns out to be a veteran of every war, or every just war, a hero who represents all that is good and noble about his country, a man who everyone has forgotten."

"Miralles."

"That's right, Miralles. Doesn't it ring a bell, what I've just said? Now tell me something else: who in Spain had ever heard of historical memory when your novel was published?"

"You're not trying to tell me that my novel is to blame for the apotheosis of historical memory? I'm vain, but I'm not stupid."

"Your novel and various other things, but your novel is partly to blame. How else do you explain its success? Why else do you think so many people read it? Because it was good? Don't make me laugh. People read it because they needed it, because the country needed it, they needed to remember its Republican past as though they were exhuming it, needed to relive it, to weep for the elderly forgotten Republican in that asylum in Dijon, for the friends he lost during the Civil War, just as they needed to weep over the things I said in my talks about Flossenbürg, about the Civil War and my friends during the Civil War: over Francesc Armenguer from Les Franqueses; Jordi Jardí, from Anglès . . ."

"You don't need to continue, I know the list by heart. And, please, don't compare yourself to Miralles."

"Why not? Do you know how many journalists, how many students came to see me in 2001 or 2002 or 2003 or 2004 or 2005 believing they had found their own Miralles, their veteran of every just war, their forgotten hero? What was I supposed to do? Tell them to fuck off? Tell them that there are no such things as heroes? Of course not: I gave them what they came looking for, the same thing you'd given them in your novel."

"The difference is that Miralles was a true hero, and you aren't. The difference is that Miralles didn't lie, and you did. The difference is that I didn't lie either."

"Really?"

"I lied with the truth, I lied legitimately, in the way that novels lie, I invented Miralles in order to talk about heroes, about the dead, to remember some of the men forgotten by history."

"And what did I do? I did exactly the same thing as you—no, I did it much better than you. I invented a guy like Miralles, except that this Miralles was alive and he visited schools and talked to children about the horrors of the Nazi camps and about the Spanish inmates there, and about justice and freedom and solidarity; this man was leader of the Amical de Mauthausen, and thanks to him people began to talk about the Holocaust in Spanish schools, thanks to him people discovered that Flossenbürg camp existed and that fourteen Spaniards had died there."

"Yeah, that's another story I know by heart, how you were working like a novelist; I've already mentioned it in the book. The problem is that you weren't a novelist, and novelists are allowed to deceive, you aren't."

"Why not?"

"Because everyone knows that the novelist deceives, but nobody knew that you were doing it. Because the novelist's deception is consensual and yours was not. Because the novelist has a duty to deceive and you had a duty to tell the truth. Those are the rules of the game, and you broke them."

"Look who's talking. Didn't you break them? How many people did you deceive with *Soldiers of Salamis*? How many people did you get to believe that everything you said in the book was true?"

"Like I said, the duty of the novelist is to get people to believe that everything he says is true, even though it's a lie. For God's sake, do I have to repeat what Gorgias said four hundred years before Christ? 'Poetry [that is to say fiction, in this case the novel] is a deception, wherein he who deceives is more honest than he who does not deceive, and he who is deceived is wiser than he who is not deceived.' It's all there. Do you understand now? I don't have anything more to add."

"Well I do. That might be true for ordinary novels, but what about true stories? What about non-fiction novels?"

"*Soldiers of Salamis* isn't a non-fiction novel or a true story."

"The narrator says that it is."

"But that doesn't mean that it is. The first thing you have to do when reading a novel is distrust the narrator. The narrator of *Don Quixote* also said that his story is a true story or a non-fiction novel and that he has done no more than translate it from the original Arabic of someone called Sidi Hamid Benengeli. That's not true, it's a joke."

"Yes, but in your case there were people who believed it."

"There are also people who believe the real author of *Quixote* is Sidi Hamid Benengeli. And that Don Quixote really existed."

"Yes, but in your case there were people who not only believed that Miralles existed, there were people who wrote letters to the clinic where he lived, who believed that you'd met him and interviewed him in the same way that all those people met and interviewed me imitating the narrator from your novel. And you didn't disabuse them, at least not always. On several occasions you even said that Miralles existed."

"He did exist, though I never met him; Roberto Bolaño met him, as I mention in the book, but by the time I was writing it, Miralles was already dead. Besides, that thing about Miralles existing was a joke too, or a manner of speaking: what I meant was that while people were reading the book, Miralles was alive, just as Don Quixote will continue to live for as long as people read Cervantes' novel. It's a joke, but it's true: that is how literature works."

"Nonsense: Don Quixote was never alive; and Miralles is dead. He was already dead when you wrote the book, although you didn't know that and nor did your friend Bolaño. And I wonder if you didn't know that Miralles was dead, if he might still have been alive, why did you not go looking for him? Why did you not look for the real Miralles, the flesh and blood Miralles, instead of inventing a false Miralles?"

"Because, in the novel, the real Miralles would have been false, while the false Miralles is the real one. Because I was writing fiction, not a true story."

"Bullshit: you didn't go looking for him because you didn't give a damn about the truth; all that matters to you is writing a good book so you can line your pockets and get into the limelight and everyone will love and admire you and think you're a great writer and all that stuff: come on, it's the same stuff that matters to me. Although, come to think of it, rather than talking about Miralles, we should talk about the fortune-teller."

"I don't want to."

"That's hardly fair: you've devoted I don't know how many pages to me, saying whatever you like, and in the brief space you allow me to talk about your affairs, you refuse to talk. You can accuse me of hiding my past all you like, of not wanting to know myself or recognise myself, of being a Narcissus, but you're just the same. Or worse. Well, fuck you—at least in this chapter. In the rest of the book you can do what you like, but right now I'm in charge. Talk to me about the fortune-teller."

"It's a disgusting story."

"Personally, I think it's funny. You write a novel in which all the characters are real, except for the fortune-teller on the local television station in Gerona, and the woman who worked as a fortune-teller on the local T.V. station sued you. You see what happens when you mix fiction with reality? People get confused."

"All novels mix fiction and reality, Señor Marco. Except for non-fiction novels or true stories, all novels do. And as for that woman, she wasn't confused. She said she was the character in *Soldiers of Salamis*, but it was all nonsense: I didn't know her, I'd never slept with her, I'd seen her once or twice on T.V., that's all. That woman tried to take advantage of the book's success, to steal the limelight."

"And she succeeded."

"She got her fifteen minutes of fame, that's true. But the judge acquitted me. In any case, it was a horrible story. We were living in Gerona at the time, it's a small town, and my family had a terrible time . . . Can we change the subject?"

"Alright: I'll do it if we can talk about your son. I like him. He seems like an amazing guy."

"He is."

"I can understand you not wanting to talk about that story. Can you understand that there are things I don't want to talk about, things I want to hide? We all have secrets, and we all have the right to hide them, don't we? Now I've told them to you because you're putting them in your book, and, you know what? I don't regret it. Tell my secrets. Don't try to use them to save me, I don't need it. Use them to stand up for me. But that's not what I wanted to say. What I wanted to say is that people in glass houses shouldn't throw stones: you did exactly the same thing I did, you made historical memory fashionable, or contributed to making it fashionable, you helped to create the industry of memory just as I did, more so than I did; but you were rewarded for it, it made you a famous writer while I was punished for it, it made me a pariah."

"It's a waste of time: I'm not going to agree with you. And you're not going to make me feel guilty."

"But you are, just as I am—maybe more so, because at least I've purged my guilt, you haven't. This is what I don't understand: given that we did the same thing, why do you get the glory and I get the shame? And please don't lie to me again: of course you feel guilty; you always feel guilty. Otherwise, why would you see a psychoanalyst?"

"I'm not seeing a psychoanalyst."

"But you used to."

"How do you know?"

"I know a lot more than you think. Besides, it doesn't surprise me that a weak, neurotic petit bourgeois like you would be constantly troubled by his conscience. I suppose the closest I came to being psychoanalysed was when we were filming *Ich bin Enric Marco*, trying to find the truth among the lies of my past. That's what psychoanalysis is, isn't it?"

"I suppose so."

"And what did you find?"

"Among the lies of my past? Nothing."

"You're a liar."

"What about you? What did you find?"

"Something small but important, something I already knew was there. Something grey, grubby, plain, mediocre and ghostly: just enough to be able to lie. That's the truth, don't you think? What we need to lie. The truth is unbearable. It's not the lie that's terrifying, what's terrifying is the truth."

"Fiction saves, reality kills."

"Exactly."

"But you can't always live with the lie."

"You can't always live with the truth. You can't live, but you have to live. That's the problem: I could live with the lie. And now, when you've finished your book, I will live with the truth, the whole truth. I don't doubt it. I can live with anything, Javier. Anything. I am Enric Marco. Don't forget that. When the scandal broke, people thought I'd run away, that I'd sink, that I'd never set foot outside again, that I'd kill myself, in fact one son of a bitch told me that's what I should do. Fuck him! Fuck the lot of them! I'm not going to kill myself, I thought. Let them kill themselves, I thought. Let the bastards who want me to kill myself kill themselves, I thought. I didn't commit suicide. I stood up for myself. And here I am. It's true: I made a mistake; we can agree, I should probably not have done what I did. But has no-one else ever made a mistake? What about the journalists and the historians who swallowed my story hook, line and sinker? Didn't they make a mistake? Is there anyone who never made a mistake? Haven't you made mistakes? And who was harmed by my mistake?"

"Millions of the dead. You mocked them. Them and millions of the living."

"That's a lie: I didn't mock anyone; on the contrary, I made that atrocity public. And I showed that nobody cared about that atrocity, that, in Spain at least, nobody wanted to know about it, no-one had cared about it before and no-one cared about it now. Do you really believe that if they'd known anything about it, if they'd truly cared about it, my lie would have passed for the truth, my deception would have been believed? Look, with your novel you proved that many people had forgotten the Civil War and in particular those who lost the war, or at least you made them believe they had forgotten, but with my imposture, I proved that in our country the Holocaust didn't exist, or no-one cared about it. Don't try to tell me I harmed anyone. I did no more harm than you did, I did it the same way you did, using the same tools you used. The difference is that you were acclaimed for doing it and I was made a pariah. That's why you are indebted to me. That's why you have to clear my name."

"I am not indebted to you, and I've already told you what I propose to do."

"And I'll tell you again, I don't need you to save me. Don't be so arrogant. Or so naive. As for saving yourself, no-one is ever saved, we're all damned. But who cares? Obviously, I don't, and I don't think you care either. I'll settle for you standing up for me. And, well, can I tell you something?"

"Haven't you already told me everything?"

"No."

"Say whatever you like."

"I had a better sense of you before I met you, when I had only read you."

"Oh, that doesn't surprise me: everyone says that. That's why I have less and less of a social life."

"I'm serious. People who don't know you, people who have only read you, think that you're humble, because you're always self-deprecating, you always mock yourself, especially in your journalism. I don't believe that. In fact, until I met you, I thought the self-mockery in your articles was a sign, not of humility, but of smugness: he feels so powerful, I thought, he even attacks himself, mocks himself; if he weren't so arrogant, I thought, if he were more humble, more cautious, less sure of himself, he'd leave the job of mocking him to others."

"It's strange, I've never thought of it that way. To me, self-mockery is the most basic form of decency, the minimum honesty you can have, especially if you write for a newspaper: after all, good criticism begins with self-criticism, and anyone who isn't capable of laughing at himself has no business laughing at anything else."

"Yes, that's what an arrogant person would say. And that's what I liked about you when I only knew you through your writings: behind that humble appearance, I could glimpse a terrible arrogance. But, now that I've met you, I know you're not arrogant at all, though you're not humble either. You have a typical petit bourgeois mentality: a neurotic mix of guilt and fear. I find your relationship with guilt funny. I remember a scene in a western I saw recently. The town sheriff has just beaten the shit out of a black man, and the whore the black guy worked for says that he's an innocent man; and the sheriff looks at them, intrigued, and says, 'Innocent? Innocent of what?' You're like that: any excuse is good enough for you to feel guilty. You have the morals of a slave; I, on the other hand, have the morals of a free man. I don't feel guilty about anything, I have overcome my guilt, and you know that and that's why you admire me. You wouldn't dare admit it, of course, but you admire me. You think of me as your hero, that's why every now and then in your book, you let slip an 'our hero' here and there."

"I hate to be the bearer of bad news: the whole 'our hero' thing is ironic; in reality it means our villain. Or at best our hero and our villain."

"And are you sure that's how your readers will understand it?"

"In the same way they understand that Don Quixote is both a hero and a fool, or that he's crazy and sane at the same time."

"You have a lot of faith in your readers."

"Of course, I write for intelligent people."

"Yes, but even idiots are going to read this book. It's about me, remember. But do you see it?"

"See what?"

"That you're worried about what your readers will say. You're afraid."

"Afraid? You're the one who should be afraid: yes, my book is about you, but I'm going to tell the truth. What you've told me but also what you haven't told me. The lies, but also the truths."

"Don't talk such nonsense: I told you everything, and anything I didn't tell you I implied, or hinted at, or suggested how you could find it out. Are you saying that you're simply recounting what I told you? Haven't you had the impression more than once that I was the one who wanted you to discover the truth, that I lived what I lived and invented what I invented so that you could recount it, as Alonso Quixano lived what he lived and invented what he invented simply so that Cervantes could recount it? Why should I be afraid of what you're going to tell? And, incidentally, have you forgotten that I am the great impostor, the great pariah, and when the Marco scandal broke, I was called every name under the sun, so now they have nothing left to call me? I'm not worried about what you're going to say; or rather, I'll benefit from it, I'll be back in the limelight, as you put it. There's no such thing as bad propaganda. Besides, I'll soon be ninety-five, do you really think that at ninety-five anyone is afraid of anything? You, on the other hand, are a mere youngster, a youngster of fifty, granted, but a youngster, and you're scared to death. You're afraid of your readers.

You're afraid of what they'll say about this book. You're afraid they'll notice that you like me, that you admire me, that you would like to be like me, to feel no guilt, to be immoral, or rather amoral, to be able to reinvent yourself at fifty-something like Alonso Quixano, change your life, your name, your city, your wife, your family and be someone else, be able to live novels rather than simply write them, free yourself of this shitty petit bourgeois morality that makes you feel guilty for everything, forces you to respect your miserable petit bourgeois principles of being faithful to truth and decency and I don't know what all, when what you most desire is to be like me, a Nietzschean hero like me, a guy who knows that there is no virtue superior to life, not truth, not decency, nothing, a guy who, at the age of fifty, having reached the pinnacle of life and when he should be preparing for death, says No to everything and fashions a life to equal his desire and lives it without caring about anything or anyone, neither his stinking moral values nor the stinking opinions of others, as Alonso Quixano does. But you cannot do that, you cannot even admit that you admire me, because I could do it. You feel panicked, your knees tremble at the mere prospect that someone might say: here comes Cercas again; just look at his books: first he defends a fascist, then he defends a psychopath, now he's defending a liar, a man who mocked millions of the dead. Tell me, how many times have people accused you of defending fascists?"

"I told you, I write for intelligent people."

"And I told you, even idiots read you. Idiots and one-dimensional moralists, as your mentor Ferraté calls them. Even the sanctimonious hypocrites who had the gall to defend your little friend Vargas Llosa. And you're afraid of them. My God, you're afraid. You're terrified that, because you spend your time defending liars, they will feel entitled to lie about you. About you and your family. That they have the right to eviscerate you and your family, especially your family. When all's said and done, in Spain, people like nothing better than watching some guy ripping the guts out of another, right? That's happened to you before, right? But that's not the only thing you're afraid of. Mostly you're afraid of damning yourself. You're afraid of damning yourself by telling my story just as Truman Capote damned himself telling the story of Dick Hickock and Perry Smith in *In Cold Blood*.

That's what you're really afraid of: you're scared shitless. You're terrified of ending up like Capote, ravaged by spite, snobbery and alcohol.
You're afraid you've made a pact with the devil in order to be able
to write this book, and you don't have the guts to just make a pact
and take the consequences, the way Capote did . . . Now that I think
about it, I know why you want to save me."

"Why?"

"To save yourself, the way Dickens saved himself by saving Miss
Mowcher in *David Copperfield*. It's childish. It's pathetic. But the idea
that you might damn yourself throws you into a panic. A terrible
panic. And there's something else that makes you panic: the idea that
people might find out that you, too, are a liar, a fraud. A liar as good
as I am—or almost—and a fraud who is much better, because I was
exposed but you haven't yet been unmasked. Both of these things
frighten you equally. Or almost. Or perhaps what frightens you is
that this is the price you've to pay the Devil to tell my story, rather
than Capote's snobbery, his spite and his booze. That people will
discover that you've spent your whole life deceiving everyone. Discover that you are the impostor, as your friend Martínez de Pisón
told you at Vargas Llosa's house in Madrid. Remember? Clever guy,
the man from Aragon. He truly had the measure of you, he realised
who you were, that what terrified you was the thought that people
would discover you aren't what you seem, and so you make a super-
human effort to try to convince people that you are what you aren't,
a good writer, a good citizen, a decent person and all that respectable
drivel. God, the effort you make, your life must be excruciating, much
worse than mine, or what people believe mine was like before I was
exposed: getting up every morning at first light, spending all day writing to keep up the imposture, so they don't catch you out, so no-one
realises, reading what you've written, that as a writer you are a farce,
a writer with no talent, no intelligence, with nothing to say, spending
every day pretending that you aren't a puppet, a brainless moron, a
pathetic human being, a completely antisocial creep and an utter bastard. Doesn't it make your head spin? Aren't you tired of pretending
that you're something you're not? Why don't you just confess, like I
did? You'll feel calmer, I can assure you, you'll feel relieved. You'll be
able to know or recognise yourself, you'll no longer be hiding from

everyone behind your writing, you'll finally be able to be who you are. I know that this is what you want. I didn't want it, but you do. Otherwise, why are you writing this book? I understand that you did everything you could not to write it, that for years you refused to write it, that you postponed the moment for as long as possible; it's only natural that you were afraid to face the truth. But now, you've almost finished it and you have no choice but to face it. Besides, deep down, you've known the truth from the first, the very moment the scandal about me broke; that was precisely why you didn't want to write about it."

"I don't understand."

"Tell me something, why did you title your article in *El País* 'I am Enric Marco'?"

"Because the film by Santi Fillol and Lucas Vermal was called *Ich bin Enric Marco*, which is German for 'I am Enric Marco.'"

"Bullshit: you called it that because you knew from the beginning that, like me, you were a charlatan and a liar, that you have all my flaws but none of my virtues, and that I'm your reflection in a dream, or in a mirror. And that's why I'm asking you to defend me, to forget about saving me and defend me, because neither you nor I can save ourselves, but in defending me you defend yourself. That's the truth, Javier. The truth is that you are me."

9

The uproar surrounding the Marco scandal far surpassed Marco's most pessimistic predictions. He, with wilful naivety, had expected a discreet scandal limited to the community of *deportados*, perhaps *deportados* and historians, or at worst the Catalan community. In reality, the scandal echoed across five continents. It was inevitable: firstly, because his deception had been astounding, secondly because anything related to the Holocaust has a universal dimension. Besides, the headline could not have been more gripping, it wrote itself and, despite minor variants, it was universal; it was also inevitable, true and devastating: "The president of the Spanish association of Nazi camp survivors was never in a Nazi camp."

But, although the shockwave from the media earthquake reached the furthest corners of the planet, its epicentre was in Spain, particularly in Catalonia, where, as the editorial in *Avui* noted, Marco was a "beloved figure." Many other newspapers devoted their editorials to Marco, including those with the largest circulation: *El País*, *La Vanguardia* and *El Periódico*. There was probably not a single media outlet in Spain that didn't pick up the story, didn't publish an article, a feature, an interview, a statement or a joke about Marco, nor a single talk-show host on radio or television who didn't offer an opinion on the case, nor a single columnist who didn't write an article about him or mention him in some form, nor a "letters to the editor" page that didn't feature a letter about him. Most of the comments were disparaging; besides impostor and liar, Marco was called every name under the sun: swine, scoundrel, bastard, crook, traitor, scum; at least two articles opined that the best thing he could do was take his own life;

in Barcelona, Neus Català, a former inmate of Ravensbrück and a member of the Amical, said that Marco had mocked the memory of the dead, while, in Paris, Ramiro Santisteban, president of F.E.D.I.P. (the Spanish Federation of *Deportados* and Political Prisoners), suggested that Marco deserved to be tried and sentenced by the Spanish courts. Marco's former enemies at the C.N.T., who, even after twenty-five years had not forgotten the turmoil caused by the internecine struggles within the union, resurrected the old accusations about their former secretary general, that he had been a government or a state collaborator, perhaps a police informant, perhaps one of those behind the Scala affair and the collapse of the C.N.T., which caused a number of journalists, as young as they were bloodthirsty, and ignorant of the political squabbles that had triggered the decline, dutifully to follow this sensational lead, attempting to uncover the only part, or almost the only part, of Marco's past that hadn't yet been exposed. In short: during these turbulent days, Marco was thrust into the limelight more than he'd ever imagined, but not for the reasons he'd imagined. In short: Marco had managed to become a beloved figure, a civic hero, a champion or a rock star of so-called historical memory, but in a few short days he became the great impostor and the great pariah.

This is what he has been ever since. In spite of that, from the beginning, Marco had his defenders. Not all of those who defended him did so to be contentious, to draw attention to themselves or to set themselves up as non-conformist conformists; some seemed to be genuine in their defence of him. Among them, there were those who rehashed the arguments used by Marco himself, particularly the argument that his lie was a good lie, or at worst a venial sin, since it had contributed to publicising truths that needed to be known, or that he had done so because the genuine camp survivors were no longer able and someone needed to step in for them. But there were also those who defended Marco by arguing that the press was engaged in an *auto-da-fé*, a shameful bloodletting intended to hide the true culprit for the deception, which wasn't Marco but the press itself, which had accepted, exploited and broadcast Marco's lies; according to this interpretation, the "Marco affair" was actually the affair of those gullible, opportunistic, incompetent journalists who felt they had been ridiculed and swindled by Marco and were now avenging themselves by pillorying him with savage cruelty. There were also people who appended to this a further argument, whereby there were impostors much worse than Marco, whose lies triggered wars, suffering and death and whose crimes went unpunished, great liars whom the media didn't dare criticise, revered and treated with kid gloves by everyone. There was no shortage of those who tried to argue that we are all impostors and that, in one way or another, we all reinvent our past, and hence everyone is tainted with Marco's guilt.

At the Amical de Mauthausen, the Marco affair triggered the worst crisis in the 43-year history of the association. As acting president, Rosa Torán attempted to control the situation and minimise the damage by giving press conferences, holding meetings and distributing statements refuting false information and defending the actions of the board of directors; and also by sending letters to every possible authority, soliciting their compassion and their support and assuring them that, despite the scandal, the work of the association was continuing. Torán had no more success than might be expected. Although the authorities feigned compassion and continued to provide financial support, and although there were some who joined the association in an attempt to buttress it in the midst of this earthquake, the fact is that respect for the organisation suffered so much that many wondered whether it would survive. The problems didn't all come from without, but also (perhaps especially) from within. Members' meetings degenerated into pitched battles: there were screams, insults, doors slammed, violent scuffles; there were innumerable attacks on the board, in which they were accused of every imaginable wrong, of having poorly managed the scandal, having known for some time that Marco was an impostor and hidden the fact for spurious or unspeakable reasons; some resigned from the board and some resigned from the association; some declared that the Amical was dead and it was necessary to rebuild it. In an attempt to finance the association, on June 5, almost a month after the Marco scandal broke, members held the first and only extraordinary general meeting of the Amical in Barcelona, at which they elected a new board, and a new president, Jaume Álvarez, a camp survivor and founding member of the association. It had no effect: although the Amical survived the Marco affair, it was

mortally wounded and its subsequent history has been one of gradual
decline, as has that of the so-called movement for the recovery of
historical memory.

But the person who suffered most from the Marco affair was
Marco himself. As I've said, the magnitude of the scandal far exceeded
his worst expectations; his response to it, however, was exactly as he'd
planned: he put up a fight, defended himself by attacking or attacked
by defending himself. In the days when the character he'd spent his
life creating seemed to be collapsing on top of him with an apoca-
lyptic rumble, Marco stood firm against the avalanche of public condemnation and abuse, and, to judge by his actions and his words, at no
point did he consider running away or hiding, at no point did he think
of retreating or surrendering, still less committing suicide, at no point
did he refuse to face the consequences. However one judges him from
a moral standpoint, this in itself is astonishing, especially considering
that he was an old man of eighty-four. It's no less astonishing that,
rather than hole up in his house for ever, or seek exile in an igloo
in Lapland, or simply put a bullet in his head, Marco gave countless
interviews to the press, radio and television, interviews in which he
was routinely accused of being a liar and an impostor, in which he was
mauled half to death. All of this simply served to magnify the scandal, which continued to grow, but Marco did not seem to care. One
might conjecture that Marco's mediopathy felt a secret jubilation at
this overexposure in the media; that may be true, but what's certain is
that he was humiliated and insulted beyond endurance and his pride
took such a knock that it's incredible he did not go under.

It's incredible, but that's how it was. Marco did not avoid a single
meeting with a single journalist. In every interview, with minor variations, he trotted out the handful of arguments which he'd contrived
or cobbled together in the days before the scandal broke and which,
gradually, as the days passed, he developed, polished and improved,
incorporating new arguments and perfecting the old ones. There
were interviews in which Marco appeared to be penitent and others
where he did not seem to repent; in most of them he seemed simultaneously penitent and unrepentant. In some of the first interviews
he granted—I'm thinking of one that was conducted on the day the
scandal broke, on Catalan public television, by Josep Cuní, one of the

most influential journalists in the country—Marco seemed at times to be nervous and indignant, almost on the brink of tears. Gradually, however, he settled down and regained his composure; gradually, without abandoning his original tenets—he hadn't lied, he had simply distorted the truth; if he had lied, then it was a good lie, a noble lie he could have claimed with Plato, a beneficial lie he could have alleged with Montaigne, a salutary or vital lie he could have excused himself with Nietzsche; a lie thanks to which he had exposed the horrors of the twentieth century to the young and had given voice to the voiceless; he had been a prisoner in Nazi jails as the *deportados* had been prisoners in Nazi camps and therefore he had a right to speak on their behalf, etcetera—influenced perhaps by some of his defenders, he began to present himself as a victim: a victim of spiteful, bitter journalists, a victim of the failure to understand or remember his virtues as a civic hero and a champion or rock star of historical memory, a victim of general intransigence, ignorance and ingratitude, a victim of Benito Bermejo and his war against the Amical or against his co-workers at Amical, a victim of the Spanish right wing who were fed up with historical memory, a victim of Mossad Jews fed up with his denunciations of the situation in Palestine, a victim of everything.

This defensive campaign (or this offensive disguised as a defensive campaign) wasn't merely public but also private. When the Marco scandal first broke, but especially as it was beginning to fade from the national media, our hero unleashed upon the world an avalanche of letters comparable only to the avalanche of accusations and insults he was receiving or had received, using writing as any writer does: to defend himself. Marco wrote to the board of Amical, to the members of Amical, to politicians at municipal, autonomous and state level, to celebrated journalists and others who were practically anonymous, and to the editors of newspapers he'd vainly tried to meet with the day before the scandal so he could give them the statement acknowledging his imposture; he wrote to public figures with whom he had some connection, to former colleagues at the C.N.T. and at FaPaC, to current friends and acquaintances and to friends and acquaintances he hadn't seen in years, to universities, cultural associations, retirement homes, penitentiaries, institutes for adult education and to groups of every kind where he had ever given a talk; in particular, he wrote to the countless secondary schools he had visited. In some schools, no doubt because his talk had had an electrifying effect, the discovery of his deception also had an electrifying effect, to the point where some of the teachers who had invited Marco to speak to their classes felt obliged to explain to their pupils that, although the old man they'd been so impressed by and some had seen as a hero was actually a liar, nothing he had told them was a lie. Marco's letters were an often bewildering torrent of excuses, self-defence and self-justification to which he sometimes appended documents that proved or were intended to prove his past as an anti-Franco resistance fighter: like the photographs of his body mottled with bruises after his beating by the police on September 28, 1979, during a protest march in favour of the defendants in the Scala affair, or paperwork appearing to prove that not only had he been tried by a Nazi court (which was true), but that he had been an anti-Nazi agitator (which was false)—Marco sent the prosecutor's report in which he was accused of high treason but not the judge's sentence dismissing the original denunciation and exonerating him of the charges. In fact, Marco's defence of himself was so meticulous that it even included symbolic gestures. Two days after the scandal broke, Marco presented himself at the office of the President of the Generalitat of Catalonia and handed over an envelope containing the Creu de Sant Jordi, the certificate, and a letter addressed to the Head of State apologising for having lied about being a *deportado*, and adding a brief account of his usual justifications. This wasn't the only thing Marco returned. Although at the time, Marco was accused of having grown rich from his deception, the only payment our man had received as a false *deportado* was 7,000 euros compensation from a foundation based in Switzerland for German companies who had profited from the use of Nazi prisoners during the Second World War; in the wake of the scandal, Marco returned the money only to have it sent back to him some months later with the explanation that, although he hadn't been a prisoner in a Nazi camp, he had been used as slave labour by the Nazis.

It was all futile: Marco fought as though his life depended on it, because the truth was his life *did* depend on it, but to no avail. He was stunned, angry and confused. He could not conceive that people wouldn't listen to his arguments, he could not accept that they condemned him out of hand, he could not bear that his status as civic hero, as champion or rock star of so-called historical memory had been snatched away, he wasn't prepared to accept that they had stripped away his persona and wanted him to return to being Alonso Quixano, and not even Alonso Quixano the Good, but Alonso Quixano the Bad. And he didn't accept it among other reasons (or perhaps especially) because he knew they hadn't truly killed off his character: they might have killed off the survivor of the Nazi camps, but there were others—the defender of the Republic during the war, the victim of the Nazi prisons, the post-war anti-Franco resistance fighter, the trade union leader at the C.N.T., the educational leader at FaPaC. Did none of this mean anything? Surely this was the life story of a hero, even if not that of a *deportado*. Surely a life of sacrifice in the service of just causes was enough to redeem a minor mistake in old age, if indeed it had been a mistake? He felt as though he'd managed to keep the house of cards standing and, in spite of that, everyone was behaving as though it had collapsed.

After agonising months of relentless struggle, in the end it was he who collapsed. Or so he says. What he says is that, seeing himself ruthlessly relegated to the rank of great impostor and great pariah, at some point he sank into depression. That may be true, though I have trouble believing it, because a guy like Marco never sinks into depression, he never sinks, full stop. Nevertheless, it's true that there came a point when he stopped fighting and sought refuge in the bosom of his family, with his wife and two daughters, and from time to time with a friend, although Marco was always a lone wolf and never had many friends. This hiatus, always assuming it was a hiatus, didn't last long, and afterwards Marco became what the scandal had made him, became what he was when I met him and, thinking about it, what he'd always been: a great impostor and a great pariah but chiefly a self-publicist, a man on a war footing, devoted to the cause of his own defence. He no longer gave public talks, but he accepted every opportunity to explain himself that was offered, beginning with interviews about his own case and cases similar to his (although Marco always fixed it so that he talked mostly about himself, seeming not to care that he could defend himself only by defending another charlatan). He attended public functions where he encountered former colleagues from his time at the C.N.T. and FaPaC; some had liked him, others had disliked him, some had admired him, others had loathed him or were indifferent to him, but all of them had followed the news of the scandal, were incredulous, indignant or embarrassed on his behalf, and now either didn't speak to him, behaved as though nothing had happened, or managed to avoid him.

Marco also attempted to recover his position at Amical. On several occasions he sent letters requesting a meeting in order to explain himself, to give his former colleagues his version of the Marco affair, to try to redeem himself in their eyes and renew his ties with the organisation; and every time he found new documents that confirmed his status as victim of the Nazis (after travelling to Germany to film *Ich bin Enric Marco* with Santi Fillol and Lucas Vermal, for example), he would send copies to the headquarters of the Amical on calle Sils as proof that his version of the facts was correct, that he hadn't lied as much as people thought. The Amical de Mauthausen did not respond to any of his letters, despite the fact that Marco resorted to every possible reason for them to readmit him, including those of the shameless charlatan and peerless trickster, suggesting that his former co-workers should help him recover his good name so that no-one would be able to criticise them for allowing an impostor to be president of Amical. On one occasion, however, he did meet with them again, or with many of them. It was at the funeral of Antonia García, who had been in what was called Convoy 927 or the Convoy of Angoulême, a train filled with Spanish Republican exiles that left the French city of Angoulême in June 1940 for Mauthausen. Marco attended the funeral because he'd had a warm relationship with the deceased, and perhaps also because he saw it as a possibility to be reconciled with his former colleagues. But if it was for the second reason, it didn't work; although some shook his hand or seemed happy to see him again, most of the members of the association were embarrassed that he attended the event, and more than one refused to acknowledge him. It's likely that no-one really understood why he was there.

Marco has spent recent years living in a perpetual state of self-justification. He has said a thousand times that he doesn't want to be rehabilitated, but that is precisely what he wants: he wants to stop being a pariah, to stop being the impostor and the liar par excellence; he wants to resume, if not his role as champion or rock star of so-called historical memory—Marco is well aware that historical memory scarcely exists now, and that his case contributed to its demise—at least his role as civic hero or exceptional individual; he wants to be allowed to contribute to the betterment of his country, and to speak to young people about truth, justice and solidarity; he wants it to be recognised that he, too, was a victim of Francoist and Nazi barbarism, someone who fought against them, and that his lie was a beneficial lie, one so insignificant that it is barely, or barely deserves to be considered, a lie; he wants it to be admitted that society as a whole treated him unjustly, that he was unfairly, spitefully, savagely abused by the media; he wants everyone to accept once and for all that he is not Alonso Quixano but Don Quixote.

And he will not rest until he succeeds. Or so he says, and I believe him. In this, the final quest in his life, Marco works alone, whenever the opportunity presents itself and with the means at his disposal, his gift with words, his talent as a charlatan, a charmer and a trickster, qualities that, despite the ravages of his ninety-three years, are largely intact; on occasion, he works with others, or has attempted to, because he doesn't spurn help from anyone and because he is aware that, having lost all his credibility, he must try to take advantage of the credibility of others, even if they don't realise it (or especially if they realise it). It doesn't matter who they are: journalists, filmmakers, writers. It makes no difference. What matters is that they have an audience, that they allow him to step into the limelight, and above all that he can persuade them to defend him, to champion his cause. The first great rehabilitation he attempted, some years after the scandal broke, was a long article entitled "The Story of a Lie," published in the magazine *Presència;* its authors were two good journalists, good people who had known him since their youth, who had admired him and who, despite their disappointment on discovering his deception, continued to consider him a friend: Carme Vinyoles and Pau Lanao. The second vindication he attempted, in 2009, was *Ich bin Enric Marco*, the film by Santi Fillol and Lucas Vermal. The last, it scarcely needs to be said, is this book.

The Blind Spot

I

In the spring of 2012, when after many years I was about to stop refusing to write this book, the newspaper *Le Monde* asked a group of writers to choose the word that best defined what we wrote; we were also requested to write a page in support of our choice. I immediately chose my word: No. And I wrote what follows.

"What is a rebel?" Albert Camus asked. "A man who says No." If Camus is right, most of my books are about rebels, because they are about men who say No (or who try and fail to do so). In some of my books, this is not very apparent, in others, it is impossible to miss: *Soldiers of Salamis* centres on a Republican soldier who, at the end of the Spanish Civil War, must kill a fascist leader and decides not to kill him; *The Anatomy of a Moment* centres on an act by a politician who, at the inception of the current Spanish democracy, refuses to lie on the ground when the members of a final Francoist coup ordered him to do so at gunpoint. The words of Dante (*Inferno*, III, 60), that serve as an epigraph to *The Anatomy of a Moment*, might serve as an epigraph to most of my books: "Colui che fece [. . .] il gran rifiuto." He who said the great No: Dante is referring to Pope Celestine V, who abdicated the papacy, but centuries later, Constantin Cavafy understood it as referring not to a single man, but to many of us. "For some people there comes a day when they have to say the great Yes or the great No." This is what most of my books are about: the day of the Great No (or the Great Yes); that is to say, the day when one knows once and for all who one is [. . .]

What about this book? What about this book that, for so many years, I didn't want to write, and am now about to complete? Is there no-one in this book who says No (or who tries and fails to do so)? Is it simply the story of a man who always said Yes, a man who was always with the majority, always in the middle of the crowd, a man who is no-one, or one who will never see the day when he knows once and for all who he is? In his talks and his public statements, Marco emphatically insisted that heroes do not exist, but by now we know all about emphasis (particularly Marco's emphasis), and we also know that in saying that heroes do not exist, what Marco wanted to say is that he was the hero. So, in this book about a false hero, is there no true hero?

Of course there is. We all know that there will always be men capable of saying No. They are very few, and besides, we immediately forget them or hide them away so that their resounding No doesn't expose the silent Yes of everyone else; but we all know that they exist. They are here in this book: Fernández Vallet and his comrades in the U.J.A., a handful of boys from the suburbs of Barcelona who, in early 1939, when Franco's troops had already taken the city, the war was lost and everybody was saying Yes, said No, who refused to give up, who refused to surrender, who refused to meekly endure the opprobrium, the indecency and the humiliation that was the lot of the defeated, and in doing so learned once and for all who they were. They are here. After more than seventy years of obfuscation and amnesia, they are here one last time. Honour to the brave: Pedro Gómez Segado, Miquel Colás Tamborero, Julia Romera Yáñez, Joaquín Miguel Montes, Juan Ballesteros Román, Julio Meroño Martínez, Joaquim Campeny Pueyo, Manuel Campeny Pueyo, Fernando Villanueva, Manuel Abad Lara, Vicente Abad Lara, José González Catalán, Bernabé García Valero, Jesús Cárceles Tomás, Antonio Beltrán Gómez, Enric Vilella Trepat, Ernesto Sánchez Montes, Andreu Prats Mallarín, Antonio Asensio Forza, Miquel Planas Mateo and Antonio Fernández Vallet.

Who else? Is there anyone else in this book who said No? Of course: Benito Bermejo. The hidden villain of this story is actually its hidden hero, or one of its heroes. Although perhaps the word "hero" is inaccurate; more than a hero, Bermejo is a just man; one of those who work in silence, with humility, integrity and tenacity, one of those men whose sense of duty, when the decisive moment comes, instils enough courage in him to say No, and if necessary to be a wet blanket and poke people in the eye, as Bermejo did when he exposed Marco at the height of the funereal celebration of memory, when the funeral industry of memory was working at full strength.

Anyone else? Let me go back to Albert Camus. The most famous quote by the French writer was something he didn't write; he said it in Sweden on December 12, 1957, shortly after receiving the Nobel Prize. In its most common (and categorical) form, it runs: "I believe in justice, but if I have to choose between justice and my mother, I choose my mother." Although he was bitterly attacked for his statement, in actual fact this is not precisely what Camus said, nor did it have the general sense that his enemies attributed to it. But that doesn't matter to me, at least not today. Today, I'll stick to this, which is more important—when the Marco scandal broke, his wife and two daughters, who must have suffered as much if not more than Marco, clung, in their way, to this quote: between an abstract principle and a man of flesh and blood, they chose the man of flesh and blood. In those end-of-the-world days for Marco, these three women stuck by him, the three of them shielded him, none of them asked for any further explanation than he was prepared to give them. More than that, on the day after the scandal broke, Ona, who was twenty-one at the time, unexpectedly called in to a morning programme on Catalan television in which her father was being attacked, and, a little later, wrote an article published in *El País* in response to an open letter written by a former member of the board of Amical, criticising her for her defence of Marco on television. Between truth and her father, Ona Marco chose her father; between truth and her father, Elizabeth Marco chose her father; between truth and her husband, Dani Olivera chose her husband. None of them relented at the time, none of them has relented since; in the many years that Marco has been the great impostor and the great pariah, no-one has heard a word of reproach from them against him, or witnessed any gesture that was other than affectionate. Fuck the truth: honour to the brave.

Is that everyone? Are there no other heroes lurking? Just a minute: What about our hero? What about Enric Marco? Is he merely a false hero? Did he never say No (or at least try and fail to do so)? Can he not be both a false and a true hero, a hero and a villain, in the same way that Don Quixote is both ridiculous and heroic, or both sane and crazy at the same time? Is it possible that the visible great villain of this book is also its invisible great hero? Is it possible that the man of the great Yes could also be the man of the great No? And, speaking of Don Quixote, who, at the age of fifty, rebelled against his lot as a country gentleman with no glory, and in order not to know or to recognise himself for what he was, and not to die like Narcissus staring into the shimmering waters of his own terrifying reflection, gave himself a hero's name and reinvented himself completely so he could live the heroic novels he had read—is there not something of similar grandeur in Marco? Did Marco not rebel too? Is his revolt against the meagreness, the narrowness and the wretchedness of life not a maximum form of rebellion like that of the rebel in Camus, the total rebellion of the man who says No and who, having crested the peak of his life, wants to carry on living when he isn't supposed to live, or more precisely, who wants to live still, in spite of everything and everyone, all that he hasn't yet lived? Is Marco's lie not a Nietzschean vital lie, an epic, totally asocial and morally revolutionary lie because it places life above truth? Did Marco not have to choose between truth and life and, flouting all the moral rules, all the norms of coexistence, all that we consider sacred and respectable, choose life? And is this resounding Yes not a resounding No, a definitive No?

2

On Friday April 5, 2013, I had a long conversation with Marco in my office in the Gracia district of Barcelona. Some months earlier, I had given up resisting writing this book and, since then, had been working on it full time. The day before I'd had a meeting in my office with Joan Villarroya, one of the most knowledgeable historians on the subject of the Civil War in Catalonia, trying to clarify what was truth and what were lies in Marco's account of his war, and on Wednesday I'd spent the day at the offices of the Amical de Mauthausen on calle Sils, looking through their archives and talking to Rosa Torán and other members of the association.

It was there that I arranged the Friday meeting with Marco. At a certain moment, overjoyed and overwhelmed by the sheer quantity of documents about our man in the Amical archives, I asked Torán whether I could photocopy them in order to study them calmly; Torán said that I could, assuming I had permission from Marco. I immediately picked up the phone and called him. I did so with some trepidation, because Marco and I had still not gotten beyond the initial phase of our relationship, when I tried my best to disguise the mixture of suspicion and displeasure I felt and Marco still wanted but didn't want me to write this book and was trying to charm me as he defended himself from my assaults, entangling me in the web of this shameless charlatan and peerless trickster, agreeing to our meetings only sparingly and doing everything in his power to control what I might find out. And so, as I dialled Marco's number to ask permission to photocopy the documents at Amical, I was afraid that he wouldn't grant it without first examining them himself.

I was wrong. Marco told me to photocopy whatever I liked; then we chatted briefly. I don't know how long it had been since our last meeting, because he was still in the process of telling me his life story, but I do know that in the past few days I'd been pressing him to meet and he'd been fobbing me off with excuses, so I made the most of this call to tell him that on Monday I was going to Berlin, where I would be spending four months as guest lecturer at the Free University; however I was careful not to tell him that, in those four months, I would be back in Barcelona from time to time, in the hope that my false long absence might trigger his cyclical desire for me to write this book and persuade him to grant me the interview I'd been requesting. The ruse worked: Marco suggested we see each other before my departure, and I seized the opportunity.

We made an appointment for Friday afternoon.

If my records are accurate, it was the fifth session we recorded, the last of the initial series. I filmed it myself. My son, who had recorded the first sessions, but had given up because he was too busy with his studies to carry on helping me, had shown me how to do it. The recording lasted three hours. When it was made, there were still many things I had yet to discover about Marco, and many others of which I was unsure. As far as I remember, I hadn't yet become obsessed with the bizarre idea that I had to save him. Let me say now that nothing extraordinary occurs or is said in this recording, or no more so than in the many other hours I filmed with Marco (during which many extraordinary things occurred or were said)—except for in the last few minutes, when Marco's story has arrived at its chronological conclusion, that is to say, the present, or what was then the present, and I'm helping him to recap and interpret some of the episodes he'd recounted during previous sessions, there is a moment when we both seem to cast aside our roles as persecutor and persecuted or besieger and besieged, and, for the first time, we establish a sort of genuine dialogue or communication. It's a strange, almost magical moment, at least for me, a sort of step change in my relationship with Marco, which is why I don't want to finish this book without recounting it, or rather without transcribing the conversation we had, in the hope that the words we exchanged might give some small glimpse of that magic.

On the video, Marco is sitting in a white Ikea armchair, and is visible only from the shoulders up; I am not visible since I'm sitting opposite him, with the camera mounted on a tripod next to me. Marco is wearing a white shirt, a blue polka-dot neckerchief knotted around his throat and a blue sweater (on his chest, out of frame, he probably has a pin emblazoned with the flag of the Second Republic); as always, his moustache is dyed, but not his hair, which is grey and thinning. Behind Marco is a bookcase filled with books and, to left and right, two windows through which the light streams morning or afternoon. But at the point of the interview I'm talking about, daylight has faded and we've turned on the lights on the bookshelf; next to Marco is a floor lamp which is also lit. I would add that, rewatching the footage, there are three things that catch my attention. The first is Marco's tiredness, unsurprising for anyone who has been talking for three hours straight as he has, but surprising for Marco; now it occurs to me that perhaps his tiredness explains not only why Marco has let me talk more than usual, but also, at least in part, the curious atmosphere of complicity or understanding that seems to pervade the scene, the feeling in that moment that I got Marco to take off his mask and show his true face. The second thing that surprises me, at least in the final minutes of the recording, is that I address Marco by the familiar *tú;* he has been addressing me as *tú* almost from the beginning but, as far as I remember, it was some time before I allowed myself to be familiar with him; this may have been the first day I did so. The third thing is, in the entire conversation, Marco doesn't once say the word "truthfully."

ME: Long ago now, someone who respects you said to me: "Enric must have suffered a lot as a boy. An awful lot. And if there's one thing he needs it's for people to love him. It's a ferocious need. And all the things he made up, all his lies, are simply a means to get people to love him, to admire him and to love him." What do you think?

MARCO *(shrugging his shoulders)*: I don't know. I've suffered so much I don't even remember any more. When I think that I was born in an asylum, that I had no mother, actually it was worse than not having a mother, I had one, but she

was insane. When I think that I barely had a father, and I
was bounced around from one house to another, from one
family to another. Did I ever tell you that one of my aunts
combed my hair with the part on the right, another with
the part on the left, and another with a centre part? You
can't imagine how angry it made me . . . Do you remember
what your father's hand felt like when you were little? I
don't. I don't remember my father ever holding my hand,
I don't remember him ever helping with my homework, or
teaching me the things he knew, how to play the accordion
or the *bandurria* for example, I don't remember ever going
anywhere with him, or doing anything with him . . . I don't
know, I think that, without realising he was an orphan, Enric
Marco suffered a lot.

ME: And that's why you so desperately needed to be loved, to be
admired.

MARCO: I suppose so, but what I was trying to say is that I have
no memory of having suffered. I assume I suffered, but
I'm not aware of it. It's strange, isn't it? I remember when
I would run out of my father's house, run away from my
stepmother, screaming: "This is all happening because I
don't have a mother!" When I did that, I was trying to say
something, wasn't I? I was trying to say that I needed a
mother, that I needed a father too, I was trying to say that I
was suffering, wasn't I?

ME: And you must have suffered during the war, and after the
war. You must have been very afraid.

MARCO: Very. But it wasn't just my fear: it was everyone's, it
was a general fear. During the war for obvious reasons;
and after the war too. A lot of people were very afraid: the
country was imprisoned, it was a country of informers, of
bribe-takers, of prostitutes. There was everything, none of

it good. And all because of this fear. In order to survive. In order to carry on living whatever the cost.

ME: You didn't talk much about this to the kids, did you? In your school talks, I mean. Maybe it would have been good if you had.

MARCO: What for? To show them how vile we can become? What would they have learned from that? No, what I told those kids is that life can be very tough, but a single dignified act can redeem you. (*Here, suddenly, Marco puts on his mask again and, mustering his energy, he launches into an anecdote pulled at random from his repertoire of glorious adventures, as though he weren't talking to me but to a vast auditorium crammed with people. When he's finished telling it, he seems once again overcome by exhaustion and once again takes off the mask. After a silence, he continues.*) I had a terrible life. I never had any luck.

ME: Your luck wasn't so bad, Enric. I'm talking about later, during the post-war period, Francoism and all that. Your life wasn't so bad, you had a job, a family, you were living much the same life as everyone else, no?

MARCO: Yes. I suppose so, yes.

ME: Until Franco died and freedom came. At that point, you must have been thinking "Fucking hell, this is the life!"

MARCO (*sitting up in the armchair and recovering his energy but without putting on the mask, smiling with a curious enthusiasm, his eyes shining, his mouth open, making a strange gesture with his arms, fast, furious, festive as he leans back*): We drank everything there was! We even drank mineral water! It was joyous! It was amazing!

ME: And at this point you began to invent a past for yourself.

MARCO: Well yes, I suppose so, yes. I felt almost obligated, the people around me, all those kids from rich families, obliged me to . . .

ME: You're referring to Salsas and Boada and Ignasi de Gispert.

MARCO: Of course.

ME: I understand. They forced you. They admired you. They saw you as a hero.

MARCO: Exactly. I didn't want to be a hero, but, as you say, I did want them to like me. Wanted them to love me and admire me. And they did love me and admire me, I think. Girls fell head over heels for me. Even much later, when I was at the Amical and more than eighty years old, there were girls of seventeen who told me they were in love with me, they more or less pestered me. And yes, I had a need . . .

ME: To be loved and to be admired.

MARCO: Yes.

ME: And creating a past for yourself as a hero was the way to be admired.

MARCO: Possibly. Probably. Yes, maybe I cast myself as a hero. Alright yes, I did. And then all this happened and I paid very dearly.

ME: You're talking about the scandal.

MARCO: Yes. And I feel very bad for Dani. *(Marco's expression changes and he suddenly gives a curt laugh.)* Did you know the French government were going to give me the Légion d'Honneur?

ME: No.

MARCO: They were just about to give it to me: they had even written the citation. Just as well they didn't give it to me! But Dani, being French, she would have been impressed, and she would have admired me all the more . . . But it was not to be: I wasn't able to give her that. I've given her many things, everything I could, you know that, but I haven't made my peace.

ME: You haven't made your peace?

MARCO: I don't think so.

ME: With her?

MARCO: That's right. I'm not saying she's not happy; what I'm saying is that this stuff about me must have hurt her terribly.

ME: And your daughters.

MARCO: More or less.

ME: You see how lucky you've been, Enric? At least in some respects. With your wife and your daughters, for example, you've been very lucky.

MARCO: Yes. Although I haven't made my peace with them.

ME: And with yourself.

MARCO: No. That's why we're sitting here talking, right? But, well, I suppose I've been a strange character, haven't I? I've led a strange life. So many things have happened to me . . .

(Here there is a long silence. Marco isn't looking at me or at the camera but at a point in front of him. He looks distracted, as

*though he were about to discover or remember something
crucial, something that would completely change or might
completely change my opinion of him, or as though he has
suddenly lost interest in the conversation. In the end, I am
the one to speak.)*

ME: Enric, tell me something: the first time you noticed that
people admired you for your past was in the late Seventies,
when you met Salsas and Boada and De Gispert and started
hanging out with university students who were more or less
anti-Franco, right?

MARCO: Yes, they were my first admirers.

ME: And later, when Franco died and freedom came and
anarchism was the fad of the moment and you were an
anarchist leader, and you found yourself surrounded by all
those young anarchists . . . Well, they must have admired
you even more, the boys and girls who were all for free love
and endless partying must have really loved you, surely this
was the moment when you triumphed totally.

MARCO: Totally.

ME: At this point you realise they love you for your past, that
a past as an anti-Franco activist, a clandestine resistance
fighter, a Republican soldier and a victim of the Nazis made
all these kids wild about you.

MARCO: Of course, the thing is I'm older than most of them, I'm
the veteran anarchist even though I'm still young, I'm the
former Republican fighter, the soldier who fought in the
Civil War, but I'm also one of them . . . I'm all these things.

ME: And they're enthralled by that. They love you for it, for
your past. Even your wife loves you for your past, she is
impressed by your past.

MARCO: Well, I don't know. She knows me, so . . .

ME: I don't mean now, I'm talking about back then. Didn't Dani
love you for your past? Didn't you woo her with your past?
Wasn't that part of your appeal for her? Didn't you say
that she admired you? I got my wife to fall in love with me
convincing her I was a writer and eventually I had to become
a writer so she'd stay with me.

MARCO: Yes, maybe. Maybe for Dani it wasn't just one more
thing, maybe for her it was important: she was a radical girl,
left-wing, anti-Franco, her mother had been in the French
resistance.

ME: For her, you were a hero too. That's why she fell in love
with you.

MARCO: Yes, maybe . . . I can see where you're heading, and
you're probably right. Probably. *(There is another silence,
though shorter than the previous one; he seems to be trying to
work out where to go next, or how to stop me continuing down
this path.)* Look, I was, I won't say an exception, but I was
different. No worse, no better: different and in any chapter
of my life there are things I'm proud of and things I'm not
proud of, and even things I'm ashamed of. It's the same with
everyone, isn't it? Especially when you get to my age. At
times, I've tried to balance things out, you know, the good
on one side of the scales, the bad on the other. And when
I do it, the scales tip in my favour, on the good side, not
the bad side, because the good weighs more than the bad.
There are things I'm ashamed of: I'm ashamed of having
abandoned my mother in an asylum, I'm ashamed of the way
I treated my first family. I'm ashamed of my lie . . .

ME: You're ashamed?

MARCO: Of course. I regret what I did; I had no reason to do it, I
don't know why I did it.

ME: You did it so people would love you. So they would admire you.

MARCO: Yes, but I didn't have to do it. And by the time Bermejo exposed me, I was tired of doing it; that's why I came clean: I was tired of lying. When Bermejo found out that I had been in Germany as a volunteer worker, I could have said, yes, that's true, but prove that I wasn't in a concentration camp, prove I wasn't in Flossenbürg. Bermejo couldn't have done it, nobody could. But I didn't. I was tired of all the lies and I wanted to tell the truth. That's why I came clean. You believe me, don't you?

ME: I don't know.

MARCO: Well, believe me, for once you have to believe me. Although at this stage I don't really care. What I'm telling you is that in my life I've done some bad things, but the rest is good, or pretty good, and it makes up for all the rest.

ME: Enric.

MARCO: What?

ME: Can I say something?

MARCO: Sure.

ME: You remember the first time we talked about this book, the book I'm writing about you now? Remember what I said to you? I said that I didn't want to rehabilitate you or exonerate you or condemn you, that that's neither my job nor the job of a writer as I understand it. You know what my job is? To understand you. (*At this point, a huge smile lights up Marco's face, and, relieved, drawing out the "o" he whispers "Good."*) Don't misunderstand me, Enric: understanding you does not mean vindicating you; it means understanding you, nothing more. (*Marco nods several times, slowly.*) But, you know what? I think I am starting to understand you.

MARCO (*sitting up slightly in the armchair and raising his arms, still nodding*): Look, I need to tell you something: if your goal is to understand me, mine is to make myself understood. And we have to take it slow, because I still have a lot of things to tell you. We can't rush.

ME: We're not going to rush. We're in no hurry. Or at least I'm not.

MARCO: Me neither. My biography is very complicated. I should probably write it myself. My daughters say to me "Don't go and see Cercas any more. Write your memoirs yourself."

ME: Your daughters don't want you to talk to me?

MARCO: No. Nor does Dani. But that's because they don't know you. I'm getting to know you. Before, I only knew you through your books and your articles. I've read them all, you know! And I agree with you on some things and not on others. But I always read your articles, I even cut them out.
     (*Here Marco puts on the charmer's mask again and launches into a spiel about my articles and my books, trying to flatter me. I interrupt him.*)

ME: Hey, Enric.

MARCO: What?

ME: Your daughters are right. I can't write your biography, nor do I want to. You are the only person who can write your biography. All that I want, as I've said, is to write a book in which people understand you, or in which at least I understand you. Besides, what interests me about you isn't just about you, but what applies to everyone, including me;

what is particular to you, you should write, Enric. Your daughters are right.

MARCO (*folding his arms, but still smiling*): And . . .

ME: And nothing. It's getting late and you should probably go, your wife will be waiting for you. I just wanted to say this: I'm starting to understand you. And that makes me happy.

MARCO. Good, good. I'm happy too.

ME: Are your daughters scared?

MARCO: No. It's just that they've noticed when I come home after seeing you, after one of these sessions, I'm out of sorts, and that worries them. But it won't be like that today; today will be different because you've said you're starting to understand me. And that makes me very happy. And I'll tell Dani as soon as I get home. I'll say to her: "Dani, I've just been with Javier and I felt completely at ease. I'm not afraid any more."

At this point Marco bursts out laughing, and then, apropos of nothing, goes back to talking about my books and my articles. I turn off the camera.

3

Did Cervantes truly save Alonso Quixano in *Don Quixote*? Am I really doing my utmost in this book to save Marco? Have I gone insane too?

Towards the end of *Don Quixote*, the bachelor Samson Carrasco, disguised as the Knight of the White Moon, defeats Don Quixote in single combat on the beach at Barcelona and demands that he return to his village. Obligated by the chivalric code, Quixote obeys and, a few days after, returns to his house "vanquished by the arm of another," as Sancho Panza says, but "victor over himself." Shortly afterwards, sick with melancholy, the knight recovers his sanity and, serene and reconciled to reality after so much fiction, with friends and family around his deathbed, knows himself or recognises himself for who he is ("I am no longer Don Quixote de la Mancha, but Alonso Quixano, whose ways have earned me fame as 'Good'"), and he abjures stories of knight-errantry. "Truly Alonso Quixano the Good is dying, and truly he is in his right mind," his friend the priest then says, as Marco himself might, and immediately afterwards, like Narcissus when he has seen his true face in the waters of the pool, Don Quixote dies.

Do I truly want to save Marco? Is it truly possible to save him? Do I truly believe that if literature cannot save a man, regardless of the mistakes he may have made, it serves no purpose? And when did I start believing this twaddle? When did I start thinking that it wasn't enough to try to understand Marco, that it wasn't enough to discover why he lied, why he invented for himself and lived out a fictitious life rather than be content living his true life? When did I start telling myself that the goal of all books isn't good enough for this book and that in the end reality might save Marco who has spent almost his whole life being saved by fiction? Am I trying to save myself by saving Marco?

I don't know. I wonder. I wonder whether, at a certain point—as I gradually became engrossed in this true story, this non-fiction novel suffused with fiction that for years I hadn't wanted to write—I might have started behaving like a sort of bachelor Samson Carrasco, determined to defeat Marco with the truth and force him to return home vanquished by the arm of another but victor over himself, whether I might have sought to compel him to recover his sanity, reconcile himself to reality, know himself or recognise himself for who he is so that, just as Cervantes transformed his book into the great disseminator of the definitive truth about Alonso Quixano, I might transform this book into the great disseminator of the definitive truth about Enric Marco ("For me alone was Enric Marco born, and I for him; it was his to act, mine to write; we two together make but one"), into a declaration that would reveal to all that Enric no longer is and no longer claims to be the man he said he was, that he abjures his fictitious heroic past as Don Quixote abjured tales of knight-errantry, that he is no longer Enric Marco, the anti-Franco, anti-fascist hero and champion or rock star of so-called historical memory, but simply Enrique the mechanic, a man as good as Alonso Quixano the Good who one day lost his mind and wanted to live more, or more than was his allotted span, who wanted to live all that he'd never lived and lied and deceived in order to do so, so that people would love him and admire him. I also wonder whether, from the moment I conceived this nonsensical goal, I might have thought or sensed that, when Marco finally recognises himself for who he is in the shimmering waters of this book, he may die like Narcissus, but he will die sane and serene and reconciled, like Alonso Quixano. And this book will then take on its full meaning.

Is that it? Is that the goal I truly set myself? And is that not an act of folly? Is it not a way of trying to write an even more impossible book than the one I intended to write? Can a book reconcile a man with reality and with himself? Can literature save anyone or is it as important and as futile as everything else, and the idea that a book might save us ridiculous and obsolete? Did Cervantes save Alonso Quixano, and in so doing save himself? Do I want to save myself in saving Enric Marco? Okay: all these questions are ridiculous, obsolete and absurd, I should be ashamed of even formulating them. And I am ashamed. But—why lie?—at the same time I'm not ashamed. I'm not ashamed at all. Because here and now, I can think of no better way to say No. No to everything. No to everyone. No, in particular, to the limits of literature, to its wretched impotence and its futility; because, yes, the way I see it is: if literature serves to save a man, then all hail literature, but if it serves only as an embellishment, to hell with literature. This is what I think: even if there's only a one in a million chance that there's a one in a million chance that my questions are not ridiculous, obsolete and absurd, and that the impossible could become possible, it's worth the effort to try. I also think that, at this stage, there's only one way to find out if Marco will be saved, if I will be saved, and that is to finish telling the truth about him, stripping him of everything as Cervantes stripped Don Quixote of everything. In other words: finish telling his story. In other words: finish writing this book.

4

In mid-April 2013, two weeks after the interview with Marco in my office in García in which I had the impression that our man had taken off his mask and that the relationship between us was changing, I had lunch with Santi Fillol in Cafè Salambó, a restaurant near my office. We hadn't seen each other in four years, not since the second time I decided I wanted to write this book and got in touch with him shortly after he'd finished making his film about Marco, and he came with me to Sant Cugat to introduce me to our man. In the meantime, we'd barely exchanged a few emails, but, in late 2012 or early 2013, Santi was one of the first people I told that I had reached the point of no return in my decision to write this book, or to stop resisting writing it. Since then, I'd tried in vain to meet with him to talk about Marco, also so he could lend me the documents, or some of the documents, that he and Lucas Vermal had put together in order to film *Ich bin Enric Marco.*

According to my diary, we met on Thursday 18, at 2:15 p.m. At the time, I'd been living in Berlin for almost two weeks as guest lecturer at the Free University, and that day I'd flown back to Barcelona to promote *Outlaws,* a novel with fiction published the previous year. My flight had landed at 1:30 p.m., which made it possible for me to arrive just on time. I was thirsty, and as soon as I took my seat on the ground floor of Cafè Salambó, facing the door onto calle Torrijos, I tried to attract the attention of a young waitress of Asian appearance and order a beer. I hadn't been there for more than two minutes when Santi appeared in the doorway with his intellectual air, his intellectual glasses and his unkempt beard, carrying a plastic bag. I waved to him, he saw me, came over and we shook hands. At that moment the waitress brought my beer and Santi asked her to bring another as he set the plastic bag on the floor. I don't remember what we talked about initially, because I was impatient to talk about Marco and nothing else mattered to me much. I vaguely remember Santi telling me that he had spent some time away from Barcelona, possibly in Buenos Aires, possibly directing a film; I vaguely remember telling him where in Berlin I was living and talking about my lectures. The waitress came back with Santi's beer and took our food order; as soon as she'd left, Santi said:

"Right, so you've finally decided to write about Enric, is that right?"

"Yes," I said.

"I knew you'd give in eventually," he said. "And I bet Enric knew too. Do you remember what he said to you that day we had lunch with him in Sant Cugat?"

"What was that?"

"Of course, Javier," he said, imitating Marco's voice, "I've always known I was one of your characters."

Santi laughed. I was stunned.

"Is that true—did he really say that?"

"As true as the fact that it's daytime and we're sitting in Salambó," he said.

"It's unbelievable. I don't remember."

"How could you possibly remember, man, you were fuming. It was like poor Enric had done something to you."

"I lost my temper," I apologised, "I suppose it wasn't the right time to write about him. My father had just died, my mother wasn't well and I was in a bad way myself. I think I got scared."

"You told me you were sick and tired of reality, that you needed fiction."

"And you told me that Enric was pure fiction. And you were right. That's why I'm going to write about him."

The waitress served the first course. Santi ignored her, picked up the bag he'd set down next to the table and handed it to me.

"I was thinking about what to bring," he said as I opened the bag, "and I came to the conclusion that this was the best thing I could give you."

Inside the bag was a computer hard drive and a case full of DVDs. "What is it?" I asked.

"It's all the footage we shot for the film," he said. "Seventy, eighty hours of Enric Marco. Maybe more, I don't remember. Barrels of crude Enric Marco. That's everything. Now, tell me about your book."

While we ate, I talked to him about my book. He listened attentively, as though his documentary hadn't jaded him about Marco, as though looking for some excuse to film him again. I explained that I was trying to reconstruct Marco's real life from beginning to end, from his birth to the moment the scandal broke, or after the scandal broke, I told him about the long sessions we had recorded in my office, about the research I was doing, the people I was contacting to check whether what Marco was saying was true or not, I told him that Marco seemed both to want and not want me to write the book, that his wife and daughters did not want me to write it.

"That's what he told us in the beginning," Santi interrupted, "that Dani didn't want us to make the film, or his daughters . . . Bullshit: Enric does whatever he likes; he doesn't care what his wife or his children have to say. The fact is, this is the only way he can charm you; what he's really saying is: you're so intelligent you'll see right through me; or, you're so clever that my wife and my daughters are afraid. And so am I. But it's a lie. Enric wasn't remotely afraid of us, any more than I think he is of you. Enric is very clever, Javier: he's a street dog who has to fend for himself, and the minute he sees you, the first thing he thinks is: 'Let's see how I can get something out of him.' That's how he is. As for his past, the truth is we focused on his time in Germany, we weren't really interested in the rest. Now, if you want to know my impression, I'll tell you. My impression is that everything about Enric is a lie: his childhood, the war, the post-war period, the clandestine stuff. Everything."

"It's possible," I said. "But lies are built on truth; plausible lies, I mean."

"You're right about that," Santi agreed.

"No-one believes pure lies," I said. "Effective lies are a mixture, they contain some element of truth. And Marco's lies were good. And that's what I'm trying to work out: which bits of his lies are lies and which are truth."

"You're setting yourself a hell of a job," Santi said, "but I'm sure it's worth the effort. Enric is always worth it. He is the motherlode that never runs out. Lucas and me, we didn't tackle the Enric of the war and the post-war years, or the Enric of the Franco regime, although we spent so many hours with him during the shoot, eventually you get a sense of it. And I can tell you, the sense you get is not that he was a resistance fighter, someone who worked with underground movements, nothing like that, you get the sense he was an opportunist, a bit of a rogue who lived it up whenever he could, money and girls and lots of nightlife."

Just then the waitress cleared away the first course, and as she did, Santi said:

"Have you noticed how much women like Enric? I've never been in a bar with him where the waitress didn't flirt with him. If he were here, this pretty little thing would already have paid him a compliment or two."

The waitress smiled without blushing, perhaps she didn't understand, and went off without a word. I asked Santi to tell me about the filming of *Ich bin Enric Marco*, of the time they had spent cheek by jowl with Enric, in Barcelona but especially on the road trip from Barcelona to Kiel, from Kiel to Flossenbürg and the return journey to Barcelona.

"Have you been to Flossenbürg yet?" he asked.

"No," I said.

"It's worth the trip. My favourite part of the whole film is the footage we shot in Flossenbürg. That's where Enric really came into his own. He'd never lived in the camp, but it was like he was at home. Much more so than in Kiel, where he'd actually lived. What's Pessoa's line? 'The poet is a faker/Who fakes with such great zeal/He even manages to fake/The pain he feels for real.' That's Enric: a poet."

Santi began to recount tales from the film shoot. He mentioned, for example, how in Flossenbürg, the director of the Memorial, whom Marco had met on his first visit to the camp, was prepared to shake his hand, but he wasn't prepared to accept the reasons Marco put

forward to justify his deception. Then he told me a story he'd heard
from Pau Lanao and Carme Vinyoles, Marco's journalist friends who,
years before the scandal broke, had published a long article about him
in *Presència*, about how, during a talk Marco was giving at a school,
they had seen him convince a neo-Nazi that his ideas were absurd, or
they knew someone who had seen it, and he also told me that a friend
of his, a film director, had told him that in the Seventies his parents
were in financial difficulties and Marco, who was secretary general of
the C.N.T. at the time, had helped them get through it.

"That's Enric too," said Santi. "On the one hand there's the con
artist, the impostor, and on the other, there's the man who'll bend
over backwards to do a favour for anyone. Enric is both: there's no
way to separate them. You either take him or leave him."

It was only then that I decided to tell Santi about the last meeting
I had with Marco in my office, just before I left for Berlin, or rather
about that almost magical moment when I'd had the impression that
Marco had taken off his mask, or it had fallen away, and that I was
seeing him as he really was and beginning to understand him. I told
Santi I suspected that the Marco he and Lucas Vermal had filmed
was not the man he was now, that the intervening years had changed
him, that he was no longer the same man who constantly needed to
justify himself, or was not entirely the same, or had begun to change
and was beginning to acknowledge his mistakes and regret what he
had done, rather than continuing to defend the indefensible, meaning
his imposture. That he'd decided to accept his mistake and apologise;
I told him that, deep down, it had probably begun the moment the
scandal broke, or just before, when, fed up with lies and tired of being
an impostor and leading a false life, Marco had admitted his deception
and had voluntarily come clean. And, now that I remember the things
I told Santi, I realise that maybe I'd already started to have an inkling
of something I only dared to think much later: that Marco didn't want
to continue hiding behind his lies, that he wanted to tell me the whole
truth perhaps because he had come to the conclusion that only by
telling the truth could he truly rehabilitate himself. More than that,
it occurs to me now that perhaps, over lunch with Santi at Salambó,
I had the first inkling of the sudden dizzying realisation I was to have
months later, one evening in late summer or early autumn, as I drove

back to Barcelona from Sant Cugat along La Rabassada having spent
the day with Marco and left him at the door of his house, when for a
fleeting moment I felt that Marco had never wanted to dupe me, that
he had never resisted telling me his story, that ever since I'd seriously
begun to study his life he had simply been testing me to see whether
or not I was worthy of his telling me the truth and guiding me to it if
I could discover what it was, that over the space of almost a century
Marco had fashioned the monumental lie that was his life not in order
to deceive anyone, or not simply in order to deceive, but so that some
future writer, with his help, might decipher it, recount it and share
it with the world, just as Alonso Quixano had created Don Quixote
and had him perform his lunatic feats so that Cervantes might decipher them, recount them and share them with the world, and that I
was certainly not using Marco as Capote had used Dick Hickock and
Perry Smith, it was Marco who was using me the way Alonso Quixano
had used Cervantes. I felt all this in a split second as I drove along La
Rabassada later that evening. I'm both happy and sad that I didn't feel
it before my lunch with Santi at Salambó, because I would have told
him about it. Instead I simply went on talking, increasingly vocif-
erous and vehement, about my most recent interview with Marco,
about what I thought I'd seen or glimpsed during it, about how much
Marco had changed recently, until I got the impression that Santi's
smile as he listened to me was about to break into a laugh.

"What's wrong?" I asked, suddenly guessing what was wrong.

"Nothing," said Santi. We were drinking coffee, having both
passed on dessert. "Do you really believe what you're saying? Oh,
Javier, you've got it bad. Do you really think that Enric came clean
because he wanted to? Enric came clean because he had no choice,
because Bermejo had caught him out and, being a smart man, he
realised the best thing he could do was tell the story himself rather
than let someone else tell it; what I mean is, he realised the best thing
he could do was take control of the debate so he could take control of
the scandal. That's what he was trying to do. As it turned out, it didn't
work, because it couldn't work, because even a liar of Enric's genius
couldn't fool everyone with nonsense about how he'd passed himself
off as a *deportado* in order to do good and give voice to the voiceless
and all that garbage. Enric take off his mask? No fucking way! Enric

never takes off his mask. He's always acting, he's always reciting what-ever speech best serves his interests. The speech he gave us was about being a victim. With you, it sounds like he's giving a speech about repentance and forgiveness. But Enric doesn't repent anything, nor does he want anyone's forgiveness. He simply thinks this is what will work best for him right now. Nothing more."

"You think so?" I said, perhaps just to say something, because I was suddenly convinced that what Santi had just said was true.

"I don't have the slightest doubt, Javier," he said. "With Enric, you can never stop thinking. If you stop thinking, you're fucked. If you come to a conclusion about him, you're fucked. If you think that you understand him and that he's taken off his mask, you're fucked, Enric always has another mask behind the mask. He's always slipping away. We think we're putting him in our stories, our films, our novels, but in reality he's putting us in his story, he's the one who can do what he wants with us. Enric is a riddle, but a curious riddle: when you solve it, he gives you another riddle, and when you solve the second, he gives you a third, and so on to infinity. Or utter exhaustion."

Lunch ended almost immediately after that, because Santi had an appointment and we said our goodbyes at the door of Cafè Salambó. I haven't seen him since. And it was several months more before I began to write this book, but I have not written a single word of it without thinking about what Santi told me that day.

5

What, then, is Enric Marco? Who is Enric Marco? What is his ultimate riddle?

In the talks and interviews he gave during his time at Amical, when he recounted his fictional heroic, exciting life as an adventurer, Marco presented himself as the incarnation of the history of his country, as a symbol, a summation or, better yet, as a precise reflection of the history of his country; he was right, though for reasons that were the antithesis of what he believed.

In the Barcelona of the Second Republic, Marco was a young anarchist when most young working-class men in Barcelona were anarchists, and he continued to be an anarchist at the beginning of the Civil War, when an anarchist revolution won a victory in the city. During the Civil War, Marco was a soldier when most young Spanish men were soldiers. At the end of the war, Marco was a loser who, like the vast majority of those who lost, accepted the sting of defeat and tried to avoid the consequences by melting into the crowd, hiding or burying his wartime past and his youthful ideals. Marco managed to evade military service, something most young men his age longed to do, and during the Second World War he went to Germany, which was a land of opportunity at the time, the country that, according to what people said during those years, was destined to win the war. Marco returned from Germany when everybody was now certain that Germany would lose the war. Marco lived through the Franco regime no differently from the vast majority of Spanish people, believing that the past was past, not taking up arms against the dictatorship, implicitly or explicitly profiting from it as far as possible in order to live the best possible life, sometimes the life of a simple husband and father, sometimes the life of a con artist and an opportunist, sometimes suffering in dire financial straits and sometimes—especially from the Sixties—enjoying the middle-class pleasures of his own car, his own house and an apartment at the beach, something many people began to enjoy at the time. Like almost everyone else, in the Sixties, Marco realised that Francoism would not last for ever, that the past was not past at all, and so he began to exploit it, inventing his forgotten or dormant or buried youth as a Republican, and after Franco's death, having reached Alonso Quixano's fifty years, he welcomed the return of freedom like most people and prepared to make the most of it; he became deeply politicised, and completely reinvented himself, falsifying or embellishing or embroidering his past, gifting himself with a new name, a new wife, a new city, a new job and a new life. And in the Eighties, like so many people after the transition from dictatorship to democracy, Marco ceased to be involved in politics, feeling once again that the past had passed and he could no longer take advantage of this, and, like most people, as democracy became established and institutionalised, he returned to his private life and channelled his activities or his concerns, not into a political party, but into a civic association. At length, in the first decade of the new century, the past returned more powerfully than ever, or so at least it seemed, and, like many people, Marco launched himself into so-called historical memory, eagerly joined this great movement, used and fostered the industry of memory and allowed himself to be used by it, apparently seeking to face up to his own past and advocating—in fact demanding—that his country do likewise, when in fact he, and his country, did so only in part, only enough to control without truly confronting the past so it might be used to other ends. And so, deep down, Marco was right to say in his talks that his personal history was a reflection of the history of his country; and yet he was wrong, not because his personal history had only the slimmest rapport with the one he recounted—a glittering, poetic history filled with heroism, dignity and great emotions—but because of the history that he was hiding—a vulgar, prosaic history filled with failure, humiliation and cowardice. Or, to put it another way, if during his talks Marco had related his true history instead of one that was fictitious, narcissistic and kitsch, he would have recounted a much less flattering but much more interesting history: the true history of Spain.

This, then, is what Marco is: the man of the majority, the man of the crowd, the man who, despite being a loner—or perhaps because of it—refuses to be alone on principle, who is always where everyone is, who never says No because he wants to be liked, to be loved and respected and accepted, hence his mediopathy and his fierce need to be in the spotlight, the man who lies to hide what he's ashamed of, what makes him different from other people (or what he believes makes him different from other people), the man guilty of the profound crime of always saying Yes. And so, the ultimate enigma of Marco is both his utter normality and his absolute exceptionality: Marco is what all men are, but in a form that is larger than life, bigger, more intense, more visible, or perhaps he is all men, or perhaps he is no-one, a vast container, an empty set, an onion whose layers have all been peeled away until there is nothing, a place where all meanings converge, a blind spot through which everything is visible, a darkness that illuminates everything, a great eloquent silence, a pane of glass that reflects the universe, a hollow that shares our form, an enigma whose ultimate solution is that there is no ultimate solution, a transparent mystery that is nonetheless impossible to solve, one it is better, perhaps, not to solve.

6

In mid-October 2013, I visited Flossenbürg with my son. I had suggested the idea some time earlier, because I needed an assistant on my visit to the camp, and a cameraman to film it; but we'd discussed the project several times and several times postponed it, and in the end it was Raül who set the date.

Things had changed considerably for him since the beginning of that year or the end of the previous year when I had begun working on this book and he had recorded my first conversations with Marco. He was still strong and healthy, he still loved cars, sports and movies; in his way, he was still a bit of a tough guy, even if he was going through a bad patch. That summer he had passed the university entrance exam, but had given up on the idea of taking film studies and decided to study something else. Now, however, having spent several weeks attending lectures, he was plagued by doubts: he wasn't sure whether he really liked the subject, he didn't know whether he had the aptitude, the stamina or sufficient interest to carry on with it. He was unsettled, a little demoralised, so to blow away the cobwebs and get his thoughts in order, he suggested we make the trip to Flossenbürg we had been talking about for months. I hadn't yet begun writing this book, but by now I had pieced together all or almost all of Marco's story, had drawn up a detailed structure of how I planned to tell it and, now heavily pregnant with it, with my waters about to break, I thought this was the perfect time to visit Flossenbürg: firstly, because I needed to do some final cross-checking that I could do only in Flossenbürg; secondly, because I remembered Santi Fillol's suggestion that I visit Flossenbürg and I sensed or hoped that maybe there I would discover something or experience something that would round off my book or give it some new or unexpected meaning, or make all the pieces fit; and thirdly, because I'd come to the conclusion that Flossenbürg was the place where I should end this book: after all, this was the place where Marco had constructed his great fiction, the location of the fiction that for so many years had saved Marco, not that of the reality that might have killed him.

We left Barcelona first thing on Thursday morning and that night arrived in Nuremberg, an hour and a half from Flossenbürg, having driven all the way across France and part of southern Germany, through Montpellier, Lyon, Freiburg and Stuttgart. The car journey gave us time to talk about everything, almost everything: having been eighteen myself, I knew that a boy of eighteen doesn't take advice from his father, or at least not explicit advice, so my plan for the trip was not to talk explicitly about Raül's confusion unless he brought it up, but to make the most of any opportunity to talk about it implicitly. I remember for example that we talked about *A Good Day to Die Hard*, the latest Bruce Willis movie that had just been released; though we hadn't enjoyed it quite as much as *Live Free or Die Hard*, we had liked it because it's the first appearance of John McClane's son, who was almost as much of a brute as his father and who helped him save the world again, rescuing the good guys and killing the bad guys; and I remember saying to Raül while we were talking about Bruce Willis (or John McClane), that the version of himself Marco had invented was the anti-Francoist, anti-fascist Bruce Willis (or John McClane). I also remember we talked about Rafa Nadal, for whom things had changed almost as much as they had for Raül, but the other way around: at the beginning of the year, when my son was full of energy, Nadal seemed worn out, he was recovering from a long-term injury, had dropped several places in the official rankings of the A.T.P., and looked as though he would never return to the man he was; but now, only a few short months later, everything had changed: Rafa was playing his best tennis, he had won a heap of tournaments including Roland Garros and the U.S. Open and was once again the world number one; I said to Raül that the version of himself Marco had invented was the Rafa Nadal of so-called historical memory, but I particularly remember that, while we were still talking about Nadal, or while it seemed as though we were still talking about Nadal, I told Raül that life has lots of ups and downs, that the most intelligent thing ever written on the subject was by Montaigne, who said it was "undulating"—sometimes up, sometimes down—and that all you could do was accept victory and defeat in the same spirit, understand that success and failure are simply two phantoms, or two impostors just like Marco, and afterwards quoting something from Archilochus, and I was about to quote Rafa Nadal, who in a recent interview had recommended not dwelling on moments of great euphoria or great drama, when I realised that I had become explicit, because Raül cut me short:

"No need to freak out, *Papi.*"

We arrived in Nuremberg at half past nine that evening and stayed in a hotel in the centre of town. Early the following day, we set off for Flossenbürg. It was a cloudless, sunny morning, and for fifty minutes we drove along the motorway. Then the sky began to cloud over, and by the time we turned off the motorway it was completely overcast. While I dictated to Raül descriptions of the landscape I planned to use in the book, and he took notes on his iPhone, we drove down a narrow road that snaked between tiny isolated hamlets, green meadows and autumn trees until eventually we arrived in Flossenbürg, an idyllic little village nestling between rolling hills and lush woodland. It didn't take us long to find the former camp. We parked in a lot near the entrance, next to a grey stone building with a red roof that, we found out later, had been the former command centre. Only then did Raül start to film. The initial footage was shot here, in the parking lot, in which I can be seen describing the journey we've just made. I'm wearing jeans and a brown jacket over a white shirt and a thick sweater. It's a cold, grey day; it looks as though it's about to rain. Behind me, you can see a group of old people entering the camp via a tunnel through the former SS headquarters.

Raül and I also enter via this tunnel. The Memorial was under repair, and while we looked for the archives and Raül filmed me, I told him about the camp: I told him that it had been opened in 1938 and had been liberated in the spring of 1945, that about one hundred thousand prisoners had passed through the gates, at least thirty thousand of whom had died, that there were various subcamps, that it was not an extermination camp but a concentration camp—I had to explain the difference between the two—and that what we could see today, the Memorial to the camp, was only a small part of the original installations, and other things like that. We reached the *Appellplatz*, the centre of the camp, the place where a roll call of the prisoners was taken every morning and evening, and where punishments, torture and executions were carried out; at either side of the square stood the two most important buildings that had survived, the camp kitchen and the laundry, which were now used to house exhibitions. We left the exhibitions for later and carried on, but, seeing the houses behind the former kitchen, so close they almost touched, Raül remarked:

"I don't know how people can live here, close to where so many people were killed."

"That was part of the camp too, actually," I said. "It's where the prisoners' barracks stood."

"Ugh."

We visited the Jewish Memorial and the chapel, and then walked down the Square of Nations, where memorial plaques commemorate the dead of each country; the Spanish plaque was emblazoned with a flag in red and gold under which there was an inscription in Spanish: "14 españoles asesinados en el K.Z. campo Flossenbürg."

"Only fourteen?" said Raül.

"That's what Marco thought," I said, "and that's probably why he chose this camp: because he thought that few Spaniards had been here, so no-one would be able to expose him. And it's true that there weren't many Spaniards who ended up here, but there were more than he thought. We now know there were at least one hundred and forty-three, of whom at least fifty-one died. This stone was probably laid very early and they decided not to change it."

We passed the Pyramid of Ashes, entered the crematorium and walked through without uttering a word. When we emerged, as we were climbing the stone steps towards the cemetery, I spoke. I don't remember what I said at the time, but it's there on Raül's record- ing, and I'm afraid it's part of the implicit advice or the sermons or harangues I had been subjecting him to ever since we had left home, although in this case I don't think my son noticed. I began by tell- ing him how, on a trip to Poland, I had visited Auschwitz, and then I said:

"When I visit these places, I don't feel depressed; on the contrary, I feel a sort of joy."

"Joy?" said Raül.

"Something like it," I said. "Have you read *If This Is a Man*?"

"No," he said.

"It was written by a guy who was a prisoner in Auschwitz, who recounts what happened there," I said, "Primo Levi, his name was."

"It rings a bell."

"I'm sure you've heard of him," I said. "He's a very good writer, and that book is one of the best I've ever read in my life. There's one particular scene I've never forgotten, at least I've never forgotten my memory of it, which probably isn't very accurate. Levi talks about how the prisoners in the camp had to line up at mealtimes so they could be served soup. And he says it was a vital moment, the most important moment of the day: if the person serving you dipped the ladle into the bottom of the vat and brought up a piece of solid food, everything was fine; but if he ladled from the top of the vat and only served you liquid, it was a disaster. The prisoners were constantly hungry and their survival depended entirely on a stroke of luck, on the reflex gesture of the guy serving them soup. Can you imagine? Ever since I've never been able to serve myself soup or watch some-one serve it to me without thinking of Levi."

We had now reached the cemetery and were walking between the graves back towards the *Appellplatz*.

"Sometimes I can't believe how lucky I am," I went on after a pause. "My father and mother lived through a war. And my grand-father and grandmother. And my great-grandfather and great-grandmother. And so on. But I haven't. People always say that football is the great European sport, but that's a lie, the great European sport is war. For a thousand years in Europe we did nothing but kill each other. And then I come along, I'm the first, part of the first generation of Europeans who have never known war. I can't believe it. There are people who say that that's all over now, that war between us is impos-sible, but I don't believe it . . . You see this place, people like you and me dying in their thousands like dogs, in the most disgusting, the most despicable way possible. It's ghastly. And Marco took all this and used it to dupe people, to step into the limelight. You know what? I don't even think he did it with any bad intention, actually I'm sure he didn't. It was sheer egotism. Me, me, me, me, me! Pure ignorance, pure mindlessness. If Marco had really known what this means, if he had truly understood, he would never have done what he did."

Back at the *Appellplatz* we went into the former camp kitchen, where there was a temporary exhibition about the history of the camp from its liberation to the present day. On the walls and in the display cases visitors moved between there were all manner of things: personal items, press cuttings from newspapers and magazines, television screens with looped projections of films, news reports, official documents. Although Marco had visited the Memorial quite frequently in the early years of the twenty-first century, there was, naturally, no trace of him in the exhibition. Leaving the former kitchen, we crossed the *Appellplatz* and went into what had been the laundry, which housed the permanent exhibition: on the upper floor there was a history of the camp from its establishment to its liberation; the ground floor and the basement were more or less devoted to the prisoners. We began our visit in the basement. There, in among the photographs of prisoners of various nationalities—including one Spanish man in a sailor's uniform named Ángel Lekuona, who had been murdered on April 10, 1945, thirteen days before the camp was liberated—there was a metal lectern with a huge tome lying open on it, where, in alphabetical order, one could read the names of all the prisoners who had so far been identified. Leafing through the book, I found the name I was looking for; next to it there was a date, 15.08.1900, and a number: 6448. I pointed to it.

"That's the prisoner number Marco appropriated," I said, then I pointed to the name next to it, "and that's the name of the guy he usurped."

"Moner Castell, Enric," Raül read aloud, then said, "Enric Moner sounds like Enric Marco."

"Exactly." I said. "That's why he chose him."

We went upstairs. There, in a glass case, was a notebook open to a page on which was a handwritten list of names; to the left of each name, there was a number and the name or an abbreviation of the name of a country, to the right, there was a series of jottings.

"Right," I said, "this is what we came to see."

"What is?" Raül asked.

I nodded to the book and, while he filmed it, I said:

"It's one of the camp registers. In here, the Nazis wrote out by hand the names and some information about each prisoner who arrived in Flossenbürg. Although this can't be the original, it has to be a facsimile, because the original books are in the National Archives in Washington. OK, now look at this."

From my pocket I took a folded piece of paper, opened it out and held it up to the camera, which now shows a close-up of the document.

"You know what this is? It's a photocopy of one of the pages in the register. It's not the page you can see in the case, which runs from prisoner number 13661 to number 13672, while this runs from 6421 to 6450. And now," I said, pointing my index finger to what was written next to the number 6448 on the photocopy, "read this."

"Span.," he read, and then abruptly turned the camera away (on the recording, the image makes a sudden, uncontrolled swipe), and then looking at me, he screamed, "Fuck, it says Marco!"

There were four or five other people in the room who turned to look at us. Raül didn't notice; he was staring at me, angry and confused; he was still recording, but the camera was pointed at the floor.

"Wait a minute, what the hell's going on?" he said impatiently, dropping his voice to a whisper. "It's true, Marco really was here? So was the guy lying or what?"

"What do you think?" I said. "Come on, start filming again and I'll explain."

Raül turned the camera on me angrily.

"This piece of paper," I said, holding up the photocopy, which reappears in close-up, "was in the archives of the Amical de Mauthausen in Barcelona. When he became a member, Marco offered it as proof that he had been a prisoner in Flossenbürg. Where did he get it? From here, obviously. On one of his first trips to Flossenbürg, Marco asked the archivists for photocopies of the pages listing Spanish names, and among them he found this one. Remember Enric Moner's prisoner number in the register? 6448. Here, where you and I read Marco, it actually says Moner. So the question is, is it a coincidence? What I mean is, did the guy who wrote Moner write the name so that—at least to you and me—it looks like Marco? Or did Marco write over Moner's name until it could be mistaken for Marco? That's what we've come to find out."

"Is it important?"

"In theory, no, but in practice, yes," I said, "at least to me. It's one thing if, like a gift from the gods, Marco found a name in the register that he could use to shore up his deception, it's a very different thing if it's a gift he gave himself. As far as I know, Marco didn't fabricate any evidence; this would be the first, or the only piece. I want to know whether one night, after he got back from Flossenbürg, he locked himself in a room in his house and, on his own, without a word to his wife, he very carefully faked the proof that he needed. And do you know how we can find out? It's simple, we just compare the photocopy with the original, which shouldn't take too long; now all we have to do is find it."

As we went up to the first floor, Raül whispered: "Jesus, you gave me a shock. Can you imagine if Marco really was here?" On the first floor, near the entrance to the exhibition, there was a desk and behind it, an attendant, and behind the attendant there was a bookcase containing books and DVDs about the camp. Since I don't speak German and neither does Raül, I asked the attendant—a man with bulging eyes, a pointy nose and a drooping moustache—whether he spoke English. He didn't, or very little. Despite this, I tried to explain to him in English what I was looking for; naturally he didn't understand me. I took out the photocopied page from the register bearing Moner's name, pointed to it and repeated the word "archive." The attendant finally seemed to understand and gestured to the floor below while he babbled something in German. Assuming that this was where the other facsimile registers were kept, or this was where the archive was, Raül and I headed back downstairs. We did not find the other registers or the archive. We went back upstairs and once again I tried to explain, slowly and enunciating clearly, what I was looking for, and halfway through my explanation he handed me a form and a pen. The form was written in English, but it had nothing whatever to do with what I was asking. I stared at the attendant, confused, and at that moment, as Raül was saying something I didn't hear, I realised that the attendant looked just like Sig Ruman, a German comedian who had been famous in the Thirties and Forties, appearing in the films of Ernst Lubitsch. I had started writing my name on the form, I don't quite know why, when I heard the attendant mention a name that was familiar.

"Yes, yes," I said, looking up from the form and nodding forcefully, "Ibel, Johannes Ibel."

The attendant gestured for me to wait and, with grave seriousness, picked up the telephone and made a call. While he was talking, Raül asked:

"Who's that?"

"Ibel? The historian in charge of the archive. I should have asked for him from the start. He's a friend of Benito Bermejo."

When he replaced the receiver, the attendant pointed to a window through which we could see the old camp headquarters and rattled off another screed of German, in which I could make out only two names, one male, Johannes Ibel, the other female, Anette Kraus.

Raül and I walked quickly across the *Appellplatz* towards the entrance of the camp while I talked about the mess we'd made with the attendant.

"The mess *you* made," Raül corrected.

"The guy looked just like Sig Ruman," I said, or rather I thought aloud.

"Who?"

I explained to Raül who Sig Ruman was, mentioned *Ninotchka* and *To Be or Not to Be*.

"You're a freak," he said.

The archive was accessed via a side door in the old command centre. We pressed the buzzer on the intercom and someone opened the door. At the end of the corridor, a girl in her twenties was waiting for us, smiling; she was thin, with pale eyes and chestnut hair pinned up; a green neckerchief all but hid her throat. As she ushered us into her office and gestured for us to take a seat, she explained in impeccable English that she was Anette Kraus, assistant to Johannes Ibel who happened to be in Dachau that day; she also offered to help us with whatever we might need. Sitting opposite our hostess in that huge office with its vast windows overlooking the entrance to the camp—an office she probably shared with various other people, though just then there were only the three of us—the first thing I asked was whether she minded if my son filmed us; Anette Kraus smiled and said no. So, while Raül began recording, I told the woman I was a writer, and that I was writing a book about Enric Marco. Obviously, she had heard of Marco, but hadn't met him as she hadn't yet started working at the Memorial during the time he was visiting or when the scandal broke. She asked me what kind of books I wrote.

"Novels," I said. "Sometimes novels with fiction and sometimes novels without fiction. This one will be without fiction."

"Of course," she said, "Señor Marco will be supplying the fiction for this one."

"Exactly," I said.

The woman seemed happy to be able to help, so I spent some time talking to her while Raül filmed us. In response to my questions, Anette Kraus explained the workings of the archive, the history of the camp and the Memorial, she told me about the database Johannes Ibel had created, and gave me some bibliographic information, clarifying certain details and dates. When the interview was over, I told her I had one last request.

"What's that?" she asked, smiling into Raül's camera.

I took out the photocopied page of the register bearing the name Enric Moner, the name that, from the way it was written, looked very like Enric Marco, explained my problem and asked whether I could see the original, or the facsimile of the original, to check whether Marco had altered the photocopy or not.

"Of course you can see it," she said.

She got up and left the office. While she was gone, Raül turned off the camera and we looked at each other anxiously. For a moment, I thought about Bruce Willis and his son saving the world.

"I'm sure it's a coincidence," Raül said.

"I'm sure it's not," I said.

After a few minutes Anette Kraus came back with a piece of paper which she set down on the desk between Raül and me and stood between us. It was a photocopy of the page I had requested; I set my photocopy next to it, Raül had forgotten to resume filming and the three of us leaned over the desk. The truth was immediately obvious. Marco had created a masterpiece: in the register the name was written not as "Moner," but "Moné," and our man had taken advantage of the providential accent to create a "c"; then, it had been a simple matter to turn the "o" into an "a," and "n" into an "r," and he had added the final "o," such that, after carefully going over the name, it was as though what appeared in the register was not "Moné" or "Moner," but "Marco"; furthermore, so that the manipulation would not be noticeable, he had also gone over the abbreviation "Span" (for Spanier—Spanish) next to the word "Moné" so that the letters of both would have the same thickness and look like they were written by the same hand. The three of us stared. Raul's camera didn't capture the moment, but I will never forget it.

"You were right," said Anette Kraus, still smiling.

And, thinking of Marco, I thought, "I knew you wouldn't let me down."

"He's the fucking master!" blurted Raül, unable to contain himself.

And, thinking about Raül, I thought: "Yes. But he is also Enric Marco."

Acknowledgements

Leonie Achtnich, Antonio Alonso, José Álvarez Junco, Joan Amézaga, José Luis Barbería, Montserrat Beltrán, Benito Bermejo, Mercè Boada, Francisco Campo, Montse Cardona, Enric y María Teresa Casañas, Julián Casanova, Manoli Castillo García, Blanca Cercas, Pepita Combas, Emili Cortavitarte, Juan Cruz, Ignasi de Gispert, Santi Fillol, Juanjo Gallardo, Anna María Garcia, Gutmaro Gómez Bravo, Xavier González Torán, Jordi Gracia, Helena Guitart Castillo, Johannes Ibel, Anette Kraus, Pau Lanao, Philippe Lançon, Frederic Llausachs, Loli López, Teresa Macaulas, Anna María Marco, Bartolomé Martínez, Bettina Meyer, Adrián Blas Mínguez, Llàtzer Moix, Adolfo Morales Trueba, Javier Moreno Luzón, Marta Noguera, Jordi Oliveras, Gloria Padura, Carlos Pérez Ricart, Alejandro Pérez Vidal, Xavier Pla, Fernando Puell de la Villa, Jesús Ruiz, Margarida Salas, Antoni Segura, Guillem Terribas, Isidoro Teruel, Rosa Torán, David Trueba, Enrique Urraca, Lucas Vermal, Joan Villarroya, David Viñals, Carme Vinyoles.

Notes

Page

8   If This Is a Man: In the U.K. *If This Is a Man* and *The Truce* are published in one volume translated by Stuart Woolf (Abacus, London, 1987). The passage referred to appears in "Postscript: The Author's Answers to His Readers' Questions," p. 442. In the USA, these two books, translated by Ruth Feldman, are published as *Survival in Auschwitz and The Reawakening* (Simon & Schuster/Touchstone, New York, 1985).

34 Outlaws: This novel was first published in Spain as *Las leyes de la frontera* (Mondadori Literatura, Barcelona, 2012).

46 *"The largest operation in the east"*: Antony Beevor, *The Battle for Spain* (Weidenfeld & Nicolson, London, 2006), p. 126, and Antony Beevor, *La guerra civil española* (Critica, Barcelona, 2005).

223 *"The masses"*: Adolf Hitler, *Mein Kampf* (trans. James Murphy).

224 *"Because enduring the camps"*: Norman Finkelstein, *The Holocaust Industry* (Verso, London, 2003), p. 81.

224 *Or the case of Binjamin Wilkomirski*: In the U.S.A. *Fragments* was published with the subtitle *Memories of a Wartime Childhood*.

227 *"sacralisation of the Holocaust"*: Peter Novick: *The Holocaust and Collective Memory* (Bloomsbury, London, 2000), published in the U.S.A. as *The Holocaust in American Life* (Houghton Mifflin, 2000). See pp. 200 and 280.

229 *"he who plays a part in a historic event"*: Leo Tolstoy: *War and Peace*, Book II, Chapter 4 (trans. Louise and Aylmer Maude).

229 *as Isaiah Berlin puts it*: Isaiah Berlin: *The Hedgehog and the Fox: An*

Essay on Tolstoy's View of History (Weidenfeld & Nicolson, London, 1953).

229 *Stendhal described a similar scene:* Stendhal, *The Charterhouse of Parma* (trans. Scott-Moncrieff).

252 *Adolfo Suárez could not have done it:* Suárez, González, Aznar and Zapatero are all prime ministers of Spain since the death of Franco.

Javier Cercas is a novelist and columnist whose books include *Soldiers of Salamis* (which has sold more than a million copies worldwide), *The Speed of Light, The Anatomy of a Moment, Outlaws,* and the novellas *The Tenant* and *The Motive.* His books have been translated into more than thirty languages and have received numerous international awards. He lives in Barcelona.

A NOTE ON THE TYPE

This book was set in Janson, a typeface long thought to have been made by the Dutchman Anton Janson, who was a practicing typefounder in Leipzig during the years 1668–1687. However, it has been conclusively demonstrated that these types are actually the work of Nicholas Kis (1650–1702), a Hungarian, who most probably learned his trade from the master Dutch typefounder Dirk Voskens. The type is an excellent example of influential and sturdy Dutch types that prevailed in England up to the time William Caslon (1692–1766) developed his own incomparable designs from them.

Composed by North Market Street Graphics,
Lancaster, Pennsylvania

Printed and bound by Berryville Graphics,
Berryville, Virginia

No.		Name		Place / DOB	Date	
21	Franz.	Heuillard	Georges	Magny en Vexin	23.2.44	
2	Sch. Slo.	Hauptman	Josef	Laibach 20.9.21.	8.10.43	21
3	Frz.	Delhonelle	Georges	Romilly 26.5.94	23.2.44	✝
4	Sch. Fr.	Allemand	Gustave	Die 7.9.02	23.2.44	3
5	Frz.	Delfosse	André Josef	Verfosse 1.2.06	23.2.44	✝ 14.
6	Sch. Slo.	Potrebujes	Josef	Florjul 6.11.05.	8.10.43	3
7	Frz.	de la Rochefoucauld	Lucien			✝ 4.6
8	Franz.	Ben-Haim	Marin	Mascara 22.1.21.	23.2.44	zurück
9	Franz.	Ferrier		La Motte 26.12.09 St Mart	23.2.44	Bundes
30	Frz.	Wal	André Francois	Gray 17.6.06 17.7.05	23.2.44	✝ 2
1	Franz.	Dufour		Borge	23.2.44	Hollerist 8.3.44
2	Slow.	Muhic	Johann	Dreznik 10.2.17	8.10.43	Lublin
3	Franz	Oudin	Pierre	Teplevilla 29.12.10	23.2.44	3.3.44
4	Slov.	Koritnik	Max	Laibach 24.6.20	8.10.43	Koritnik 3.3.44
5	Schweizer	Mortier	Henri	Vevey 13.1.20	23.2.44	
6	Sch. Fr.	Lefevre	Georges Marin	27.11.98	23.2.44	3
7	Franz	Anthoine	Francis	Marnacy 4.6.12	23.2.44	26.2.44 Joh. ges
8	✕					
9	Jug.	Drasler	Valentin	Laibach 6.2.20	8.10.43	8.3.44 Lublin
40	Slov.	Jaksa	Felix Henri	Selo 29.5.03 1.12.06	8.10.43	8.1.45 Etms
1	Franz.	Bezy-Salen		Firenze	23.2.44	2.3.45 Bergen
2	Franz.	Hique	Alfred	St. Germain 2.3.94	23.2.44	✝ 19.
3	Frz.	Boch	Constant. Josef	St. Singolph 31.12.16 30.11.09	23.2.44	✝ 18.
4	Span.	Fernandez		Simon 23.7.10		3.3.44
5	Franz	Benod	William	Meung-Loire	23.2.44	26.2.44
6	Sch. Fr.	Shadefaux	Marcel	Fontailler 8.1.99	23.2.44	3
7	Franz	Rohmer	Pierre	Duisburg 8.4.07	✝	zurück 10.4.
8	Span.	Moni	Henri	Figueras 15.8.00	23.2.44	3.3.44
9	✕					
50	Sch. Slo.	Kremzar	Davorin	Laibach 1.12.13	8.10.43	4